The Future of the Soviet Empire

THE FUTURE
OF THE
SOVIET EMPIRE

Edited by
Henry S. Rowen and Charles Wolf, Jr.

Foreword by
Donald H. Rumsfeld

AN INSTITUTE FOR CONTEMPORARY STUDIES/
ST. MARTIN'S PRESS PUBLICATION
NEW YORK, NEW YORK

Library of Congress Cataloging-in-Publication Data

The Future of the Soviet empire / edited by Henry S. Rowen and Charles
    Wolf, Jr.
    p.   cm.
    Bibliography: p.
    Includes index.
    ISBN 0-312-01347-7 : $27.50. ISBN 0-312-01348-5 (pbk.) : $12.95
    1. Soviet Union—Foreign relations—1975- 2. Soviet Union—
Politics and government—1982- 3. Soviet Union—Economic
conditions—1976- 4. Soviet Union—Social conditions—1970—
5. Anti-communist movements. I. Rowen, Henry S.   II. Wolf,
Charles, 1924-
DK289.F87   1987
947.085'4—dc19   87-20737
                                                  CIP

First U.S. Edition

10 9 8 7 6 5 4 3 2 1

To Jan Erteszek
Whose knowledge, insight, and personal experience
motivated this book

Table of Contents

Part I
Political and Moral Dimensions

Part II
The Decline of Economic Performance

Part V
The Future of the Empire

List of Tables and Figures

Foreword

The Soviet Union has suffered seventy years of rule based on a doctrine involving the supremacy of the state over the individual. This state, erected on the soil of Russian historical precedent, has created one of the world's two military superpowers. Its continued existence — so different from counterparts in the rest of the world — has depended on keeping the Soviet people in a permanent state of crisis. But as Vladimir Bukovsky points out in this book, the permanent crisis, predicated on external threats and internal vigilance, has lost much credibility with Soviet citizens.

There are many manifestations of social sickness in Soviet society: alcoholism, poor health, destruction of the environment. And the Soviet economy has been stagnating for decades. General Secretary Gorbachev does not hesitate to announce these facts with great vigor. It is clear that the Soviet system is in the midst of both a social crisis and an economic crisis.

These tensions within the Soviet system make it appear that some kind of reversion to a more normal civic existence, closer to that of the less dictatorial systems, could conceivably take place. And something like that is what Gorbachev seems to have promised the world with his "perestroika" and "glasnost" initiatives.

"Perestroika," meaning restructuring, is obviously needed. "Glasnost," meaning "publicity" or "openness," has great (although far from universal) appeal in Soviet society, for if there is an idea whose time has come, it is the opening up and loosening up of Communist systems. For the Soviet Union to move away, to some degree, from its highly centralized, repressive, and militarized society, and adopt a more open system, political and economic, would fulfill the dreams of many of its citizens, as well as many foreign observers. But can this happen?

Many people hope that this is happening, and hopes can affect expectations and condition behavior. Of course, we must respond to positive Soviet initiatives. But many observers in the United States and in Europe are acting as if Gorbachev's speeches have already fundamentally changed the Soviet Union and East-West relations. There is much evidence that such an interpretation is at least premature and may turn out to be quite false.

We hail Gorbachev while forgetting the lessons of Lenin and Khrushchev, Stalin and Brezhnev. The Russian dissident Vladimir Voinovich, in analyzing "glasnost," has cited an appropriate precedent even further back, warning of the parallel between Gorbachev and Tsar Alexander II, who ruled in the middle of the last century. Only when it had become clear that certain basic reforms, such as the liberation of the serfs, could no longer be avoided were these reforms decreed. Alexander's liberalism, however, gave rise to terrorism, his own assassination, a strong political reaction to the right, and eventually, the catastrophe of the Bolshevik revolution.

The primary argument for caution comes from history. The Soviet Union has had previous liberalizations, which have come to disappointing ends. Khrushchev's dethronement of Stalin was followed by Brezhnev's revival of Stalinism. Lenin's New Economic Policy, which partially restored a free market, was followed by Stalin's forced collectivization. And liberalizers in the Kremlin are not immune to foreign adventurism: Khrushchev followed his anti-Stalin actions by suppressing the Hungarian Revolution of 1956, and Lenin accompanied his reforms with the forcible joining of the independent state of Georgia into the Soviet Union and the erection of a Soviet puppet state in Mongolia. Today, the Soviet occupation of Afghanistan continues.

Clearly, we would be mistaken to perceive change in the Soviet Union as a process resembling change in the United States. Conceivably, ongoing changes could lead to a heightened Russian nationalism that would threaten the peace of the world no less than Leninist revolutionary ideology.

Still, remarkable events are occurring in the Soviet Union. They are most dramatically evident in the realm of cultural activities. More diversity in novels, plays, and films is now possible. In addition, nationalist groups are more openly voicing their beliefs, and controversy on projects that damage the environment is widely apparent. This new wind is refreshing.

But where will it lead? No one predicted even five years ago that steps such as Gorbachev is initiating would occur. The West would doubtless be cheered by the news that Gorbachev had suddenly abolished the secret police apparatus. But as dissidents point out, under Khrushchev the discretionary power of state "organs" was markedly curbed, but that did not prevent Brezhnev from staging a spectacular series of Stalin-type show trials of dissidents. There are grounds for wondering how far the Gorbachev moves will go and what will succeed them. One even wonders how long Gorbachev will remain in power.

It has been the goal of the editors and authors of this book to illuminate these matters. Professors Rowen and Wolf have joined their own considerable prior work and experience on Soviet matters with the expertise of some of the most knowledgeable thinkers on Soviet affairs today. These two scholars, with their collaborators and the Institute for Contemporary Studies, have sought to provide a profile of Soviet power and the factors that have put it in turmoil in its seventieth year. The detailed picture they have assembled of Soviet strengths and weaknesses, as well as prospects and uncertainties, are no less cogent for being sometimes contradictory, reflecting the Soviet reality. *The Future of the Soviet Empire* raises some of the most important issues facing United States foreign policy in the years ahead. In their lengthy concluding chapter, the editors outline several alternative policy directions that we might take. Their evaluations of the respective merits, as well as shortcomings, of the alternatives can be usefully pondered by those on all sides of the emerging policy debate, both in the United States and abroad.

We hope "perestroika" and "glasnost" will have positive outcomes; however, we must be prepared for the likelihood they will not. To cope with whatever comes will take faith in freedom, a clear understanding of Soviet history, the forces now at work in that society, and a keen awareness of the basic interests of the Western democratic societies. In all these areas, the present volume will, I hope, be recognized for its contributions.

Donald H. Rumsfeld

Chicago, Illinois
October 1987

Preface

As the United States nears the end of the Reagan presidency, we find ourselves faced with new challenges from the power that, since the Second World War, has been our main world competitor—the Soviet Union. The "glasnost" offensive of Soviet party chief Mikhail Gorbachev is only one such challenge.

As the example of "glasnost" shows, the Soviet system today must face its own challenges as well: an overseas empire that is not easy to control; disaffection among the young; and thorny problems involving economics, population, and minorities.

The people of the United States and our political leadership must not close our eyes to the problems the Soviet Union has produced in its own sphere and in relations between nations. It is of the greatest importance that our citizens and our policy planners possess an accurate and sufficiently deep understanding of the internal and external stresses of the Soviet power complex.

It was in awareness of this need that the Institute for Contemporary Studies commissioned two of the country's leading authorities on the Soviet Union, Drs. Henry S. Rowen and Charles Wolf, Jr., to assemble this volume. Drs. Rowen and Wolf have drawn together an impressive roster of scholars on Soviet society, ranging from a major Soviet dissident intellectual, Vladimir Bukovsky, through a number of nationally and internationally known analysts.

The Institute for Contemporary Studies is grateful to Drs. Rowen and Wolf for the fine work they have done, and is proud to present this work to the public.

We believe this study will contribute greatly to the broadening of knowledge and perspective needed in our country as it faces the Soviet empire in these, the closing years of the twentieth century.

> Robert B. Hawkins, Jr.
> President
> Institute for Contemporary Studies

San Francisco, California
October 1987

The Future of the Soviet Empire

1

Henry S. Rowen and Charles Wolf, Jr.

Introduction

Winston Churchill once observed that "Russia is a riddle wrapped in a mystery inside an enigma." Although the quotation remains apt today, some things have been learned in the nearly five decades since the original Churchill speech. At least part of the mystery has been solved, and some of the enigma has been penetrated. Puzzles and obscurities still exist, but we know a lot more now about economic, political, social, and military conditions and mechanisms within the Soviet Union and the Soviet empire abroad.

To be sure, a new set of puzzles has recently emerged in conection with the dramatic reforms espoused by Mr. Gorbachev since he assumed the Soviet leadership in 1985. These reforms, many of which were enacted into law in mid-1987, generally propose a considerable devolution of economic decision making from central to regional authorities and to enterprise managers. In the process, the reforms would free some prices from central control, legalize certain private services, and introduce wholesale trade as an alternative to administrative distribution of industrial supplies. The new puzzles associated with these measures—many of which recall the short-lived reform efforts of the New Economic Policy in the early 1920s and the Khrushchev era of the late 1950s and early 1960s—concern whether, how far, and how long the reforms will be implemented, and with what effects on the Soviet systems.

Without exaggerating what we know or minimizing how much we don't, our aim in this volume is to take stock of the Soviet system and the Soviet empire. In particular, we seek to appraise strengths as well as weaknesses, contradictions as well as consistencies—and to use the evaluation of present circumstances as a basis for assessing the empire's future prospects, including implications for U.S. and Western policy. Toward this end, the successive chapters—contributed by authors who are both knowledgeable and distinguished—address the political, social, economic, and military elements of weakness and decline on the one hand, and of strength and expansion on the other. We consider both the domestic Soviet Union—the inner empire—and the Soviet empire in Eastern Europe and the Third World.

Among the controversial matters addressed in this volume, the use of the term "empire" to characterize the Soviet system is one of the less troublesome. Examination of the classical literature on empires and imperialism—including the abundant Marxist-Leninist writings on the subject—suggests that, with very few modifications, the term fits the Soviet case quite comfortably. For example, the salient criteria that scholars have used to define empires include two characteristics that are of central importance in the Soviet empire: first, governance by a ruling class, specifically the *nomenklatura* of the Communist Party; and second, the essential role of military might in the acquisition and maintenance of imperial control.

In the concluding chapter, we use the assessments presented in the preceding chapters as background for developing suggestions for U.S. and Western policies. In the late 1940s, those policies were appropriately labeled "containment." In time that policy eroded, and what has evolved is a complex—if not confused and contradictory—mix of competitive, more or less mutually supportive, actions toward the Soviet empire. We propose moving beyond containment, working toward the central aim of seeking to change, or at least significantly modify, the specific attributes of the Soviet system that seriously threaten world freedom and peace. We do so without illusions about the difficulty that outside nations inevitably face in trying to affect the course of that rigid and insular system, although perhaps the difficulty is slightly eased by Mr. Gorbachev's declared policy of "openness." The concluding chapter is, of course, our responsibility, not that of the individual chapter authors.

Thus, the book's aims are ambitious, and the reader will not be surprised that a gap exists between our reach and grasp. Although our assessment is extensive, it is not all-inclusive. Some relevant matters are omitted, while others have been covered only in limited detail. One omission is the absence of explicit consideration of recent developments in China and their potentially significant political, economic, and even military consequences for the Soviet Union. Also, we have given only limited attention to issues of nationality as they may affect social and political stability in the Soviet Union. Two additional items are even more critical: our virtual neglect of the pervasive and possibly increased strength and influence of the state security organs (especially the KGB) in the Soviet power structure, and our neglect of the complex and perhaps shifting relationships among the Party, the military, and the KGB in their respective influence on Soviet policies.

Notwithstanding these and other limitations, the book's coverage is distinctively comprehensive. Part I, *Political and Moral Dimensions*, begins with chapter 2, "The Political Condition of the Soviet Union," by former Soviet dissident and writer Vladimir Bukovsky. His chapter is a broad and insightful overview of the current Soviet system, providing a general frame of reference for much of the material in subsequent chapters. It addresses the conflict of ideas within the Soviet Union; the central role of the Party in the "double structure" of the Soviet state; the continued role of ideology backed by military power and threat; the evolution, power, and privilege of the ruling class—the *nomenklatura*; the system's military and imperial successes, and its economic and social failures. Bukovsky also addresses the erosion of belief in the system and confidence about its future, coupled with powerful forces of inertia and stability within the system; the absence of a consequential dissident movement; and the nearly universal belief within the Soviet Union that nothing fundamental in the system is likely to change.

Chapter 3, "The Unsettled Condition of Eastern Europe," by Professor Charles Gati of Union College and Columbia University, examines present conditions in Eastern Europe. It analyzes the region's deep-rooted and widespread resistance to Soviet dominance, the resulting absence of political legitimacy for the communist governments of Eastern Europe, and the strong cultural influence of the West: the pull of Western economic systems and Western European standards of living. In opposition to these are the centripetal forces exercised by Moscow, by the internal communist parties in Eastern Europe, and by the coercive control apparatus of the Soviet military and the state security organs. Professor Gati also emphasizes the dilemma posed by the essential role of the Soviet Union in maintaining the Eastern European communist regimes, on the one hand, while the legitimacy of these regimes rests on their independence from Moscow, on the other. He describes the significant local variations that exist within this highly circumscribed set of relationships, as well as the options for Western policies to assist present and latent centrifugal tendencies in the area.

Chapter 4, by Dr. Francis Fukuyama of the RAND Corporation, deals with "The Political Character of the Overseas Empire." This chapter describes the differing characteristics of the regimes that constitute the extended Soviet empire from Cuba to Vietnam, as well as Angola, Ethiopia, Mozambique, South Yemen, Afghanistan, and other "fraternal" states, and it traces how they reached their current status in the empire. Dr. Fukuyama also considers the variety and types of relationships between these states and Moscow; the process by which the extended empire has grown; the forces holding it together, as well as those promoting fragmentation; and the empire's prospects in light of the evidently mixed assessments by the Soviet leadership of the empire's gains and losses.

Chapter 5, "Marxism-Leninism in the Third World," by Professor Herbert Ellison of the University of Washington, provides a brief history of Marxist-Leninist liberation movements and the role of nationalism and rural insurgencies in the communist path to power in the Third World. Dr. Ellison emphasizes the strong appeal of the Marxist-Leninist model to Third World elites who seek to acquire or maintain political power through the communist party and its ideology as instruments of revolution, despite the poor economic performance of the communist model in its actual operation. Among the factors considered by Dr. Ellison as contributing to the expansion of the Soviet empire are the dismantling of the colonial empires, the expansion of Soviet global military and political power, the Soviet provision of military and economic aid, and the conditions that Moscow imposes in return for this support. Finally, he considers the mixed returns realized by the Soviets from their export of assistance for local acquisition and exercise of power. His prognosis for the extension of the Soviet empire is ambivalent, although generally less favorable from the U.S. and Western point of view than is that of Dr. Fukuyama.

Part II focuses on *The Decline of Economic Performance*. Chapter 6, by Professor Richard Ericson of Columbia University, analyzes "The Soviet Economic Predicament." Professor Ericson begins with a description of the Soviet economic system of centralized directive planning, implemented through detailed coordinating instructions—a system of commands, instructions, constraints, and priorities issued from above in the vast Soviet hierarchy. His description covers the major agencies and institutions involved in the process. In effect, he finds that the process and participants lie at the root of the present Soviet economic predicament: the strengths of the system lie in its ability to achieve central priorities, both economic and noneconomic; its myriad weaknesses lie in its inability to take account of true opportunity costs, its pervasive inefficiency, and its perverse incentives. He also analyzes the secular decline in Soviet economic growth over the past twenty-five years, the negative rates of growth in total factor productivity, the near stagnation of per capita output in recent years, and the prospects for reform and improvement under Gorbachev. While fundamental improvement would require a thorough and drastic alteration of the system, this, in turn, would compromise the essential purpose of the Soviet structure and of its ruling groups.

Chapter 7, "The Costs and Benefits of the Soviet Empire," by Dr. Charles Wolf, Jr., of the RAND Corporation, begins by defining the term "empire" as it applies to the Soviet Union. Dr. Wolf suggests that the Soviet empire consists of three different empires: the inner empire, embracing the fifteen distinct national republics of the Soviet Union; the geographically contiguous parts of the empire – that is, Eastern Europe and, more recently, Afghanistan; and the empire abroad, from Cuba to Vietnam, and including various Third World Marxist-Leninist states, "vanguard" states, and others that are simply categorized as "progressive" or "revolutionary." This chapter provides estimates for the period from 1971 to 1983 of the costs that the Soviet empire imposes on the Soviet economy and the benefits that the Soviet leadership attaches to the empire. The costs include subsidies, arms supplies, military and economic aid, export credits, support for destabilization activities in the Third World, and the incremental burden of direct Soviet involvement in operations in Afghanistan. The military, political, and strategic benefits associated with the empire explain the willingness of the Soviet leadership, even when the economic system is under serious strain, to sustain its imperial efforts while seeking to reduce their costs.

Part III surveys *The Growth of Soviet Military Power and Resistance to It*. Chapter 8, written by Dr. James Roche of the Northrop Corporation and Dr. Bruce Porter of the Board for International Broadcasting, addresses "The Expanding Military Power of the Soviet Union." Viewing Soviet military power as the key to the Soviet Union's international status, the chapter also stresses the key role of military power in sustaining Soviet hegemony in Eastern Europe and providing the Soviet Union's principal attraction as an ally and mentor for countries in the Third World. The chapter surveys the range of Soviet military forces and their remarkable growth over the past two-and-a-half decades. It reviews the expansion and modernization of nuclear and nonnuclear forces and evaluates Soviet ability to project military power abroad, now and in the future. Drs. Porter and Roche also focus on the political uses of Soviet military power to maintain the empire in Eastern Europe, to prevent German reunification, to intimidate Western Europe, and to defend against an attack from the West. The growth of Soviet power projection capabilities is treated in detail as the crucial element in Soviet support for "national liberation" movements and for the expansion of the Soviet empire abroad. The chapter also points out that not only does Soviet military power help to sustain and extend the Soviet empire, but the empire's existence also increases Soviet military power by providing bases for forward operations, as well as proxy forces to assist in those operations.

Chapter 9, "Resistance Movements in the Soviet Empire," is by Charles Waterman, a private consultant and formerly a senior official in the Central Intelligence Agency. In the early 1970s, seven of the world's nine major insurgencies were Marxist-Leninist; currently, only four of fourteen are of this complexion, while six are anti-Marxist-Leninist. This chapter focuses on the emergence of insurgent movements of varying types, intensity, and scale in many parts of the Soviet empire, noting that the six anti-Marxist-Leninist insurgencies include elements motivated by allegiances other than those to democratic, pro-Western values and forms. Nevertheless, the political strengths and symbols represented by these movements put most of the Marxist-Leninist governments in the extended Soviet empire under considerable stress. Hence, they are a new phenomenon that raises questions about the previously assumed inexorable advance of so-called "progressive" forces in the Third World. Mr. Waterman considers the experience of the resistance movements, their prospects for intensification or regression, the extent to which they depend, directly or indirectly, upon external financial support, and the possible scope for resistance movements in other parts of the Soviet empire.

Part IV is concerned with *Social Conditions in the Soviet Union and the Empire*. Chapter 10 by Mikhail Bernstam, a senior fellow at the Hoover Institution, deals with "Trends in the Soviet Population." The chapter begins with an analysis of vital statistics in the Soviet Union and in its fifteen component national republics. Dr. Bernstam finds that life expectancy at birth for Soviet males is currently at about the mid-1930s' level of U.S. white males, and for Soviet females, about at the early 1950s' level of U.S. white females. Life expectancy in the Russian Republic for males is the lowest in the Soviet Union as a whole, having fallen in the first half of the 1980s to just over fifty-nine years, slightly lower than in Colombia, Ecuador, the Philippines, and Thailand. Dr. Bernstam's analysis finds explanations for these demographic trends in deteriorating health and safety conditions, increased work hazards, and lagging or unequally distributed sanitary improvements in rapidly growing cities. He also provides projections of population changes within the Soviet Union into the next century, including estimates of the declining absolute, as well as relative, numbers of Russians in the total Soviet population. His novel explanation for relatively high nonwhite fertility rates views this phenomenon as a well-calculated effort at "un-modernization": the substitution of a preferred primary economic activity (the family farm) for the economic mode of industrial wage labor, which produces inferior living standards under Soviet conditions. Dr. Bernstam also considers the possibly explosive grievances of the European nationalities — especially the Russians — and their fear of relative depopulation compared to the growth of the non-Slavs, and the extent to which this pattern may pose a risk for the survival of the Soviet empire in the future.

Chapter 11 by Nick Eberstadt, visiting fellow at the Center for Population

Studies at Harvard University, addresses "Health of an Empire: Poverty and Social Progress in the CMEA Bloc." Dr. Eberstadt presents a general overview of the official estimates of macroeconomic performance in the non-Soviet countries by the Council for Mutual Economic Assistance (CMEA). While the data suggest a general pattern of declining performance, Eberstadt comments critically on the quality of the underlying data and their general unreliability. Instead, he focuses on social conditions, especially the health of the respective populations, as likely to be more accurate indicators of the performance of these systems. Although, unlike the Soviet Union, there has been no recorded rise in infant mortality in Eastern Europe as a whole, life expectancy declined in Eastern Europe in the mid-1980s from what it had been in the mid-1960s – in sharp contrast to the substantial improvement in the same period in Western Europe. In comparison with health conditions in Western Europe, the health problems of Eastern Europe look like a less virulent, but nonetheless distinctly recognizable, version of the Soviet health "malaise." Eberstadt's discussion also includes a comparative treatment of public expenditures on health care and total expenditures on hard liquor in the Eastern European countries and Western Europe.

Eberstadt also surveys health statistics in Cuba and Vietnam, identifying significant statistical anomalies in the Cuban data. He concludes by noting that poor performance in levels of domestic health and poverty may only marginally constrain a mobilized country in its attempts to project power abroad.

Part V, *The Future of the Empire*, deals with various scenarios that may impend over the next ten to twenty years for the Soviet empire and their implications for U.S. and Western policy.

Chapter 12, "Where Is the Soviet Union Heading?" is written by Dr. Dennis Ross, formerly at the University of California at Berkeley and presently at the National Security Council. Dr. Ross reviews the current Soviet situation, stressing the central importance of the system's declining economic performance, as well as the social, demographic, political, and institutional factors that have contributed to this decline. He is more inclined than several of the other chapter authors to forecast that Gorbachev's indicated lines of less-than-systemic reform may well have moderately successful payoffs for the economy's future performance. Dr. Ross then considers the fairly strong Soviet motivations for improving relations with the United States, and suggests how this may be translated into mutually beneficial agreements in the areas of arms control, restraint on Soviet activism in the Third World, and certain types of internal change within the Soviet Union.

Chapter 13, by editors Professor Henry Rowen of the Graduate School of Business and the Hoover Institution, Stanford University, and Dr. Charles Wolf, Jr., addresses "The Future of the Soviet Empire: The Correlation of Forces and Implications for Western Policy." This concluding chapter is divided into four segments: a balance sheet covering the strengths and weaknesses of the system; an evaluation of trends in these strengths and weaknesses as they seem likely to develop over the next ten to twenty years; a brief outline of several different scenarios covering possible futures of the Soviet empire—including "more of the same," a possible shift to "market socialism" reflecting the Gorbachev reform efforts, a centrifugal movement of the nationalities, and foreign adventures and expansion; and, finally, a formulation and evaluation of alternative directions for U.S. and Western policy, together with our views of the preferred policy choice among these options.

Our recommendation involves acceptance of the basic lines of present policy, but urges that substantial modifications be made. The strategy is directed toward the three components of the Soviet empire (the *inner empire* within the Soviet Union, the *contiguous* Eastern European and Afghanistan component, and the *extended empire* overseas), employing four broad sets of policy instruments: military, economic, diplomatic, and people-oriented. The recommended strategy is divided into "Three Tracks."

Track 1: consists of vigorous competition on the security fronts against threats to U.S. allies on the Soviet periphery and to the continental United States, as well as increased efforts to contain and prudently reverse the overseas empire.

Track 2: encompasses formal relations on the diplomatic front, together with strictly nonsubsidized relations on the economic front.

Track 3: encompasses supportive actions directed toward the peoples of the empire to expand their information access, to encourage large- scale bilateral exchanges involving the peoples of the Soviet Union (preferably those who are not members of the *nomenklatura*), to promote links between Eastern European enterprises and Western firms, and to provide contact with and support for anti-Marxist-Leninist and legitimate anti-communist movements in the *overseas* Soviet empire.

Part I

Political and Moral Dimensions

The Political Condition of
the Soviet Union

The Crisis of Ideology

The imminent downfall of the Soviet regime has been announced in the West almost every decade since the Bolsheviks seized power in Petrograd seventy years ago. Indeed, by the standards of the Western democracies they were always in a deep crisis in the sense similar to that of traditional Marxist-Leninist teaching, which states that "the world crisis of capitalism is historically predetermined." But, apparently, whatever the problem of a given society, it does not become a "crisis" unless it is perceived as such by those who matter. Consider these examples:

- The loss of some 50,000 American lives in Vietnam created a national crisis, while comparable Soviet losses in Afghanistan seem to cause little concern in Moscow;

- At the same time, the Kremlin perceived as real threats to the Soviet system such "trifles" as a relaxation of political censorship in Czechoslovakia and the appearance of a new trade union in Poland;

- Communist takeovers in Southeast Asia and in several African and Central American countries left the American public quite indifferent, while a minor episode with hostages in Iran became a turning point in the American political mood;

- Mass unemployment during the Great Depression shook the foundations of American society while, at the same time, several millions were starved to death in the Soviet Ukraine without any awareness of a crisis.

Clearly, "those who matter" in the United States do not matter at all in the Soviet Union, and vice versa. In a country where every life is supposed to be dedicated to a long-term ideological goal—the worldwide triumph of socialism over capitalism—the short-term well-being of the people means nothing. In the Soviet system, a crisis can only mean a serious challenge to the fundamental principles upon which the regime was built—described by the terminology of Marxism-Leninism. Richard Pipes[1] is probably closer to the truth than he suspects when he ironically describes the current Soviet situation using Lenin's definition of a "revolutionary situation":

> for a revolution to take place it is not enough for the exploited and oppressed masses to realize the impossibility of living in the old way, . . . it is essential that the exploiters should not be able to live and rule in the old way.[2]

Of course, Lenin's "revolutionary situation" does not necessarily mean a revolution exists, only the possibility of one. The outcome will depend heavily on the degree of "impossibility" of living and ruling in the old way, as well as upon the rulers' ability to reform. However, "those who matter" in the USSR already clearly perceive the existence of a Soviet crisis. In his speech to the Plenary Session of the Communist Party of the Soviet Union (CPSU) Central Committee in April 1985, Mikhail Gorbachev ruled out any alternative except radical changes in the Soviet economy:

> The historical destiny of our country and the position of socialism
> in the modern world will largely depend on the direction we take
> now. . . . There is simply no other way.[3]

But there are no starving crowds or dead bodies along the roads, no riots or clashes with the police, virtually nothing to show or hide on the evening news. Nonetheless, the stagnation of production and general backwardness of the Soviet economy has threatened the cause of socialism in the world. The hard-earned advantage in the "correlation of forces" may be lost to "world capitalism."

The current crisis and its implications for internal developments in the Soviet Union are described by Prof. Zaslavskaya in her famous "Novosibirsk Document"[4] in unusually frank and clear Marxist-Leninist expressions. This influential scholar—Gorbachev uses many of her definitions in his speeches—sees the cause of the Soviet economic problems in "the lagging of the system of production relations, and hence of the mechanism of state management of the economy which is its reflection, behind the level of development of the productive forces."

Lest somebody might have doubts, Zaslavskaya quotes a classic Marxist formula describing what actually happens in a time of contradiction between productive forces and the system of production relations: "There ensues either a period of acute socioeconomic and political cataclysms within the given formation, which modify and readjust production relations to the new mode of production, or there comes an epoch of a general crisis of the given social formation and of its downfall caused by a social revolution."

Nor should we believe that the socialist formation is a miraculous exception to this general rule; "attempts at improving production relations, bringing them into greater correspondence with the new demand of productive forces, . . . cannot run their course without conflict."

So, the Soviet people should brace for a new spell of class struggle in their classless society—or a struggle of "interest groups," as Zaslavskaya tactfully calls them—because "radical reorganization of economic management essentially affects the interests of many social groups, to some of which it promises improvements, but to others a deterioration in their position." And no class (or "interest group") in history has been known to give up its position without a struggle.

Not surprisingly, Zaslavskaya becomes vague and inconsistent, even evasive, when she defines the "social group" whose interests are antagonistic to the goal of social progress, and whose position, therefore, must "deteriorate" in the forthcoming class struggle. She speaks about an "intermediate link of the management" that has acquired more rights and responsibilities than those on the top and at the bottom; and about some bureaucrats on the top who do not want to have more responsibilities requiring better professional qualifications than they have. She mentions some officials who "occupy comfortable positions with high income and vaguely defined responsibilities," and she describes the general tendency of the Soviet system to reward the docile rather than the more gifted and efficient.

However, a description of general human characteristics and tendencies cannot substitute for a clearly defined social group that, in Marxist terms, shows similar economic interests and occupies a certain place in the production relations. She comes close to naming this mysterious group when she says that the "central element in the system of production relations is the dominant form of ownership of the means of production"—a classic Marxist formula. Should she go a bit further and name the culprit, she would not be an influential Soviet scholar anymore, but a dissident, because every schoolboy in the Soviet Union knows that under socialism the means of production belong to the Communist Party apparatus, acting on behalf of the "proletariat."

This is exactly the "interest group"—or "new class," as Milovan Djilas called it long ago—the bureaucrats who occupy comfortable positions, with high incomes and vaguely defined responsibilities, who reward the docile instead of the gifted, and whose interests are opposed to a radical reorganization of economic management. When Zaslavskaya speaks about the need to shift from "administrative methods to economic means of management"; and when Gorbachev, echoing her, speaks about the need for more "independence and rights" to be given to the enterprises; when he, finally, says that "it is impossible to achieve any tangible results in any sphere of activity as long as a Party official substitutes for a manager . . ."[5] one has little doubt whose interests must be affected by this reorganization.

The emerging dilemma is truly paradoxical: If the Party retains its control over the economy, the cause of socialism will be endangered and finally lost. If, however, the Party loses its control over the economy, it will thereby lose its control over Soviet society, and there will be no cause of socialism in our world.

If the inevitable end of socialism can be predicted by the implacable logic of Marxist-Leninist analysis, then, indeed, we are witnessing a crisis of the system.

The Soviet State: Dual Structure, Dual Purpose

The Soviet state emerged as the first compromise between revolutionary ideology and reality, a compromise the communists had to make in order to survive.

As soon as the Bolshevik victory within the borders of the former Russian empire had been secured, it was obvious the rest of the world was not going to follow the example. There was not a single sign that the world socialist revolution was soon to come. Attempts in Hungary, Germany, and Italy failed. An attempt to speed up the "historically inevitable process" by invading Poland also failed miserably: the Red Army was defeated, while Polish proletarians rallied behind their bourgeois government instead of revolting and joining forces with their Russian brothers.

Everywhere in postwar Europe, economic conditions were gradually stabilized. Even Lenin had to admit by 1921 that the world proletarian revolution had been "delayed." This was a major defeat for Lenin personally and for the cause of socialism in general.

For Lenin it was a failure of his own pet theory, his main contribution to Marxism, according to which Russia was merely a "weak link" in the chain of world capitalism, and the Russian Revolution was to serve as a trigger for a general revolution in Europe, particularly in the industrially developed countries. His personal authority was thus at stake; the October Revolution was his personal gamble, initially opposed by almost all of his colleagues. The question remained: was it just an adventure or the beginning of a new era?

The longer the new era was delayed, the less likely it was to occur. A long shadow of a doubt was cast on the true nature of the Russian Revolution. If it was a real socialist revolution as predicted by Marx, it was bound to be repeated in all developed capitalist countries "within the reasonably near future";[6] it would signify a real historical change, as had been true of the change from feudalism to capitalism, and from slavery to feudalism before that.

The whole edifice of Marxism started to crumble right in front of the victorious proletarians, who believed in it as a religion, and who had just destroyed their country to achieve their victory, murdering a few million people in the process. The question remained: was it just a slaughter, or would history justify the casualties?

It was even worse for the cause of socialism because its very survival appeared threatened: "For our victory to be secure and lasting, we must achieve victory for the proletarian revolution in all, or at least a few, of the main capitalist countries," said Lenin at that time.[7] Otherwise, the "class enemies," both outside and inside, could be expected to seize the opportunity of "strangling socialism in its cradle."

The internal "class enemy" was already rearing its head all over the country. Peasants were in revolt against the "war communism" policy. Sailors and proletarians followed in Kronstadt and Petrograd. The country, still overwhelmingly agrarian, had been virtually ruined by civil war. Fortunately for the cause of socialism, the external class enemies showed less interest in finishing it off, "because the capitalist world is progressively decaying and increasingly disunited."[8]

So sure were communists of the forthcoming world revolution that they did not try even to anticipate any of these problems, let alone to prepare a workable program. Even the most fundamental problems had not been discussed among their theoreticians because "for a Marxist, relying on European revolution is a must."[9]

Needless to say, there could be no way back and the revolutionary ideology could not be abandoned. Instead, Lenin proclaimed a new policy "of switching from a strategy of assault to one of a siege."[10] "We are in the position of people who have to keep retreating in order, in the end, to seize the offensive."[11]

Internally, it was the New Economic Policy (NEP); externally it was "peaceful coexistence," diplomatic relations, and even concessions to foreign capitalists, which, Lenin insisted, did not mean "making peace with capitalism."

Indeed, it was not peace. First, the Communist International declared "that the fate [of the revolution] in the West would depend entirely on the progress and strength of the revolutionary movement in the Eastern [colonial] countries,"[12] a view accepted by Lenin. Basically, the idea was that the surplus value stolen from the workers of colonial and dependent countries, plus the plunder of the natural resources of those countries, had allowed the developed capitalist countries to bribe their workers, thus aborting the original Marxist scenario. Since that time, the main thrust of the Soviet revolutionary efforts has been directed to the Third World, creating a huge machinery of subversion with its own logic and dynamics.

Second, because of their fabled inability to unite, the capitalist states offered the Soviet regime an opportunity to exploit their own "contradictions." In particular, it became possible to conduct a dual policy, one through official diplomatic channels, another through the Comintern. As Lenin stated it: "We must declare our wish for immediate resumption of diplomatic relations with the capitalist countries—on the basis of complete noninterference in their internal affairs. . . . In fact, they will be beside themselves with joy, will throw open their doors to us—and in will march our Comintern agents and Party spies to infiltrate their countries, dressed up as diplomatic, cultural, and trade representatives."[13]

The Comintern developed into a huge machinery of disinformation and subversion, as indispensable for the cause of socialism as the "revolution in the East."

Although these changes helped Lenin overcome what he called "the biggest internal political crisis Soviet Russia ever faced,"[14] more fundamental problems continued to haunt the Soviet system long after his death.

Central to these problems is an inherent contradiction between the *state* and a *revolutionary ideology*. Socialism promises a complete elimination of class structure and, therefore, elimination of the state as an "instrument of class oppression." There would be no crime and no police, no army, and no national borders in the perfect society, no private property and inequality. How is this possible in a single underdeveloped, predominantly agrarian country, encircled by powerful capitalist states? According to Lenin's own theory, the state is supposed to "die out" under socialism; yet its power must grow in order to survive and to promote revolution in the world.

- The state is interested in increasing productivity; yet the ideology demands elimination of inequality and imposes a principle of reward through collective social benefits, as well as strict central control of the economy.

- The state must establish good relations with other countries, particularly if one expects to attract foreign investments. It needs stability in the world and stability in its foreign relations; yet ideology seeks to subvert them by spreading revolution and turmoil.

- The state needs the development of science, culture, and education to compete in the world market; but its ideology recognizes the universal values and declares science and culture to be class-oriented, serving the interests of the ruling class. It rejects bourgeois culture and must protect the population from its influence.

- The state needs calm and stability, a governmental structure and order, a just system of law, and citizens' conformity to it, while ideology pushes to keep the "masses" in a revolutionary fervor, expecting world revolution as an advent of eternal happiness. Being a revolutionary force, it cannot rule by law, which is based on recognition of at least some inalienable rights of its subjects, but only by coercion. Its purpose is to remake man into a new creature, *Homo Sovieticus*.

In short, communist ideology was created to destroy (and later rebuild) the world, not to compete or coexist within it. A "socialist state" is thus a contradiction in terms, which ultimately can never be reconciled.

The contemporary Soviet state has evolved precisely out of these contradictions, according to dialectical laws.

The new system of government was proclaimed a "dictatorship of the proletarians," which in practical terms meant a dictatorship of the "advance-guard of the proletarians"—of the Communist Party—ruling on behalf of the proletarians. By that time the proletarians—industrial workers and poor peasants—constituted barely 10 percent of the population, while the Party members constituted about 10 percent of the proletarians.[15] Leaving aside the terror needed for such a tiny minority to rule dictatorially, partocracy[16] became the only solution to resolve the contradiction.

Thus, there is always a Party "shadow government"—the Central Committee of the CPSU and its respective departments—which oversees and works in accordance with ideology behind the backs of all other governmental institutions. And a network of Party cells penetrates every institution, from top to bottom, in order to guarantee that each Party directive will be carried out to the letter.

The Foreign Ministry of the USSR, like the foreign ministry of any normal state, is preoccupied with its professional duties of maintaining relations with other states, promoting trade, negotiating agreements, and, in general, advancing Soviet state national interests. At the same time, the International Department of the Central Committee promotes world revolution everywhere, making sure that the interests of communist ideology are given priority over any consideration of normal diplomacy.

The Ministry of Education is concerned with preparing specialists in every sphere of activity, but its counterpart in the Central Committee is concerned with making a good builder of communism out of every student. And the Central Committee's task gets priority when it comes to promotions and appointments, ideological content of educational programs, etc.

The Ministry of Defense is supposed to be concerned with defense of the country and with training good soldiers and officers. But a parallel department of the Central Committee, acting through the Chief Political Directorate of the Army, makes sure that these soldiers are good *Soviet* soldiers, the liberators of humanity from the chains of capitalism.

The Ministry of Culture is supposed to attend to the promotion of arts, literature, and entertainment. But it is subordinate to the Department of Propaganda of the Central Committee, which ensures that its real concern is effective propaganda for communist ideology. Accordingly, it became a ministry of political censorship, weeding out "wrong" tendencies and promoting the "right" ones. There is no such thing as "culture," only "socialist culture" and "bourgeois culture."

Even the intelligence service, apart from its "normal" duties of collecting military and strategic information about potential enemies, has a task of ideological subversion: disinformation, organization of mass movements, "liberation movements," international terrorism, drug smuggling, etc. — in short, the organization of any activity that might destabilize, confuse, or scare the external world into submission. Internally, it evolved into a powerful secret police force.

This dual structure, established in every sphere of life, on all levels — national, district, regional, local, with vertical and horizontal subordination — is a perfect instrument of control and an ideal system of government for the dual purposes of the Soviet state: to maintain socialism within and to spread it without. For the Soviet state is not a traditional state: it is the material and operational base of the world socialist revolution. Internally, it maintains a regime of occupation; externally, a state of permanent ideological war. One is impossible without the other.

Ideological Warfare Backed by Military Power

As much as a "socialist state" is a contradiction in terms, the Soviet man, a kind of a "revolutionary conformist," is also an irreconcilable contradiction. This new humanoid, *Homo Sovieticus*, is supposed to be seething with revolutionary zeal while working, resting, rearing children, or waiting for five years for a flat to live in. He must be filled with ever-consuming "class hatred" toward the American capitalists, while observing the governmental villas and the party bosses' limousines, or while waiting in line to get a pound of rotten potatoes.

Clearly, such states of mind can be maintained only in a completely isolated country, where people do not know their own history and cannot communicate with each other except through official channels. Yet, it is impossible to live and compete with the outside world, let alone spread the revolution across the globe, if the country is totally isolated. It must be a kind of "semiconductor," which exchanges lies about Soviet life for lies about the outside world.

The nation must constantly be kept on the edge of a catastrophe, of a crisis, to make the system work. What can provide that condition better than the permanent threat of war?

Constant hostility to the outside world and a permanent threat of war fit perfectly into communist ideology and its dogma of inevitable class struggle. The basic thesis is simple: the socialist state, which is promoting the liberation of the brother-proletarians in the capitalist world, can only be a deadly threat to the capitalist system. As such, it is a constant target of its plots, aggressive plans, and provocations. The Soviet state is not an aggressor, according to this doctrine; it is simply on the side of the exploited masses, who fight for their liberation against their greedy rulers. The mere existence of the socialist state (and, particularly, its every success, whether a huge construction project or fulfillment of a five-year plan) is a ray of hope for the oppressed proletarians in the capitalist countries and is a threat to the existence of capitalism.

The Soviet people must work hard because each success is a new blow to the common enemy. They must be disciplined. They must not tell the enemy their shortcomings or their secrets. They must be vigilant; and, because the enemy may be nearby, they must inform on each other. They must not relax; they must defend themselves—therefore, their army must be the best. Above all, they have no right to demand justice or equality, mercy or prosperity, until the crisis is over—until, that is, world capitalism has been destroyed.

Such propaganda is administered to every Soviet person, from cradle to grave, through all forms of media, arts, and education. This is a crucial element of the Soviet system, fostering secrecy, mutual suspicion, and the incentive to work for less, while making demands for improvements in material living standards or individual rights illegitimate. The system, finally, turns human beings into ideological warriors. In reality, the system is much more important than the Marxist-Leninist teaching itself, which is ridiculed by people in every walk of life.

To be believable and effective, propaganda must bear some relation to reality. To survive, the Soviet regime needs the *constant threat of war, international tension*, and *certain tangible proofs of its successes in the world conflict*.

On the other hand, a world war, particularly a nuclear one, would be a complete disaster for the Soviet system. Let us remember that only months after Hitler's attack on the Soviet Union in 1941, several million Soviet soldiers had surrendered to the enemy, something totally unprecedented in Russian history and quite out of character for the Russian people. The reason was simple: those conscripted peasants and workers refused to defend the communist regime, with its collective farms, purges, and Gulags, even though they knew next to nothing about the Nazi regime. Needless to say, a war with a democratic country will certainly produce even more defections.

Let us suppose, for the sake of argument, that the Soviet military machine engages in a war with the Western democracies. This could not plausibly be presented as another Great Patriotic War, and the army would probably soon disintegrate. If it advanced into Western Europe, the poor soldiers would see more food and consumer goods than ever before in their lives. All of them would be looting and drinking. None of them would willingly fight or return home.

If NATO were strong enough to prolong such a hypothetical conflict, the Soviet economy would not be able to sustain the military effort. Fear, mass desertion, and an economic collapse, which are bound to happen in a prolonged war with the democratic world, make it extremely unlikely that the Soviet Union would ever try to solve its internal problems through a foreign war.

Even less attractive is the prospect of a nuclear war. If the Soviet system needs anything in the West, it is technology, goods, and credits, not a gigantic stretch of charred earth. Above all, the leadership must fear that even a few nuclear explosions on Soviet territory would finish it by disrupting the system of centralized control over the population. Thus, as long as the West has the will and the means to defend itself, there will be no world war. But there will be no peace, either.

Because the Soviet regime needs the threat of war for its survival, and yet cannot survive an actual war, the purpose of Soviet military might is to *project the threat of force*, not fight. Then, in the shadow of its force, it can employ its most powerful and successful weapon—ideological warfare. The bigger the shadow, the better.

The main principle of the ideological war is to claim sovereignty over your enemy's population, and then communicate directly with this population over the head of its government. In essence, you pose as protector against an illegitimate, oppressive, or unjust government, and in doing so, you make the government look illegitimate, oppressive, and unjust. This principle implies a two-prong policy: one with the hostile government, another with the population, which is friendly and protective. The object of ideological war is to generate civil war or civil disorder, or to use already existing civil disorders to increase your influence and, finally, to take over the country. A more modest goal might be to create a constituency that will advance your interests. Your objective in this case is to change your neighbor's policy, to modify his behavior, or even to force certain changes.

Needless to say, the Soviet system is perfectly suited for conducting ideological war. Although the Soviet Union wages this war against the entire noncommunist world, it differs slightly in two large areas: the Democratic Industrial World and the Third World. In the 1920s, when it became obvious that the world revolution was "delayed," the main center of revolutionary activity was shifted to the Third World countries, where ideological war was waged for a kill. Revolutions followed in China, Vietnam, the Middle East, North Africa, etc. There was no need for actual projection of Soviet force, only for help to the indigenous revolutionary movements.

Colonial revolutions have caused considerable trouble in the democratic countries, occasionally bringing an acute political crisis, such as in the United States during the Vietnam war or in France during the liberation of Algeria. These revolutions, nevertheless, never developed into a serious economic crisis of the type predicted by Marx. No increase in class struggle in the metropolis occurred. Meanwhile, most of the world's colonies gained independence. By that time, the huge Soviet machinery of "liberation" had acquired its own self-importance and logic. It became a part of the Soviet state and the Soviets' most effective weapon of foreign policy. Its next operational concept was aimed at several strategically important areas: the Persian Gulf (Ethiopia, Somalia, South Yemen, Afghanistan); Southern Africa (Angola, Mozambique, Namibia); and Mexico and the USA (Cuba, Nicaragua, El Salvador). It developed useful helpers (Vietnam, Cuba) and clusters of mutually dependent socialist countries. It involved East European satellites in the process. Today the distant colonies are a large part of the socialist world and cannot be "dropped" at will.

Most importantly, they became the only tangible measure of success the Soviet system could produce—the only proof that communist ideology is still correct and world revolution is still in the making. Besides, in the areas of expansion a direct clash with American interests often occurs, producing an additional source of tension and another opportunity to show Soviet superiority over "enemy number one."

This, of course, is a powerful reminder to the sullen majority back at home that the threat of war is real and that the communist forces are still strong.

This message is especially important for the numerous nationalities of the Soviet empire. War is always a risk, and ideological war is no exception. Countless Kazakhs, Uzbeks, Lithuanians, Estonians, Ukrainians, Armenians—to say nothing of the Eastern Europeans—are watching Soviet adventures in the Third World with great interest: one day the tide of war might turn the other way. (Some of these nations were occupied only recently, during World War II, and armed resistance continued until the early 1950s.)

Thus, the Soviet Union seems to be trapped in its own expansionist policy because a collapse of a communist regime anywhere in the world may set an example to many, triggering a chain reaction. Lenin's own theory seems to turn against his disciples: where is the weak link in the chain of socialist countries: Afghanistan, Poland, or Nicaragua?

And so it goes, a vicious circle: the inherent instability of communist regimes drives them further on, around the world in search of a new target—even though it strains their economy and makes them more vulnerable. [17]

Meanwhile, in Europe, ideological war has been conducted much more modestly. The second strategic decision made by Lenin in 1921 concerned the developed capitalist countries, still the ultimate target though not an immediate one. This strategy called for "peaceful coexistence." It did not mean, of course, anything like peace in the bourgeois sense. No such nonsense as friendly cooperation and relaxation can really exist between the class enemies. But the revolution was delayed, leaving a backward and half-ruined country facing powerful enemies. The task, therefore, was: a) to neutralize the class enemy, while b) strengthening the country by developing its industry, and c) quietly preparing infrastructures necessary for a forthcoming revolution.

Accordingly, a more mild form of ideological war was selected for Europe: not to foment a civil war, but to organize and strengthen the forces sympathetic to Soviet Russia. Consequently, by the end of 1921, Lenin launched, through the Comintern, a new "United Front"—a broad alliance of revolutionary forces with the nonrevolutionary, "progressive" forces of social democracy, the reformist trade unions, groups of fellow travellers, and "useful idiots" among intellectuals. This was a long-term policy.

On the other hand, capitalists were given broad concessions and long-term trade agreements, on very good conditions, to create a vested capitalist interest in the survival of the Soviet Union. Curiously enough, Lenin viewed it as a purely political ruse: "So, in negotiating the concessions, our own primary interests were political. . . . The economic aspect was secondary." [18]

Little did he know at that time how important this "secondary aspect" would later become. Practically every "industrialization" project carried out during the subsequent five-year plans was made possible by imported Western technology. [19] From that time on, Soviet dependence on Western technology and know-how continued to grow until it became a major Soviet vulnerability.

The need for a constant threat of war and international tension—both currently necessary for the Soviet regime's survival—did not exist in Lenin's time. Communist ideology was still sufficiently attractive in Europe, and revolutionary zeal had not yet subsided at home. Soviet propaganda about the "capitalist encirclement" and about "class struggle" was still effective. As Lenin remarked:

So how come that from all our contacts with bourgeois Europe and

America, it is always we who have been the gainers and not they? Why always they who have been afraid to send delegations to our country, and not we to send our delegations to theirs? And, from these they have dared to send, we have always managed to lure some of its people (however few) to our way of thinking.[20]

But as the communist ideas became less attractive, the Soviet population grew more cynical and the Soviet regime had to rely on fear and the threat of war as substitutes for revolutionary zeal and devotion. The European peace movement, organized in the best traditions of the "United Front" and similar infrastructures, is fueled by fear of a nuclear holocaust, not by a sympathy with the cause of socialism. The emergence of nuclear weapons as a new factor in international relations gave an additional dimension to "peaceful coexistence," with the "struggle for peace" being perceived by the Kremlin as a substitute for "class struggle." And when the Soviet people watch on their television screens millions of Europeans demanding unilateral nuclear disarmament or protesting against placement of American missiles in Europe, their fears are reinforced and their willingness is strengthened to accept the Soviet regime as a lesser evil than destruction. After all, "better Red than dead" is a far more realistic proposition in the East than in the West.

These changes in the equation of ideological war have occurred since World War II, as the Soviet population and especially the peoples of "liberated" Central Europe lost their belief in the socialist revolution. This myth was destroyed during the war, when millions of Soviet soldiers saw Europe and lived in occupied territories without commissars breathing down their necks. Stalin himself had to admit the complete failure of communist ideology when he appealed to the nation at its most difficult moment in 1941, invoking Russian national tradition and religion and carefully avoiding any socialist phraseology. Throughout the war, anti-Western propaganda was abandoned because of the Great Alliance, while high-quality American goods destroyed all talk about "rotten capitalism."

On the other hand, the brutal Soviet subjugation of Central Europe has considerably reduced pro-Soviet sympathies in the West. The iron curtain fell, perpetuating the division of Europe. And from that time on, the Soviet regime has had to rely on the fear of its military strength to advance its influence. With the American presence in Europe and, later, with the organization of NATO, this projection of force could work only if it was greater than the American one. Hence, military competition between the United States and the USSR became an important feature of the ideological war. A shift in the balance of power can decide the destiny of Europe, because political behavior will follow the shift: either Western Europeans will impose a "self-occupation" upon themselves, Finnish-style, or the Central Europeans will progress to a Finnish status or beyond. The latter, of course, would begin the Soviet empire's disintegration.

Accordingly, one final change has occurred in the ideological war: the Soviet regime no longer promises to liberate proletarians from the chains of European capitalists. Instead, it poses as a protector of all Europeans against American imperialism.

To sum up, the survival of the Soviet regime depends today on three permanent factors:

1. International tension and the threat of war;
2. Military competition with the West—mostly the United States; and
3. Expansion in the Third World.

It also depends on Western technology, goods, and credits, without which it cannot continue to compete militarily with the United States, or expand further in the Third World. This dependence has become an unplanned fourth factor that slowly becomes more and more important. To compensate for it, the Soviet Union needs the threat of war more than ever—as the best "export" it can offer in exchange for technology and credits. Thus, Soviet foreign policy must fluctuate from détente to cold war and back. Its cycle works as follows: after reaching a maximum point of tension and deriving all possible advantages from the "struggle for peace," the Soviet Union "sells" peace to the West for a maximal profit and declares détente. Since the system cannot relax without eroding, it uses this pause to improve its military balance with the West, and expand further in the Third World, thus fostering a new tension. And so on.

Of course, such a fluctuating *modus operandi* is not perfect. Ideally, the Soviet regime strives to reach absolute superiority, and simply "collect a tax" from the West, under the blackmail of the threat of war. As it is, it continually extends control over a few more countries at a time. However, the decline of the Soviet economy endangers even this imperfect process. Within ten to fifteen years the Soviet Union may become a second-rate power, incapable of military competition with the United States, unable to project its force and, therefore, incapable of generating a plausible threat of war. Collapse of its Third World and, later, its European satellites is likely to follow, setting off a chain reaction *within* the USSR.

The Crisis of the Dual Structure

The dual structure of the Soviet state did not appear overnight, but evolved during the 1918–21 Russian Civil War, and the subsequent struggles within the Party. Initially, Party control over the governmental apparatus was justified with the

argument that most of the existing functionaries were untrustworthy "class enemies." During the Civil War, most of the Red Army officers were former czarist
officers conscripted by the communists on Trotsky's urging, to serve as
voenspetsy—military experts. Since these officers were fighting their former colleagues in the White Army, instances of "treason" were likely. Therefore, political commissars were appointed to each unit.

The same was true in other spheres of life; old czarist teachers and engineers,
although maintaining their posts, were perceived as "class enemies" and mis-
trusted. The Party was small (estimates show 115,000 members on January 1,
1918; 250,000 in March 1919), and consisted mostly of uneducated people (even
by 1927 only 1 percent of them had graduated from universities, 8 percent had
basic schooling, while over 25 percent were registered as "self-educated," and
2 percent were completely illiterate),[21] as benefits a party of proletarians.

The latter point is not a joke, but a very serious contradiction that was never
resolved. On the one hand, a party of proletarians ruling on behalf of the working class should include a clear majority of workers in its ranks. So workers "from
the factory" were the clear priority in recruitment and enjoyed especially favorable conditions for joining the Party. On the other hand, as soon as they became
full members of the Party, they were promoted to leadership on all levels, thus
ceasing to be workers. Demand for "real proletarians" in the Party was so great
that only complete imbeciles were left without opportunities for advancement.
This practice has continued almost until the present, creating an ill-educated and
incompetent Party bureaucracy.

In due time most of the old "specialists" were replaced by new "Soviet specialists," often Party members. Thus, in the army only 4,500 former czarist officers
were still serving by 1930,[22] out of 50,000 on duty. The number of Party "specialists" in the governmental apparatus increased from 5 percent in 1923 to 20
percent in 1927. But the practice of Party "control" through political commissars
created conflict between the more competent specialist and his Party controllers,
usually less competent but obviously more influential.[23]

Spheres of competence were defined vaguely: a Party leader was supposed
to "lead, but not to interfere." The considerable resentment thus accumulated was
voiced at the 1923 Party Congress by People's Commissar for Trade Leonid Krasin, an old companion of Lenin, who, on behalf of the "People's Commissars
as a whole," suggested that "Government should govern, while the Party should
conduct propaganda."[24] After 1923 this conflict became an essential part of the
internal struggle in the Party; General Secretary Stalin defined the "proletarian
dictatorship" as the *rule of the Party apparatus over both the Party and the government apparatus*.[25] Control of the apparatus was the main advantage against
the opposition.

Stalin had to build his personal authority in tough competition with old revolutionaries, who as late as 1927 constituted three-quarters of the leadership, while being only 1.4 percent of the total membership. By combining promotion of new members with purges of the old, and by increasing the power of the Party apparatus, Stalin consolidated his own power. This meant the creation of many new positions of control and a more extensive dual structure. In 1925, the apparatus constituted only 2.5 percent of the membership, while by 1939 it had reached 10 percent.[26] After the mass terror of the 1930s, the domination of the Party over the state could not be challenged. Its power became enormous, its privileges huge. Naturally, by that time it consisted of careerists without any real ideological commitment. In 1939, 70 percent of its members had joined after 1929, and only 8 percent had joined before 1920;[27] total membership was 1,589,000, and at least half were educated. Thus, the dual structure was complete by the end of the 1930s, with its inner core, the apparatus, reaching maximum power.

A new class of bosses, of professional leaders and organizers, was what Stalin sought, a

> certain type of Order of Sword Bearers (Knights Templars) inside the Soviet State, directing its every organ and spiritualizing its activity.[28]

Indeed, they were and remained the very embodiment of revolutionary ideology, its priests and caretakers. For they are nothing without it but cynical parasites. But as long as the ideology reigns, they are omnipotent. There is no law, human or natural, that they cannot override. As a famous Stalinist wrote,

> Our task is not to study the economy, but to change it. We are not bound by any law. There are no fortresses Bolsheviks cannot storm.[29]

In 1939, at the 18th Party Congress, it was decided that specialist departments of the Party's Central Committee responsible for the different branches of industry should be liquidated because they only "increase[d] confusion by competing with each other," and by taking on the functions of economic institutions. This, it was argued, undermined the independence and sense of responsibility of the directors of enterprises. However, the result was totally opposite: being used to strict Party control, enterprise management seemed to be in complete confusion. After so many years of terror and purges, nobody showed initiative or took responsibility. Performance of the enterprises went sharply down and "reorganization" was quietly killed.[30]

After Stalin's death, the appalling state of the Soviet economy forced Premier Nikita Khrushchev to attempt different reorganizations. He tried to subordinate the Party to the economy, so to speak, by giving priority to economic factors over ideological ones. He split the District Party Committees (*Obkomi*) into an Agricultural and Industrial *Obkom* for each district; he recreated *Sovnarkhoz*, the Councils of the People's Economy (thus weakening central control). All to no avail. The people he shifted and shuffled were the same old Party bureaucrats and his haphazard "reforms" only multiplied the bureaucracy.

Eventually Khrushchev was pensioned off as a "voluntarist" who had rocked the boat too much, but the problem refused to disappear with him. Under the next leadership the economic functions were separated. Unlike Khrushchev, who was tormented by the need to reconcile the two opposite drives in the dual system, Kosygin represented the interests of the government (therefore, the need for reforms), while Brezhnev embodied the interests of the Party apparatus. However, it soon became clear whose interests were more important. Kosygin's reforms turned out to be modest: all he achieved was to insist that enterprises should be self-sufficient and should generate profits rather than losses. Even this simple wisdom was never fully accepted. Kosygin's reforms were watered down by the Party apparatus and then quietly sabotaged by the middle management of the bureaucracy.

The long years of Brezhnev's reign saw the ultimate triumph of the partocracy. Not only did he outlive Kosygin, but he also was the first General Secretary in Soviet history to write proudly in the new Soviet Constitution (1977) that the Communist Party is, indeed, the supreme ruler of the Soviet Union and of its every institution. However, Kosygin's efforts were not entirely in vain. His reform campaign generated debate in the hierarchy, and a barely noticeable split occurred between two trends: "managers" and "ideologists" (the actual terms used). Certainly, there was no questioning the ideology. Rather, the two sides argued how to better achieve the same goals. Thus, one side argued that, according to Marx, economic relations are the essence of history, a material force that moves society. And we are Marxists, aren't we? Therefore, management efficiency should be paramount. Indeed we are, replied the other side, the ideologists—but did not Lenin write that the "ideas which come to possess the masses are a material force"? And we are Leninists, are we not? Therefore, ideological guidance is most important.

Nevertheless, a number of interesting industrial experiments were carried out in the 1960s, and were written up ecstatically in the Soviet newspapers. The early euphoria passed, for the experiments illustrated all too clearly the superiority of capitalist methods over socialist methods. It was clear that, if extended country-wide, although they would lead to a more rapid economic growth, they would also restore those "ulcers" of capitalism with which Soviet propaganda so loves to frighten people: unemployment, inflation, and "the anarchy of production." That is, it would be a market economy, and the state would no longer maintain its control over economic life. More importantly, it would render Party control of the economy both superfluous and impossible.

In the ensuing muffled war, waged under the banner of economic reform, the Party apparatus used every means to suppress its opponents, including judicial repression.[31] But the decisive stroke involved the West. As an alternative to broad internal reforms, the ideologists proposed détente. They gambled on obtaining extensive economic aid and a trade boost from the West. *Why introduce dangerous reforms if you can get what you want from abroad?*

One must not assume that this disagreement erupted between members and nonmembers of the Party, or that the Party bureaucracy had only one opinion, while the government functionaries were moved by another. Anyone in a position of power must become a Party member, and positions within the hierarchy are often determined by chance. But in every society there is a certain notion of decency, or a criterion of dignity that is accepted by anyone with a modicum of self-respect. Nobody can explain how this came about, but "decent" people in the Soviet Union do not join the Party simply for a Party career. Those who do are widely regarded as "backward" types incapable of attaining a normal, "decent" profession. However, it is an entirely different matter when a good specialist is forced to join the Party. So, there is a dual path: one individual can become director of an enterprise because he is a good Party member, while another becomes a Party member because he is a good enterprise director.

Managers belonged to the latter group, and ideologists to the former, but one cannot tell them apart by their official biographies. Most Soviet officials in either are required to have a complete higher education in economy, technology, or industrial processes; most must have experience in both Party and governmental work. And the closer to the top, the more indistinguishable they become from the outside.

Rank and file members in the Communist Party do not enjoy enormous privileges, but they have a better chance of being promoted, whatever their profession might be. The key positions in every community, in every occupation, are always filled by Party members. They constitute the ruling elite on all levels. Accordingly, they have a dual loyalty: first and foremost, to the Party which promotes them; second, to the enterprise, institution, or department they work for. The second structure—the Party apparatus—runs parallel to the local, regional, district, republic, and Central committees. There are currently 18 million Party members, roughly 6.5 percent of the population, or about 10 percent of its adult component. The ruling elite, the *nomenklatura*, is about 3 million, families included.[32] Other estimates go as high as 5 million.[33]

It is impossible to determine how many are "ideologists," but they are a formidable force. It does not matter what they believe in; much more important is what they stand to lose. Their status being conferred by the Party, and not by their skills or talents, they could not remain on the same level in any other socio-political system (if, indeed, such a level of power and privilege exists anywhere else). Besides, many might be held responsible for corruption and crimes they have committed in the service of the regime, if the regime ever changes dramatically (as happened in Poland during the heyday of Solidarity). For these reasons, they prefer a long decline, a slow death, if the demise of the system should become inevitable. Although both sides seem to agree that some reorganization is necessary, radical economic reforms mean an immediate ouster and a loss of status for the partocracy. By contrast, a continuous decline in the economy, dangerous as it is, would mean only a *gradual* defeat for the Soviet camp, with the ultimate catastrophe coming perhaps fifteen to twenty years from now. Even if radical reform can "save the cause of socialism" (which is questionable), they would still prefer the slower scenario. Understandably, the idea of reform makes them uneasy—who knows if the process can indeed be managed?

On the other hand, the "managers" apparently believe they do not stand to lose anything except their ideological chains. Being good specialists, better educated and more confident, they believe they will remain at the same level (or even improve their status) in a more competitive society. Members of the top echelon in the *nomenklatura* probably hope to become the sole masters of the country if they can manage to remove the partocrats. They may become that in the long run, but let us have no illusions: these "reformers" are simply more energetic, more self-assured, and better educated communists than the old partocrats. Being "specialists," they are used to relying more on calculations than on political intuition, and they are willing to run the risk of reforms in order to "save socialism." Being younger, they do not want to preside over the downfall of their regime. It is less clear, however, how much they understand of the system's limitations or the possible consequences of needed reforms.

Even if Gorbachev is a proponent of radical reforms, he will find himself in the same situation as Khrushchev twenty years ago. His reforms will have to be conducted through the same Party apparatus whose power he will strive to diminish. The General Secretary has no other instrument of control over the country, and by reducing its power he will be reducing his own, too.

Ever since Stalin established his own power, by establishing the power of the apparatus over the Party, and that of the Party over the country, any significant change in Soviet life must start with the apparatus. Indeed, during Andropov's brief reign, according to some accounts, "hundreds of persons who held real power either in Moscow or in the provinces were removed. Thousands of middle-echelon officials were replaced or shifted to other duties."[34] This "purge" continues, but even if Gorbachev places people like himself in every position of influence in the country, he is bound to discover what Napoleon discovered when his brother Jerome, whom he appointed to be a "king" of conquered Spain, became a real king in due time. After all, Khrushchev was removed by the people he had chosen and promoted when they felt he had gone too far.

Structural constraints make far-reaching reforms impossible. But if they do not go far enough, they will not work. Where is the border between these two? The time when the government could govern, leaving the Party to conduct propaganda (as Krasin suggested), passed long ago. Once revolutionary enthusiasm died, the Party had to rely on an exclusive right to promote and to dismiss, to enrich and to impoverish any individual in the country. If people are promoted according to their talents and rewarded according to their performance, who will bother to join the Party? And if they do not—where is the reform?

So far, Gorbachev has not unveiled a plan for reorganization. We can only guess its main features, from hints in his early speeches.[35] Amidst invigorating appeals for better discipline, he reemphasizes Kosygin's principle of "self-sufficiency," which this time must be introduced "in reality"; he threatens to eliminate many bureaucratic governmental institutions and hints at a possible return to the Khrushchevian version of the *Sovnarkhoz,* or regional economic authorities. His constant subject is a need to give more rights and independence to enterprises, the simplification of central planning, and a "revolutionary shift to state-of-the-art technology." It looks like a fairly minimal adjustment within the system.

His other ideas are bound to be more controversial. Thus, his remedy for agriculture is believed to be wide introduction of a "family-based productive link system" (*zveno*), a system that was tested in the experiments of the 1960s but which, in spite of spectacular results, had been rejected as an attempt at restoring capitalism.

Some of his statements are quite radical:

> We should take measures that would strengthen the consumer's impact
> on the technical level and the quality of production. We ought to rad-
> ically improve price formation . . .

It remains to be seen, however, how much of this "radicalism" will actually be introduced into Soviet economic life.

Clearly, there is no overlap between what goes too far ideologically and what goes far enough economically. Such is the nature of the system. As soon as merit, professional skills, and real prices are introduced, the dual structure of the Soviet state will collapse. A writer becomes prominent because his books are popular among readers (not among leaders); an enterprise becomes successful because its product is in great demand; a student becomes just a student, a teacher—a teacher, and a government—merely a government. At such a point ideology will disappear, along with the Party apparatus.

The introduction of "market socialism" in Hungary and the rapid modernization of China have created additional pressure (and temptation) regarding similar changes in the Soviet Union. But these are poor examples. The huge shadow of the Soviet Union prevents Hungarian society from going too far politically with its economic development. Nobody wants a repetition of 1956. But who is going to pull back the Soviet Union if it strays too far?

Chinese reforms are just beginning and their further development or results are uncertain. There is, however, a very important difference between the Soviet Union and China: the latter need not ponder the repercussions of its reforms on a closely guarded "socialist commonwealth of nations." Developments in Central Europe have always gone further than in the Soviet Union (Poland and Hungary in 1956, Czechoslovakia in 1968, etc.). This centrifugal tendency will grow even stronger, because now the Soviet regime needs its satellites as an economic buffer during the present period of economic stagnation and costly reorganization. This strains the economy of Central Europe through the process of "further economic integration and international division of labor."[36] Can the Soviet regime combine liberal economic reforms at home with tough policies in Central Europe (let alone with crushing popular unrest in these countries)?

Such will be a particularly difficult task during a period of détente, which the Soviet regime desperately needs to achieve the goal of a "revolutionary shift to state-of-the-art technology." In fact, they need much more; according to Gorbachev they need:

> joint development [with the West] of new technology, planning and construction of [new] enterprises and exploitation of raw materials' resources.[37]

Of course, they hope to enjoy economic cooperation with the West without relaxing their internal "cold war" climate. Today, however, this may prove difficult to achieve. The Western public might, by this time, have learned something from the previous spell of détente. Also, the need for more initiative from the people in order to make reforms work, combined with an external détente, could make maintaining the internal "cold war" difficult.

In short, limiting factors and possible grave consequences outweigh any drive for radical economic reforms. Desperately needed reforms may result in a loss of control over the economy. Reforms, needed because the Soviet economy cannot sustain the huge military apparatus and the effort of maintaining or expanding its external empire, may lead to an erosion of the external empire, reversing the momentum and threatening the internal empire of the Soviet Union. Reforms are needed to sustain military competition with the West, but they may require a prolonged period of détente with all the dangerous consequences that would entail.

Accordingly, two variables are enormously important: first, the behavior of the West; second, the behavior of the Soviet population. If the West provides help on a great scale and places no preconditions involving internal systemic changes on its transfers of technology, equipment, and consumer goods, then the Soviet regime can get away with a policy of minimal change and will continue its "class struggle" for another decade or more before its next crisis. That is, *the scale of its reforms is inversely proportional to the scale of conditions of Western economic assistance.*

If the West continues to help perpetuate the existence of the Soviet external empire by recognizing Soviet client-states and providing them economic help (Central Europe, Mozambique, Ethiopia, Angola, and, perhaps soon, Vietnam), then the price of the empire will continue to drop and the risk of collapse will be diminished, slowing the drive for radical changes in the Soviet economy. If, on the contrary, the West disassociates itself from these countries and supports resistance movements, then the drive for improving the performance of the Soviet economy must increase, producing, in turn, desirable internal changes.

A similar effect is produced by the American rearmament program and, particularly, by the Strategic Defense Initiative. If the Americans abandon SDI, the pressure for reform will be reduced.

Finally, a second variable — the response of the Soviet population. How far must the forthcoming reforms go to gain their enthusiasm? How big must new incentives or popular belief in the stability of the reforms be to stimulate productivity to a required level? Will the Soviet people be deceived once again by propaganda and by their rulers' television performances? Can they be simultaneously enthusiastic about reform and frightened into submission without a threat of war? In the final analysis, the extent and success of reforms will depend on the popular reaction.

Exhaustion of Materials: Human and Physical

Of all the elements in Soviet society, the human being is the most neglected. Socialist ideology deals with classes, social groups, and "collectives." The individual is absorbed in the collective and then, supposedly, is reborn, completely transformed as a function of the statistical average. While in a nonsocialist country, the prosperity of the whole is measured by the prosperity of each individual, Soviet citizens are supposed to define their wealth in the context of the common wealth of the society.

Therefore, in 1918, the first major economic decision made by the "proletarian vanguard" was nationalization of all enterprises; the second was the establishment of centralized state planning (GOSPLAN) as a substitute for market relations; the third was the introduction of a system of "leveling" benefits to proletarians, i.e., collective rewards through social benefits (free education, free medical care, etc.).

Whatever revolutionary enthusiasm among the masses might have existed in 1917, their response to this new system was lukewarm; by 1923, productivity had dropped to 60 percent of the prerevolutionary level (although the market-oriented New Economic Policy was already in operation and some wage incentives had been reintroduced), and production reached only 25 percent of the average in the period just before the Revolution.[38] Later, however, egalitarian "leveling" was abandoned. By 1934, the gap between highest income to lowest was a ratio of 29:1.[39] However, this did not include "rewards" for "productive" labor. Through the period of the Stakhanov movement and beyond during the 1930s, the higher productivity of the pacesetters was used to set *production norms*, not *wages*. Once the state (or, rather, the Party) became the sole distributor of (insufficient) goods, favors, and privileges, they rewarded *loyalty*, not *productivity*. Those who were more "loyal" were more "equal." Money had little importance, and good relations with management and Party bosses became essential for survival. A popular book of the 1930s tells a story of an underground millionaire who, travelling with a suitcase of money, could not live decently or even buy basic things because he did not belong to a "collective."[40]

Soviet economic development meant the rapid industrialization of the country, i.e., the development of heavy industry, engineering, and energy supplies. From the standpoint of Marxist theory, socialism can be built only in countries with a sizeable proletarian class created by industrialization. Further, heavy industry was an indispensable basis of military force, needed in a world of "capitalist encirclement"; and finally, economic independence from world capitalism is impossible without a strong industry. As a result, Soviet capital goods production, by the beginning of the 1940s, increased four times over the level of 1928, while production of consumer goods trailed far behind.[41] By and large, heavy industry worked full blast for continuous self-reproduction.

This process made people even more dependent on the state (Party) distribution system because consumer goods were in permanent shortage. An *extensive economy* emerged, with huge capital investments and low return on investment. An increase in production could be achieved only by building more and more low-profit enterprises. In due time, such economic expansion reached its natural limit, with a permanent shortage of labor and capital. The economy survived only thanks to wholesale exploitation of natural resources (oil, gas, gold, etc.), a skimming of the easily accessible, low-cost upper layers. Thus, by the 1980s, extraction of practically all major natural resources in the country was becoming more costly, leaving the country with reduced means for expansion, and with shrinking hard currency resources.

On the other hand, persistent labor shortages led to further exploitation of the workers. A number of legal restrictions were introduced in the 1930s–50s, including the internal passport system, laws on "parasitism," punishment of those who changed jobs too frequently, and a wide use of prison labor in the unproductive branches of industry. The latter created an economic need for mass repression under Stalin (up to 20 million prisoners in the late 1930s),[42] which continued as an indispensable part of the Soviet economy. Although the number of prisoners decreased in the 1960s–70s to 4–5 million, a much bigger number of petty offenders (those sentenced to up to three years of imprisonment) were sent to work at "construction sites for the people's economy."

At present, even the ruling Party has to admit that:

> Further movement along this course in a situation where the possibility of involvement of labor, raw materials, and natural resources in production is reduced, will only lead to [an] increased number of unfilled jobs, to an excessive growth of expenditure for development and transportation of mineral resources, and for protection of the environment. This way of development has no positive prospects now: more and more investment would yield less and less results. In the present conditions, this would be a dead end.[43]

Developments in Soviet agriculture were even more disastrous. Communists could never make up their minds about what to do with the peasants, who because they earn their living with their hands cannot be regarded as a class of capitalists; on the other hand, they were not "proletarians" because they owned the "means of production." This puzzle has never been satisfactorily solved and peasants were vaguely defined as a class with "petit-bourgeois instincts."

This ambiguity was reflected in subsequent political decisions. The Revolution was made by peasants who, attracted by Lenin's promise of immediate division of the land, abandoned an unpopular war in 1917 to get home for the loot. There followed Lenin's policy of war communism and confiscation of agricultural produce, which produced peasant revolts and hunger riots. Lenin changed course and introduced the New Economic Policy; within a year, agricultural production reached three-fourths of the prewar level. But this meant loss of state control; workers were less well off than peasants, and industrial investment lagged.

So, by the beginning of the 1930s, the NEP was ended and war was again declared on the peasantry. Agricultural production again dropped dramatically; "collectivized" peasants did not want to produce. Starvation ensued on a vast scale and was used to break the peasants' will to resist (exactly as is now taking place in Ethiopia).

Soviet agriculture never recovered from this genocide, economically or morally. Although the 1928 level of production was surpassed by the end of the 1930s, this was achieved by increasing the acreage of arable land. Indirectly, Stalin recognized the defeat of his policy in agriculture when in 1935 he allowed collective farmers to maintain private plots, a restricted number of individually owned cattle, and permission to sell their produce legally in the cities. By 1937–38, these tiny private plots (3.3 percent of arable land) accounted for 21 percent of all agricultural output in the country.[44] By the mid-1970s, the share of privately produced goods grew to 30 percent.

Paradoxically, when Brezhnev decided to increase agricultural production in the mid-1970s by investing more in it and by raising payment to the "peasants," the production of agricultural goods decreased in inverse proportion to investment. With more money being paid for the same work and little to buy, the farmers simply decreased their private production.

Thus, both industry and agriculture reached the point of exhaustion; further expansion became impossible. Today the country must rely on imports of grain, technology, and credits to survive.

Even nature seems to have been exhausted by seventy years of communist rule. Unlike in the West, where public opinion prevents or rectifies the worst excesses of industrial pollution, there were no forces in the Soviet Union to stand in the way of the state. The very idea that nature should be "protected from man" was totally alien to the revolutionary philosophy. "We cannot wait for favors from nature. Our task is to take them from her." This was the slogan of the "proletarians," who believed that, in the appropriate conditions, one can make a pear out of an apple and a government minister out of a cook. Seventy years later, this philosophy has created a major environmental catastrophe: Chernobyl is only its best-known example.

By the end of the 1970s, air pollution in the Soviet Union had reached a "threatening level" in more than 1,000 cities; a level of "immediate danger for health" in over 100 cities; and a level ten times higher than that indicating "immediate danger" in about 10 cities.[45] Total economic damages caused by air and water pollution at the end of the 1970s were estimated by official Soviet experts to be 20 billion rubles, and by 1990 may reach 120 billion. Soviet rivers carry to the Baltic Sea about 20 times more pollutants than the Rhine delivers to the North Sea. Since land reclamation is expensive, only about 8 to 12 percent of the land destroyed by quarries and other methods of exploitation of mineral resources is annually reclaimed. Thus, about 77,200 square miles of territory had been destroyed by the end of the 1970s, with an additional 400 square miles being destroyed each year. Another problem is the rapid depletion of forests.

More land is destroyed by huge artificial lakes and seas created by hydro-electric power stations. The area submerged by these lakes equals 46,320 square miles. Soil erosion has made unusable a staggering 243,180 square miles of once excellent fields (with biological productivity being reduced by 80 to 90 percent). Komarov has calculated that the total land lost is equal to the territories of England, France, Italy, West Germany, Switzerland, Belgium, Holland, and Luxembourg combined.[46] An estimated 100 to 200 years will be needed to restore it.

Soviet policies have also destroyed rivers, turning them into stinking swamps. All this failed to produce the required amount of hydroelectric energy when the water level dropped. Evaporation, agricultural irrigation, and rapid expansion of industry aggravated the problem further. Natural lakes and seas—the Aral Sea, the Sea of Azov, the Caspian Sea—may shrink greatly or simply disappear by the next century. The ecology of the Black Sea is already damaged and will be damaged further. Shortage of water will affect development plans in industry and agriculture.

The main solution pursued is to continue building canals, dams, and lakes. Thus, the waters of the Danube are going to be diverted northward, and proposals—now abandoned—would have turned the course of northern rivers (Pechora, Sukhona, Onega, and North Dvina) to the south via the Volga. There are also proposals to redirect the waters of huge Siberian rivers (Ob and Irtysh) to Central Asia, through a canal 1,500 miles long. Both projects would have cost about 35 billion rubles (undoubtedly with the widespread use of prison labor).[47] Scientists predict that these gigantic projects would not have saved the south, but would have destroyed the fragile northern ecosystem.[48]

This background of general hopelessness and environmental destruction is necessary to understand two widespread human reactions to Soviet reality: degeneracy and dissidence.

One must remember that at least three generations have been born and have grown up under this system, watching the slow destruction of their country, culture, and fellow citizens. There is hardly a family that has not experienced repression at some time. For three generations these people have been obliged to listen and to repeat the obvious lies of official propaganda and to be cheerful at the same time because it is antisocial not to be cheerful in a socialist paradise. This contradiction alone, between reality and propaganda, is sufficient to produce a profound psychological trauma, to say nothing of ever-present fear, suspicion, and misery.

One of the main goals of the Soviet regime was always to convince the population that they are in a no-win situation: there is no escape from their misery, either physically or emotionally. There is no way to improve their situation or to escape abroad, and any initiative is severely discouraged. This pattern is known in experimental psychology as "learned helplessness" and leads to the inability of the subject to discover *how* to escape, even when escape is available.

One has to employ medical terminology because Soviet reality is not simply a matter of disillusionment, lack of prospects, apathy, or resignation. It is a biological exhaustion, a fatigue of human material. The signs are high infant mortality, low birthrate (below replacement rate among the Russians and some other nationalities), and an exceptionally high percentage of children born physically and mentally handicapped (about 6 to 7 percent by the end of the 1970s and projected to be 15 percent by the end of the 1990s).[49] The latter is partly caused by massive environmental pollution but largely by alcoholism, which is the most common escape-reaction.

Contrary to popular belief, the current epidemic of alcoholism has little to do with traditional Russian drinking habits. A Russian prerevolutionary encyclopedia[50] says that in 1905 about 50 percent of men and 95 percent of women were total abstainers; per capita consumption was much smaller than in the United States today. A document smuggled from the Soviet Union in 1985[51] showed an enormous increase in alcohol consumption. Although it is hard to believe, it is there asserted that, in 1979, only 0.6 percent of men and 2.4 percent of women were abstainers, and 5 percent among young people under age 18. In 1983, it reported, there were an estimated 40 million medically certified alcoholics; and that number is estimated to be growing to 80 million by the year 2000, or 65 percent of the working population.

The second main reaction—dissidence—should not be understood simply as narrow political disagreement. Professor Zaslavskaya explains it as follows in the "Novosibirsk Document":

> Even with the most rigid regimentation of behavior in the economic sphere, the population is always left with a certain choice of reactions to governmental restrictions, which it does not necessarily . . . accept. Hence there is a possibility of overt and covert conflicts between interest groups and the society as a whole. When the established norms and rules affect the vital interests of certain groups of the population, . . . the latter often find a way to shirk restrictions and to satisfy their demands. When the state takes more strict measures to curb undesirable types of activity, the population responds by finding more subtle patterns of behavior to secure satisfaction of

its demands in the new conditions, etc. Thus, reciprocally oriented behavior and interactions, of the state on the one hand, . . . and of socioeconomic groups on the other, represent an important part of the social mechanism of economic development.[52]

Needless to say, the same kind of implicit "dialogue" occurs between the regime and society in all spheres of life. In the economic sphere, this "dialogue" has led to a "black market" of semilegal activities, corruption, and theft of public property. In other spheres it has led to cultural, religious, nationalist, and political dissent.

The black market and corruption permeate every aspect of Soviet life, from top to bottom. Shortages of consumer goods, food, services, and materials have made it necessary for the people to develop their own system of distribution. The government has tried to fight it tooth and nail (since the early 1960s, a wide variety of these activities have been punishable by death), but the system grows. It has developed into a huge and intricate network of underground business activity, private industry, and corruption. The system of internal Soviet trade, many official enterprises, and a large portion of the police have become involved in it.[53] Quite often Party bosses and top governmental executives become involved, or are bribed to cover it up. Few have been caught. During the eighteen years of Brezhnev's reign, the top echelon of power became practically immune. One can only guess what effect this has had on corruption.

To the population, the effect has been quite profound. If nothing else, people became less dependent on official favors and state distribution while becoming more and more cash-oriented. Consider the following, admittedly crude, estimate: the official average income in the country is about 160 rubles a month, and official governmental prices are calculated to allow people to barely make ends meet. However, little in the way of food and consumer goods is available in the shops, while in the black market their prices are three to four times (often five to ten times) higher than those established by the state. Since nobody dies of hunger or goes around naked, many actual incomes must be much higher — many people must be making 500 to 1,000 rubles monthly. When we hear that the black market price of blue jeans was 250 rubles in 1979, and they were "selling like hotcakes," when we know that the prices of Soviet cars are in the range of 8,000 to 15,000 rubles, what else can we think? One cannot buy them with a 160 rubles monthly salary.

To sum up, the past seventy years of communist rule have destroyed any trust that may have existed originally between the rulers and the people. The latter can hardly expect significant improvements from any within-the-system reforms because the system has outlived itself. But, even if the system is dismantled, it

may take a couple of generations before the country recovers and a huge, degener-
ated portion becomes replaced. Collective farmers have to relearn how to be peasants, "proletarians" have to learn how to be workers, surviving craftsmen have
to teach their skills to the new generations.

Gorbachev cannot count on these millions of "medically certified alcoholics"
to sober up suddenly and to become high-output Stakhanovite workers, even if
he pays them five times the present wage. If they were capable of such feats of
production, workers already would have joined one or another of the semilegal
businesses existing in the country. The best Gorbachev can use them for will be
on the construction of a 1,500-mile-long canal from Siberia to Central Asia, and
of thirty-two dams on the White Sea, as some authors have suggested.[54] Gorbachev's reforms must appeal to those who are interested in improving their personal income, who therefore must compete with the black market. In a way,
Gorbachev's reforms will help the black market. Two obstacles currently curb
its activity: one cannot spend a lot of money in the Soviet Union, and, above
all, one cannot do it openly. Both obstacles will have to be removed if increased
material incentives are to be introduced. Besides, Gorbachev's main idea—to
reduce control over enterprises and to give them more initiative—implies even
more "uncontrolled" interactions between underground capitalism and the state
enterprises.

In short, Gorbachev is going to learn what Lenin discovered sixty-five years
before him: that the "market place is stronger" than socialism. It is of some interest
to note what Gorbachev wants to do with the economy; it is far more interesting
to see what the economy will do with Gorbachev. Whatever he does is bound
to increase already growing inflation and, therefore, create conditions for widespread industrial unrest. Whatever his intentions, his actions will strengthen the
existing trends.

3

Charles Gati

The Unsettled Condition of Eastern Europe

The unsettled condition of Eastern Europe remains a problem for all parties having an interest in the region and its future. The problem is a critical one for the unreconciled people of Eastern Europe. It is agonizing for the communist regimes there, which are caught between the imperative of satisfying Moscow's demands and the desirability of advancing their countries' national interests. It is serious for the Soviet Union, which has yet to find a formula that would make the region both subservient and stable. And it is embarrassing for the West, which is unable to overcome its positional disadvantage and has not advanced significantly its stated goals of Eastern European independence and democratic evolution.

Eastern European Realities

No reasonable observer can entertain doubts about the political sentiments and aspirations of the people of Eastern Europe. These sentiments and aspirations were expressed clearly in East Berlin in 1953; in Hungary in 1956; in Czechoslovakia in 1968; and in Poland in 1956, 1970, 1976, and most dramatically in 1980–81. Although each of the popular outbreaks, some violent and some peaceful, displayed features characteristic of the particular country involved, they shared a number of common features as well. Above all, they aimed at extricating Eastern Europe from excessive Soviet domination and sought to initiate a process of pluralistic evolution. In the case of Poland, all outbreaks aimed at economic renewal as well.

The obvious explanation for deep-rooted and widespread opposition to Soviet domination is that the people of Eastern Europe want to control their own destinies. After all, prior to World War II they enjoyed a period of national independence which, however short-lived, is deeply ingrained in their collective consciousness. A more nuanced explanation begins with the observation that while the people of Eastern Europe are used to living in the shadow of a great power, they are not used to accepting such massive penetration of their daily existence as presently demanded and enforced by the Soviet Union. Thus, according to this view, what they actually seek, and would certainly welcome, is no more than a measure of independence or semiautonomy, an historically familiar condition that would allow them to assume their role of maneuvering between great powers and at the same time to develop domestic institutions more closely resembling traditional patterns and practices.

To understand persistent popular resistance to Soviet hegemony, a key consideration remains the absence of "authentic revolutions," and hence of political legitimacy in Eastern Europe. The people in Moscow's Eastern European empire, unlike some of their counterparts in Russia, China, Cuba, or Yugoslavia, did not participate in an indigenous or native communist revolution after World War II, nor have they experienced one since. Their "revolution" of 1944–45 was essentially exported to their homelands by Soviet power. Furthermore, either they were denied the opportunity to vote against the new order, or when given such an opportunity—as in Hungary in 1945 and Czechoslovakia in 1946—the majority voted against a Soviet-style, one-party hegemony and for a multi-party, pluralistic political system. In the eyes of their subjects, then, the Eastern European regimes have lacked legitimacy from the beginning.

Popular opposition to Soviet-style communist rule in Eastern Europe also stems from economic dissatisfaction. True, the standard of living is higher in Eastern Europe than it is in the Soviet Union, perhaps a third higher in the region as a whole. As of the mid-1980s, living conditions—as measured either by incomes or by the availability of goods—were considerably better in the German Democratic Republic (GDR), Hungary, Czechoslovakia, and even Poland than they were in the Soviet Union, with Bulgaria and especially Rumania lagging behind. But, rightly or wrongly, Eastern Europe's relative standing vis-à-vis the Soviet

Union is largely irrelevant to the people of the region, who tend to compare their standard of living with Western neighbors. The question for people in the GDR is not how much *ahead* they are in comparison with the Soviet Union, or for that matter in comparison with any other state in the Soviet empire; the question they ask is how far *behind* they are in comparison with West Germany. Similarly, Hungarians make the comparison with Austrians, Czechs with West Germans, Poles with Scandinavians, and so on. As a result, they—correctly—conclude that the economic system imposed by the Soviet Union has failed to match the results achieved by their capitalist neighbors in Western Europe. As a result, too, they blame the Soviet Union as much as their own regimes for economic mismanagement, including high prices, low-quality goods, persistent shortages in most countries, and—especially in Rumania but also in Poland—the frequent unavailability of even the most basic necessities of life.

Still another reason why the people of Eastern Europe remain unreconciled has to do with their at least partial exclusion from the mainstream of Europe. The very term *Eastern Europe* is alien to the residents of Prague, Warsaw, Berlin, or Budapest. They regard themselves as *Central* Europeans, who have had to join a new political configuration called Eastern Europe only because they ended up in the Soviet sphere after World War II. When it comes to culture, in particular, they regard their contributions as part and parcel of a broader European civilization; many of the great European musicians and writers of past centuries, they point out, accomplished what they did in such Central European centers of culture as Vienna and Prague, Berlin and Budapest.

In trying to overcome their predicament, Eastern Europeans have resorted to one of two political strategies during the past several decades. They have opposed the communist regimes *from without* by methods ranging from quiet participation in unofficial discussion groups and human rights organizations to organizing illegal demonstrations and even outright rebellions. Their often heroic and dramatic activities have indicated a deep desire to bring about fundamental, systemic changes in Eastern Europe, on the assumption that it is neither desirable nor possible to reach genuine and lasting agreements with the communist authorities. Others, considering any confrontation futile, have sought to oppose the communist regimes *from within*, aiming less at systemic transformation than at the gradual reform of the existing system. They assume that the most that the Soviet Union may be expected to tolerate in Eastern Europe is a measure of liberalization of the Soviet-type political and economic order. This kind of change, in turn, can best be achieved by individuals feigning support for the regimes' general objectives and thus making themselves politically palatable in order to gain a measure of influence and then to improve conditions in some small ways. Needless to say, the activities of such people usually go unheralded and unappreciated. In fact, neither strategy has worked well, which is why there is permanent tension between the ruled and the rulers in Eastern Europe.

The Transfer of Power

For several years after World War II, it was easy to generalize about the rulers of Eastern Europe. Nearly all of the top leaders were "Muscovites"–communist revolutionaries and ideologists who had spent the 1930s and the wartime years as exiles in the Soviet Union, working for the Communist International, preparing for their return to and their new postwar role in Eastern Europe. Returning home in the wake of the Red Army, they were joined by the so-called "home communists," many of whom had played a leading role in anti-Nazi resistance movements in their native lands. Minor and early differences between the Muscovites and the home communists aside, the communist leaders of Eastern Europe were united in their fanatic allegiance to, and unquestioned acceptance of the "leading role" of, the Soviet Union's Communist Party and its greatly admired, even adored, leader, Iosif Vissarionovich Stalin.

Since Stalin's death in 1953, more so in some countries than in others, such unquestioned allegiance has given way to a greater variety of official policies and attitudes in Eastern Europe. Generally speaking, while the region's regimes have continued to satisfy Moscow's demands for "bloc cohesion," some of them also have sought to respond to popular pressures by adopting policies more in line with their countries' particular "national interests." At one time or another during the past several decades, almost all Eastern European regimes have developed policies and embraced ideological orientations that, to a greater or lesser extent, diverged from those of the Soviet Union. They have done so neither because they ceased to be communists nor because they necessarily meant to become disloyal to the Soviet Union, but because they concluded that in order to obtain a measure of stability in their respective countries, they had to take exception to some of Moscow's least effective or least justifiable patterns and approaches.

Since the mid-1960s, the Rumanian regime of Nicolae Ceausescu has gone the farthest to exploit nationalist aspirations by following a foreign policy course considerably different from that of the Soviet Union. Rumania refused to participate in the Soviet-led military intervention in Czechoslovakia in 1968, and it has criticized the undeclared Soviet war against Afghanistan since 1979. It has not allowed Warsaw Pact military exercises to take place on Rumanian soil. Alone in the Warsaw Pact, Rumania defied the Soviet boycott of the 1984 Los Angeles Olympics as it has the Pact's diplomatic boycott of Israel. Rumania also has maintained cordial state-to-state as well as party-to-party relations with the People's Republic of China. However irritating to Moscow, these policies and gestures nevertheless have failed to satisfy the Rumanian people's longing for autonomous or semiautonomous existence because they have been accompanied by such widespread domestic repression, including religious and cultural intolerance, and such chaotic economic conditions as to make Rumania one of Europe's harshest dictatorships.

Also since the mid-1960s, the Hungarian regime of János Kádár has stressed economic reform and political accommodation. The economic reform has especially affected the country's agriculture. Although peasants remain in the collective farms, they have a large say about farm leadership, production, produce marketing, and—within limits—the prices they charge for their products. Such changes have resulted in higher agricultural prices, but also in the easy availability of food for both domestic consumption and export—a rare development in the Soviet bloc. Without making similar changes in the country's industrial sector, the Kádár regime also has allowed private enterprise to mushroom in service areas such as repair shops, restaurants, local transportation, and the like. All in all, Hungary's pragmatic approach to Marxist economic theory, despite serious setbacks in the 1980s, has proved to be quite successful.

In the political realm, Kádár's so-called "alliance policy" has signified grudging tolerance of prevailing sentiments and conditions such as the apparent popular hatred for everything Russian, widespread contempt for communist ideology, and a pervasive sense of nostalgia—especially among urban intellectuals—for belonging to "Europe." The alliance policy means that the regime is prepared to accept, work with, and even promote to positions of some importance everyone except those who openly and explicitly challenge its claim to legitimacy. Reflecting that policy, Kádár has reformulated the Stalinist dictum—"He who is not with us is against us"—to say, "He who is not against us is with us." The substantial difference between the two formulations has made Kádár and the political order he has built the envy of Eastern European and perhaps even Soviet reformers.

Poland's communist leaders have retained or developed several institutions and policies that cannot be found elsewhere in the Soviet bloc. The relative autonomy of the Catholic Church, with its extraordinary following and influence, is a *fait accompli* even Moscow has come to tolerate. Throughout the postwar decades, much of Polish agriculture has remained in the hands of private farmers. Before, during, and even since the dramatic rise of the Solidarity movement in 1980–81, Polish intellectuals always have managed to express themselves more freely than their counterparts elsewhere in Eastern Europe. Since 1981, still stubbornly refusing to conform, they have published and circulated thousands of weeklies and monthlies that castigate the regime of General Wojciech Jaruzelski for its incompetence and failures, and that advocate a variety of radical solutions for the country's future. As a result the condition of Poland is paradoxical: while it remains, as Warsaw wits put it, the freest barracks in the Soviet camp, the overwhelming majority of the people — actively or passively — reject the regime's concessions as altogether insufficient.

Until the 1980s the communist regime in the GDR was Moscow's most loyal ally in the Warsaw Pact. Its domestic political arrangements still resemble Soviet patterns. Yet in the economic realm East Berlin has sought to find an organizational model somewhat more in line with what is expected to work in this economically quite advanced country. Accordingly, East Germany's economy has been "streamlined" rather than "reformed," meaning that the regime has reduced the size of the bureaucracy by eliminating unnecessary middle management and has begun to introduce high technology to make the economy more efficient. As in Hungary, private enterprise has taken over some of the small service industries. Because of the relatively advanced stage of the East German economy and because of the interest and willingness of West Germany to be a steady supplier of technology and credit to the East Germans, there has been a substantial expansion of inter-German economic relations in the 1980s — even during a time of poor relations between the Soviet Union and West Germany. Thus, for the first time since the end of World War II, the otherwise loyal communist regime of Erich Honecker has had to face the choice between pursuing its national interests by maintaining cordial relations with West Germany or pursuing its international duties and obligations by following all the twists and turns in Soviet foreign policy toward the West.

The Bulgarian and especially the Czechoslovak regimes show few if any signs in the 1980s of their need or desire to do anything differently from the Soviet Union. There have been reports of Bulgarian attempts to change the terms of Soviet-Bulgarian trade and indeed to reduce Sofia's economic dependence on Moscow, with Bulgarian leader Todor Zhivkov allegedly hoping to make his country "the Japan of the Balkans." As for Czechoslovakia, the promising reforms of the 1968 "Prague Spring" are gone, the dream of creating "socialism with a human face" is gone, the fervent hopes of Czechs and Slovaks to rejoin Central Europe are gone. What remains is a sullen, defeated people who are ruled by an unimaginative, lethargic government and the most orthodox communist party in the Soviet bloc.

All in all, there has come to be both uniformity and diversity in Eastern Europe. Like the Soviet Union itself, the six countries of the region are ruled by communist parties, and their economies borrow heavily from the centralized Soviet model. Political rights do not exist and individual freedoms occasionally are given, never granted. But precisely because some Soviet policies are duplicated only "to a greater or lesser extent," it is possible to speak of the region's diversity as well. Not the satellites of the past, some Eastern European regimes are even making common cause with one another—forming informal mini-coalitions—within such multilateral institutions as the Warsaw Pact and the Council for Mutual Economic Assistance in order to advance their countries' national interests.

Eroding Influence

For the Soviet Union, Eastern Europe does not constitute a "sphere of influence" in the classical meaning of the term. The region is certainly more than a buffer zone and a political or military asset. Economically, it is almost certainly a liability. If Eastern Europe were merely a "sphere of influence" for Moscow, the region's states would long have been allowed to emulate Finland's postwar understanding with the Soviet Union.

Such an understanding would have resulted in Eastern European foreign policies so carefully pursued as to avoid alienating or perhaps even irritating the Soviet Union; but it would have also resulted in considerable independence, if not complete freedom, for the Eastern Europeans to fashion domestic political and economic institutions that would suit their traditions and interests. An Eastern Europe so construed would not have joined Western military, political, or even economic organizations and alliances; indeed, it would have offered the Soviet Union a sphere of cordial and respectful states mindful of the security interests of their big Eastern neighbor.

Having gained the condition of semiautonomy, such a "Finlandized" Eastern Europe would have been more stable and its people less preoccupied with the now overriding issue of anti-Sovietism, and the region's new status also would have advanced Moscow's other foreign policy objectives in Western Europe and elsewhere. Instead of the present condition of "communist encirclement" by hostile people and ostensibly fraternal regimes, the Soviet Union could have obtained a neutral belt along its western border, ranging from Finland in the north to Yugoslavia in the south, and hence would have gained a measure of genuine security.

But there are no indications that Moscow ever has considered the possibility of granting Eastern Europe such a "Finlandized" status. Indeed, the Soviet concept of a "sphere of influence" significantly differs from the classical meaning of the term for three reasons. One is that for the Soviet leaders real influence is synonymous with control. The second is that for the Soviet leaders control over Eastern Europe has become synonymous with control over the Soviet Union itself. The third is that the Soviet leaders are limited by ideological precepts to accept what they would regard as a "historical regression" from the "socialist commonwealth" of the present era to a neutral "sphere of influence."

Unable to devise fresh initiatives, Moscow has sought to maintain its Eastern European empire by inducements when possible, by force when necessary. In the 1970s, for example, the Soviet Union found itself compelled to sustain the Eastern European economies through favorable credit arrangements and apparently vast trade subsidies. By the end of that decade, the economic cost of the region rose to as much as about 2.5 to 3 percent of the Soviet gross national product (GNP), essentially doubling during that decade. Since the very beginning of the Warsaw Pact, Soviet military contributions to the Pact—measured by GNP per capita—have outpaced Eastern European contributions by a factor of at least two to one and possibly three to one. Such Soviet "sacrifices" should be understood to have been made in order to buy political stability in this volatile region.

Soviet control is also maintained through the penetration of the Eastern European armed forces and internal security apparatuses. In Czechoslovakia, for example, a good number of security agents in the mid-1960s were reportedly "two check" employees, meaning that they were paid a salary by the Czechoslovak government and by the Soviet government as well. The training of high-ranking Eastern European military officers in the Soviet Union and the integration of the region's armed forces into the Warsaw Pact are also meant to ensure that these armies remain or become reliable instruments of Soviet policy.

Of course, one of the most effective mechanisms of Soviet control always has been Moscow's ability to determine the composition of the Eastern European *nomenklatura*: its ability, in particular, to select party leaders who would loyally and pliably implement Soviet goals. Back in the 1950s, the Soviet leaders could simply call a few Hungarian leaders to Moscow and "recommend" the replacement of Matyas Rakosi by Imre Nagy as Prime Minister; the decision was made then and there, and there was nothing unusual about it. Today, it is not self-evident that a similar "recommendation" automatically would be accepted or immediately carried out. The Soviet Union must now rely on more subtle methods of persuasion and pressure to get *its* people into positions of authority. Normally, Moscow still gets its way, especially when it comes to the position of the General Secretary (or First Secretary) of an Eastern European communist party. However, there were reported instances in 1985 when a high-ranking party official who was considered to be "Moscow's man" lost his position (e.g., Polish Politburo member Stefan Olszowski), or when a high-ranking party official who was not regarded by Moscow to be fully trustworthy kept one (e.g., Hungarian Central Committee Secretary Matyas Szuros).

In the final analysis, however, it is the threat of Soviet military intervention that keeps Eastern Europe in line. After all, Moscow has demonstrated over the years that while it may not be trigger-happy and while it may regard military intervention as a last resort, it is prepared to protect its dominion irrespective of cost and consequence. Because Eastern Europeans do not doubt Moscow's determination and because they want to avoid hopeless confrontations, there have been relatively few cases when the Soviet leaders actually intervened—only a "few cases," that is, when viewed against the background of pervasive discontent and deep-rooted anti-communist and anti-Soviet sentiments.

With all these efforts, the Soviet Union successfully has maintained its ultimate control over Eastern European developments. At the same time, however, the Soviet bloc Stalin built has been transformed from one based on a common ideology with an acknowledged—and admired—center of power to one in which the pursuit of national interests has become a significant fact of political life. What has taken place, then, is the gradual erosion of Soviet authority over the less-than-ultimate issues of Eastern European economics and politics. Moscow's twin goals of bloc cohesion and regional stability remain beyond reach.

Moreover, the erosion of Soviet authority in Eastern Europe has become a source of considerable division, and perhaps even a sense of helplessness, in Moscow. In mid-1985, for example, an authoritative article in *Pravda* sought to deny the legitimacy of different national interests among members of the bloc, arguing against "revisionist" views—as advanced by the Hungarian, East German, and Romanian communist parties—which stressed the special role of "small and medium-sized" countries in the improvement of East-West relations. "What question can there be of any mediation by particular socialist countries in resolving disagreements between the USSR and the U.S.," *Pravda* asked, "if on key international questions the foreign policy of the USSR and of the Marxist-Leninist nucleus of world socialism is identical?" But two months later the authoritative Soviet foreign affairs weekly *New Times*, in an article written by a Central Committee member, took a more nuanced position. At the present stage of development, the article noted, each communist party must find the appropriate balance between fulfilling its "international obligations" to the bloc and also pursuing its national interests. Though couched in somewhat obtuse communist jargon, such a public debate about Eastern Europe had never before taken place in the Soviet Union.

But the most revealing, if puzzling, aspect of Soviet–Eastern European relations in the 1980s has been Moscow's inability to reverse, stop, or even slow down the process of national assertiveness in the region. Moscow has not been able to oust the more "pragmatic" Eastern European communist leaders from high leadership positions anywhere. There has been no significant recent realignment in the Eastern European countries' foreign trade patterns due solely or primarily to Soviet political pressure. High-level meetings between the leaders of Eastern and Western Europe had taken place before Soviet leader Mikhail S. Gorbachev decided to hold such meetings with leaders of Western Europe and the United States (even if Erich Honecker and Todor Zhivkov did have to postpone their visits to Bonn in 1984). The meaning of what constitutes "socialism" is still differently interpreted in Bucharest, Budapest, East Berlin, and Warsaw on the one hand, and in Moscow (as well as in Prague and Sofia) on the other.

The main reason for such diversity—and for Moscow's problem of empire management—is conceptual. The Soviet goals of Eastern European subservience and stability are inherently contradictory. The goal of subservience to and conformity with Soviet policies requires harsh demands and pressures; the goal of Eastern European stability requires respect for each country's own interests. Unable to choose between its conflicting goals, the Soviet Union has sought to muddle through in order not to disturb the uneasy status quo for small, short-term gains. But Moscow cannot be satisfied fully with the result: over four decades after its formation the Soviet bloc in Eastern Europe is alive but not well.

Western Perceptions

The West and particularly the United States also has had a conceptual problem in dealing with Eastern Europe. For reasons of genuine idealism as well as domestic politics, the West has upheld maximalist objectives with respect to the future of Eastern Europe—the objectives of freedom for the people and independence for the states of the region. But at least since the 1956 Hungarian revolt, the West has actually pursued more limited, even minimalist objectives, seeking as it has no more than "humane conditions" for the people and only a "measure of independence" for the states of the region. The resulting gap between rhetoric and policy has caused some confusion as well as differences between the United States, which has tended to give voice to its idealism, and its more pragmatic Western European allies.

In practical terms, the main issue in the United States has had to do with the proper implementation of the official policy of "differentiation." In a nutshell, this policy—as affirmed by several administrations—consists of two propositions. First, by peaceful means, the United States will encourage those Eastern European regimes that, by treating their people more decently than the Soviet Union, show signs of respect for at least certain human rights. Second, by peaceful means, the United States also will encourage those Eastern European regimes that are willing to take distance from at least some of the least justifiable Soviet foreign policies and positions.

The consistent or vigorous implementation of differentiation has been opposed frequently by conservative critics, who consider differences among communist states to be insignificant and believe that this policy—by implicitly accepting the postwar status quo—offers far less than the dissolution or even the transformation of the Soviet empire. Human rights advocates of a liberal persuasion also have tended to find fault with differentiation, arguing that Western rewards should be denied to violators of human rights, including those in Eastern Europe—even if their foreign policy runs counter to the Soviet Union's. In recent years, such maximalist views—conservative and liberal—have converged in a growing congressional sentiment to deny Rumania most-favored-nation (MFN) tariff status, something that country had enjoyed since 1975. Moreover, the United States has actually denied Hungary, the other Warsaw Pact recipient of MFN, the opportunity to purchase a new telephone exchange from a West German–Austrian consortium in the 1980s, doing so on the grounds that a few of the American-made, presumably high-technology, components should not be sold to a member of the Warsaw Pact.

It seems that the policy of differentiation is in trouble because it satisfies neither the conservative nor the liberal longings for political and moral clarity. After all, it aims to reward, in however small ways, communist regimes that are not on our side and that only try to be a little less tied to the other side. On the assumption that something is better than nothing, the policy takes into account the West's substantial positional disadvantage in Eastern Europe and thus does not seek to obtain more than marginal influence in Moscow's front yard. That may well be the most that can be had under prevailing geopolitical circumstances; indeed, the policy of differentiation may well be the only realistic alternative to empty rhetoric and pathetic posturing. But it lacks emotional appeal; it offers no quick solution to the problems of Eastern Europe.

As to the Western Europeans' approach to the Soviet bloc, their criteria for Western rewards—certainly the Federal Republic's criteria—are mainly economic and only partly political. For, unlike the United States, which never has had extensive commercial ties with Eastern Europe, the Western Europeans always have had a natural trading relationship with their Eastern neighbors. Since the 1970s, the Federal Republic of Germany has become the leading Western trading partner of every Eastern European state; after the Soviet Union, it is the second most important one for most of them. For Western Europe, therefore, trade with the East has *economic* significance, and hence the expansion of ties with Eastern Europe widely is regarded as a positive and desirable goal even for commercial reasons alone.

Western Europe's political objectives tend to be modest and mainly long-term oriented. To the extent such a generalization can be made, Western Europeans do not believe that Moscow can be either charmed or pressured out of Eastern Europe, nor do they assume that significant changes in Eastern Europe can take place without Soviet concurrence. Accordingly, while waiting for a breakthrough in Soviet attitudes or in East-West relations, either of which may be years or decades away, Western Europeans seek a Western "presence" in Eastern Europe in order to maintain at least the appearance of an organic relationship between the two halves of Europe. Without expecting much to be gained in the short run, they seek to encourage the more tolerant regimes in the region to follow the path of détente between the small and medium-sized states of Europe, East and West.

Given the condition of different Western interests and approaches, it is hard to tell how much influence Western policies have had on the evolution of Eastern Europe. Arguably, Western policies may have had less impact than has the West's very existence; it has even been said that it matters less what the West *does* than what it *is*. While that may be an unduly critical appraisal of Western foreign policies, it is clear that the West does lack powerful instruments of policy to overcome its positional disadvantage vis-à-vis the Soviet Union. And since no policy can succeed without a prudent balance between ends and means, it seems that a realistic Western policy should aim at encouraging evolutionary or within-system changes rather than seek noble, desirable, but unrealizable objectives.

4

Francis Fukuyama

The Political Character of the Overseas Empire

Categorizing the Soviet Empire

As the Soviet Union begins its fourth decade of active involvement in the Third World, it finds itself the patron and leader of a large and extremely heterogeneous overseas empire.[1] It is nearly impossible to generalize about a group of countries that at one time or another has included communist Vietnam and Cuba together with mixed-economy states that have substantial private sectors, such as Syria and Iraq; with regional, well-developed, diversified economies and powerful military forces, such as those of Egypt, Indonesia, and India; and with the tiny, backward, and poverty-ridden "Marxist-Leninist" regimes of Benin, Guinea-Bissau, and Cape Verde in West Africa. Indeed, under a broad definition of "client" as any country that accepts some form of Soviet patronage, the list could be expanded to include some regimes formally tied to the United States, including Turkey, Iran under the Shah, or Argentina—which during the period of military rule after 1976 had substantial economic and political dealings with Moscow.[2]

This diverse empire, however, does lend itself to a certain degree of categorization. As the Soviet Union responded to the opportunities offered by the changing Third World environment after World War II, its strategy evolved as it tried to cultivate first one and then another type of state. Like the layers in an archaeological dig, the current heterogeneity in the states associated with Moscow represents successive accretions of allies from earlier periods of Soviet foreign policy. And as in the case of an archaeological excavation, a simple effort to group similar types of Soviet client regimes in some sense recapitulates the history of postwar Soviet policy in the Third World.

The Soviets do not, of course, possess an "empire" in the strict sense of political sovereignty, or even (with the sole exception of Afghanistan) in the sense of physical presence and political control. At one time or another all Soviet allies have acted contrary to Soviet wishes or in some way have demonstrated their "independence" of Moscow. "Empire" is used here in the looser sense—when clients depend on Soviet support, share substantial areas of common interest (or at least share more common interests with one another than with the other superpower), and look toward Moscow for patronage and protection.

Bearing this definition in mind, it is possible to group the empire's constituent members according to their political consanguinity to Moscow, that is, by the degree of cooperation that exists between patron and client. As it turns out, the Soviets themselves are very conscious of the often minute differences in the political character of their clients and distinguish between them on the basis of their willingness to collaborate with the rest of the "socialist community" (i.e., the Soviet bloc). Soviet writers on the Third World have established an elaborate conceptual structure within which to classify their Third World friends, based (not surprisingly) on the ideological nature of the regimes involved. While the exact terms vary from author to author, there are at least four major categories: socialist countries, socialist-oriented countries, national democracies, and capitalist-oriented countries. The Soviet "overseas empire" can be said to encompass the first two of these categories, with some countries from the third category participating from time to time.

The Soviet hierarchy is useful for describing their network of Third World allies, not only because it corresponds to real differences in the nature of Soviet clients, but also because it provides insight into the Soviets' own perception of their activities. It so happens that there is also a chronological order to these political categories; most clients falling into the group of national democracies were acquired during the 1950s and 1960s, while the bulk of the socialist-oriented states joined the empire during the 1970s. Each of these terms will be discussed in turn.

The Socialist States. At the top of the Soviet hierarchy are those developing states deemed genuinely socialist,[3] i.e., on the level of the USSR itself and the other states of "real socialism" in Eastern Europe. The socialist countries are governed by formal communist parties,[4] have declared Marxism-Leninism as their ideology, and are at a level of development sufficient to permit implementation of the major socioeconomic transformations dictated by the program of scientific socialism. There are only two developing countries that consistently qualify as socialist countries in Soviet eyes: Cuba and Vietnam. At times the Soviets have also included North Korea, Mongolia, and Vietnam's satellite, Laos, in this group, but the practice is not uniform.[5] Inclusion among the ranks of the socialist states is clearly a mark of the trust the Soviets have in the reliability and staying power of the Third World leaderships involved. It also seems to reflect a willingness to make a substantial economic commitment; Cuba and Vietnam are the only Third World full members of the Council for Mutual Economic Assistance (CMEA) and benefit from the latter's "leveling up" policy.

The Socialist-Oriented States.　　Underneath the tier of the socialist states are the so-called "states of a socialist orientation" or, alternatively, those said to be on the "noncapitalist path of development." This somewhat loosely defined group is said to number between fifteen and twenty-five and includes many of the Soviet clients acquired during the 1970s, such as Afghanistan, Angola, Ethiopia, Mozambique, the People's Democratic Republic of Yemen (PDRY), and Nicaragua. One feature that the majority of socialist-oriented states have in common with socialist states is that they have declared Marxism-Leninism as their governing ideology; a few others (such as Libya, Tanzania, and Algeria) proclaim a left-wing but non-Marxist socialism and are included in the group.

The Soviets emphasize their support for the socialist-oriented states, in terms of both what they say (according to Yuri Andropov, "most close to us are the states of a socialist orientation") and where they put their development and military assistance. Nonetheless, Soviet unwillingness to admit this group into the charmed circle of fully socialist states despite their rhetorical commitment to Marxism-Leninism reflects at times serious Soviet doubts about the credentials of the local leadership. In most cases the Soviets believe that these countries' level of socioeconomic development is too low to permit the development of a true working-class and mass-based communist party; socialism is merely declarative and not yet implemented in actual policy. The lower prestige accorded such states is evident not only in formal Soviet pronouncements that rank Third World countries,[6] but also in the facts that the USSR has limited its economic commitments to them and has not permitted any to hold more than observer status in CMEA.[7]

The National Democracies.　　This group of countries alternately has been referred to by the Soviets as "bourgeois nationalists" or the right wing of "revolutionary democracy." For example, included in this group at one time or another were Egypt under Nasser, Indonesia under Sukharno, India, Somalia (prior to its abrogation of its friendship treaty with the USSR), Ghana, Mali, Burundi, and Zambia. The national democracies generally proclaim vaguely left-wing but non-Marxist-Leninist ideologies that tend to be more nationalist than socialist in character,[8] doctrines such as African socialism, pan-Arabism, or more recently Islamic Marxism. While national democratic regimes are explicitly non-communist and have frequently jailed or persecuted local communists, they also tend to be strongly anti-imperialist in foreign policy. Many national democracies proclaim their nonalignment and are active in the nonaligned movement but in fact have collaborated extensively with the Soviet bloc; in the cases of Egypt and Somalia, treaties of friendship and cooperation with the USSR were actually signed.

The Capitalist-Oriented States.   The Soviets recognize a final category of Third World countries, those with capitalist economic systems and political alignments with the West. These include states such as Pakistan, the Philippines, Saudi Arabia, Brazil, and Argentina. While none of these states would be considered part of the Soviet "overseas empire," this has not prevented the USSR from having extensive economic and even political dealings with them.

While these four categories are useful for understanding the hierarchy of Soviet clients, they are not all-inclusive; it is difficult to know where to place a state like the Islamic Republic of Iran, which seems to be the ally of neither superpower. Nonetheless, the categories do identify common characteristics among Soviet clients and map out the varying degrees of political influence exercised by the Soviets. In the following sections I will describe how these different groups came to accept Soviet patronage and the types of relationships they have with Moscow.

Where the Overseas Empire Came From

Since the Soviets today consider only a handful of Third World states genuinely socialist, it is difficult to generalize about their origins. Nonetheless, much of the groundwork for the contemporary categories was laid by Stalin. Of the four states (excluding Mongolia) that at some time have fallen into this category, one came to power in the immediate postwar period (North Korea), and the liberation wars leading to the formation of two others (Vietnam and Laos) were begun at that time as well.[9] In the immediate aftermath of World War II, Stephen Sestanovich has pointed out, Soviet policy toward the colonial world (there were very few independent Third World states at the time) was not a low-key one, as many people assume.[10] Stalin sought protectorates over Libya and the Horn of Africa, threatened Turkey in hopes of obtaining a revision of the conventions governing the Turkish straits, supported the Chinese communists after they defeated the Kuomintang and the Vietminh in Indochina, tried to establish an independent pro-Soviet communist republic in northern Iran, and gave Kim Il-Sung the go-ahead to invade South Korea. These major Soviet initiatives tended to revolve around allies that were 1) orthodox communists, and 2) on the periphery of the Soviet Union. Stalin believed that leaders of newly independent nations, such as India's Nehru and Egypt's Nasser, were bourgeois puppets of the colonial powers, and for this reason he preferred to support orthodox communists.

Khrushchev and the National Democracies.   The bulk of the clients falling into the category of "national democracies" were acquired during the tenure of Nikita Khrushchev as First Secretary. It was Khrushchev who opened Soviet foreign policy to the national democrats by negotiating the famous arms deal with Egypt's Nasser in 1955 and announcing the possibility of "many roads to socialism" at the 20th CPSU Congress in February 1956. Khrushchev subsequently applauded the work of the Nonaligned Conference in Bandung, Indonesia, and established aid relationships with Afghanistan, Syria, Indonesia, India, Iraq, Ghana, Mali, and other noncommunist Third World countries. Most Soviet clients that still fall in the category of national democracies, such as India and Syria, began their association with Moscow during this period.

Khrushchev recognized that national liberation struggles throughout the world, though not led by communists, were universally anti-Western in character and that European and American positions could be undermined at low risk and with a relatively small Soviet expenditure of political and economic capital. Many national democracies still were engaged in conflicts with Western states and eagerly sought Soviet support. For example, Nasser's nationalization of the Suez Canal led directly to his appeals for Soviet support against the tripartite British-French-Israeli attack on Egypt during the 1956 Suez crisis. While Nasser was hardly a communist, his resentment of British colonialism and his promotion of pan-Arab nationalism put him squarely at odds with Western interests throughout the Arab East.

Most national democracies were led by pre-independence nationalist movements that had come to power on their own and had a broad popular legitimacy. The Soviets did not have to intervene militarily to bring them to power or keep them there. Thus, in the absence of global military power projection capabilities, the Soviets faced vast new possibilities for extending their influence to distant, noncontiguous regions. The Soviet Union encouraged the national democrats' anti-imperialism primarily through the transfer of arms out of its own enormous stockpiles. Moscow also provided economic assistance—a value in the 1950s and 1960s that was greater than that of arms transfers. But this tended to be concentrated in a few large showpiece projects with high political payoffs, such as the Aswân High Dam in Egypt,[11] and was politically less salient than weapons deliveries. During this period the Soviets did not attempt to intervene directly in their clients' internal affairs or try to help them build orthodox socialist institutions, but took a more laissez-faire attitude. Thus, apart from engaging in polemics with Nasser, Khrushchev did nothing to prevent the latter's suppression of the Egyptian Communist Party in 1958 or a similar persecution of local communists by Iraqi president Abd al-Karim Kassem in 1960.

This is not to say that the Soviets were unconcerned about their clients' internal ideological character. Khrushchev and others maintained what was in retrospect a highly overoptimistic belief that their clients would undergo something of a natural evolution from incoherent nationalism to scientific socialism. The Soviets at this point took Marxism-Leninism quite seriously as a workable doctrine for political and economic development. They hoped that its inherent superiority over capitalism would be sufficient to ensure its spread in the Third World, and they believed that it would not be necessary to intervene more directly to ensure the creation of socialist institutions in Third World countries. However, the only state that followed this line of development to full-fledged socialism was Castro's Cuba.

Brezhnev and the Socialist-Oriented States.   As noted earlier, most of the socialist-oriented states—including the present regimes in Angola, Mozambique, Afghanistan, the PDRY,[12] Ethiopia, Benin, Guinea-Bissau, Cape Verde, and Nicaragua (as well as the Bishop regime in Grenada)—all came to power during the 1970s, most of them in the period of intense Soviet activism in the Third World between 1975 and 1979. This came about as the result of a shift in Soviet strategy toward Marxist-Leninist parties, coinciding with the breakdown of the last major European colonial empire, that of Portugal in Africa. As the authoritative handbook, *The World Communist Movement*, edited by the Central Committee's International Department First Deputy Chief, Vadim Zagladin, put it,

> It is possible today even to speak of two groups of countries of a socialist orientation and of a second generation of revolutionary democrats, who are closer to scientific socialism. The distinctiveness of the new group of countries of a socialist orientation (Angola, Ethiopia, Afghanistan, Kampuchea, the PDRY, and others) is that they have to build the economy virtually from scratch. . . . The political

regimes of this group of countries are distinguished by great clarity of class positions. A process of the coming into being of new revolutionary parties, which at their congresses have declared their adoption of Marxist-Leninist ideology, is under way there.[13]

The Soviet Union and its socialist bloc allies such as Cuba and East Germany were instrumental either in bringing these regimes to power, as in the case of the cooperative intervention in Angola in 1976, which allowed the Movement for the Liberation of Angola (MPLA) to triumph over its Western and Chinese-backed rivals, the National Front for the Liberation of Angola (FNLA) and the National Union for the Total Independence of Angola (UNITA), or in keeping them there, as in the support rendered to the Ethiopian Dergue when Ethiopia was invaded by Somalia in 1977. Moscow supported Vietnam militarily and politically prior to its 1979 invasion of Kampuchea, and in Afghanistan, the Soviet Union intervened with its own forces in December 1979 to keep the People's Democratic Party of Afghanistan in power.

The shift in Soviet emphasis away from the Khrushchev-era national democracies toward the socialist-oriented states was a fully self-conscious decision on the part of the Soviets, the rationale for which was developed at length in the Soviet theoretical literature on the Third World. The shift came about as a result of the perceived weaknesses of the national democracies from the standpoint of Soviet interests. In the late 1960s and early 1970s, Moscow suffered a number of setbacks in the Third World. Many Khrushchev-era clients, including those in Algeria, Ghana, Mali, and Indonesia, were overthrown in coups; the Indonesian Communist Party was suppressed at enormous human cost with the downfall of Sukharno in 1965. In July 1972, Soviet advisers were expelled from Egypt, Moscow's oldest and most important client, leading to the total elimination of Soviet influence from that country by the middle of the decade. Even in the case of states that did not desert the Soviet camp, Moscow's national democratic allies had foreign policy agendas that frequently had little to do with those of the Soviets. Hence Moscow found itself drawn into unwanted confrontations with the United States in the Middle East Wars of 1967, 1970, and 1973; at odds with Syria over the latter's intervention in Lebanon in 1976; and bickering with Iraq over arms purchases from France and other matters.

The Soviet analysis of these weaknesses led them to two conclusions. The first was that where Moscow had the choice, it ought to favor Marxist-Leninist over non-Marxist-Leninist groups—a reversion to the Stalinist policy, though applied much more flexibly in practice. Unlike the Khrushchev-era national democracies, the second-generation socialist-oriented states "enhance cooperation with the socialist countries to a new level and deliberately promote the expansion of such cooperation," while rejecting "the idea of a 'third way,' and the thesis of the special features of the 'African' or 'Arab' personality."[14] Since Marxism-Leninism is an inherently internationalist doctrine, the socialist-oriented states should, all other factors being equal, be more prone to cooperate with the foreign policy goals of the Soviet Union than the national democracies.

The second weakness in the first-generation states noted by the Soviets was their lack of a strong organizational base. Most national democracies were led by charismatic individuals—often, like Nasser, former military officers—who had made names for themselves in the independence struggle, but who failed to institutionalize their rule. The result was that when that individual was overthrown in a coup, the Soviets had no one to fall back on, which led to the collapse of their position in the country. In the days of Stalinist orthodoxy when Moscow worked entirely through communist parties, this problem, of course, did not arise. In the absence of a regular communist party, the solution favored by Soviet theorists was to encourage their Marxist-Leninist clients to form vanguard parties after coming to power. Vanguard parties were meant to be highly centralized Leninist organizations that would give the Soviets some assurance of political continuity in the face of changes in the leader or leaders at the top, as well as provide them with alternative points of influence.

With the exception of the Vietnamese Communist Party (and its affiliates in Laos and Kampuchea) and the PDPA in Afghanistan, none of the new socialist-oriented states that received Soviet support in the 1970s started out as orthodox communist parties. Most began as national liberation movements fighting colonial rule and at some point came to declare Marxism-Leninism as their guiding ideology. The Front for the Liberation of Mozambique (FRELIMO), for example, adopted Marxism-Leninism only after the assassination of its first president, Eduardo Mondlane, in 1969 and the subsequent takeover of the group by Samora Moises Machel. The MPLA in Angola started off as a Marxist organization that maintained close ties to both Moscow and the Stalinist Portuguese Communist Party in the 1960s.[15] All of the Soviet-supported national liberation movements in Lusophone Africa were heavily influenced by the writings of Amilcar Cabral, the theoretician in Guinea-Bissau who developed a kind of homegrown African Marxism, modified to meet local conditions.[16] In South Yemen, the National Liberation Front, which took over power from the British in 1968, was initially not a Marxist group but a coalition whose constituent members espoused everything from Nasserism to Marxism. While the NLF and its successor, the United Political Organization of the National Front (UPONF), moved steadily leftward under the influence of Soviet and East German advisers in the early to mid-1970s, the Yemeni Communist Party remained organizationally separate until 1978.[17]

Least organizationally developed of all the new Soviet clients was the ruling military council, or Dergue, in Ethiopia. The "revolution" in Ethiopia started out as a revolt among young army officers in reaction to the Haile Selassie regime's incompetence dealing with the drought and famine of 1974; it initially proclaimed a local ideology called, in Amharic, *hebrettesebawinet*. The officers around Mengistu Haile Mariam began moving leftward in the direction of Marxism-Leninism only after an internal palace coup that took place in February 1977, and they remained the chief political force in Addis Ababa.[18] In Nicaragua, the three main tendencies of the Sandinista Front for National Liberation (FSLN) were all Marxist organizations, but organizationally they were separate from the orthodox pro-Soviet communist party (the Socialist Party of Nicaragua, or PSN) and much more sympathetic to Cuban theories of armed struggle and guerrilla war.

As a result of Soviet urging, formal vanguard parties were formed in Angola and Mozambique in 1977 and in South Yemen in 1978. Soviet pressure to create a party was most evident in Ethiopia, where the Committee for Organizing the Working People of Ethiopia (COWPE) was established on December 18, 1979. The military rulers of Ethiopia understood quite well Soviet motives in urging them to establish a vanguard party and resisted Moscow until the formation of the Worker's Party of Ethiopia in September 1984, the tenth anniversary of the revolution.

Opportunism. While this historical account presents a neat picture of the evolution of the Soviet overseas empire throughout the stages of emphasis on socialist, national democratic, and socialist-oriented clients, a certain number of Soviet–Third World relationships do not fit this structure and can only be explained by Soviet opportunism. For example, Libya under Colonel Gadhafi was cultivated by Moscow after the shift in overall emphasis to the socialist-oriented states in the early 1970s in the wake of the oil crisis and Libya's growing radicalism, despite the fact that Gadhafi never espoused Marxism-Leninism. His theory of the "Third International Way" in the so-called *Green Book*, as well as the recklessness of his support for a variety of terrorist and revolutionary organizations around the world, traditionally have been suspect in Soviet eyes and yet are supported generously by the Soviets in view of his hostility to Western interests and his purchases of over $20 billion in Soviet arms (all for hard currency, substantially improving the Soviet balance-of-payments situation).[19]

The fact that Argentina was governed, after 1976, by a repressive right-wing military junta did not prevent Moscow from cultivating close economic ties with Buenos Aires, particularly after the Carter administration's embargo on grain sales to the USSR. On a political level, the Soviet Union supported Argentina before the United Nations Human Rights Commission and against Britain in the 1982 Falklands war, while counseling moderation to the pro-Soviet Argentine Communist Party.[20]

Finally, only opportunism can explain Moscow's courtship of Ferdinand

Marcos and his wife in the wake of American criticism after the assassination of Benigno Aquino and congratulations (virtually the only ones) after the Marcos "victory" in the February 1986 election.

Degrees of Consanguinity

The nations of Eastern Europe that were occupied by the Red Army after 1945 served as the model for near-total Soviet control over countries within its empire. For the first decade or two after the war, the Eastern European satellites marched lockstep with Soviet foreign and defense policies; Stalin could remove the Rajks, Kostovs, Slanskys, and Clementises from local leaderships at will. Soviet control was based not only on the presence of the Red Army (whose ultimate sanction was intervention, as in Hungary), but in the penetration of local party and military organizations by the secret police. The only communist parties not subject to such control were those that had come to power through their own efforts, such as those in Yugoslavia and China.

The problem for the Soviets in the Third World is that they never have been able to create a physical presence overseas that would permit them to duplicate the degree of control they once possessed in Eastern Europe. Instead, Soviet influence rests on a combination of factors. The most important, perhaps, is ideology or the inherent willingness of the local client to collaborate with the Soviets and to follow the model provided by the Soviet state. Another factor is the client's dependence on material aid or services that the Soviet Union is able to supply, or rather, relatively more able to provide than the other superpower. The Soviet Union also can provide its friends with political support in international forums like the United Nations. Soviet military power serves as a residual source of protection for regimes under attack either externally or internally and is effective even when there is only a potential threat. Finally, Soviet influence derives from Moscow's ability to penetrate the local society, either through overt control mechanisms such as the police and army or through indirect channels such as the training of soldiers, students, and cadres.

Moscow and the Socialist States.   Moscow receives the highest degree of cooperation from the socialist states of the Third World, particularly Cuba. The Cuban role in promoting Soviet interests in the Third World does not need to be elaborated here; suffice it to say that Cuba, aside from constituting the Soviet Union's major outpost in the Western Hemisphere, made possible the coming to power of the entire second generation of socialist-oriented states by intervening in Angola, Ethiopia, Nicaragua, and a host of smaller countries in Africa,

Latin America, and the Middle East. But Soviet-Cuban cooperation did not always exist and cannot be taken for granted; examination of past relations between the two countries reveals the interplay of all of the factors outlined above.

In the first decade after Castro came to power, relations between Moscow and Havana were not particularly good, in spite of Castro's evolution into an orthodox communist. Castro, like the Chinese, early on proclaimed his intention of arriving at true communism sooner than the Soviets themselves, and he pursued radical policies both at home and abroad. Criticizing both the Soviets and the pro-Soviet Cuban Communist Party (the Partido Socialista Popular, or PSP) for being too conservative, he supported a wide variety of guerrilla groups throughout Latin America in the 1960s and advocated heavy reliance on armed struggle as an instrument of revolutionary change. The Soviets for their part regarded Castro as a "putschist" and an infantile left-winger, and went so far as to embargo oil shipments to Cuba in 1968 in response to Castro's purging of the pro-Soviet "microfaction" led by Annibale Escalante.

The Cuban-Soviet cooperation that emerged in the 1970s was made possible only through ideological shifts on the part of both Havana and Moscow. Following his disastrous effort to achieve a 10,000,000-ton sugar harvest in 1969, which had seriously disrupted the Cuban economy and led to ever-increasing dependence on Soviet subsidies, Castro abandoned ambitions of arriving at communism sooner than the Soviets and reintroduced material incentives and other Soviet-style economic policies.[21] In foreign policy as well, the guerrilla movements supported by Cuba in the 1960s ended in failure, proving correct Soviet contentions that uprisings by local *focos* were premature and would lead only to greater repression. The Soviets for their part felt they had to protect their left flank as they moved toward détente with the United States in the early 1970s and became more interested in supporting national liberation movements like the MPLA in Angola, which formerly had been backed by the Cubans.

Since that time Cuban and Soviet foreign policies have become much more closely aligned, but even subsequently there have been instances of disagreement, for example, over Havana's continued support for the Eritrean separatists fighting the central regime in Addis Ababa. Cuban collaboration with the USSR arises not from any type of physical control exercised by the large Soviet presence in Cuba but rather from a variety of factors indigenous to Cuba itself, including ideology, Castro's personal ambition to play a worldwide revolutionary role,[22] the Cuban armed forces' need for an external mission after their disengagement from domestic administrative functions in the late 1960s,[23] and the economic benefits derived from the Soviet subsidy.

In East Asia, Vietnam has collaborated extensively with the Soviet Union, providing Moscow with base facilities at Da Nang and Cam Ranh Bay. Vietnam forms one anchor of Moscow's policy of encircling and containing China, threatening pro-Chinese and pro-Western groups in Southeast Asia, and tying down Chinese forces in the South. But like the Chinese Communist Party itself, the Vietnamese communists came to power primarily through their own efforts in a decades-long struggle against the Japanese, French, and Americans. They consistently have shown themselves to be prickly nationalists, and their collaboration with Moscow has been the result of Hanoi's acute dependence on Soviet military and economic assistance in the wake of the American withdrawal from Indochina in 1975, rather than an ideologically motivated desire to place themselves in the Soviet camp. No sooner had Vietnam's economy begun to adjust to the dislocations caused by absorption of the South, creation of the "New Economic Zones," and the forced departure of over a million of the South's most productive workers, than Vietnam invaded Kampuchea and began absorbing the costs of maintaining an army of 170,000 men in the field in a prolonged counterinsurgency campaign. As a result of its conquest of Kampuchea, Vietnam also had to worry about a military threat from China, for which only the Soviet Union could act as a viable counterweight. The Vietnamese remain, by all accounts, highly nationalistic and distrustful of the Soviets; Soviet access to Da Nang and Cam Ranh Bay reportedly came only after hard bargaining during the negotiations over the Friendship and Cooperation Treaty in November 1978.[24]

The limitations of Soviet influence over its socialist Third World allies is also evident in the case of North Korea. North Korea traditionally has been much more of a Chinese than a Soviet client, although ultimately Pyongyang has been answerable only to itself. The reasons for this are largely historical: the North Koreans believe that Stalin tried to dominate their party after installing them in power in 1945, encouraging them to invade the South in 1950 and then abandoning them (unlike the Chinese) when the United States repulsed the invasion and moved north. The regime of Kim Il-Sung has developed the doctrine of *chu'che*, or self-reliance, in response to the failings or perceived failings of its communist superpower patrons. The Soviets, in turn, have been highly distrustful of Kim's single-minded pursuit of reunification, keeping him on a short leash to minimize the risks of confrontation with the United States,[25] and they doubtless have been annoyed by Pyongyang's effective default on its billion-dollar debt. Soviet unwillingness throughout the 1970s to supply North Korea with weapons that were routinely provided to noncommunist clients in the Middle East spurred resentment in Pyongyang and the creation of a domestic arms industry whose exports have been shipped to various parts of the Third World. The North Koreans thus appear to be acting as independent entrepreneurs more than as proxies for the Soviet Union when selling weapons to countries like Iran. This situation may be changing, however. Following Kim's visit to Moscow in 1984 (his first in seventeen years), Moscow agreed to supply North Korea with MiG-23 jets, a major upgrading of Pyongyang's capabilities. The Soviets evidently have forgiven the earlier North Korean debt, and there have been rumors to the effect that Kim Il-Sung's son, Kim Chong-Il, may soon be invited to Moscow. The Soviets may be hoping to take advantage of China's warming ties with the United States, Japan, and even South Korea to establish a firmer foothold in North Korea. Even if pursuing its own interests in promoting arms sales, North Korean interests overlap quite substantially with those of the USSR; the fact that North Koreans have shown up in places like Grenada suggests a more extensive degree of cooperation dating back to the 1970s.

Moscow and the Socialist-Oriented States.   As noted above, Moscow shifted its emphasis to the more radical, Marxist-Leninist, socialist-oriented countries in the 1970s because of perceived weaknesses in its policy of support for the first-generation national democratic clients, weaknesses both in the regimes themselves and in the degree of influence the Soviets could achieve over them. Because the new socialist-oriented clients had declared Marxism-Leninism their governing ideology and because Moscow and its socialist bloc allies began helping them build vanguard party organizations and other elements of a centralized Leninist state, the Soviets hoped to create a group of clients 1) more naturally inclined to cooperation with the "socialist commonwealth" and 2) less subject to backsliding and reversal through coup d'etat, Western blandishments, or a simple change of heart on the part of the leadership.

Active Soviet bloc involvement in Leninist state-building marked a significant shift from Soviet policy in previous decades, which had been characterized by a relatively hands-off approach toward the internal politics of clients. In the 1970s the Soviets, Cubans, East Germans, and other bloc allies supplemented traditional arms and economic aid transfers with more direct forms of intervention. At first this consisted of military power projection to help clients (like the MPLA) come to power in the first place, or to help sustain them. But the initial effort was followed by large contingents of advisers to assist in such tasks as the training of party cadres, staffing of economic ministries, creation of popular militias to offset the power of the regular armed forces, writing of socialist constitutions, etc. Essentially, the Soviets were able to offer Marxist-Leninist Third World clients a package deal of security services, providing them with the political/military means to seize and to hold power.

Perhaps the most important of these services was the organization of secret police apparatuses to secure the regime against potential coup attempts, or, in extreme cases, to actually remove a deviating leadership. The East Germans played a particularly important role here, helping establish the Department of Information and Security of Angola, The National Security Service in Mozambique, the General Directorate of State Security in Nicaragua, the Libyan Mukhabarat, and other police organizations in Ethiopia, the PDRY, Guinea-Bissau, San Tome, and Grenada.[26] From an early point the Cubans were aware of the importance of protecting the character of a regime through the creation of an effective security apparatus and in the 1960s had provided presidential guards for Massamba-Debat in the People's Republic of the Congo and for Sekou Toure in Guinea-Conakry. In light of the military coups against Soviet clients in Ghana and Mali, the Cubans went on to establish popular militias in Sierra Leone, Equatorial Guinea, and South Yemen.[27]

The socialist-oriented states that the Soviets and their allies have put into place through these varied activities have been more politically reliable as a group than the earlier generation of national democrats. This is evident in a number of respects. Five of the new Marxist-Leninist states signed friendship and cooperation treaties with the USSR shortly after coming to power: Angola on October 8, 1976; Mozambique on March 31, 1977; Ethiopia on November 20, 1978; Afghanistan on December 20, 1978; and the PDRY on October 25, 1979. In addition, communist Vietnam signed a similar treaty prior to its invasion of Kampuchea on November 3, 1978.[28] A number of socialist-oriented states also have signed bilateral friendship treaties with other Eastern European states such as East Germany, and in 1981 Libya, Ethiopia, and the PDRY signed a tripartite treaty of cooperation. These treaties in themselves do not constitute binding obligations on either signatory, as Moscow's inaction in the face of China's 1979 invasion of Vietnam proved, but they are political symbols of a willingness to be aligned politically with the Soviet Union. While a number of other national democratic clients have also signed friendship and cooperation treaties, including (at one time) Egypt, Somalia, Iraq, India, Syria, and most recently North Yemen, these were most often done with much greater reluctance, in response to some urgent foreign policy need.[29]

In the military sphere, the socialist-oriented states have proved much more willing to cooperate with the Soviet Union than their national democratic predecessors. The Soviet armed forces have obtained access to Dahlak Island, Massawa and Assab in Ethiopia, Perim Island and Socotra in South Yemen, as well as base facilities in Aden, an airfield in Luanda, Angola, and the Mozambican ports of Maputo, Beira, and Nacala. Again, the difference between the later and earlier generations of Soviet clients is a matter of degree. Soviet forces in previous decades had access to facilities at Alexandria, Egypt; Berbera, Somalia; Tartus and Latakia, Syria; and the like. But such access generally was granted only grudgingly by national democratic clients, in the case of Egypt as an act of desperation to compensate for Israel's demonstrated military superiority in the Six Day War.

It is in the realm of support for like-minded Marxist-Leninist groups in other regional conflicts that the socialist-oriented states have shown the greatest willingness to collaborate with Moscow. In this sense Soviet support for Marxist-Leninist states becomes self-sustaining, since groups brought to power turn around and become bases for further Soviet bloc activities. Every one of the new socialist-oriented states that came to power in the 1970s has shown an interest in sponsoring other revolutionary movements. Angola at one time or another gave sanctuary and assistance to the South West African People's Organization fighting for Namibian independence and the Front for the Liberation of the Congo in Zaire, while Mozambique helped Robert Mugabe's ZANU guerrilla group prior to the Zimbabwe settlement and the African National Congress (ANC) struggling for black rule in South Africa. The PDRY for a long time sponsored the National Democratic Front seeking to overthrow the regime in North Yemen, and the Popular Front for the Liberation of Oman and the Occupied Arab Gulf (PFLOAG), and served as a major logistics entrepôt during the Soviet/Cuban airlift to Ethiopia in 1977–78. Ethiopia supported Cuban efforts to suppress forces loyal to Selim Rubai Ali in the PDRY and has hosted groups trying to subvert the Sudan, while Nicaragua has played a role in sustaining the constituent groups of the Farabundo Marti Liberation Front in El Salvador.

Soviet bloc efforts to make these gains in some sense irreversible through vanguard parties, secret police, and other Leninist instruments of centralized state control have only partially succeeded. It is possible to point to several clear-cut Soviet successes in providing regime security, mostly on the level of protecting or removing individual leaders from power. Libya's Gadhafi, for example, has survived at least two assassination and coup attempts over the past decade thanks to the East German–trained bodyguard protecting him. In June 1978, President Selim Rubai Ali of South Yemen was removed forcibly by security forces organized by the East Germans, after he indicated a desire to move closer to the pro-Western states of the Persian Gulf. While Rubai Ali's hard-line pro-Soviet successor Abd' al-Fattah Ismail was removed from the PDRY Politburo in April 1980, Moscow's influence apparently was strong enough to force his return to the YSP Central Committee Secretariat in February 1985.[30]

Still, the new Leninist institutions in the Third World are less than perfect. When fighting broke out between the Hassani and Ismail factions of the Yemeni Socialist Party in January 1986, the Soviets supported first one and then the other side when it appeared that Ismail was going to win. While Moscow's interests were in the end preserved, the Soviets and East Germans were not able to control the fighting and were embarrassed by the ensuing bloodbath, which revealed the tribal mentality of the Yemeni leadership underlying its veneer of Marxism-Leninism.

Another example is provided by Mozambique. The fact that it possesses a formal Marxist-Leninist vanguard party and East German–trained internal security forces has not been sufficient to prevent it from turning to its formal colonial masters, the Portuguese, to meet its security needs and from signing the Nkomati Accord with South Africa, under which Maputo dropped its support for the ANC in return for an end to South African support for the Mozambican National Resistance (Renamo). Indeed, simultaneously with Nkomati the Mozambicans began dismantling a number of their counterproductive socialist innovations such as collective farms; it is no longer clear in what sense Mozambique still constitutes a Soviet client. Similarly, the new vanguard Workers Party of Ethiopia set up under Soviet tutelage remains by most accounts no more than a front for the military, which retains real political power in the country;[31] Soviet distrust of Ethiopian pretensions to being a true Marxist-Leninist country are evident in the remarks made by Grigory Romanov at the ceremony marking the founding of the WPE in September 1984.[32]

But perhaps even more unsettling for the Soviets than evidence of backsliding by local Marxist-Leninist leaderships is the frontal assault being waged on them by internal armed resistance groups.[33] The fact that many socialist-oriented regimes of the 1970s (including Angola, Mozambique, Afghanistan, Nicaragua, and Ethiopia) are under attack by anti-Soviet guerrilla groups has been noted widely by now, most prominently by President Reagan in his October 1985 speech to the United Nations General Assembly. That it is the socialist-oriented states, rather than the national democracies from the 1950s and 1960s, that are subject to insurgencies is not accidental but springs directly from their common characteristics. The second-generation Marxist-Leninist clients all have tended to be small, weak states at low levels of economic development even for Third World countries. Soviet ability to bring such clients to power and reshape their internal institutions along Leninist lines, while enhancing Moscow's influence and control, also has served to undermine Soviet legitimacy in the eyes of client populations. As noted earlier, the national democrats, for all their weaknesses and internal instability, generally were governed by regimes that had come to power through their own efforts and therefore enjoyed a certain broad popular legitimacy. The same could not be said for the new socialist-oriented states, several of which probably would collapse quickly were Soviet and Cuban forces to withdraw.

Strengths and Weaknesses of the Empire

The Soviet Union's principal strength in the Third World is its ability to provide its clients with security, that is, a comprehensive package of goods and services that allows them to seize and hold onto political power. In the early years of the postwar era, this package often consisted of nothing more complicated than large quantities of used weapons from Soviet stockpiles. While these weapons were often not particularly sophisticated when compared to those available from the West, they were suited to the technical level of Third World armies and were provided in very large quantities given the context of the regional conflicts into which they were introduced. Capitalizing on the easy gains to be had from support of national liberation movements, Moscow could back states seeking independence from European colonial tutelage, with the consequent rapid expansion of Soviet influence.

By the 1970s, this security package had become much richer and more sophisticated, responding to the requirements of new clients (many of which tended to be small and backward by comparison). The Soviets not only supplied arms but also provided direct intervention by Cuban or in extreme cases Soviet troops if that was required, internal security training and forces, assistance in setting up disciplined political parties, and the like. Moscow acted as the clearinghouse through which specialized services by the different bloc allies could be coordinated, while it also provided logistic and financial support for these varied operations.

The package of military/security measures was highly effective and continues to be the Soviet Union's chief attraction as a patron. But by the early 1980s, the Third World's own agenda had changed. With the withdrawal of Portugal from Africa in 1974–75, the last of the great European colonial empires collapsed and, with the exception of a few minor separatist groups and organizations like the PLO, national liberation was no longer an issue. The principal preoccupation of most Third World countries turned to economic development, and in that sphere the Soviet Union had much less to offer.

This was not for lack of a policy and a theoretical model of economic development. The traditional Soviet view, enunciated first in Lenin's *Imperialism—the Highest Stage of Capitalism* and later elaborated in a somewhat modified fashion by Third World economists themselves as the *dependencia* theory, maintained that economic ties on the part of Third World countries with developed capitalist economies, in the form either of trade or investment, were inherently exploitative. Capitalist countries could not create wealth in the less developed world; they could only extract it, usually in the form of natural resources. The Ricardian theory of comparative advantage and the international division of labor was held to be unjust because it locked the Third World into permanent dependence on the capitalist world. The solution to this problem was protectionism and autarkic industrialization with help from the socialist bloc, i.e., the cutting of economic ties with the West, nationalization of foreign investment, import substitution, and the like. Economic organization was to be centralized along

Soviet lines, leading to the creation of a balanced industrial economy.

There were two problems with this theory: first, it did not work, and second, it proved to be very costly to the USSR. Both points were demonstrated amply by the case of Cuba, which had an important effect on subsequent Soviet policy. As a result of American sanctions and Castro's own preferences, in the early 1960s Cuba was torn abruptly from the Western international economic order and from the United States, its dominant trading partner, and integrated very quickly into the socialist system. Castro made all the mistakes possible in a command economy: in the first few years after the revolution he invested in a number of large, expensive industrial projects that played to none of Cuba's comparative advantages and turned out to be highly inefficient. Then in the late 1960s he staked his prestige on expanding sugar production and producing a 10,000,000-ton sugar crop. This too was a costly failure, but in each case the Soviet Union had to pick up the bill. By the early 1980s, Soviet economic assistance to Cuba amounted to some $4 billion per year.[34] The rapid reorientation of the Cuban economy away from the West did not permit Cuba to be "exploited," much to its detriment, and forced the USSR to pick up the tab instead.

Clearly, the Soviet Union gets many political benefits from its relationship with Cuba, and it would be very difficult to argue that the Soviet leadership thought even the $5 billion annual subsidy (including an additional $1 billion in arms aid) too high a price. But just as clearly, the Soviets cannot afford many more Cubas, and much of Moscow's subsequent policy toward the Third World has reflected a clear preference to make clients pay their own way to the extent possible. On a theoretical level, many Soviet developmental economists now appear to have rejected many elements of the traditional Soviet development model, and they argue in favor of a more eclectic one that combines socialist and market-oriented solutions. While Soviet economists still posit autarkic development as an eventual goal, their almost universal advice to clients is to go slow and avoid massive disruption of ties with the West through nationalizations, import substitution, and the like.[35] On a practical level, the Soviets increasingly have insisted that clients pay their own way. For example, the Angolans reimburse Moscow for arms through the hard currency earnings of the Gulf Oil operation at Cabinda, Vietnam sends guestworkers to the Soviet Union, and Mozambique and Ethiopia export coffee and other agricultural products to the USSR and permit Soviet ships to fish in their territorial waters. It is clear from a reading of Soviet communications that economic assistance to the Third World is very controversial in high Kremlin leadership circles, and that in recent years important voices in the Politburo have urged a lower level of resource allocations to less-developed clients.[36]

Economic stringency caused by the competing demands of the domestic Soviet economy would be bad enough for the Soviet position, but it coincides with the manifest failure of the Soviet model of economic development where Soviet clients have tried to apply it. It is now a well-known fact in Africa and elsewhere that the poorest and most backward countries are the socialist ones; not only have they failed to grow as rapidly as more market-oriented economies, but in cases such as Mozambique and South Yemen they have experienced declining agricultural output, both absolutely and per capita, for several years in a row.[37] In both cases poor performance can be tied to efforts to collectivize agriculture along Soviet lines (if perhaps against the advice of the Soviet experts on the ground). The severe drought and subsequent famine that struck the Sahel in 1984 was made much worse in Ethiopia as a result of the Dergue's efforts to create agricultural cooperatives; and while the response of the Western world to the famine was quick and generous, Ethiopia's patron, the Soviet Union, could only supply military transport aircraft—a fitting symbol of Moscow's role in the Third World. The poor performance of socialism in the Third World has been accentuated by comparison to the spectacular performance of certain capitalist-oriented states in the 1970s, particularly in the Far East.[38] The protectionist industrialization policies advocated by the likes of Raul Prebisch a decade or two earlier have been supplanted by market-oriented solutions and an emphasis in many places on traditional activities such as agriculture. These shifts are evident in the two largest countries of the Third World, China and India, and are likely to become of long-term concern to the Soviets.

All of this leaves a somewhat confusing picture for the future. While all Third World states want economic development, their leaderships want political power as well. The Soviets now seem to show a clear preference for a situation in which their clients remain aligned with the Soviet bloc politically and militarily but turn to the West for development assistance, investment, and the like. In contrast to Cuba, Nicaragua has been advised to go slow in cutting its ties with the West and to rely heavily on the continuing goodwill of the West Europeans. Owing to a certain conceptual confusion in Western policy, many well-intentioned people in the West seem inclined to go along. Nonetheless, to the extent that the Soviets are seen primarily as purveyors of political/military security, it is likely that Soviet influence will remain restricted to small, weak states at a relatively low level of socioeconomic development. Some Soviet officials, such as the Central Committee International Department's Karen Brutents, have gone even further in advocating a shift in Soviet policy away from these weak, socialist-oriented states toward the larger, geopolitically important capitalist-oriented states like Mexico, Argentina, and India. But Moscow is caught in a bind: the larger and more inherently influential the client, the weaker will be its influence and control and the fewer goods and services it will be able to provide. All of this suggests clear-cut opportunities for Western policy in the Third World in the future.

5

Herbert J. Ellison

Marxism-Leninism in
the Third World

Liberation Movements, Peasants, and Nationalism

In the early 1920s Joseph Stalin proclaimed the goal of Soviet policy for what today is called the Third World:

> . . . the road to victory of the revolution in the West lies with the liberation movement of the colonies and dependent countries against imperialism.[1]

This statement was a dramatic departure from the dominant party view that communism would succeed first in the advanced industrial countries. The Russian Revolution itself was viewed as a temporary aberration caused by the impact of World War I and Russia's unique economic development.[2]

But the revolution expected in Germany did not arrive, and Europe had achieved a new political stability. Meanwhile, "liberation movements"– nationalist and anti-colonial movements seeking political independence and economic and social reform—were an emerging and powerful force for change from North Africa to China. In these movements was the "weakest link" in the world capitalist system, "the road to victory of the revolution in the West."

To examine communist ideology in the contemporary Third World, we should begin with three paradoxes of the Marxian revolutionary legacy. First, the mass workers' parties inspired by Marxism—the modern socialist and social democratic parties—abandoned violent revolution for parliamentary reform. Second, the communist parties, which derive from Russian Bolshevism and remain committed to revolution, stress the central role of an elitist, authoritarian revolutionary party—not the spontaneous rising of disaffected workers—in the acquisition and consolidation of revolutionary power. Third, the popular movements used by those parties to acquire power have been chiefly agrarian and nationalist, not proletarian. Exploring these paradoxes reveals a great deal about the successes and failures of communism in the Third World and its prospects.

The formation of modern communism was greatly influenced by the fact that Lenin undertook a socialist revolution in a predominantly agrarian society. He saw his party as the agent of a tiny minority—the emerging industrial working class—not of the great peasant majority. In his view Russia's future lay with the proletariat and with socialism. The existing social and economic structure in the countryside was the legacy of Russian feudalism, and the expression of peasant aspirations in the Russian populist slogan "Land and Liberty" an illusion. Russia must proceed, he believed, through a stage of capitalist development, including capitalist concentration of landholding, as preparation for its eventual march toward socialism. Hence, Lenin had no sympathy for land redistribution and peasant smallholding as a final agrarian program. But as a revolutionary strategist he perceived the enormous importance of the peasantry as a force for change in Russia. And when, in March 1917, the collapse of czarist power opened the way to the peasant's version of the Russian Revolution—the spontaneous mass seizure of the remaining lands of the nobility—Lenin co-opted that revolution as a force against the existing order, and, having come to power in October, incorporated the change in the land law of the new regime.

Thus, while Lenin joined forces with the insurgent peasants, his plans for agrarian socialism were alien to them. This conflict of purpose was apparent in the period of war communism (1918–20), when peasant resistance to socialization of land and grain requisitioning brought a collapse of agricultural production and a retreat from socialist programs. It was even more brutally apparent when Stalin took the course of socialization of agriculture in 1928 and peasant resistance was crushed by violence and famine.

The communist agrarian dogma—that the land must be socialized—has usually been concealed from the peasantry in countries where communist parties have competed for political power and has been applied only when power was successfully consolidated. The results have been disastrous: frequently devastating famine, or at least severe disruption of food production, followed by formation of an inefficient and underproductive agricultural system. Yet the crucial point has been the difference between peasants' pre- and postrevolutionary perceptions of communist objectives. In advance of the revolution, the communists have often been the most outspoken advocates of agrarian reform, appealing to the peasants' wish for land redistribution or other benefits of revolutionary change.

Hence, regions of the Third World in which demands for agrarian reform remain a major force of popular discontent continue to be targets for communist political organizers, who either work directly among the peasants or ally with noncommunist agrarian leaders. The most recent edition of the Soviet International Department's key publication, *The World Communist Movement*, stresses the elements of peasant discontent in Third World countries—with the landlords, their governments, foreign producers, and agricultural products purchasers— and outlines ways in which communist parties can and should build cooperation with the peasants, noting that "the peasantry was the earliest ally of the proletariat."[3]

Lenin's approach to nationalism and to nationalist movements demonstrated the same mixture of ideological dogma and political opportunism that was apparent in his agrarian policy. He accepted Marx's concept of proletarian internationalism, was hostile to the socialist parties' support of their national war efforts in World War I, and insisted, in the organization of both the domestic communist party and the international communist movement, upon subordination of national parties to the leadership and interests of the world movement.

Yet there was another, more opportunist side to his policy. Lenin's political opportunism in the use of nationalism was demonstrated in his approach to non-Russian nationalist movements in the prerevolutionary multinational Russia. Their concept of revolution was to overturn Russian rule and achieve self-government, a program based on nineteenth-century nationalist ideology. For Lenin such aspirations were politically reactionary. The future belonged to the proletariat, and the proletariat, as Marx had shown, "has no homeland." Yet in the context of the struggle against autocracy nationalist movements were a progressive force because they contributed to the strength of opposition and the prospects for successful revolution.

When revolution came, and the collapse of the old regime opened the way for separation of several of the non-Russian peoples from the Russian state, Lenin first affirmed the principle of self-determination and then reneged on it, using political intrigue and military force to reunite as much of the former empire as possible within the new Soviet state. He thus made it clear that nationalism was a force to be encouraged and exploited in the struggle against noncommunist governments, but suppressed and controlled when communists came to power.

Lenin's main competitors in the Russian social democratic movement did not understand the degree to which he had modified the views of conventional European Marxism in adapting it to the key realities of the Russian empire – that it was predominantly peasant and multinational. Nor did most European communist leaders of the interwar period understand or appreciate the efforts of Lenin and his successors to apply their revolutionary doctrine and experience to the non-European world. The conflict between "Easterners" and "Westerners" in the Comintern during the 1920s was essentially between European communist leaders, who clung to the view that future communist revolutions would occur in the industrial countries of Europe, and Soviet party leaders, who saw a special relevance of the Russian revolutionary experience to the future of the non-European world.[4]

Communism in Asia between the Wars

Most of the examples of communist activity in Third World countries today have their antecedents in Soviet and Comintern policies of the interwar years. The extension of communist revolution to Asia following the Bolshevik Revolution was initially confined mainly to territories that had been part of the prewar Russian empire (Transcaucasus and Central Asia) or its dependencies (Outer Mongolia). Communist political control in these areas was achieved primarily by military conquest, although communist organizers – Russian and local – and communist political methods and propaganda were used in the process. The absolute priority of acquiring political power in Leninist doctrine permitted all instruments, as it permitted all alliances.

As in Europe and Asia, Russian military action was used to extend communist revolution beyond prewar borders. In the spring of 1920, following the conquest of Azerbaijan, Russian ships and troops entered the Persian Caspian port of Enzeli to assist the formation of a Soviet republic in the province of Ghilan –whose troops then marched on Teheran with Soviet support. The invaders were defeated by Persian forces led by the nationalist military leader, Reza Khan, and the Soviets withdrew from Persia under British pressure.[5] Such use of Russian troops in support of revolutionary insurgents abroad has been a repeated pattern of Soviet international behavior and a basic technique for the spread of communist revolution.

Communist revolution "from below" was accompanied by an equally important policy of appeals for state-to-state cooperation with new Asian nationalist regimes. The vast extent of the European colonial empires limited the number of Asian states with which direct diplomatic dealings were possible; these were Turkey, Persia, Afghanistan, China, and Japan. For most of the remainder of Asia diplomatic relations were possible only with the colonial powers themselves: Britain, France, the Netherlands, Japan, and the United States. Exceptions to this division were Outer Mongolia, conquered by Red Army forces in 1921, and Tannu Tuva, only nominally an independent Central Asian republic. But the Soviets pursued the available opportunities with some energy, their declared aim being "to destroy the capitalist front by means of organizing the revolution and revolutionary fighting forces behind the capitalist line."[6]

The independent Asian regimes were the first targets of Soviet policy. The Soviet government pointed proudly to its disavowal of the imperial claims of the czars and its equal treatment of non-Russians within the Soviet state. Further, it offered independent Asian regimes cooperation against the Western powers. In Turkey the aim was to reduce Anglo-French influence and achieve an alliance; in Afghanistan and Persia to diminish British influence. Unfortunately, though debt renunciation and abdication of property claims were accepted cheerfully and friendship treaties signed, it was soon clear that mistrust of Russia and communism was high and that the Turkish and Afghan governments were playing off Soviet Russia against the Western states, while suppressing internal communist activity.

Focus on China

Thus Soviet leaders learned early on the difficulty of winning nationalist leaders to their cause. They had better luck in China, however, where, in 1923, they signed an agreement of cooperation with the Chinese Nationalists (Kuomintang) to provide Soviet military aid and advisers to assist the Nationalists in uniting the country under their banner.

Unlike the Turkish and Persian nationalist leadership, the Chinese Nationalists were not masters in their own land, and desperately needed military and organizational assistance to achieve their goal. The Soviet-Chinese agreement therefore became a milestone in the history of communism — a three-party relationship between the Soviet government, the Chinese Communist Party, and the Nationalists. Originally developed in Java by Dutch communist Fritz Maring, this became for the Soviets a strategy of "Third World" revolution. The strategy assumed that the best way to broaden the support of a small communist party was to link it with the dominant mass movement and then to work within that movement for influence and control, making a revolution from within. In China, the strategy failed when the Nationalist leadership, fearing communist and Soviet conspiracy, purged their party and military organizations of communists and suppressed communist labor organizations. The communists responded to this with experiments first with communist organization in the cities and then, under the leadership of Mao Zedong, a peasant-based, guerrilla-defended enclave state in Kiangsi province, thus beginning the long struggle to replace the Nationalists by civil war.

The experience in China in the 1920s and 1930s thus encompassed all elements of the developing communist strategy and tactics for Third World revolution: 1) government-to-government agreement and cooperation, using the prestige and resources of the Soviet state; 2) a united front between the local communist party and the dominant mass nationalist movement, followed by extensive Soviet military aid, including Soviet specialists; and 3) urban and rural insurrection against the nationalist government, followed by the formation of an enclave guerrilla state.

It is significant that none of these enterprises involved serious modification of Leninist ideology. For Lenin, the acquisition of political power had always been the primary goal, and all else was means to achieve it. The wide range of his formal and tacit political alliances, both in the prerevolutionary period and in the Russian Civil War—including alliances with nationalist movements—provided ample precedent for alliance with the Chinese Nationalists. What Mao later contributed was the practical application of these ideas to China, borrowing ideologically chiefly from Lenin's *Two Tactics*, his *Imperialism*, and the special papers and resolutions of the Comintern. Mao's commentary on *The Peasant Movement* in Hunan demonstrated his special understanding of the crucial importance of the peasantry and of peasant revolution.[7] His example and leadership provided a model for the adaptation of Leninism not only to China, but to much of the rest of the world.

The Instruments of Revolution

There were other sides to Moscow's early efforts to spread communism to Asia, albeit none with the short-term impact of the work in China. One of the major tasks was the establishment of communist parties. Those in Turkey, Persia (Iranian Communist Party), and Java (Indonesian Communist Party) were founded in 1920; the Chinese and Korean in the following year; the Indian in 1925; and the Indochinese in 1930. The actual strength of these communist parties varied greatly. The Turkish and Persian governments persecuted their parties severely, and British policy in India delayed both the organization and growth of the party, which remained outside the mainstream of Indian political life. The Indonesian party formed an early alliance with the nationalist movement (Sarekat Islam), broadening its popular base; although this alliance subsequently collapsed, the party was the main organizer of insurrection against Dutch authority and a continuing ideological influence on the nationalist movement. The Japanese party was dissolved in 1924 following police harassment, reformed in 1926, and gained support during the economic depression of the early 1930s. It was then suppressed by the military regime during the period 1933–45. Suppression of the Korean Communist Party by the Japanese sent its senior leadership into exile in the Soviet Union from which it returned only at the end of World War II. All of these conformed to the Comintern requirements of accepting the Soviet ideological and organizational model and full subordination to the power of the Soviet-controlled Comintern Executive Committee.

The Soviet Union also concentrated heavily on training students from Asian countries. The Communist University for Workers of the East (KUTV), founded in 1921, provided travel and study expenses for students from Japan, Korea, Indonesia, and India. Chinese students were trained at the Sun Yat-sen University in Moscow. Other institutions also supported Asian students and conducted research on Asian countries. Many of the students from these institutions later became prominent leaders in Asian communist parties.

Also important in Asia was the work of the Communist Trade Union International (Profintern), founded in 1921, which was somewhat successful in winning labor leaders and workers to the movement. The Peasant International (Krestintern), organized in 1923, sought to provide communist leadership for peasant organizations in Asian countries. (Ho Chi Minh, the Indochinese communist leader, was a member of the presidium of Krestintern.) Through the Comintern and the other international organizations, and through the communist parties, the Soviets organized an extensive propaganda campaign in Asia, focusing their attack on the colonial system and stressing the theme of class warfare.

The Japanese Challenge

During the 1930s the Soviet Union searched urgently for diplomatic means to avoid conflict with Germany and Japan. In Moscow's view, which saw the international communist movement as one body and the security of the Soviet Union as a common obligation, it was natural to make heavy use of Asian parties to support Soviet security. For this purpose the Soviet-controlled Comintern was instrumental in the employment of the Popular Front, a policy whose most important Asian application was the effort to achieve cooperation between the Chinese

Nationalists and communists for resistance against Japan—a policy that had only limited success. In the long run, however, the main gain of the 1930s was the consolidation of the Chinese communist enclave in Shensi Province following the Long March of 1934–35. It was the sole example from the interwar years of a phenomenon that would spread widely during and after World War II, the building of a "state within a state" as base and training center for the conquest of national power.

War and Revolution: Second Act

World War II brought new opportunities for the communist parties of the Asian countries occupied by Japan. As in Europe, the communists were uniquely equipped to organize and lead armed resistance to occupying forces. They had substantial numbers not only in China, where their armed resistance against both the Nationalist government and the Japanese dated to the early 1930s, but also in Burma, Malaya, Indochina, Indonesia, and the Philippines. Given favorable geography (mountains, jungle, or other remote areas), communists were able to organize and train guerrilla forces and to prepare the political organization and administration to take power at war's end. Their methods of organization were those used in similar political and social conditions in the wartime Balkans (Yugoslavia, Albania, and Greece), and these in turn had been borrowed from an earlier Comintern-directed resistance against the fascists in Spain.[8]

The main issue on which the communists based their appeal in wartime Asia was nationalism—resistance to an enemy occupation force. Since the struggle was for national independence, it also implied future struggle against restoration of prewar colonial control. Hence it provided an immediate pretext for common effort and strengthened enormously the long-term program. Though resistance appeared earliest and was strongest in China and among the Chinese in Malaya, it appeared elsewhere later in the war, or at its end. At that point, with the Japanese removed from the picture, the communists sought to capitalize on their previous efforts by leading the struggle against restoration of Western colonial rule.[9] The wartime cooperation with noncommunist political parties, and the communists' presentation of themselves as the most uncompromising of nationalists, had greatly expanded their support.

Yet the communists had not organized and fought to put noncommunist nationalists in power. With the Japanese gone, the first enemy was the returning colonial power—the British, French, Dutch, and (in the Philippines) the Americans—and where such a challenge existed the cooperation with noncommunist nationalists was continued. But with that victory won, the stage was set for communists to strike for independent power against their former allies. The shift took place earliest in China, where the communists abandoned all political cooperation with the Nationalists by April 1946. It came later in Burma, Indonesia, Malaya, and the Philippines. In all cases the communists fought against nationalist leaders for varying periods of time, most until the early 1950s.[10]

Korea and Vietnam were special cases. In North Korea the communists were simply installed in power by the Soviets, as they were in East Germany. Their subsequent effort to unite the entire country under their own rule was the counterpart of the battle of the communists against noncommunist nationalists elsewhere in Asia. In Vietnam, the end of the war found the communists in control of the resistance movement and dominant in the political negotiations with the returning French. But the French refused to surrender power to Ho Chi Minh and the Vietminh; the Vietminh fought for eight years to achieve independent political power in North Vietnam (1954) and an additional twenty to gain control of the entire country.[11]

From Revolutionary Offensive to United Front: The "New" Policy

The mid-1950s brought major changes in communist policies in the Third World. Conquest of power in China, North Korea, and North Vietnam were impressive achievements, but elsewhere communist offensives were abandoned (Burma, Indonesia, the Philippines) or crushed (Malaya and Korea). The time had come for the return to a united front strategy, for building new Soviet ties with the Third World, and for restoring and broadening the political base of communist support, especially political cooperation and alliances with noncommunist parties.

From the viewpoint of communist interests, the political stabilization of postwar Asia was similar to that of Europe. Viewing all such stabilizations—however long—as temporary, the Soviets now sought a strategy appropriate to changed circumstances, counting not only on their own moral and material support, but also on that of the newly expanded company of communist states, especially China.

Reviewing the more than three decades that have passed since the end of the Korean War, it is clear that communism in the Third World has expanded enormously as a political force—that it has won a number of major victories, has suffered serious reverses, but on balance has achieved an impressive extension of its influence and power. Communists have come to power in thirteen countries, comprising a population of about 140 million. With the exception of South Vietnam and Ethiopia, most are rather small countries, but they are spread over

East and South Asia (South Vietnam, Laos, Cambodia, and Afghanistan), the Middle East (People's Democratic Republic of Yemen), Africa (Angola, Benin, Congo, Ethiopia, Mozambique, and Zimbabwe), and Latin America (Cuba and Nicaragua). Most of these countries occupy important strategic locations from which further revolutionary initiatives can be, or have been, undertaken.

Dismantling Empires

A number of factors have favored communist Third World initiatives. Perhaps the first of these has been the dismantling of the colonial empires. In the interwar years the colonial states had usually crushed communist political activity, and equally importantly had blocked Soviet diplomatic contacts with the subject population. The end of colonial control often – though not always – brought freedom of political organization and activity for the communists. And the advent of self-government brought opportunities for them to seek power, either in the unstable transition period from dependence to self-rule, or over the longer term, as internal divisions (political, ethnic, and religious) and failures of leadership produced political instability. [12]

Although in India, the transition from a colonial state to a dependency with a strong political leadership and developed governing bureaucracy and army made for an orderly transfer of power, other transitions were not as smooth: the Belgian Congo, for instance; the hasty British withdrawal from East of Suez in the late 1960s; or the sudden collapse of the Portuguese African empire following the overthrow of the Caetano government in 1974. These abrupt and ill-prepared power transfers provided communist parties the opportunities to strike for power comparable to those available in wartime resistance movements and postwar anticolonial struggles.

Soviet Global Power

A second factor creating new opportunities for Third World communism was the advent of Soviet global power, and with it the capacity (including the capacity of fellow communist states) to provide aid and protection to other communist movements, a process accompanied by a decline in Western ability or will to counter Soviet initiatives.

The development of Soviet global power, and its impact on the prospects of Third World communism, was a gradual process. Diplomatic relations with the Third World reopened when the reclusive Stalin was replaced by the travelling Khrushchev-Bulganin team—representing a new Soviet leadership eager for direct contact with Third World leaders. The main targets of the new policy were Egypt and India, and the Soviet offerings were arms and economic development aid. The Soviets sought to develop expanding ties with a wide range of countries in Asia, the Middle East, Africa, and Latin America.

The updated version of the Leninist theory offered by Moscow and local communist parties stressed that the old colonialism had been only superficially dismantled; it had been replaced by a subtler "neocolonialism" that continued to control the destinies of Third World countries by powerful levers of economic and cultural control; and that Soviet economic and military support were available to those states seeking to end their dependence and pursue an "independent" policy in cooperation with the Soviet Union to expand "the zone of peace."[13]

The policy sought to use the prestige and resources of the USSR in combination with internal efforts by local communist parties. From the viewpoint of the latter, the policy shift was doubtless welcome, since the Stalin "two camps" theory of the postwar era had treated the new nationalist leaders as lackeys of the Western states and Soviet hostility had damaged the images and interests of local communist parties. Now the formerly scorned nationalist leaders were praised and wooed. And, as in China in the 1920s, they were described (assuming, of course, that they adopted an anti-Western policy) as a progressive group leading "national democratic states." In 1963, after a few years' experience with the policy, a new concept was added—that of the "revolutionary democratic state"—to distinguish those states that not only pursued an anti-Western foreign policy but also adopted socialist economic and social measures and gave freedom of action to their communist parties.

Appeal of the New Line

Thus the prospects of communism in the Third World brightened in the 1950s and 1960s. The tripartite Soviet strategic formula was to attack Western "neocolonialism" (a useful reformulation since the United States had no visible colonies); to offer economic and military aid; and to urge adoption of internal policies that would, over time, favor the interests of communist parties. The policy had considerable appeal to Third World intellectuals and many of their leaders, although the extent and the effectiveness of the appeal varied greatly. Certainly for peoples of Asia and Africa, for whom Western colonial power was still a recent memory or a continuing reality, the anti-Western theme was appealing. The concept of neocolonialism, with its emphasis on Western economic preponderance and manipulation, was similarly appealing for newly independent states whose economies were often heavily dependent on the export of a limited range of products to Western markets – a relationship in which they had little control over price or market stability. And for the numerous companies whose own economic management (often based on ill-conceived measures of socialization) had failed, it was tempting to blame neocolonialism rather than themselves.

Both the economic analysis and anti-Western aspects of neocolonialism were appealing – a timely adaptation of Leninist dicta on imperialism to the contemporary scene. The socialist ideology of the Soviet leaders and local communist parties was also attractive to Third World intellectuals, most of whom subscribed to some form of socialism combined with nationalism. Thus a Third World leader such as Egypt's Nasser was an easy target. Nationalist and socialist in ideology, he was hostile to Israel (and therefore to the United States as Israel's main supporter) and to Britain (because of her former position in Egypt and her continued role at Suez).[14]

Problems of Alliances with Nationalists

Two persistent problems for the Soviets and the Egyptian communists from 1955 to 1972, when the Soviets were expelled from Egypt, were the Egyptian government's refusal to grant freedom to the Egyptian Communist Party and the uncertainty of its commitment to the Soviet Union. The situation is essentially the same as that of Syria and Iraq today, both of which have gone further than Egypt in their collaboration with the Soviets.[15]

Clearly these are problems with no solution. For both sides there is a gamble. Third World leaders who accept large-scale Soviet aid run the risk of developing disabling dependencies – both economic and military. Exclusive dependence on Soviet military supplies frequently sets limits to policy initiatives, as it did with Nasser and Sadat in Egypt, and more recently with Assad in Syria. There is often serious concern about the dangers of such cooperation leading to the expansion of Soviet regional military and political power – a concern expressed in recent years by many leaders in Africa, the Middle East, South Asia, and Latin America. Even close collaborators of the Soviets, such as Assad, have felt deep concern about the Soviet position in South Yemen, especially as it is combined with a growing regional military and naval power. The growth of such concerns was an important element in the decision of Sadat to expel Soviet advisers and reorient Egyptian policy toward the United States. It has also recently motivated leaders in Syria, Iraq, and India, among others, to broaden their sources of arms supplies and reduce the Soviet role.[16]

Third World leaders have other major concerns in their military and economic cooperation with the Soviets. Cooperation inevitably involves the presence of large numbers of Soviet military and other specialists.[17] Like the Chinese Nationalists of the 1920s, other Soviet collaborators have discovered that military cooperation brought Soviet political influence within their military organization, and that specialist training of their nationals—locally, in the Soviet Union, or in other communist countries—carried a large dose of political indoctrination. Nor were such leaders slow to learn that Soviet technical and trade officials often had dual roles.

Leaders of more-developed Third World countries were better equipped to contain the unwanted elements of Soviet influence—whether by simultaneously limiting the activity of the local communist party, diversifying arms supplies and sources of economic aid, or other means. But leaders of less-developed or smaller countries—Afghanistan, South Yemen, Ethiopia, Angola, or Grenada—were much more vulnerable to development of both a powerful Soviet influence and internal communist political power. Moreover, even the more sophisticated and skillful of Third World leaders often found that the policies for which they sought Soviet military aid in the first place involved them in accelerating conflicts (Egypt and Syria with Israel, Iraq with Iran, Ethiopia and Somalia with one another, India with Pakistan, etc.) that only increased their arms dependence.[18] This is doubtlessly why in recent years the provision of arms and of military training has become the main ingredient of Soviet Third World policy. No other policy—certainly not general economic aid—offers comparable political returns.

How does the gamble appear from the Soviet side? The question has not often been seriously evaluated in Western scholarly and general literature.[19] Yet it is an immensely important question to answer carefully in any assessment of the prospects of communism in the Third World. Those prospects are strongly dependent on a complex structure of factors in addition to Soviet policy: political, social, and economic trends in Third World countries; policies of Western countries; developments in the international economy; effectiveness and appeal of local communist parties; etc. But the future of communism in the Third World will be heavily dependent upon the commitment and policies of the Soviet Union and other communist states.

Clearly the Soviets are aware of the uncertainty of results from their Third World policy efforts. They write constantly about those policies and have an impressive array of specialist institutes and publications dealing with developments in those areas, including political, economic, and social trends that favor or disfavor their own policies and clients. There is ample evidence that they are informed and realistic about the problems they face. They have written for fifty years about the unpredictability and frequent unreliability of the "national bourgeoisie" as Soviet collaborators and communist allies in Third World countries.

Obviously it was possible for them to survive betrayal by Chiang Kai-shek and Sadat without losing confidence that long-term trends are in their favor. Their assessment has clearly led to continued commitment of energy and resources, albeit with allowances for resource limitations and evaluation of success and failure in specific situations.

The Future of Soviet Commitment

Some contemporary Western commentary—both scholarly and journalistic—has cast doubt on the continued commitment of the Soviets to Third World communist revolution. The arguments tend to fall into identifiable categories. The first is economic; namely, that the costs of sustaining Third World revolutions—whether the heavy economic subsidies to Cuba, Vietnam, and Ethiopia, the military aid costs to many countries, or the high costs of intervention in Afghanistan—have become too large to justify. The Western view usually stated is that the grave weaknesses of the Soviet economy are such that future expenditures of this kind must be reduced.[20]

The argument is not convincing. It has not been sustained by close analysis of such costs within the larger context of Soviet resources and expenditures; it has not been compared with Soviet support of comparable activities at an earlier time when funds were presumably even scarcer; it does not look at the many advantages gained from the expenditures—military, strategic, and even economic; and (perhaps most telling of all) it projects an exclusively economic basis of analysis into a Soviet milieu where political concerns are always first priority.

A second argument uses the phrase "limits of empire" to epitomize its analysis. The main notion is that every historical empire has eventually reached the outer limit of its capacity for expansion, and that surely seems to be the case with the Soviet empire today. The notion of limits is defined partly in terms of resources, and even more in terms of the resistance of states on the periphery of the empire to the expansion. While there is indeed evidence of mounting regional concern about the expansion of Soviet power and influence among many African and Asian leaders and evidence of efforts to shift policies on alliances and arms to strengthen regional security and diminish arms dependence, such policies really cannot set effective limits to the extension of communism in the Third World. There is always a regional division of opinion and regional conflicts for the Soviets to exploit.

Moreover, the term "empire" is misleading when applied to the Soviet relationship to Third World states. With noncommunist client states the structure of the relationship—limited treaty agreements combined with economic and/or military aid arrangements—is not greatly different from that which other powers maintain, though the policy aims are different. With communist states such as Cuba, Vietnam, or the People's Democratic Republic of Yemen (PDRY), the costs are high but so are the advantages – bases in the Caribbean, Southeast Asia, and the Middle East, respectively – each a crucial region for the global power relationship with the United States and a vital position for support of political developments in countries where opportunities present themselves.

What the Soviets export in foreign communist revolutions – in the Third World as elsewhere – is a system for acquiring and maintaining power that is then operated by locals.[21] The enterprise has become costly where either protracted resistance to the consolidation of communist power (Korea, Vietnam, Angola, Nicaragua, Ethiopia) or subsequent internal conflicts within the communist leadership (Afghanistan and Cambodia) or counterrevolution (Afghanistan, Nicaragua) have developed.

It is important, however, to estimate the impact of such costs against the background of Soviet traditions and habits of calculation. The Soviets paid a heavy price – and fought fierce guerrilla resistance – in establishing their control of Central Asia during the 1920s and in reestablishing it in the Baltic states and the Ukraine after World War II. Outside their own national boundaries, the main direct military burden in Third World countries has been borne by local communist-led military forces, or, in some recent cases, by Cubans. Except for Afghanistan, Soviet costs have been in the form of military supplies and general economic aid. Moreover, they have sensibly encouraged continued economic participation of capitalist countries where such participation reduces Soviet obligations and involves no serious danger to their political interests. They have also welcomed aid in food supplies from capitalist states – particularly important in Ethiopia (and elsewhere in Africa), as it was during the early stage of consolidation of communist power in Russia. Experience suggests that the Soviets are willing to bear very high costs when they are confident of the policies of the local communist leadership and confident of communist control of political power, however severe the external challenges to that power.

Recent Revolutionary Action

The absence of new communist revolutions in the Third World in the 1980s is sometimes interpreted as a full or substantial withdrawal of the Soviets from such activity. Broader historical perspective would support the view that what has declined, probably only temporarily, is opportunity rather than interest. In the Americas, Grenada was lost but El Salvador is still a question, while the Nicaraguan revolution continues to consolidate its position with extensive Cuban and

Soviet aid.[22] The combined Cuban-Nicaraguan base for further revolutionary action in the region provides an immensely powerful lever for future policy. In the Horn of Africa every effort has been made to build a full-fledged communist party and governmental apparatus in Ethiopia, and in Southern Africa the Soviets and Cubans have sought to eliminate the challenge of Savimbi in Angola, to support revolution in Namibia, and to work for the isolation and overturn of the South African government.

The 1970s were extraordinarily active and successful. The prime success was, of course, the conquest of South Vietnam by the North Vietnamese made possible by Soviet military aid. Others include the opening of Portuguese Africa, Soviet-Cuban support of the Movement for the Liberation of Angola (MPLA), in Angola, the close ties with the radical military coup in Ethiopia, the communist domination of the victorious Sandinista revolution in Nicaragua, and the guerrilla war mounted in El Salvador and elsewhere in Central America.

The first half of the 1980s was a quiet period, with continuation of earlier conflicts but without the appearance of significant new ones. Afghanistan was a festering sore—not only an intractable guerrilla war in which Soviet anti-insurgency action appeared to be both enormously destructive and ineffectual, but also an action generating anti-Soviet sentiment from Damascus to Djakarta.[23] The Iranian revolution, which the Soviets had endorsed, turned sharply anti-Soviet over Soviet arms aid to Iraq and in 1983 brought a severe crackdown on the Tudeh (pro-Soviet communist) party.

Future Prospects

A review of communist fortunes in the Third World in recent decades must acknowledge successes and failures and the trends that would argue for more or less opportunity in the future. The picture varies greatly throughout the Third World. East and Southeast Asia have witnessed spectacular economic growth, which has not only reduced social and economic problems favoring revolutionary politics, but has also challenged fundamentally the communist claims to leadership in economic progress. Impoverished Vietnam, Kampuchea nearly destroyed by ultracommunist fanaticism, and China recovering from the vagaries of Maoist economic policy by application of profit incentives and rapidly expanding economic interaction with capitalist states hardly provide inspiring examples for winning political converts to the communist model.[24] In noncommunist Asia, including India, the trend is away from socialist economic measures and toward competitive markets and individual economic incentives. The successes of Japan, South Korea, Taiwan, Hong Kong, and Singapore are the inspiration—even to some degree for China. Here the communist opportunities are likely to come in the exceptional cases—such as the Philippines—where a mix of factors including a major communist guerrilla insurrection and a very difficult transition from the Marcos to the Aquino leadership has created great political instability.[25]

The opportunities in East and South Asia are modest compared to those in Southwest Asia, the Middle East, and Africa, not to mention the Americas. They exist in the countries and regions whose political future is profoundly uncertain, and in which a combination of domestic and foreign (Soviet and other communist) influences will likely have an important role: Iran, the Arabian peninsula, Southern Africa, and Central America. Soviet spokesmen frequently deride the views of those in noncommunist countries who accuse them of exporting revolution. Obviously no one has the ability to create a revolutionary situation. But recent years have brought a huge growth in the capacity of the Soviets and their allies to exploit revolutionary situations around the globe.

This capacity includes many elements: expanding diplomatic contacts and influence, many of these functioning, as in parts of Africa, for the first time in the last ten to fifteen years; a greatly expanded and restructured apparatus for liaison with communist parties (also much increased in number) in Third World countries through the International Department; expanded resources for training of Third World students in the Soviet Union, such as the Patrice Lumumba/ Friendship University in Moscow and many other specialist institutions; a huge and expanding armaments industry, and the ability to cultivate alliances by meeting military needs; large resources for economic and technical aid (albeit often inferior to those offered by Western competitors); a company of generally supportive allies who have developed important specialties, such as the East Germans in security matters; and the ability to provide direct military support (including the portable Cubans) to clients by air and sea as needed.[26]

To use the business phrase, the Soviets offer a full-service package for a wide range of clients. Not the least important component is what might be called "protection services"—the services whose purpose is to provide protection for communist revolutionaries against interference from the "imperialists." One element, chiefly handled by the International Information Department of the Central Committee, is the creation of favorable public opinion abroad to thwart interventionist action.[27] The other is the broad protection provided by Soviet global military power, an element whose deterrent influence on the behavior of the United States and other countries has probably received too little attention.

Historically, the most important factor in blocking communist victories—or in protracting and raising the cost of the struggle to achieve them—has been intervention, including military intervention, by opposing powers. Examples since

World War II include the British suppression of the Greek communist insurrection in 1944–45 and the communist insurrection in Malaya in the 1950s, and the American role in Iran, Korea, Guatemala, Cuba, the Dominican Republic, Vietnam, El Salvador, Nicaragua, and Grenada.[28] Clearly a small country is no match for an internal rebellion, whether instigated by the unpopularity of a regime (e.g., Batista in Cuba or Somoza in Nicaragua) or by a powerful domestic guerrilla movement — or both-heavily supported by the Soviet Union and/or other communist states. It was precisely this fact that initiated development of the American postwar containment policy.

But that policy and its context have been greatly transformed since Vietnam. The burden of its implementation is now almost wholly on American shoulders, with scant help and much criticism from allies. Since Vietnam, it is almost unthinkable that anything like the Korean or Vietnamese wars of containment could be mounted again. The modest but decisive Grenada action does not invalidate this. It seems difficult to convince Congress and the American public to provide modest support for anti-communist forces in Central America and Angola, even as Soviet-delivered and supplied Cuban forces move about Africa by the tens of thousands.

Whatever the wishes of an American president — present or future — his capacity for containment action against communist-organized revolutions or *coups d'etat* is far less than that of any president between Truman and Johnson. The Reagan administration notwithstanding, the presidential power in such matters has diminished.

The situation is also affected fundamentally by the transformation of the Soviet-American power relationship. The achievement of parity in ICBMs by the late 1960s, the acquisition of Soviet regional superiority in nuclear and conventional weapons in Europe and East Asia in the 1970s, and the building of a Soviet naval and air power with global access have all radically altered the military balance. Whatever other factors were operating, the change in the military balance alone greatly limits the American containment capacity and, by implication, increases the Soviet capacity to sponsor, sustain, and protect communist revolutions abroad.

There is a tendency in contemporary Western commentary to give a low rating to prospects for future communist revolution in the Third World and to emphasize the factors favoring Western influence in that area: dynamic economies and technology; enormous capital resources for development; and the steady expansion of democratic rule — most recently and impressively in the major states of Latin America. The present period appears to be one of those eras when the achievements and prestige of the industrial democracies are viewed with favor. It is too tempting to claim that they have demonstrated the superiority of their economic and political model and that the rest of the world will follow suit—when it can.

It would probably be wiser at such a time not only to reexamine closely the variety of contexts in which communists have acquired power in the Third World, and the instruments they used, but also to emulate the admirable habit displayed in Soviet political documents and scholarly studies of taking the long historical view.[29] The Soviets seem to feel that the competition has only seriously begun—and perhaps they are right.

Part II

The Decline of Economic Performance

6

Richard E. Ericson

The Soviet Economic Predicament

The Nature of the Predicament

In the latter half of the 1970s the Soviet Union, along with most of the industrialized world, experienced a distinct deterioration in economic performance. The rates of growth of gross national product (GNP), industrial output, factor productivity, consumption, investment, and even defense procurement fell dramatically.[1] This situation has aroused much comment in the West, revolving around the rubric of "crisis in the USSR," and evident concern within the Soviet Union, where it seems to be viewed as the manageable consequence of a difficult transition from "extensive" to "intensive" economic development.[2] Yet the early 1980s brought still further deterioration in economic performance that was halted only by a vigorous campaign for social and economic discipline, a campaign initiated and pursued under the new leadership of Andropov and then Gorbachev. As a consequence there was a return in 1983–85 to the better rates of growth of the mid-1970s.

Although respectable for a developed Western economy, this performance remains unacceptable to the current Soviet leadership. For example, the draft of the 12th Five Year Plan was rejected by Gorbachev in June 1985 as providing for insufficient growth and development of the economy. Major programs have been announced for raising the standard of living, for restructuring and re-equipping industry, for accelerating technological change, for raising product quality, and for expanding the economic rights and responsibilities of produc-ers.[3] Gorbachev has said that significantly better performance is essential, that current levels are unacceptable, and that hard decisions and changes will have to be made.[4] Evidently an economic predicament of serious dimensions is perceived.

The predicament runs deeper than shown by the worsening indices of per-formance alone. Those declines undercut the legitimacy of the political and socioeconomic system, one in which the leadership arrogates to itself ultimate wisdom, absolute authority, and final responsibility for the nature and direction of development of the polity. The legitimacy of such a system depends in part on its ability to make demonstrable progress toward the overriding social, politi-cal, and economic goals of the society for which the leadership speaks. This involves demonstration of the superiority of centrally planned socialism by making steady progress in the "material basis of communism," carrying out the "progres-sive" transformation of society, as defined by the current program of the Com-munist Party of the USSR, and overtaking the developed capitalist world. The legitimacy also rests, in part, on the success of that leadership to preserve and extend the socialist and progressive blocs of nations and of Soviet superpower status. The health and growth of the Soviet economy is the foundation upon which the pursuit of these objectives rests.[5] Thus, the deterioration of economic per-formance gnaws at the legitimacy of the entire system.

Until 1975, the economic performance of the Soviet system made claims of superiority plausible. In spite of perceived problems of microeconomic in-efficiency, the Soviet economic system achieved rapid urbanization and indus-trialization, supported a total war effort, recovered from wartime devastation, and rapidly narrowed the development gap behind advanced capitalist countries in output and national income.[6] There was, however, a steady and disturbing decline in microeconomic indices of performance throughout the postwar period that could be explained only partly by the "recovery phenomenon." In the late 1950s and early 1960s declining economic performance, though still impressive by Western standards, led to major—if temporary—structural changes (Khrush-chev's *Sovnarkhoz* system, abolished in 1965) and some economic reforms (the Kosygin Reforms of 1965–67, and their continuing modification) that apparently rejuvenated growth and productivity.[7] These gains, however, were short-lived, as the statistics of Table 1 indicate. By the mid-1970s, indices of economic performance resumed their slow but steady decline, with the deterioration becoming more rapid at the end of the decade.

By the late 1970s, it was obvious that the economic situation had become critical, though the nature and depth of the crisis were subject to differing interpretations.[8] As indicated in Table 2, both Soviet and Western measures of Soviet economic performance reached unprecedented lows during 1979–82 as the 10th Five Year Plan fell far short of its goals and the 11th opened with two years of stagnation. A fall in the rate of growth of output, increasingly tight resource and factor constraints, and a collapse of factor productivity combined with exogenous shocks to produce the most serious economic situation faced since the end of the New Economic Policy (NEP, 1927–29).

Although Tables 1 and 2 seem to show comparable Soviet and Western macroeconomic performance during much of the past decade, they were still correctly interpreted with alarm. In particular, the steady decline to 1982 was significant in dashing hope of soon overtaking the West, as was reflected in the revised Third Party Program. Furthermore, these numbers are apt to be seriously inflated, as many Soviet authors have recently noted.[9] The reasons include significant price inflation, particularly in machine building and construction, one-sided errors in aggregation, and the inclusion of useless production and waste in the net output figures, all driven by the strong incentives throughout the economic system to exaggerate output and performance. Thus, aggregate Soviet economic performance was undoubtedly worse than Tables 1 and 2 indicate, while at the same time showing an alarming deterioration.

Not only did overall performance deteriorate, but the traditional microeconomic inefficiencies and distortions of the system became more acute and disruptive. Supply and transportation bottlenecks became more frequent, waste in intermediate product and materials use and quality problems became more prominent, inventories and unfinished construction grew even in the face of diminished investment, and the waste and inefficiency in agriculture became increasingly obvious and damaging.

Each of these problems was recognized in the Soviet Union and attempts were made to deal with them. These included changes in priorities, changes in administrative procedures, and modifications to the planning and control system that had served so well for so long. An initial reaction was to deal with each problem through a new decree.[10] The fuller response, as we shall see, has been to try to reinvigorate the system, to reorient it toward the pursuit of subtler, more qualitative goals. The primary issue facing the Soviet leadership is whether the entire economic mechanism, the planning and administrative system, is up to the task. In spite of great official optimism, voices of doubt have been raised in

TABLE 6-1 **Average Annual Rates of Growth** (*percentages*)

Index	1951–60	1961–65	1966–70	1971–75	1976–80	1981–83	1981–85*
Soviet							
National Income Produced	10.1	6.5	7.6	5.7	4.2	3.6	3.4
National Income Utilized	NA	6.5	7.1	5.1	3.9	3.6	3.3
Investment	12.6	5.2	7.4	6.6	3.4	6.2	2.6
Consumption	NA	7.0	10.1	6.9	5.4	2.7	3.3
Industrial Output	11.7	8.6	8.5	7.4	4.4	3.6	3.7
Agricultural Output	7.9	2.3	3.9	2.4	1.7	0.7	1.2
Labor Productivity	13.5	6.5	7.9	4.9	3.5	3.4	3.3
Labor in Industry	10.3	5.2	6.5	6.7	3.4	3.0	NA
Western							
GNP	5.6	5.1	5.3	3.8	2.7	2.6	2.2
Industrial Production	9.5	6.8	6.4	5.9	3.2	2.7	2.3
Total Factor Productivity	1.9	0.6	1.1	–0.5	–0.8	–0.4	–1.0
Total Labor Productivity	NA	3.4	3.2	4.4	1.9	2.2	NA
Total Capital Productivity	NA	–3.4	–2.0	–4.0	–4.1	–3.5	NA
F. P. in Industry	NA	–0.5	0.3	0.6	–1.3	–1.3	NA

NA = Not available.

F.P. = Factor Productivity.

*Preliminary estimates.

Sources: Soviet data are calculated from Central Statistical Administration of the USSR (CSU), *Narodnoe Khoziastvo SSSR*, various issues; 1985 data are from CSU Report of Plan Fulfillment, *Ekonomicheskaia Gazeta* 6 (February 1986). Western data are from CIA, *Handbook of Economic Statistics* (Washington, D.C.: U.S. Government Printing Office, 1984); 1981–85 data are from JEC, U.S. Congress, "The Soviet Economy Under a New Header (Washington, D.C.: U.S. Government Printing Office, 1986), and are calculated at factor cost in 1982 prices whereas previous data are based on 1970 prices.

TABLE 6-2   **Average Annual Rates of Growth** *(percentages)*

Index	1979–82	1981	1982	1983	1984	1985*
Soviet						
National Income Produced	3.7	3.9	3.7	4.2	3.2	NA
National Income Utilized	3.1	3.2	3.6	3.6	2.6	3.1
Investment	1.0	0.9	11.0	4.9	−1.5	−0.1
Consumption	3.1	4.0	1.2	3.1	4.0	4.3
Industrial Output	3.4	3.4	2.9	4.2	4.2	3.9
Agricultural Output	−0.4	−1.1	5.5	6.1	0.0	0.0
Western						
GNP	1.6	2.2	2.6	3.5	1.5	1.6
Industrial Production	2.4	2.4	2.3	3.4	2.9	2.8
Agricultural Production	−0.9	0.5	6.1	6.3	−0.5	−0.6
Total Factor Productivity	−1.3	−0.8	−0.5	0.0	NA	NA
Total Labor Productivity	0.9	1.3	1.7	2.2	NA	NA
Total Capital Productivity	−6.1	−4.0	−3.5	−3.1	NA	NA
Net Investment	NA	1.0	11.2	5.0	1.9	2.7

NA = Not available.
*Preliminary estimates.
Sources: See Table 6-1.

the Soviet Union, calling for far-reaching changes in the economic system.[11] To the extent that the system itself is a major source of the current difficulties, it indeed will be necessary to make more radical changes than have been attempted.

The causes of deteriorating performance are manifold and closely related to, and indeed dependent on, the nature of the Soviet economic system. The cheap resources, surplus labor, and massive investment opportunities on which previous growth had been based were essentially exhausted by the mid-1970s. Exogenous factors such as the weather and population growth had taken a turn for the worse, and the aging capital stock was increasingly inadequate to the requirements of a changing technology. (These negative factors more than offset the large improvement in terms of external trade stemming from the sharp increase in energy prices during this period.) However, more than just a confluence of negative circumstances was involved. The problems caused by these objective factors were aggravated by decisions on the volume and allocation of investment, defense expenditures, and the general inflexibility and aversion to innovation and change characteristic of the Soviet economic system.[12] Thus, exogenous, policy, and systemic factors all played a role in the economic difficulties of the late 1970s, though their impact is subject to varying interpretation.

Although there is some recognition of these factors expressed in the Soviet Union, the response of the leadership has been, so far, quite conservative and only modestly successful. Strong emphasis has been placed on hard work, discipline, and individual responsibility for results; expectations of performance at all levels have been raised. Priority has been given to retooling industry with advanced technology, raising the output of agricultural and consumers' industrial goods, and increasing the variety and quality of goods available. Individual incomes and rewards are to be tied more closely to productivity increases and to meeting planned objectives (including the introduction of new technology and increased quality of goods and services).

The whole program revolves around the "large-scale experiment," initiated by Andropov, that extends the economic rights and responsibilities of enterprises, and that was to be broadened under Gorbachev to all industry on January 1, 1987.[13] Although this program is only beginning to be implemented, the discipline campaign and the associated management changes in top leadership have had a noticeable impact. The significant recovery of performance in 1983 apparently has been maintained, with some slippage, in the succeeding two years. (However, one has to note that part of the reported improvement may be an artifact of reporting; many managers are likely to be trying to look good to the new bosses.) The Soviet leadership clearly hopes and expects this performance to be significantly better in the 12th Five Year Plan, which began January 1, 1986, as the full impact of the new measures comes to be felt. If so, they will have found a way out of their economic predicament.

There is good reason to believe that so easy a solution is not to be found. The programs and policies of Gorbachev in no way alter the essential nature of the Soviet economic system. To the extent that the fall in performance is *systemic* in nature, these new measures are apt to prove inadequate to the challenge. If they fail to increase the rate of growth of GNP and productivity, the rate of innovation and technological change, and the level of economic efficiency, they will leave the Soviet Union in an increasingly serious situation. For at current levels of economic performance there is no hope of catching up to, never mind overtaking, the developed capitalist world, or of developing the material basis for communism.

The current level of development is too low to support a claim of success for the Soviet system and to justify the sacrifices asked of the Soviet people. Without a significant improvement in performance, questions of the system's legitimacy may become serious. Further, extremely difficult choices will have to be made on the allocation of an insufficiently growing national product; these choices will raise questions about the maintenance of the empire and superpower status. All these questions will become more acute and the predicament sharper, to the extent that Soviet leaders are unwilling to consider true systemic changes. For they are then faced with a Sisyphean task: reversing the slowdown without abandoning the essential character and objectives of the Soviet system, without sacrificing centralized social control, the "leading role of the Party," and indeed their own positions and well-being. This, I believe, is the true Soviet economic predicament.

The Soviet Economic System

To comprehend the momentous problem facing Gorbachev and the new, younger leadership of the Soviet Union, it is necessary to understand the nature of the economic system they inherited, largely intact, from Joseph V. Stalin. For the difficulties with which they must deal are largely systemic, while those that are exogenous are significantly worsened by the nature of the system's economic interaction. Moreover, the working of this economic system has so far negated all efforts at "conservative" economic reform, leading to a rejection (revocation or neutralization by decree) of those measures incompatible with its essential nature.[14] Thus, all "reforms" and "improvements" attempted during the last thirty years have failed to reverse the steady deterioration of economic performance and indeed may have accelerated it. This implies that radical reform of the system, of its basic nature and principles of operation, may be needed for a sustained improvement in its performance.

How It Functions.   The Soviet economic system is best described as one of centralized directive planning implemented through detailed coordinating instructions. Subordinate operational agents have little autonomy in determining what to do, or even how to do it. Their activity is bound by a network of commands, instructions, constraints, and priorities issued from above. Subordinates provide information and suggestions that may greatly influence commands, yet they are rigidly bound by them once issued. All wisdom and authority ultimately reside with the central organs, though the fine details of implementation must necessarily be delegated to operational units. The political leadership, and the central planning organs that serve it, must know best and must decide in great detail what society needs and what must be done to meet those needs.

The logic of the system is clearly reflected in its economic institutions and procedures.[15] Direction and control of economic activity, and the Soviet claim to socialism, are helped by the overwhelming size and importance of the "socialized" sectors. The state owns all natural resources and almost all of the reproducible capital—including land, minerals, buildings, machinery, equipment, and inventories—and conducts virtually all activity in industry, mining, construction, transportation, wholesale trade, communications, health, research and development, and education. The state and cooperative sectors produce, respectively, over 47 percent and 41 percent of the value of final output in agriculture, the remainder being provided by the private sector. These two socialized sectors also control 70 percent and 28 percent, respectively, of retail trade; and the state owns three-fourths of urban, and one-fourth of rural, housing space—the remainder again being in the private sector.

The legal private sector is quite small, restricted as it is to small-scale agricultural activity, the construction of private housing, arts and crafts, and the provision of some professional and personal services. There is also a significant amount of illegal private economic activity, and it seems to be growing in importance, although we have no firm, reliable measure of its size or impact. [16] Even the private sector, however, is subject to substantial control by the state political and economic apparatus.

The priorities of the political leadership are maintained through a vast and complex administrative structure. This consists of a number of overlapping hierarchies that gather information, disseminate instructions, coordinate interactions, manage change, and monitor and enforce commanded performance. At the apex stand the highest Party and government organs, the Politburo and the Praesidium of the Council of Ministers. The government, i.e., the Council of Ministers, and a vast array of central planning and control agencies are responsible for translating the objectives and policies of the political authorities into consistent and realizable plans. These central agencies comprise over twenty state committees, functional ministries, and agencies, each dealing with a particular economic function, such as GOSPLAN (planning), GOSSNAB (materials and equipment supply), GOSSTROI (construction), GOSKOMTSEN (prices), GOSKOMTRUD (labor issues), GKNT (science and technology), SEL'KHOZTEKHNIKA (agricultural equipment), the State Bank (GOSBANK), the Central Statistical Administration, the Ministry of Finance, the Committee of Peoples Control, etc.

Below these are over fifty "branch" ministries. These include four food and agriculture ministries, nine ministries for different kinds of construction work, twelve ministries for different kinds of machine building, and nine ministries—including three machine building—primarily producing for the military. [17] Each is further divided into departments (GLAVKI or main administrations; industrial associations) by region or more specific output category. Each department is in turn solely responsible for providing planning information and implementing plans and instructions within its specific "branch" of the economy. This ministry/department structure is duplicated for about half of the branch ministries—called "union-republic ministries," within each of the fifteen Soviet Socialist

Republics, introducing a regional dimension to administration and leading to dual subordination for those associations and enterprises. Ministries whose activity does not involve significant regional considerations, e.g., heavy and military-related industries, are called "all-union ministries," and have no counterparts within the republics.

At the base of this hierarchy are the organizations that do the work: the actual production, construction, transportation, distribution, and trading activities in the economy. These are associations (*ob'edineniia*) and enterprises (*predpriiatiia*) subordinate to either ministries or local governmental organs, and collective farms and consumer cooperatives. For example, there are about 44,000 industrial enterprises, almost 20,000 of which belong to about 5,000 production or science-production associations, 22,000 state farms, 26,000 collective farms, 10,000 interfarm enterprises, 1,000 agro-industrial associations, 27,000 construction organizations, and almost three-fourths million wholesale and retail trade organizations. Their detailed activities must be planned and controlled by the central authorities to achieve the goals of the Soviet state and society.

Alongside this organizational pyramid there are a number of parallel monitoring and control hierarchies, including the Party, the banking system, State Arbitration, Peoples Control, the material and equipment supply system, and the monitoring system for military output of the Ministries of Defense and Defense Industries. Each serves to insure proper reporting of information and proper implementation of central instructions. They are outside the direct economic chain of command, but have important powers of investigation and intervention in order to insure that the commands and intentions of the central authorities are followed. Indeed, the local Party organizations are the ultimate representatives and interpreters of central priorities and desires at the local, operational level.[18]

The orchestration of this complex structure requires extensive, detailed planning. This entails a continuous process of "explicit administrative guidance of production, distribution, investment, and consumption."[19] The task is overwhelmingly large, involving many tens of thousands of major operational units regarding tens of millions of production and distribution processes, and over 24 million products during some given interval of time. Thus, it must be simplified by aggregation and subdivision along the administrative lines of the hierarchy and by restricting the planning period. The operational plan is limited to a one-year period, while much less detailed developmental plans cover a five-year period.[20] Aggregation and administrative partitioning of the task, however, also create massive planning coordination problems. Coordination, to the extent that it is achieved, arises out of direct interaction at the highest levels and the efforts of the primary planning organ, GOSPLAN.

The actual process of planning involves iterative communication and bargaining among the central organs, between these and the ministries, and along the economic chain of command within each particular branch of the economy. It begins with a series of directives from the top outlining the goals and tasks that are interpreted by GOSPLAN in a set of "control figures" that set specific targets and priorities, and constrain and guide other central and subordinate agencies. These figures are elaborated in increasing detail down the hierarchy, becoming more specific targets and commands to operational subordinates. However, they are based only on prior information available to superiors about subordinates' capabilities and hence need not be consistent or even feasible. Operational units respond to these assignments by requesting the capital and material resources needed to do them, and thus reveal information about their own capabilities. This is accompanied by extensive bargaining as the central authorities strive for maximal performance while subordinates seek easier tasks.

The outcome is a set of revisions for each of the branches of the economy that must be made broadly consistent for a workable national economic plan. The central organs, in particular GOSPLAN and GOSSNAB, work to get at least a rough, tolerable balance of planned supplies and demands for all products and resources as they draw up a final draft of the plan. The plan is submitted to the highest authorities; when approved it becomes a set of binding commands to the branch ministries. These are disaggregated down the administrative hierarchy into directives to all organizations at each level. The final stage ends with an exhaustive set of commands, targets, allocations, operational instructions, and constraints that touch on every aspect of the economic activity of the operational units at the base of the hierarchy. At that level it becomes the *Tekhpromfinplan* and material supply plan which commands every aspect of the technological, production, and financial activity of each enterprise and its economic interactions with other organizations.

Alongside runs a parallel process of financial planning. This is primarily handled by the Ministry of Finance, which draws up the State Budget of the USSR, including all republic and local budgets, and by GOSBANK, the sole bank of the USSR, which draws up, among other plans, credit plans, cash plans, and the balance of incomes and outlays of households. A branch of the GOSBANK controls financial operations of every state organization. Financial planning is, however, of decidedly secondary importance since all nonprivate economic activity is, in principle, subject to direct physical planning and control. Its primary purposes are to provide a check of the implementation of plans by monitoring financial flows ("control by the ruble") and to channel and constrain nonplanned economic activity in the cooperative and private sectors.[21]

This implies that money must have a very limited, passive role in the Soviet economy. Within the state sector it is merely an accounting entry in the books of the State Bank to be transferred between accounts in response to legitimate, planned exchanges between state organizations. Money is only physically used for interaction between the state and nonstate, and within nonstate, sectors—in particular for wage payments and for consumer purchases. Thus, the task of financial planning "is to assure that individual enterprises and households . . . have enough (but not too much) money to buy the goods and services intended for them in state output and supply plans."[22] By the logic of the system, money exists only to facilitate planned economic activity and should not have an independent influence over economic decisions.

The logic of the system also implies a limited and passive role for prices. They are primarily used for measurement, accounting, and control purposes, though they have an impact on income distribution and a generally undesired influence on production decisions. Prices, including wages and salaries, are administratively set and controlled by hierarchies under the direction of GOSKOMTSEN and GOSKOMTRUD, respectively. They are highly differentiated according to administrative (*not* economic) criteria and remain fixed for extremely long periods. Commodity prices are generally set on a "cost-plus" basis and include turnover taxes and handling charges. They are meant to cover average costs of production in each branch of the economy so that enterprises might be "self-financing" with "profit" a useful measure of performance. There is some effort to set consumer goods prices to limit demand to planned output levels. However, prices bear no real relationship to relative use values or scarcities, and they reflect central priorities only in the most aggregate terms. This is hardly surprising in view of the overwhelmingly complex task of keeping prices for over 24 million goods aligned with their true and constantly changing economic values. Further, price inflexibility is useful for measurement and physical control; aggregates retain their physical meaning and financial flows reveal true actions, rather than reflecting price changes. Yet to the extent that prices influence decisions, they cause bad choices because they provide irrelevant or incorrect information about relative values and scarcities.

Actual economic activity in the Soviet state and cooperative sectors is generated by the attempts of operational economic organizations to carry out their given commands. In a complex social economy with a high degree of specialization and interdependence, this involves hundreds of millions of microeconomic relations and interactions, including precise specification and timing of production and transfer activities in full operational detail, in a continually changing economic situation. Were plans fully consistent and perfectly feasible this would pose no problem, and the only performance question would be of the efficiency and optimality of the plan. This is far from the case.

Due to the complexity of the planning problem, the naturally limited information gathering and processing capability of the central authorities, extreme time pressures, and continual changes in economic situations, detailed operational plans are rarely consistent, while central plans are so only at the most aggregate level. The problem is aggravated by the fact that the information on which plans are based is frequently intentionally distorted by subordinates seeking "easier" assignments against which their performance will be judged. In this game, the central authorities consciously pursue a policy of "taut" planning, i.e., pressuring subordinates by assigning ambitious targets and limiting the resources provided, largely in pursuit of rapid growth and development and partly to counter the distortions of subordinate organizations. This further aggravates consistency and feasibility problems. It also means that plans must be continually changed and these changes often make matters worse.

These shortcomings imply that operational organizations have greater autonomy than the logic of the Soviet economic system would indicate. Even the most detailed plan must be aggregate in relation to reality, so subordinates have much latitude in interpreting commands. This latitude, this power of interpretation, is vastly enhanced as inconsistent plans lose power to affect behavior. When it is impossible for them to do what was commanded, subordinates must make critical choices and trade-offs on the spot. Their choices are informed not only by the plan, but also by the interpretation of the desires of superior and monitoring organs, by the implicit priorities in the material incentive system, and by the parochial interests of the subordinates. They are motivated by the need for at least the appearance of plan fulfillment, of satisfying superiors that everything possible was done in their interest; by the material and "moral" rewards associated with success; and by the desire to accomplish all this as easily as possible.

In an interdependent system, such choices have a considerable impact on the other organizations that depend on the output. These decisions taken by subordinate producers (enterprises) create problems because they are isolated by the administrative hierarchy and hence are taken in ignorance of, and complete indifference to, social objectives. Subordinates care only about assigned plan targets, the communicated priorities of superiors, and their own narrow area of responsibility. The plan that should coordinate them as frequently isolates them, leading to decisions and behavior that are quite dysfunctional from the perspective of the whole economy, even though they are perfectly legitimate and rational given the information and constraints of the acting agent.

As a result, commands to subordinates are of necessity frequently changed. This generates additional inconsistencies, further expanding the possibility for uncontrolled (unplanned) and potentially undesirable actions. The logic of the Soviet economic model dictates that these actions be subject to strict central control. Yet that is physically impossible – a fact with profound consequences for the performance of the economic system.

The salient characteristics for understanding recent performance of the Soviet economic system can be summarized in nine areas:

1. A hierarchical structure of authority in which choices must be made and conflicts resolved at a level superior to all sides of the issue.

2. Rigid, highly centralized planning of production and distribution, and a commitment to maximal resource utilization implying tautness and pressure in planning.

3. Formal rationing in physical or quasi-physical terms of producers' goods and services.

4. Exhaustive price control, yielding multiple and contradictory systems of inflexible prices.

5. Incentives geared to meeting the plans and desires of evaluating superiors and not to the economic consequences of decisions taken at levels below the very top.

6. Absolute and arbitrary control by superiors of the norms, indices, and parameters of plan assignments, performance evaluation, and rewards.

7. The lack of any legal alternatives to given economic relationships and the inability of any subordinate to legally alter these relationships.

8. The lack of any "liquidity" or flexible response capability (eg., reserves, excess capacity) in the system, and in particular the lack of any true "money."

9. The systematic separation (due to the hierarchical structure) of the loci of efficient action in any situation. In particular, the dispersion of usable data and their separation from decision-making authority is critical to the functioning of the system.

Strengths and Weaknesses. Both the strengths and weaknesses of the Soviet economic system derive from these characteristics. The strengths lie in the system's ability to achieve central priorities, both economic and noneconomic. It is very good at pursuing clear, well-defined objectives that can be expressed in measurable, quantitative, and communicable terms, and yield large observable changes. Such a system facilitates the massive mobilization of scarce resources and their exclusive concentration on achieving these central objectives. Further, their simple nature allows the generation of appropriate plans and commands and verification of their proper pursuit. Thus, the system is quite *effective* in attaining simple and clear-cut aims. The building of major heavy industrial capacities and, indeed, of whole sectors, the collectivization of agriculture, the postwar reconstruction of industry, the development of an unprecedented military-industrial complex, and the maintenance of the world's last true empire – all are examples of this effectiveness. These tasks are all the easier when they entail catching up, replicating an existing or previous economic structure or achievement. For then the problems of knowing what to do, when and how to do it, and whether it was properly done are solved by reference to a working model, by exploiting the "advantages of backwardness."[23] Thus, the early stages of industrialization are particularly helped by the Soviet system, as is the whole process of "extensive economic growth," involving massive increases in inputs used in essentially the same ways.

Accompanying these advantages are a number of shortcomings. As the system pursues a few priority objectives, there is little control over, or even knowledge of, the economic costs involved. Commanded goals are attained regardless of sacrifices in lower priority, and there is no way for those at the top to know whether that success was worth achieving. The central authorities cannot monitor all important costs—in particular, true opportunity costs—yet they are the only ones with a true interest in knowing them. It is they for whom the economy functions, in whose interests choices must be made. Yet they necessarily lack the information, the physical capability, to make all the choices that they must to achieve social goals.

In all but a very few priority areas, the central authorities can only indicate what is desirable and what needs to be done in general terms and must leave the details to subordinates. The nature of the system isolates and blinds all agents to the consequences of their actions. Thus, subordinates with no idea of true opportunity costs are forced to make decisions in pursuit of the ill-understood objectives of superiors that have a wide-ranging impact on other organizations in the complex economy. ·

As the Soviet economy grows and develops, the problems facing the central authorities become more difficult. This is because of a dramatic increase in the complexity of the economy. Successful development, industrialization, and advance of technology brings growing specialization, division of labor, and mutual interdependence of all economic units. This means an increasing number of factors that must be considered and incorporated into planning—as well as an increasing number of subordinates to implement those plans. Thus, economic development implies the necessity of explicit conscious management of an ever-growing number of operational agents. It leads naturally to ever-growing problems of economic efficiency, a growing loss of control by the central authorities, and a steady reduction in the effectiveness of the pursuit of priorities.

A more complex economy requires a more elaborate administrative structure and hence a longer chain of command and wider spans of control. This removes the center even further from real economic activity, dissipates the impact of commands and instructions through the hierarchy, and requires that even more be left to ill-informed and irresponsible subordinates. Objectives become more refined and harder to communicate, priorities proliferate, coordination becomes more difficult, and monitoring of subordinate activity becomes much harder. New opportunities and problems arising in the system become increasingly difficult to keep track of and hence tend to be ignored with growing frequency. The few priorities whose implementation can still be insured become progressively less important to the overall functioning of the economy as they become a smaller part of the total. Hence, the center tends to lose control — and thus effectiveness — in achieving its priorities. All of the causes of inefficiency are aggravated by the growing complexity that accompanies, and indeed defines, successful economic development.

Causes of Deteriorating Performance. This process explains much about recently deteriorating economic performance. The inherent *inefficiency* of a centrally planned and command-administered economic system has slowly come to dominate its *effectiveness*. Methods and institutions, effective at an earlier, simpler stage of development, no longer generate desirable outcomes. The system is becoming ever less adequate for the needs and flow of economic activity — though the desire for control forces its maintenance. The natural consequence is an increase in clearly dysfunctional behavior of subordinates, increasingly obvious waste and inefficiency, slowing economic growth, slowing and then declining factor productivity, and ever more frequent failures to achieve proclaimed priorities. This is the situation in the Soviet Union today, as Gorbachev and others repeatedly emphasized during the 27th Party Congress.

Of course, there are many "objective," nonsystemic factors that can be pointed to as the immediate causes of current Soviet economic difficulties. These causes have been classified as exogenous factors; consequences of a maturing economy; and strategic planning decisions.[24] While some are at root truly exogenous to the Soviet economic system, many are a consequence of the way it operates, and all have been severely aggravated by the nature of the system.

These exogenous factors include the unusually bad weather of the late 1970s and early 1980s, demographic shifts leading to a sharp drop in increments to the labor force, and external economic and political conditions limiting Soviet access to trade and credit. Bad weather had a direct impact on the agricultural, food processing, and transportation sectors that was magnified by the lack of reserves and the rigidities inherent to the system. In addition, the structure of the system led to a delayed and inadequate response to the crisis. Similarly, demographic trends have long been clear, yet the system has continued to move along the old path, failing to adjust the structure of capital and production to meet them. The system has shown itself also incapable of adjusting to world markets, except for the purchase of high-priority inputs (e.g., grain and items of advanced technology), leading to an inability to export little more than energy products. The Soviet ability to import has suffered a further dramatic decline as the price of its primary export—oil—has fallen to below $20 per barrel.

The consequences of a maturing economy include depletion of the resource base, which leads to energy and raw material shortages, and an aging and increasingly obsolete capital stock. Both arise from the extensive growth and the aversion to innovation the system fosters, the waste of resources it rewards, and the ignorance of obsolescence and opportunity costs the system imposes on decision makers. Capacities are left in use far longer than is rational, resources are wasted on repairing obsolete capital, and investment is dissipated on countless projects that are long delayed in completion. Thus, the economy has "matured" far faster than it should have due to the wasteful repetition of past methods and structures in the pursuit of rapid growth of measurable outputs.

Policy Decisions.   The final set of "objective" factors involves planning and policy choices. The most important of these was the decision to cut growth targets for the 10th and 11th Five Year Plans and, in particular, to cut the growth of fixed investment.[25] This was an attempt to command an increase in efficiency and productivity by reducing material and capital inputs while maintaining the growth of final output. This challenged the pattern of extensive growth and bet success on the unobservable actions of subordinates without changing the system that renders proper, efficient, and innovative action impossible. The natural consequence was disruption of the flow and growth of production, generating shortages and bottlenecks that multiplied throughout the economy. Raw materials and industrial intermediate products, and the energy, construction, and transportation sectors, were particularly hard hit by this during the late 1970s and early 1980s.

Another policy decision derivative from the nature of the system has been the continued absolute priority of the military sectors; this is true in spite of an apparent reduction in the growth rate of military procurement. Not only does the military absorb 15 to 17 percent of Soviet GNP, but it has first claim on the highest-quality material inputs, capital, labor, and transportation services, and on about a quarter of the capacities of the machine-building sectors.[26] Further, the more broadly defined security sector (which includes support for Cuba, Vietnam, etc.) probably commands over 20 percent of GNP and has a much greater impact on industrial production activity. The priority of this sector protects it from negative outside impacts and mistakes in plans, and insures that it will function properly because it receives a disproportionate share of support from the central authorities. The rest of the economy, however, is further disrupted because it must act as a buffer to protect the military economy from disturbances.

Another strategic planning decision that was taken during the late 1960s, and maintained to the present, has been to increase imports of advanced technology and equipment from the West in order to speed up the rate of technological progress and innovation and maximize the "advantages of backwardness." This strategy appears to have failed, again for systemic reasons. Due to the unique structure of the Soviet economy, the model they were attempting to copy wasn't very relevant to the Soviet needs or factor and resource endowments. The system obscured true opportunity costs and made the assimilation of the new technology extremely difficult; it disrupted established patterns and worked against the interests of subordinate agents who inevitably control implementation in all but the highest-priority situations. The consequence has been massive waste of expensive imported technology together with no noticeable improvement in productivity or rates of growth.

A last set of policy decisions that may have had a negative impact concerns the continual adjustment of procedures and institutions that has taken place since 1965. These changes constitute a "treadmill of reforms" that, however, never challenged the underlying logic of the Soviet economic system.[27] Some changes, largely of an administrative nature, have survived (e.g., the ministerial system, state committees, associations), but most have proved to be inconsistent with the logic of the system and hence have been modified or rolled back (e.g., enterprise control over investment and incentive funds and production targets). Indeed, all attempts at enhancing the autonomy and discretion of enterprises have led to increases in hoarding, in simulation of outcomes, in distortion of product mixes, and in self-serving manipulation of incentive funds. Further, these repeated changes in the economic mechanism have increased the uncertainty facing everyone. This allows more room for dysfunctional decisions and aggravates the worsening of economic performance.

Despite all these problems the Soviet economy is in no imminent danger of collapse. The predicament is not one of potential collapse but of slowly increasing obsolescence of the economic foundations of Soviet power. The highly centralized system can easily maintain current levels of output; enforce the achievement of major, measurable priorities; and probably produce some expansion in the level of economic activity. It has a strong capital and resource base and a compliant labor force that can be used to maintain Soviet economic and military power well into the future. But its economic system *is* in danger of becoming an anachronism before it begins to lose economic potential and power. The true economic predicament is one of potential system-induced stagnation under a relatively growing burden of "empire," of maintaining political and military power and superpower status. This implies a long-run threat of eventual loss of legitimacy, empire, and international status to which the Soviet leadership cannot, and indeed will not, remain indifferent.

The Soviet Response and Future Prospects

The problems arising from this economic predicament have come to occupy the center of attention of the new Soviet leadership before and during the 27th Party Congress at the beginning of the 12th Five Year Plan. There is a sense of deep urgency in Gorbachev's frequent speeches and statements about the state and future of the economy, as well as a declared commitment to undefined "profound structural" change. There is a growing emphasis on the need to reinvigorate the economy, to stimulate initiative and innovation, and to modernize the structure of capital and production in order to take full advantage of the ongoing "scientific-technological revolution." There has been a flurry of activity, including the replacement of much of the top- and middle-level economic leadership, the consolidation of the machine-building and agricultural ministries, the rewriting of the draft of the 12th Five Year Plan and guidelines to the year 2000, the announced continuation of the "large-scale economic experiment" and its extension to all industry, new decrees stimulating technological innovation and enterprise initiative, and a new "Comprehensive Program for the Development of the Production of Consumers' Goods and Services." There is also the prospect of further and deeper changes and policies to come in the aftermath of the Party Congress from February–March 1986 and the Central Committee Economic Plenum of June, 1987.

Gorbachev's Strategy.   Despite this rhetoric and activity, nothing truly new came out of the 27th Party Congress, and the concrete steps taken so far have been quite conservative. They are little more than a natural extension of Brezhnev's July 1979 program to improve planning and the functioning of the "economic mechanism" and of Andropov's "large-scale experiment" begun in five branches of industry in 1984. The Gorbachev strategy for dealing with the economic predicament can be broken down into two stages. The first, dealing with the immediate situation, involves the traditional emphasis on the human factor, i.e., on personnel changes, "state, plan, and labor" discipline, a businesslike attitude, and the work ethic. This is to be accompanied by changes in policies to deal with the most pressing economic problems of waste, slowing productivity, lack of innovation, and slow technological change. These changes relate particularly to the targeting of investment, whereby the machine-building industries, equipment production, and the re-equipping and rebuilding of existing plants are to receive priority over new construction, regional development, and the other sectors of the economy.

The second stage involves a longer-term "restructuring of the economic mechanism" in order to address what are perceived as the basic causes of the economic stagnation. It is to include a streamlining of the central planning apparatus, a centralizing of authority at the expense of the branch ministries, the computerizing of the economy, a restructuring of the price system on the basis of "quality" rather than cost, and an expansion of the economic rights and responsibilities of enterprises based on quality- and innovation-oriented incentives. The core of this program to date is the extension of Andropov's experiment to all civilian industry and two military production ministries on January 1, 1986, and to all industry in 1987 along with the true implementation of the various earlier decrees aimed at "improving the functioning of the economic mechanism."[28] These measures once again alter the indices for evaluating plan performance and the parameters of the incentive system; declare the need for stability of plans and indices over a five-year period; increase the extent of central planning and material balancing; expand the role of enterprises in the formulation of plans; increase enterprise control over incentive and investment funds; increase the economic accountability of subenterprise organizations; and increase enterprise responsibility for contract fulfillment and the level of product quality.

Organizational changes have been promised—such as the recent amalgamation of eleven machine-building ministries under a State Bureau and of five agriculture-related ministries and SEL'KHOZTEKHNIKA into a new State Committee on Agro-Industrial Complexes (GOSAGROPROM), together with a significant reduction in central ministerial staffs—in order to put more power in the hands of the top Party and government authorities. This is accompanied by a declared intention to reduce the role of the ministries and local Party organizations in the operational management of economic activity, which is now to be left to newly "responsible" enterprises and associations under the supervision of the higher central authorities. Finally, this stage of the strategy seems to involve increased CMEA (COMECON) integration, giving the Soviet Union access to more high-quality investment goods, and a lessening of the subsidization of the empire in general and Eastern Europe in particular.

There is very little to this program that is new, aside from its scope and the energy with which it is being introduced. Most aspects had been tried during the preceding "treadmill" of reforms and experiments with no evidence of lasting success. Yet this program contains some hints of systemic change—hints that something more will follow after Gorbachev has fully consolidated his power. In particular, the August 4, 1985, Decree opens a crack in the rigid allocation of production materials by giving priority to enterprise-determined research and development (R&D) and retooling and reconstruction needs.[29] Further, there is talk of legalizing parts of the "second economy," of encouraging private initiative and reward in agriculture, and of introducing the reorganization of enterprises as a form of "socialist bankruptcy." These, however, remain mere hints of future possibilities.

Will the Reforms Make a Difference?   These reforms may well aggravate existing difficulties. The attempt to make the Five Year Plan operational is apt to place an unbearable burden on the capabilities of the central authorities. Binding "control figures" on the formation of one-year enterprise plans are apt to be even less realistic and relevant to the actual situation. This is particularly true of any attempt to draw up binding material balances over a five-year period. Further, the weakening or elimination of middle levels of the planning and management hierarchy can only add to the already unmanageable burden on the central authorities. The increased use of computers and new "mathematical methods" of planning is also only apt to make things worse; the size and complexity of the problem are well beyond the capability of even the most advanced technology, the information base is woefully inadequate, and hence its use will give precise, accurate answers to increasingly irrelevant problems. Thus, Gorbachev's economic strategy is most likely to render planning ever more inflexible and irrelevant.

The Soviet hope is that this can be avoided by significant devolution of responsibilities to the operational organizations—associations, enterprises, cooperatives, etc. Yet none of the sources of dysfunctional subordinate behavior has been seriously addressed. Incentives are still geared toward meeting plan targets, prices are still rigid and irrational, resource allocations are still administratively rationed, horizontal interactions are still rigidly planned and assigned, and the hierarchical structure of the economy still isolates operational units—both from the data to make proper decisions and from their consequences. Thus, the expansion of the powers of implementing agents is apt only to make their assigned tasks easier, to "insure" themselves, and to simulate outcomes when necessary. Enterprises may be more able to achieve planned and contracted investment, assortment, and quality goals, but those goals are more apt to be irrelevant or counterproductive. Local technological efficiency under the current program is likely to work against economic and allocative efficiency. The announced changes in pricing do nothing to alleviate this problem because prices are still administratively fixed, only now on the basis of technical quality rather than economic criteria. And the resultant disruption, inherent in any change, can only further distort economic behavior and lower performance in the eyes of the central authorities.

This does not mean, however, that Gorbachev's strategy cannot be effective in yielding a short-term boost to performance. The stress on the human factor can be particularly important, for example in the appointment of better managers, the "discipline" and anti-alcoholism campaigns, and the tying of individual reward to the performance of the immediate collective. These, as well as the campaigns to enforce strict contract compliance and technical quality standards, are likely to yield a gain in technical, if not allocative, efficiency.[30] Thus, the "large-scale economic experiment" will undoubtedly have an early positive impact on performance until subordinates learn how to take full advantage of it for their own interests, how to manipulate and exploit the new norms, incentives, and targets. Only after several years of improved economic performance will the dysfunctional aspects become sufficiently widespread and visible to demand a central response.

There are three other areas in which policy changes could have a noticeable positive impact on performance: investment priorities, the price structure, and imports from the West. Targeting investment to loosen constraining bottlenecks, such as raw and processed materials and energy supplies, along with the tightening of state, plan, and labor discipline, has already improved performance in the mid-1980s. Gorbachev's new priorities for investment include the machine-building sectors, the renovation of existing plants, and the introduction of new equipment and technology, all of which should help raise the technological level and technical efficiency. The restructuring of prices to reflect more closely the opportunity cost of aggregate commodity groups should also help. Thus, the prices of energy inputs and new "progressive" products and technologies have been raised, the prices of substandard and obsolescent products reduced. There is the possibility that agricultural and food prices will be raised, consumption subsidies reduced, and the basic capital charge increased. Finally, there is the possibility of a greater opening to the West, allowing the use of imports to break critical bottlenecks. Already imports account for 35 percent of machinery investment goods, and their doubling might raise GNP growth by another 1 percent per year.[31] However, because none of these changes address the most fundamental causes of the Soviet economic dilemma, they promise no more than a temporary improvement of performance.

Dilemmas in Modernizing the Capital Structure. There are also limits to what policy changes can do without a major change in the capital structure of the economy. The modernization sought by Gorbachev will require massive investment for the introduction of new technologies and the rebuilding of obsolescent capital stock in every sector.[32] Thus, Gorbachev has called for a doubling of the rate of investment growth during the 12th Five Year Plan, raising the volume of investment by 15 to 18 percent by 1990. Yet, unless his overall economic growth targets (e.g., GNP up by 4.7 percent per year) are met or exceeded, there are apt to be too few resources to support such investment growth without sacrificing defense or newly proclaimed consumption priorities. Both investment growth and the use of the resulting capital stock will be limited by a lack of complementary labor inputs; additions to the working-age population during the next decade will be lower than during any previous period and less than one-third those of the early 1970s. The rate of investment is further limited by the capacity limits of the machine-building metal-working (MBMW) construction materials and construction sectors. These obstacles are made even more formidable by the high priority of the defense sectors and by the costs of the empire. For example, the military sectors absorb some 15 to 17 percent of Soviet GNP, over 20 percent of the output of metals, and over 25 percent of the MBMW industries' output, as well as the highest-quality labor, capital, and material inputs.[33]

Imports of advanced machinery and technology from the West might seem to be the way to open this supply bottleneck. Yet the collapse of energy prices, led by oil as low as $12 per barrel, has significantly undercut the Soviet ability to earn foreign exchange. Without significant borrowing, the Soviet Union will be unable to maintain current agriculture import levels, never mind increase industrial imports. So far there has been little indication of Soviet willingness to dramatically increase their foreign debt for this purpose, and speeches at the Party Congress stressed the need to rely on internal sources.

Some of these obstacles to modernization, however, have been addressed in Gorbachev's priorities. The key role of the machine-tool industries in the investment process, and particularly for the introduction of new productive, labor-saving technologies, is clearly recognized in the drive to re-equip existing enterprises and retool all industry. In order to implement a "scientific-technological revolution" in Soviet industry, the machine-tool sectors are to be modernized through an increase in investment of over 80 percent during the 12th Five Year Plan. Because these sectors absorb about 25 percent of all industrial investment, this implies that more than the total increment to investment in industry will be allocated to these priority sectors. This, together with the 12th Five Year Plan commitment to increase investment in the fuel/energy and agro-industrial complexes by 47 percent and 22 percent respectively, implies reducing the total amount available to the rest of the economy by about 8 percent.

This is a risky strategy. As noted above, transportation became a serious bottleneck in the late 1970s. In particular, the railroads, responsible for over 70 percent of Soviet industrial transport, are old and overused; both their fixed and rolling stock require renovation and replacement. Yet only minimal resources and a strong dose of "discipline" have been committed to their improvement. Agriculture is another perennial problem area, characterized by high costs, particularly low productivity, slow growth of "quality food" output, and general output instability. Together with its supporting industries, agriculture absorbs better than one-third of all investment (27 percent directly) and subsidies greater than half of the value of its net output, yet seems to call for still greater investments to deal with its problems. Further, resource extraction and processing—particularly energy—sectors cry out for massive investments while their costs—especially investment costs—are rising dramatically as more accessible sources are exhausted. There is particularly a need for the development of infrastructure in remote source regions and for the development of transportation to areas of use. Falling oil production requires massive investment to re-equip industry to use plentiful gas supplies. Lower-quality coals must be used on the spot and the resulting energy transported, requiring massive investment in energy generation and transmission facilities. Finally, there is a vast backlog of unfinished construction that requires heavy investment to be brought to completion.

Gorbachev's priorities clearly de-emphasize these other needs, though some investment resources seem already committed through the Brezhnev Food Program and the Energy Program. In particular, Siberian development and the Baikal-Amun railroad (BAM) seem to have been put on hold. The policy changes are resolute, thorough, and consistent, yet fraught with risks due to the breadth of the economic problem. But more seriously, they still seem only to address the consequences of the economic predicament and not its fundamental causes.

The Need (and Poor Prospects) for Radical Decentralization. Attacking the roots of the problem would require a radical decentralization of authority responsibility. The central authorities must allow operational organizations to have detailed information of time, place, and circumstance at their disposal to make needed trade-offs, to choose and change priorities, and to pursue opportunities, including making their own investment decisions. This means that they must have the right to select their own line and scale of economic activity, choose their own "partners" (especially suppliers), set and change prices in response to economic pressures, and survive, prosper, or fail as a consequence of their own choices and activities. Operational organizations must be self-motivated, self-interested, and ultimately responsible for their own well-being in order for them to have a proper incentive to exploit fleeting opportunities, to take advantage of the changing economic situation in ways that are not wasteful and/or destructive of material wealth.

The superior-subordinate relation between central planners and enterprises must therefore be abandoned, along with any attempt at serious price control; enterprises making their own decisions must face prices reflecting true relative scarcities. The central authorities must allow true competition among producers and users and allow economic activity to provide its own reward. They must abandon the increasingly futile attempt to control economic activity and socioeconomic development in detail, and leave it as the largely unintended outcome of the interaction of independent economic agents. Planning must become macro-economic and indicative, rather than microeconomic and directive. The central authorities must no longer command performance, but must rather guide or encourage desired economic activities and developments through the use of what the Soviets call "economic levers," i.e., market and/or financial instruments. Ultimately they must leave economic responsibility in the hands of the operators if they want them to act responsibly.

The nature of these changes underlines the depth of the predicament. Clearly they cannot be made because they attack the very nature and legitimacy of the system. Such a reform is tantamount to declaring the Soviet socialist system an outright failure. Politically it would disperse power, weakening and de-legitimizing the role of the *nomenklatura* and the Party. The central authorities would lose a significant amount of control over the nature and direction of economic develop-ment and even more control over the actual allocation of resources. Those intermediate-level administrators who must insure that the needed changes are properly implemented would lose even more power and status from doing so. Thus, those who alone could implement such far-reaching changes would suffer tremendous, direct loss from making them.

The gains to such a reform are, by contrast, diffuse and elusive. Further, such changes would carry dramatic distributional consequences. There would be great economic gains and losses among autonomous organizations and the individuals that comprise them, and the social contract with Soviet citizens would be jeopardized as employment and income security could no longer be guaran-teed (although welfare "safety nets" could be provided). This could engender potentially explosive discontent. Economically, there would be massive adjust-ment problems and perhaps major disruption of economic activity as organiza-tions learned to function and coordinate their activities in the new economic environment. Finally, there is apt to be in the eyes of the central authorities a loss of direction, a growth of anarchy and corruption, and an exploitation of market power by those economically strong, as the Hungarian and Chinese experiences indicate.

These are just some of the immediate and serious costs. They are sufficiently large as to make any attempt at such reform highly unlikely in the near future. Further, the short-run success of the first stage of Gorbachev's program and of the potential policy changes noted above is apt to make any far-reaching changes appear unnecessary and even less desirable. Thus, there was little reason to expect any far-reaching reform to come out of the Party Congress, and, indeed, none was proposed there. This situation, however, is apt to further aggravate the eco-nomic predicament in that delay may imply greater risks to, and hence cause fur-ther delay of, true reform.

In sum, the Soviets are unlikely to solve their economic problems. There is an inherent contradiction between innovativeness and efficiency on the one hand and centralized control on the other. Soviet economic problems, however, are not fatal, and the economic prospect is not system-threatening—at least in the next ten to fifteen years. The system is still effective at achieving major well-defined priorities, as the maintenance of a second-to-none military establishment and the replacement of U.S.-Western compressors by Soviet ones in the Orenburg gas line demonstrate. There is no danger of an economic collapse or a serious weakening of the economic foundations of the empire. Indeed, the system seems quite capable of steady, if not spectacular, economic growth with some slight acceleration in the immediate future due to Gorbachev's program.

We can therefore expect Soviet economic performance in the next five years to be better than that of the last ten, even if it falls short of that expected by the Soviet leadership. With some luck and reasonable weather, initial GNP growth rates of around 3 percent are plausible during the early years of the 12th Five Year Plan, as are positive growth rates of combined factor productivity. This should allow most of Gorbachev's priorities and investment goals to be met, though without achieving the ultimate outcomes he desires and expects. However, without further structural reform, GNP growth is apt to taper off to about 2 percent per year by 1990, implying only 1 percent growth per capita, again thrusting the economic predicament to the front of the Soviet agenda. Without radical change, the Soviet economy will then settle into a state of increasing obsolescence and very slow growth. Such a situation might threaten the legitimacy of the system and its leadership, and eventually pose a threat to the maintenance of the Soviet empire.

The longer-run prospects facing the Soviet economy are thus bleak. There is little chance of more than a temporary respite from the poor performance of the last decade, and indeed the agricultural and energy sectors are apt to present even greater problems. Industry will be renovated and modernized to some degree, yet left to function in the straitjacket of the same system. Current bottlenecks will be loosened, but others will arise. Enterprise autonomy will cause more problems than it resolves, and again be rescinded as it comes into increasing conflict with the rigidities of the system. After a brief boost from enforced labor and plan discipline, factor productivity will again stagnate, and the growth will return to its recent unsatisfactory levels.

The goals of the revised Third Party Program, in particular the building of the material basis for "communism," will appear increasingly unattainable. In an increasingly desperate effort, the State and Party leadership will roll out a steady stream of policy changes, economic "reforms," "restructurings," and "improvements"—all, however, without lasting impact. For the core of the difficulty lies in the logic of the Soviet economic system. Fundamental improvement can come only from a thorough, drastic alteration of the economic system. Yet the replacement of the economic system would destroy the legitimacy, the whole purpose, of the Soviet political, social, and economic structure, and of its ruling groups. That is the true economic predicament. It is far deeper than the mere deterioration of indices of economic performance and far less tractible.

7

Charles Wolf, Jr.

The Costs and Benefits of the Soviet Empire

Defining the Empire[1]

The terms "empire" and "imperialism" are familiar, frequently used, and unremarkable when employed in Marxist-Leninist rhetoric to describe—usually with derogatory tones—the international role of the West and of the United States. Use of the same terminology in the West to characterize the expansion of Soviet influence and activity abroad, however, is less standard and, especially in Western Europe, much more controversial. This contrast is paradoxical because the familiar use is now anachronistic, whereas the nonstandard and controversial use has a ready application. Indeed, the Soviet bloc is the only effective, functioning empire in existence today.

The Soviet Union is an empire both in the traditional, general sense and in a unique modern sense. The general sense implies a special degree of influence, control, or constraint exercised or imposed by the imperial power over the component parts of its empire. That this control varies widely across the different parts of the Soviet empire is no more peculiar to it than to the Roman, Ottoman, British, or Japanese empires of the past.

The Soviet empire also has certain distinctive features. Indeed, there are three Soviet empires: 1) the empire "at home," lying within the geographic boundaries of the Soviet state; 2) the geographically contiguous part of the empire—that is, Eastern Europe and, more recently, Afghanistan; and 3) the empire abroad. This chapter deals with the costs and benefits to the Soviet Union of maintaining the latter two components of its empire.

The empire "at home" has been the subject of several prior studies.[2] This use of the term derives from the fact that the Soviet Union is a multinational state consisting of over sixty separate ethnic groups and fifteen distinct national republics dominated by the largest and strongest, the Russian Soviet Federated Socialist Republic (RSFSR). The internal empire was created by the eastward expansion of czarist Russia in the nineteenth century, and enlarged by the communist state following the Leninist revolution.

The contiguous part of the external empire consists of the satellite countries of Eastern Europe: Poland, Hungary, Czechoslovakia, East Germany, Rumania, and Bulgaria (all of which are members of the Council for Mutual Economic Assistance [CMEA] and of the Warsaw Pact), and Afghanistan. The countries of Eastern Europe were areas of Russian influence under the czars, but the Soviets have expanded this traditional influence to the point of quasi-sovereign control.

The second part of the external empire lies further abroad, outside the limits of former czarist influence. In Cuba, Vietnam, Angola, South Yemen, Ethiopia, Syria, Mozambique, Libya, Nicaragua, and North Korea—some of which are officially Marxist-Leninist, the others simply "progressive" or "revolutionary"—Soviet influence varies in both nature and degree.

My definition of the external empire includes countries that are satellites, allies, spheres of influence, or simply more or less friendly and cooperating regimes. This is not overly broad, however; variety has characterized all empires. Moreover, as J. A. Hobson remarks, there have always been "quibbles" about the meaning of the term "imperialism" and a "sliding scale" of political terminology.[3] His point is no less relevant to the current Soviet empire than it was to the nineteenth-century British empire.

Another characteristic of the Soviet empire is that the imperial power is usually exercised through the Communist Party of the Soviet Union (CPSU) and the associated communist parties of the other parts of the empire, rather than through formal governmental channels. Thus, for example, the International Department of the CPSU plays a more active and important role than the Soviet foreign ministry.

The Soviet Union has three institutionalized mechanisms for sustaining both

Soviet predominance and a reasonable degree of cohesion within the empire: 1) the ideology of "socialist internationalism," managed by the International Department of the CPSU in concert with the foreign parties; 2) the internal state security organs, overseen by the KGB with training and support often provided by the East German state security apparatus and occasionally by North Korea; and 3) provision of military planning, training, and operational support by the Soviet military establishment: indirectly, in the form of logistical support and equipment for Cuban, Vietnamese, North Korean, and other "fraternal" states; and occasionally through direct employment of Soviet combat forces, as in Afghanistan. The military leaderships of the component states are, for the most part, trained in the Soviet Union's Voroshilov Military Academy to insure their reliability and compatibility.[4]

Controversy over using the term "empire" of the Soviet Union has arisen in both the scholarly and the political arenas. In the scholarly arena, for example, Besançon has objected that such usage doesn't conform to the historical meaning of the term. In his view:

> an empire, in the classical sense of the word, displays generally the following features: it is run by a privileged people; it relies mainly on military strength; it is relatively indifferent to the previous social structure of a submitted people, and does not seek to transform it; it acknowledges the legitimacy of other competing empires. None of these criteria applies to Soviet domination.[5]

Of Besançon's four criteria, the first two surely apply to the Soviet empire. The "privileged people" who run things (especially in the International Department of the CPSU and its counterparts) are the *nomenklatura*. And military strength is an essential part of the control mechanism. Without the direct use of Soviet forces, the threat of their employment, or (more frequently) indirect use of indigenous military forces trained and supported by the Soviet Union or its Cuban associates, there would be no external empire.

Besançon's third criterion—indifference to indigenous social structure—admittedly does not apply to the Soviet case. Even traditional empires, however, were not indifferent to preexisting indigenous social structure. The empires of Greece, Rome, and France, for example, viewed their imperial missions as in part cultural: to spread their "cultures" throughout their domains. Inevitably, this cultural infusion affected social structure.

As to Besançon's final criterion, it is not true that other empires have always acknowledged the "legitimacy" of competing empires. For example, the Ottoman empires and the empire of the Chinese Middle Kingdom (with its "mandate of heaven") assumed an exclusive claim to legitimacy.

In the political arena, the dispute over the aptness of labeling the Soviet bloc an "empire" stems from the view, widespread in Western Europe, that the term should be avoided because it is inflammatory and provocative, whether or not it is accurate. The inference is then drawn that, if the term is employed, the Soviets will respond by intensifying the cold war, which will lead to greater tension and to the deterioration of East-West relations in general, and of U.S.-Soviet relations in particular.

European anxieties are intensified when the noun "empire" is preceded by the adjective "evil," the phrase President Reagan used to characterize the Soviet Union. Yet the president had good reason to use it. The dictionary says "evil" means "offensive," "causing harm," and "not good morally." Such adjectives are not inappropriate with respect to the Soviet empire.

Furthermore, European worries about Soviet reactions to such rhetoric are overdrawn. They impute Western (or, as the Soviets would say, "bourgeois") sensibilities to the Soviet leadership. The Soviets aren't so thin-skinned. It is an article of central importance in the indoctrination of the Soviet *nomenklatura* that Western sensibilities should be rejected in shaping the attitudes and behavior of the Soviet elite.[6]

The Benefits of the Soviet Empire

Maintenance and expansion of the Soviet empire—or the advancement of "socialist internationalism," as the Soviet ideological vocabulary would have it—undoubtedly ranks high among the foreign policy objectives of the Soviet Union. This statement, of course, does not answer the question of whether and how the Soviet imperial enterprise competes with other concerns of the Soviet leadership: the Soviet military, the state security system, and industrial and agricultural investment. It says only that the empire's resource claims—channeled by the Politburo through the CPSU's International Department—are among the purposes for which top Soviet decision makers must establish priorities.

That high value is placed on the imperial enterprise can be inferred from the large economic costs the Soviet Union has incurred in maintaining the empire. If the benefits imputed to the empire were not high, the leadership would be unwilling to bear such heavy costs. I will discuss these costs below.

Benefits from the empire can also be assessed indirectly by considering the military, intelligence, political, and strategic Soviet interests the empire serves.

Military Benefits.   The Soviet empire multiplies the effectiveness of Soviet military forces in several tangible and calculable ways.[7] Soviet naval bases at Camranh Bay in Vietnam, Socotra Island in South Yemen, and Cienfuegos in

Cuba enable Soviet forces to deploy for longer periods of time in the China Sea, the Indian Ocean, and the Atlantic than would be possible otherwise. If, for example, these units' home port were, say, Vladivostok or on the Baltic Sea, transit times for ship refueling, repair and maintenance, and crew rest and rehabilitation would increase substantially. The result would be reduced time-on-station or an increase in the size of the force needed to maintain equivalent striking and patrol capabilities. Vietnam and Cambodia, therefore, are especially valuable participants in the Soviet imperial enterprise.

Soviet air bases in Afghanistan (notably in Kandahar) as well as Soviet facilities in Ethiopia and South Yemen provide potential staging areas that enhance the capabilities of the Soviet air force (for example, by bringing them within striking distance of the Straits of Hormuz) and Soviet ground, naval, and air forces (by bringing them within easy operational range of the Horn of Africa). This increases potential Soviet access to and control of oil reserves in the Persian Gulf. Without such forward basing, Soviet combat aircraft would require additional in-flight refueling or would have to trade reduced firepower for increased on-board fuel supplies or reduce their operational range. Forward bases thus multiply the effectiveness of present Soviet air capabilities and reduce the cost of achieving specified military capabilities.

Obviously, basing Soviet air and ground units in Eastern Europe improves Soviet security by extending the perimeter to be defended. But in addition, forward forces give the Soviet Union a politically useful military lever in Western Europe. Stationing the equivalent of thirty-two ground divisions and substantial air force support in Eastern Europe enables the Soviet Union to launch sudden, deep strikes against the West, and it reminds the West just how close to home Soviet power lies. (This does not deny that Soviet forces in Eastern Europe – ground divisions especially – are there primarily to maintain political control in this most important part of the Soviet empire. It also does not gainsay the fact that Soviet ability to rely on these forces as an effective threat against Western Europe may be limited by their crucial role in maintaining political control in Eastern European countries themselves.)[8]

The Soviet Union derives tangible military benefits from the opportunity to develop and test both equipment and tactics under combat conditions in parts of the empire where military operations by Soviet forces are under way (e.g., currently in Afghanistan). This does not mean the principal reason for the Soviet invasion of its satellites is to acquire a combat zone for such purposes. Nevertheless, the opportunity to conduct combined operations using airborne command posts, helicopter gunships, and small infantry units, to test chemical weapons, and to battle-harden ground forces is a major benefit that comes with having an imperial sphere of influence.

Finally, the empire offers the Soviets the chance to train and logistically support allied or "proxy" forces that can be deployed instead of, or in conjunction with, Soviet units. These forces can be used to sustain communist control where it is contested or fragile (for example, in Angola, South Yemen, and Nicaragua) and to strengthen communist-led insurgencies in other areas. In effect, such proxy forces increase the Soviet Union's capacity to project military power in circumstances where direct deployment of Soviet forces is not possible or is deemed imprudent.

Intelligence Benefits.   Expansion of the Soviet empire during the past decade has been accompanied by an increase in the scope of Soviet intelligence operations abroad. One estimate places the increase between 1971 and 1980 in the number of Soviet KGB and GRU (military intelligence) agents abroad at 25 percent, with a further increase of about 7 percent between 1981 and 1983.[9] Most of these increases probably would have occurred even without expansion of the empire, and many of the additional agents have, in any case, been placed in countries outside the empire. Moreover, some of this growth results from the Soviet "standard operating procedure" of assigning the KGB to monitor *non*-intelligence Soviet personnel stationed abroad. When the number of non-intelligence personnel abroad goes up, the number of KGB personnel grows as well.

In any event, expansion of the Soviet empire has afforded Soviet intelligence agencies numerous additional points of contact, listening posts, and sources of information. These additional resources enable the Soviet Union to acquire a greater quantity of useful military and technological intelligence.

Political and Strategic Benefits.   The political benefits from the empire are less tangible, less quantifiable, but probably more important than even the military benefits.

According to Marxist-Leninist ideology, the growth of "socialist internationalism" is an ineluctable response to capitalist imperialism. Although the original Marxian theory has been revised in many ways, accretions to the international socialist fold are essential ingredients in Leninism, and hence in the system's claim to legitimacy. Such accretions undergird the self-esteem of the leaderships of the Soviet Union and "fraternal" states. Many Soviet leaders see the task of maintaining and expanding the empire as the "historically inevitable process" through which international socialism will triumph in the world. The empire is thus a source of reassurance to the Soviet leadership. Expansion of Soviet hegemony also appeals to ethnic Russian nationalism and pride. Finally, expansion aids the leadership by contributing to the sense of urgency and crisis on which the system's internal cohesion and control feeds.

It is worth noting that the Soviet leadership never disavowed the doctrine on the need to support "wars of national liberation," either during the heyday of détente in the 1970s[10] or during the more recent twisting and turning of Soviet policy under Gorbachev. The Brezhnev Doctrine, which proclaimed the irreversibility of historical "processes" that bring socialist revolutions to political power, likewise remains in effect. These two tenets of Marxist-Leninist thinking—support for wars of national liberation and the Brezhnev Doctrine—reveal the high political value placed by the Soviet leadership on maintaining and augmenting the empire.

Lastly, maintenance and expansion of the empire clearly figure in Soviet strategic competition with the United States. In this strategic calculus, the gains and losses of the two sides register prominently with the respective leaderships. That Grenada did not become part of the socialist international fraternity was an outcome uncongenial to the Soviet Union; that Angola remains part of that fraternity is equally uncongenial to the United States.

Vladimir Bukovsky has cogently summarized the political and strategic importance of the empire to the Soviet Union in noting that the empire has become

> the only tangible measure of success the Soviet system could produce, the only proof that the communist ideology is still correct and the world revolution is still in the making. Besides, in the areas of expansion, there is often a direct clash with American interests and, therefore, an additional source of tension, another opportunity to show Soviet superiority over "enemy number one."[11]

The Costs of the Soviet Empire

Estimating the Relevant Costs. In the estimates below, the costs of the empire are defined as costs incurred by the Soviet Union to maintain or increase control in countries already under Soviet domination, to acquire influence in countries that are candidates for expanded Soviet control, or to thwart or subvert countries opposed to it.[12] Some costs are incurred in activities and in countries that are clearly *outside* the confines of the Soviet empire. When considering the latter, it is helpful to view the Soviet imperial enterprise as analogous to a large business enterprise: some costs represent investment in "research and development" (R&D) for new fields of endeavor. Like R&D in the business world, some of these efforts will be ineffective and may be terminated or deferred; others may be expanded if the initial results warrant.

There are three principal kinds of costs. The first is the total or full cost of activities that relate exclusively to acquiring and running the empire. Examples are the trade subsidies created by exporting fuel to Eastern Europe in the 1970s at prices below the world market price and importing Cuban sugar and East European machinery at prices above those prevailing in world markets.

The second kind of cost is the incremental cost of activities that, although principally connected with the normal running of the Soviet system at home, can be attributed in part to the empire. An example is the cost of Soviet military operations in Afghanistan over and above the regular peacetime cost of Soviet military forces (which for reasons to be discussed below are not counted here as a cost of the empire). Incremental costing of such activities treats the costs of maintaining the internal Soviet system and defending the Soviet state as "fixed" (i.e., they are determined independently of the empire), whereas the costs assignable to the empire are variable. [13]

The third sort of cost is tangible investment or capital projects directly related to the external empire. For example, construction of roads to the Afghan border and improvement of airports and roads within Afghanistan should properly be considered as costs of the empire, even though they may be used in the future for purposes other than maintaining influence in that country. [14]

The cost of the empire for the period from 1971 to 1980 has six components, including: 1) trade subsidies; 2) economic aid and 3) military aid (both estimated at their opportunity cost prices, but net of aid repayments and net of hard currency military sales); 4) export credits, construed as Soviet balance-of-payments surpluses; and 5) the extra cost incurred by Soviet military forces in Afghanistan over and above what they cost in their normal basing and operational modes. The sixth component consists of a part of total Soviet covert and related activities that, on a series of arguable but plausible assumptions, can be assigned to the imperial enterprise. [15]

Except for the incremental cost of Soviet military forces in Afghanistan and the net cost of Soviet military aid, I have excluded the large direct cost of the Soviet military establishment, even though it is clear that spending for the military and spending for the empire are often complementary. (For example, control of Eastern Europe depends heavily on the thirty-two active Soviet divisions there. Similarly, expansion of the navy and other Soviet projection forces during the past two decades has contributed to the empire.)

The complex relationship between Soviet military spending and empire spending thus raises the familiar and intractable theoretical problem of joint products and joint costs: where two or more products (in this case, military power and maintenance and expansion of the empire) result from the same activity (i.e., supporting the military or running the empire), apportioning the costs is arbitrary. Estimates of total Soviet military spending are provided for comparison with my estimates of the mainly nonmilitary costs of empire. But I do not attempt to assign any specific portion of military costs to empire costs. Thus, the assumption is made that the size, composition, and equipment – and hence the cost – of Soviet military forces are independent of the empire, an assumption justified less by its compelling logic than by the arbitrariness of imputing to the empire a specific part of total military costs.

Two other limitations about the costing methodology should be noted. First, if it were possible to do so, the extra cost incurred by the Soviet Union in supporting Cuban and East German allied or "proxy" forces should be included. Because the available data do not allow me to separate these costs from the cost components referred to above, Soviet costs for these allied forces appear in the estimates only to the extent that they are already subsumed in one of the six categories.

Second, in principle, allowance should be made for economic offsets to these estimates of the cost of the empire to make the latter truly *net* costs. (Alternatively, the offsets could be placed in the category of benefits.) I make allowance to only a small extent (for example, by subtracting from the total value of Soviet military aid the part that represents hard currency sales). It has not been possible to allow for certain other offsets – for example, the asset value of debts owed the Soviet Union, labor supplied to the Soviets by client states at wages below its marginal products, and direct payments to the Soviet Union for services (military or technical) rendered to parts of the empire. A still more elusive offset is the use of some parts of the empire, such as East Germany, as channels for acquiring Western technology. Ideally, all of these elements should be included in a cost model or treated as benefits. It is likely, however, that such offsets would necessitate only modest adjustments in the estimates. Moreover, any adjustments would probably be more than compensated for by elements of empire costs not included, such as the cost of supporting Cuban and other proxy forces.

Empire Cost Estimates for 1971–83. Using the methods described above, estimates are made of the cost of the Soviet empire. The dollar and ruble[16] expenditures summarized in the following tables and figures cover the periods 1971 to 1980 and 1981 to 1983. Costs are broken down for the six cost components and for three regions: Eastern Europe; Cuba and Vietnam; and Afghanistan and the remainder of the Third World. Figures 1 and 2 show total empire costs, average costs, and compound annual rates of growth (or decline), in constant dollars and rubles, respectively, for 1971–80 and 1981–83. The vertical lines above and below the regression curves show the range of the annual estimates. Midpoints are indicated by asterisks.

Figure 1 shows that the costs of the empire in constant 1981 dollars rose at

FIGURE 7-1   **Cost of the Soviet Empire in Billions of 1981 Dollars, 1971–80, 1981–83**

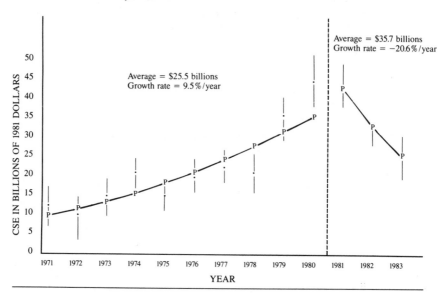

an annual rate of 9.5 percent from 1971 to 1980, reaching a peak of about $44 billion in 1980. Costs then declined from 1981 to 1983 at an annual rate of nearly 21 percent. In 1983, the costs stood at $28.6 billion, a decline of more than 35 percent from 1980. (This sharp decline resulted from the Soviet decision to reduce its trade subsidy to Eastern Europe by 40 to 50 percent. The decision was prompted by a 15 to 20 percent drop in the world price of oil. The Soviets also raised the price of their oil exports to Eastern Europe.) Despite the decline, average costs were substantially higher in the period 1981–83 ($35.7 billion) than in the preceding decade ($25.5 billion).

The picture changes sharply when costs are expressed in rubles rather than dollars, owing to persistent overvaluation of the Soviet foreign trade ruble. Because some of the components of empire cost (notably trade subsidies and military aid) represent forgone hard currency earnings, allowance for overvaluation of the ruble boosts the ruble-to-dollar exchange rate used in converting from dollar empire costs to ruble costs.[17]

As Figure 2 indicates, the cost of the empire in constant 1980 rubles rose from about 8.6 billion in 1971 to approximately 45.9 billion in 1980, an average annual growth rate of 17.2 percent.[18] By 1983 it had declined to about 27.5 billion, a decrease of 40 percent. The annual rate of decrease for the period 1981–83

FIGURE 7-2   **Cost of the Soviet Empire in Billions of 1981 Rubles,
1971–80, 1981–83**

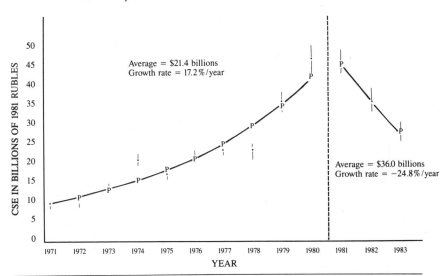

was -24.8 percent. For the decade 1971–80, average annual cost was 21.4 billion rubles; between 1981 and 1983 the average was 36.0 billion rubles.

Although the cost of the empire is larger when calculated in rubles rather than dollars, from 1981 to 1983 it declined at nearly the same annual rate: about 25 percent, compared with 21 percent in dollars. In 1983, both cost in dollars and cost in rubles had returned to roughly the levels they had reached in the period 1978–79.[19]

The ruble estimates are more significant than the dollar estimates for two reasons. First, converting the hard currency components of empire costs into rubles produces more accurate estimates of the real economic cost of the empire than using the official ruble-dollar exchange rate to arrive at dollar estimates. Second, the Soviet leadership undoubtedly thinks in terms of rubles in its decision making and pays careful attention to the high value in rubles of its hard currency costs.

To gauge the cost of the empire, it is useful to compare it with Soviet gross national product (GNP) and Soviet military spending.[20] Figure 3 shows the time paths for the ratios of ruble cost of the empire to GNP and to military spending. I also show the corresponding logarithmic regressions and average growth rate figures for these ratios that result from splitting the 1971–83 period into two seg-

FIGURE 7-3   **Ruble Costs of the Soviet Empire Compared to GNP and
Military Spending**

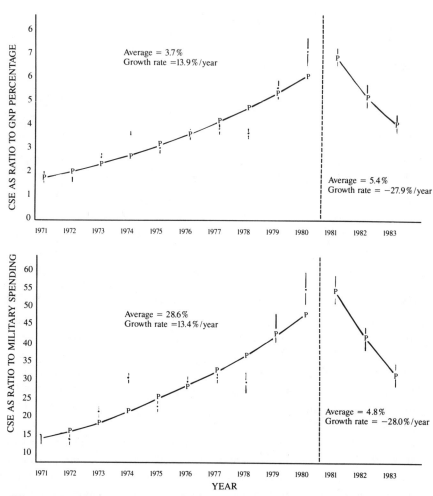

ments. The first segment covers 1971–80, when the cost of the empire generally increased as a percentage of GNP and military spending. The second segment covers 1981–83, when these percentages decreased substantially. The vertical lines above and below the fitted curves indicate the ranges of the annual estimates.

As Figure 3 reveals, the cost of the empire rose as a proportion of Soviet ruble GNP from 1.8 percent in 1971 to a peak of 7.2 percent in 1980, remained

TABLE 7-1 **Composition of Soviet Empire Dollar Cost, 1971–83**
(percentages and billions of current dollars)

	1971	1975	1980	1981	1982	1983
Trade subsidies (%)	11.0	45.5	52.0	45.5	45.4	40.4
Trade credits (%)	16.4	2.9	15.0	22.7	18.7	21.4
Economic aid (%)	10.8	4.6	2.1	3.1	3.7	5.2
Military aid (%)	18.8	20.1	18.3	16.2	16.4	12.4
Afghanistan operations (%)	–	–	2.1	2.4	3.2	4.3
Covert and destabilization activities (%)	43.0	26.9	10.8	10.1	12.7	16.2
Total cost of empire (in billions of current dollars)	6.40	12.45	40.53	43.20	35.70	29.15

Source: Charles Wolf, Jr., Keith Crane, K. C. Yeh, Susan Anderson, and Ed Brunner, *The Costs and Benefits of the Soviet Empire* (Santa Monica, Calif.: The RAND Corporation, 1986) pp. 19–33.

near that peak in 1981, and declined sharply thereafter to 4.0 percent of GNP in 1983. For the decade 1971–80, the cost of the empire averaged 3.7 percent of GNP. Between 1981 and 1983 it averaged 5.4 percent.

A similar pattern holds for the cost of the empire in relation to military spending. It rose from 14.2 percent of military spending in 1970 to 54.3 percent in 1980, then declined sharply to 30.8 percent in 1983. Despite this decline, the average ratio of the cost of the empire to military spending was higher in the period 1981–83 than in the preceding decade: 28.6 percent for the period 1971–80, and 41.8 percent in 1981–83.

In sum, the cost of the Soviet empire peaked in 1980, declined slightly in 1981, and fell more sharply in 1982 and 1983. The same pattern applies to the ratios of empire cost to GNP and military spending. These peaked at about 7 percent and 54 percent, respectively, in 1980, declining thereafter to 4 percent by 1983 for the former and to 31 percent for the latter. (For reasons discussed earlier, the corresponding ratios for the dollar calculations are much smaller — approximately one-half those for the ruble estimates.)[21]

Component Costs of the Soviet Empire. While the total cost of the Soviet empire was decreasing in the period 1980–83, its composition was changing. As Tables 1 and 2 indicate, trade subsidies as a proportion of total cost decreased markedly: from 52 percent in 1980 to 40 percent in 1983, in dollars; and from 62 percent to 53 percent, in rubles. Trade credits rose as a proportion of total

TABLE 7-2   **Composition of Soviet Empire Dollar Cost, 1971–83**
(percentages and billions of current rubles)

	1971	1975	1980	1981	1982	1983
Trade subsidies (%)	20.8	56.9	61.8	56.1	56.0	52.5
Trade credits (%)	13.0	1.8	8.6	14.9	12.4	15.3
Economic aid (%)	8.6	2.8	1.2	2.1	2.4	3.8
Military aid (%)	35.3	25.1	21.7	20.0	20.2	16.1
Afghanistan operations (%)	–	–	1.2	1.6	2.1	3.1
Covert and destabilization activities (%)	22.3	13.3	5.4	5.4	6.8	9.2
Total cost of empire (in billions of current rubles)	7.22	14.61	45.95	47.25	39.00	30.25

Source: See Table 7-1.

cost, increasing in dollars from 15 percent in 1980 to 21 percent in 1983, and in rubles from 9 percent in 1980 to 15 percent in 1983.

Military aid—the difference between total military deliveries and hard currency sales—declined as a proportion of cost. Although total military deliveries remained high ($10–11 billion), hard currency sales rose sharply. The remainder of military deliveries—the aid portion—thus fell: in dollars from 18 percent of total empire cost in 1980 to 12 percent in 1983, and in rubles from 22 percent in 1980 to 16 percent in 1983.

During the period 1981–83, all other components of empire cost (incremental costs of military operations in Afghanistan, economic aid, and covert and related destabilization activities) increased both in absolute amounts and as proportions of the total cost of the empire. Tables 1 and 2 show the changing composition of the total cost, in dollars and rubles, respectively, for the years 1971, 1975, 1980, and 1981–83.

Regional Distribution of Empire Costs.   During 1980–83, the regional distribution of Soviet empire costs also shifted. As the burden the empire imposed on the economy fell in absolute amounts, the proportion of the total spent in Eastern Europe fell from about 64 percent in 1980 to 52 percent in 1983. At the same time, the share incurred in Vietnam and Cuba rose from about 17 percent to 28 percent. The share of the total cost of the empire devoted to Afghanistan and other Third World countries remained nearly constant (20 percent) during the period.

Table 3 shows the regional distribution of total cost among three groups: the Warsaw Pact countries of Eastern Europe; the non-European members of

CMEA (Cuba, Vietnam, and Mongolia); and Afghanistan and other Third World countries, including Angola, Nicaragua, Ethiopia, South Yemen, North Korea, Syria, Libya, Cambodia, and Laos. Except for the costs of covert and related destabilization activities, all component costs discussed previously appear in Table 3 and are attributed to one of the three regional groups. Because I have not been able to attribute the costs of covert and related activities to particular countries or regions, they are excluded from the table.

As Table 3 indicates, the share of total empire cost incurred in the CMEA countries (Eastern Europe plus Cuba, Vietnam, and Mongolia) has remained fairly constant at 80 percent. As noted previously, however, within the CMEA "family" the emphasis has shifted from the Eastern European members of the Warsaw Pact to the outlying CMEA members Cuba and Vietnam.[22] The share received by the rest of the Third World has remained more or less constant during the period; compared with its share in the mid-1970s, however, this group's position has improved: from about 14 percent to more than 19 percent of the total.

It is tempting to infer from these changes in relative shares that they reflect the importance or priority accorded different regions by the Soviet leadership. This inference is unwarranted, however. The regional shares of total cost depend on a complex set of considerations, of which the importance of a particular country or region to the Soviet leadership is but one. These considerations include, for example, the extent to which the Soviet Union can reconcile its continued influence and control in particular parts of the empire with diminished resource transfers; the pressure it is able and willing to put on local leadership to boost exports to the Soviet Union; and the linking of imperial subventions to political, military, and other noneconomic benefits from particular members of the empire.

Changes in Empire Costs: Explanations and Implications. During the early 1980s Soviet empire costs declined appreciably. By 1983 they had fallen about 33 percent in constant 1981 dollars from their 1980 peaks (from about $44 billion to $29 billion), and by 39 percent in constant 1980 rubles (from 46 billion in 1980 to 28 billion in 1983).

Nevertheless, despite the declines, the cost of the empire remained substantial in both absolute and relative terms. In 1983 it was still 4 percent of ruble GNP and 1.6 percent of dollar GNP, having declined from over 7 percent of ruble GNP in 1980 and 3 percent of dollar GNP. It amounted to 30.8 percent of Soviet military spending, in rubles, compared with 54.3 percent in 1980; in dollars, it was 12.2 percent in 1983, down from 20.4 percent in 1980.

This reduced cost of the Soviet empire was still more than twice the corresponding cost of the U.S. "empire," however. Table 4 compares U.S. and Soviet costs, in 1983 dollars. Soviet costs have been adjusted by subtracting the costs

TABLE 7-3 Regional Distribution of Empire Cost, 1976–83 (billions of current U.S. dollars and percentage shares)*

	1976	1980	1982	1983
Eastern Europe (Warsaw Pact and CMEA)	7.39–8.58 (64.5–67.9%)	20.61–25.84 (61.9–65.9%)	14.84–19.17 (59.8–56.6%)	10.76–15.11 (49.4–55.6%)
Trade subsidies[1]	4.41–5.60	16.48–21.71	10.45–14.78	6.51–10.86
Trade credits[1]	1.17	2.81	3.17	2.76
Economic aid[5]	1.81	1.32	1.22	1.49
Military aid[6]	—	—	—	—
Cuba, Vietnam, Mongolia (CMEA)	2.36 (18.7–20.6%)	6.04 (15.4–18.1%)	8.11 (23.9–28.4%)	6.80 (25.0–31.2%)
Trade subsidies[1]	1.36	1.99[2]	3.59[2]	3.10[2]
Trade credits[1]	0.48	1.66	1.67	1.34
Economic aid[5]	0.34[1]	0.57[1]	0.79[4]	0.85[4]
Military aid[6]	0.18	1.82	2.06	1.51
Total CMEA	9.75–10.94 (85.2–86.6%)	26.65–31.88 (80.0–81.2%)	22.95–27.28 (80.2–80.5%)	17.56–21.91 (80.6%)
Afghanistan and other Third World countries[3]	1.70 (13.4–14.8%)	6.56–7.36 (18.8–20.0%)	5.65–6.60 (19.5–19.8%)	4.23–5.28 (19.4%)
Trade subsidies[1]	negligible	—	—	—
Trade credits[1]	—	1.62	1.90	2.19
Economic aid[5]	0.24[1]	0.28[1]	0.52[4]	0.68[4]
Military aid[6]	1.46	4.26	2.56	0.62
Military operations in Afghanistan[7]	—	0.50–1.20	0.67–1.62	0.74–1.79

TABLE 7-3 continued

	1976	1980	1982	1983
Total[8]	**11.45–12.64**	**33.31–39.24**	**28.60–33.88**	**21.79–27.19**

* All figures are in billions of current dollars except where percentages are shown. Where percentage shares are indicated, the calculated ranges are derived as the ratio between the low end of the regional dollar estimate and the low end of total empire cost, and conversely for the high end of the range.

1. Charles Wolf, Jr., K. C. Yeh, Edmund Brunner, Jr., Aaron Gurwitz, and Marilee Lawrence, *The Costs of the Soviet Empire* (Santa Monica, Calif.: The RAND Corporation, 1983); and Charles Wolf, Jr., Keith Crane, K. C. Yeh, Susan Anderson, and Ed Brunner, *The Costs and Benefits of the Soviet Empire* (Santa Monica, Calif.: The RAND Corporation, 1986). Trade subsidies for Vietnam not estimated because of insufficient data.

2. Cuba only.

3. Includes North Korea, South Yemen, Angola, Nicaragua, Syria, Libya, Cambodia, Laos, as well as other Third World countries. See also CIA, *Handbook of Economic Statistics* (Washington, D.C.: U.S. Government Printing Office, 1984 and 1985).

4. From CIA, *Handbook of Economic Statistics*, 1984 and 1985.

5. Economic aid is estimated as aid deliveries (rather than "extensions") net of estimated repayments.

6. ACDA, *World Military Expenditures and Arms Transfer*, 1985. Estimates for Eastern Europe derived by subtracting Soviet Arms *imports* from Warsaw Pact arms imports, and assuming that the remainder is arms aid supplied by the Soviet Union. See pp. 90, 123.

7. See Wolf et al., 1983 and 1985.

8. Totals exclude estimated costs of covert and related destabilization activities.

TABLE 7-4   **Comparative Costs of the U.S. and Soviet "Empires"**
(billions of current dollars and percentages)

	1981	1982	1983
U.S. economic aid	4.2	3.9	4.0
U.S. military aid (budgetary and nonbudgetary)	3.6	5.4	6.6
Export-Import Bank loans (net of repayments)	2.1	0.8	0.3
Total	9.9	10.1	10.9
Ratio of total to U.S. GNP (%)	0.3	0.3	0.3
Adjusted CSE* as dollar share of Soviet GNP (%)	2.4	1.8	1.3
Adjusted CSE* as ruble share of Soviet GNP (%)	6.1	4.9	3.6

*Soviet empire costs (CSE) adjusted by removing costs of covert operations and destabilization activities.

Sources: Office of Management and Budget, "National Need: Coordinating International Relations: Outlays," in *Budget of the United States Government* (Washington, D.C.: U.S. Government Printing Office, 1983, 1984, and 1985). GNP figures from JEC, U.S. Congress, *Economic Indicators* Washington, D.C.: U.S. Government Printing Office, 1985).

of covert and related destabilization activities, making the Soviet estimates more nearly comparable to the U.S. estimates. With this adjustment, cost of the Soviet empire was about $25 billion in 1983. The cost to the U.S. of maintaining its "empire," in contrast, was $10.9 billion. These expenditures amounted to 1.3 percent of Soviet dollar GNP (3.6 percent of ruble GNP) and 0.3 percent of U.S. GNP.

What accounts for the substantial decline in Soviet empire costs in the early 1980s? Four possible explanations are worth considering: 1) reduced economic needs and demands by the empire; 2) lower value assigned the empire by the Soviet leadership; 3) automatic operation of the five-year moving-average pricing formula used by the CMEA countries in intra-CMEA trading arrangements;[23] and 4) greater resource pressures resulting from growing stringencies in the Soviet economy.

There is no evidence for the first hypothesis. In fact, the economic predicaments of the Eastern European countries, as well as of Cuba and Vietnam, worsened or showed only modest improvement.[24] In general, the 1980s have been marked by stagnant or diminished economic performance of centrally planned, Soviet-type economic systems relative to market systems. Poland, Rumania, Cuba, Vietnam, and North Korea are the most striking examples. But the pattern holds throughout the Soviet empire.

There is also little evidence to support the second hypothesis: namely, that the political, military, intelligence, and general strategic benefits derived from the empire by the Soviet Union have become less important to the Soviet leadership in the 1980s. Indeed, it is at least as likely that the military and political benefits discussed earlier have grown in the eyes of Soviet leaders, for the reasons mentioned above by Bukovsky.[25]

The third and fourth hypotheses, therefore, are more likely to explain declining empire costs in the early 1980s.

Between 1980 and 1983, world oil prices declined by 15 to 20 percent in real terms. Because of this, the five-year moving-average pricing formula for Soviet oil exports to the CMEA countries of Eastern Europe produced a smaller subsidy on those exports. By 1983, the prices charged Eastern European countries were only 13 percent below the prices charged Western European importers.[26] Although Soviet subsidization of trade with Eastern Europe has continued, it increasingly has taken the form of paying above-market prices for machinery imports from Eastern Europe and sugar imports from Cuba. Charging below-market prices for oil exports has played a small and diminishing role.

The fourth hypothesis is even more persuasive. Economic stringencies surely have given the Soviet leadership stronger incentives to monitor and control the real economic costs of the empire and their burden on the Soviet economy. The CIA has estimated that the Soviet economy in 1980 grew at a rate of 1.7 percent, in 1981 at 1.9 percent, in 1982 at 2.6 percent, and in 1983 at 3.7 percent.[27] Some independent estimates suggest these figures may be too high, and that the actual figures on average may be 1 to 2 percent lower.[28] Estimates of Soviet real economic growth during the remainder of this decade are about 2 percent per year, which is about 40 percent below the estimated growth rate during the 1970s. From 1980 to 1983, per capita consumption in the Soviet Union grew only slightly if at all.[29] Finally, the severe problems besetting the Soviet economy—declining productivity of both labor and capital inputs, rising capital-output ratios, and the perennial and pervasive problems of incentives and rigidity in the system as a whole—are well known and amply documented.[30]

That the decline in cost of the Soviet empire has been influenced by serious stringencies in the Soviet economy, rather than simply by the workings of the CMEA pricing formula, also is suggested by the decrease in components of total cost other than trade subsidies during the first three years of the 1980s. For example, trade credits declined from $9.8 billion in 1981 to $6.3 billion in 1983. Military aid net of hard currency repayments also declined during this period.

Finally, the Soviet economic predicament is suggested by one other factor bearing on empire costs: from 1980 to 1983, Soviet real economic growth was slower, while empire costs were declining, than during the 1970s when those costs were higher. According to our earlier study of the trade-off between empire costs and the growth of defense and civil production, each drop of 1 percent in the cost of the empire as a proportion of GNP should be expected to raise the attainable annual growth of civil production by 0.3 percent or of military production by 0.6 to 1 percent.[31] Yet while the cost of the empire as a proportion of GNP was, according to our estimates, decreasing by 2 to 3 percent (from about 7 percent to 4 percent), the rates of growth in *both* Soviet civil and military production actually fell. Slow Soviet growth in the early 1980s despite lower empire costs is not inconsistent, however, with our earlier conclusion; lagging Soviet growth probably led the Soviet leadership to reduce these costs. Had the cost of the empire not been reduced, Soviet economic growth in the 1980s would have been even lower.

In sum, although maintaining and expanding the Soviet empire probably still commands a high priority in allocating Soviet resources, it came under strain in the early 1980s. This situation is likely to continue for the rest of the decade, especially in view of the sharp drops in world oil prices in 1985 and 1986, which eroded Soviet hard currency earnings by 30 percent or more. In these circumstances, the cost of the empire for the rest of the 1980s is likely to demand tighter constraints and more careful monitoring and control by the Soviet leadership. The Soviets may prove ambivalent about managing the imperial enterprise. On the one hand, they may emphasize self-reliance among the members of the empire and less access to Soviet benefactions. On the other, they may continue their willingness to devote resources to exploiting opportunities for expansion. Perhaps the dilemma will be resolved by the emergence of more exacting criteria for determining which opportunities are to be construed as genuinely promising.

The task of managing Soviet imperial operations can be likened to that of managing any large enterprise. The challenge is to keep costs down while pursuing multiple, sometimes conflicting, objectives. In periods of "prosperity"– the 1970s, for example, when oil prices were rising and hard currency earnings were high – management is more concerned with objectives than with costs. In "recession"– the 1980s, for example – these priorities are likely to be reversed. Viewed in this light, it is possible, although not demonstrable, that lower empire costs may in part reflect greater managerial efficiency. Indeed, the tighter resource constraints facing the Soviet Union may have prodded the leadership into taking advantage of previously unexploited opportunities for improving efficiency.

Part III

The Growth of Soviet Military Power and Resistance to It

8   *Bruce D. Porter and James G. Roche*

The Expanding Military Power of the Soviet Union

Empire implies might, and might means military power. During the four decades since the end of World War II, the Soviet Union has emerged as a military power of the first rank. It has acquired a massive arsenal of strategic nuclear weapons, unsurpassed in sheer destructive potential by any other force in the world. Its land armies are large, robust, and well equipped; its navy has become the first blue-water force in Russian history; and its capacity to project power beyond Soviet borders has grown exponentially. Coupled with a tenaciously expansionist approach to world politics, these military forces have enabled the USSR to pose a serious challenge to the West generally, but particularly to the preeminence of the United States in the international order.

Military power is both a key—indeed, perhaps the only key—to the USSR's current international status and the principal means by which the Soviet empire abroad has been built and maintained. The countries of Eastern Europe have remained in the Soviet orbit not because they are attracted to the discredited ideology, stagnant economy, low standard of living, or sterile official culture of their neighbor to the east. Pro-Soviet regimes in the Third World such as Vietnam, Cuba, Angola, Ethiopia, and Afghanistan are allied with the USSR not out of either admiration or charity. Military power is the one business at which the Kremlin truly excels. It is the all-important instrument of coercion that sustains Soviet hegemony in Eastern Europe and accounts for most of the USSR's attraction as an ally and mentor to countries in the Third World. Without it, there would be no Soviet empire.

World War II was the pivotal event that made possible the Soviet Union's rise to superpower status, as well as its acquisition of a twentieth-century overseas empire. The war destroyed a rival European aspirant to world empire, Nazi Germany, and drained the former imperial powers of Europe – Great Britain and France, especially – of their resources, military strength, and political will. The war accelerated the end of the Imperial Age, setting in motion powerful social and political forces by which dozens of new, independent nations were carved out of the former colonies of Europe. By 1945, only two powers remained in the world with sufficient strength and desire to compete for preeminence in the international order: the Soviet Union and the United States. Not by coincidence, they were the two major powers that had largely stayed out of the race for distant empire in the previous century (they had both concentrated, instead, on pushing their national borders outward into sparsely populated hinterlands). The United States was by far the stronger of the two at the end of the war, with its territory and industrial base untouched by the conflict; the Soviet leadership, however, possessed the ambition and political will to challenge U.S. predominance, notwithstanding the massive task of postwar reconstruction it faced.

There were other, more direct ways in which World War II made possible the USSR's emergence as a superpower after 1945. Despite the frightful toll exacted by the conflict, the pressures of war had given impetus to a vast expansion of the Soviet industrial base and to its thoroughgoing militarization. Huge stockpiles of surplus weaponry gave the Kremlin an opportunity for moving into the Third World as a major arms supplier for the first time. The war also represented the Soviet government's one unequivocal victory on behalf of the nation – a source of legitimacy and public support it did not have in the past, and one it has drawn on ever since.

But Soviet successes in the decades following 1945 cannot be explained by the experience of World War II alone. The foundations for Soviet military power were laid well before 1941. From the earliest days of Bolshevik rule, military power played a central role in shaping the character of the new Marxist-Leninist state, and the interwar period from 1917 to 1941 marked a critical stage in Soviet Russia's military development.

The October Revolution of 1917 began as an armed uprising and achieved ultimate victory through the application of raw military force. While Lenin's political genius was the key to the uprising, Leon Trotsky's organizational genius as Commissar of War made the military victory possible. Hammered together from remnants of the czarist army and from ragtag citizen volunteers, the Red Army became a seasoned military force that accomplished an astonishing number of tasks during the Civil War. It defeated three White armies; it invaded and occupied Byelorussia, the Ukraine, Armenia, Azerbaijan, and Georgia; it enabled the Soviet leaders to gain control over the Moslem borderlands and the Far East; and it even attempted, unsuccessfully, to invade Poland and establish a Red government in Warsaw. By November 1922, five years after the Revolution, the Red Army had extended Soviet rule over most of the territory of the former Russian empire, essentially reforging the dynasty that had disintegrated in 1917–18. Soviet military power thus spared the Russian empire from the dissolution that befell every other multinational empire of the nineteenth century.

While numerous factors contributed to the Bolshevik victory, credit for the establishment of Soviet rule belonged more to the Red Army than to any other factor. The early Bolsheviks knew this, and the lessons they drew from the Civil War shaped their future attitude toward the uses of military power. In the early days, the Bolshevik leaders believed that world revolution was imminent, and that it would come about primarily through domestic revolutions in the capitalist countries — not through any show of force by the Red Army. But when the Civil War had ended, and the world revolution failed to materialize, the Bolsheviks were forced to turn to the less romantic business of running a country and considering how to defend its vast borders from the same historical threats Russia had always faced — now magnified by a gaping ideological void between all that was Soviet and all that was non-Soviet.

It has become almost commonplace for historians to observe that Soviet Russia was militarily weak in the interwar years. The low technological and scientific levels of Stalinist Russia, the poor performance of the Red Army against Finland in the opening campaigns of the Winter War (1939–40), and the disastrous losses to Hitler's armies in the first months of Operation Barbarossa are often cited as evidence of the same. But this portrayal is incomplete and misleading unless other elements of the picture are included. Because Lenin and his fellow Bolsheviks recognized the importance of military power and the role of science in achieving it, they placed great emphasis on military research and development (R&D) from the beginning. The 1920s saw the Soviets conducting remarkably advanced experiments and research in rocketry, aerodynamics, and nuclear physics, in some instances on a level equalling anything then being done in the West. During the first period of Soviet-German rapprochement that followed the signing of the Rapallo Treaty in 1922, the Soviets also profited greatly from secret cooperative efforts with the Weimar German army.

By the mid-1930s, the USSR was manufacturing its own aircraft engines and building fighter planes (the I-15 and I-16 models) that consistently outmaneuvered their German equivalent (the Me-109V) when flown in combat at the outset of the Spanish Civil War; by 1939, the Soviet Union was producing 700 to 800 warplanes per month, more than Japan and roughly equal to the number being produced by Nazi Germany. By the outbreak of the war with Germany, the Soviets had built an army larger in size than the Nazis, equipped with more tanks and airplanes, and on a technological level equal to or only slightly inferior to that of the invaders. These facts are often forgotten because of the massive defeats that the German Blitzkrieg wrought on the Soviets during 1941.

The disaster of 1941, however, should be attributed more to political than to military factors. Stalin's mindless purges of the Soviet officer corps from 1937–38, and his refusal to countenance the possibility of a German invasion and hence to allow preparations to meet it, were critical factors in the stunning reversals of 1941. Yet when the very real interwar achievements of Soviet military R&D and the Soviet defense industry are kept in mind, the postwar resurgence of Soviet military power makes sense.

The mushrooming of Soviet military power that occurred after World War II took place in three principal dimensions: first, strategic nuclear weapons, the possession of which gave the USSR claim to superpower status and enabled it to meet the United States on roughly equal terms in the diplomatic arena (particularly after the achievement of nuclear parity in the 1970s); second, traditional land and sea forces configured for large-scale conventional conflict on the Soviet periphery, the existence of which, even prior to 1945, had given the USSR its status as a European power, and which have remained a critical component of the world balance of power ever since the war; and third, power projection forces (or mobility forces), suitable for extending the USSR's military reach to points far beyond its borders.

All three dimensions of military power played a role in the establishment and maintenance of the Soviet Union's global empire after 1945.

The USSR as a Superpower:
The Centrality of Nuclear Weapons

The central security problem that faced the Soviet leadership following World War II was the U.S. monopoly of nuclear weapons. The Americans were still ostensibly allies, but Stalin was not sentimental in such matters, and he probably knew full well that the alliance could not last; certainly his behavior on the world scene did not suggest a desire to preserve it. The U.S. nuclear stockpile was not large, and the Soviet nuclear program was proceeding at full pace, but in the meantime the Kremlin needed something to counterbalance the nuclear trump card of the United States. That proved to be the Red Army in Europe. The rapid demobilization of U.S. forces and their return to the United States by the millions left the western part of Europe potentially at the mercy of a massive Soviet conventional attack. The Soviets never seriously contemplated such an attack, of course; they were too busy rearranging the political face of Eastern Europe. But uncertainty about Soviet intentions played a heavy psychological role in the early postwar years, and hastened the course of events that led to the founding of NATO. The pattern that developed, in fact, has persisted to our day: Western Europe cowed by Soviet military power and forced to rely on U.S. nuclear power for its shield against the threat of an attack that is probably not contemplated, but cannot be discounted.

If nuclear weapons in the hands of the United States was the Kremlin's greatest security problem in 1945, nuclear weapons soon became the cornerstone of Soviet military power and the focus of Soviet doctrine and thinking. Through tenacious effort and singular concentration on the nuclear component of the military equation, the Soviet leadership and General Staff led the USSR past three key milestones: the production of its own nuclear weapon, achieved in 1949; the construction of a secure second-strike force, achieved by the mid-1960s; and the development of a potential first-strike capability, which began to emerge in the late 1970s and early 1980s, as the Soviets deployed large numbers of long-range, highly accurate, heavy ICBMs carrying multiple warheads. By reaching these milestones, the Soviet leadership transformed their central security problem into the foremost lever of Soviet power and influence in the world. The Soviet strategic nuclear buildup amounted to the largest single acquisition of offensive military power in the history of the modern world, and it remains the greatest single military achievement of the Kremlin to date.

The importance of nuclear weapons for the Soviet Union is immense, for if such weapons had never been invented, the USSR would not be a superpower. It would remain a European power—indeed, the largest and strongest European land power—but its power would not reach much beyond the European landmass. Even on the continent, its capacity to intimidate and threaten would be limited—for in a prolonged conventional war, the superior industrial base and mobilization capacity of the United States would still enable the New World to play a balancing role in Europe similar to that Great Britain played during the eighteenth and nineteenth centuries. Nuclear weapons changed all this. Perhaps useless for defense, they are the ultimate offensive weapon. They enable the USSR to threaten the U.S. industrial base directly, thus substantially negating the superior U.S.

potential for long-term mobilization. They give the Soviet Union a club to hold over the head of the Europeans (or any country in the world it chooses to intimidate). Most important of all, by counterbalancing U.S. nuclear power, Soviet strategic nuclear forces substantially restore the political potency of Soviet conventional superiority in Europe.

Soviet doctrine on nuclear weapons has placed a heavy emphasis on the importance of heavy, land-based ICBMs. The Soviets were first to recognize the "revolution in military affairs" wrought by the marriage of nuclear warheads with long-range rocketry. Though the full implications of the Soviet buildup of land-based ICBMs did not become apparent until the 1970s, when their levels of accuracy began to be appreciated, the foundation for that buildup must have been laid a full decade or so earlier – in other words, not long after the technical feasibility of ICBMs was demonstrated.

In 1960, three years after Sputnik, the USSR possessed only a handful of first-generation ICBMs, with warheads in the megaton range; the bulk of its strategic nuclear power remained in its bomber force. During the following decade, however, this ratio turned about dramatically, as the Kremlin undertook a massive buildup of its ICBM forces. By 1970, the USSR possessed 1,427 ICBMs, each with one warhead. These missiles amounted to over three-fourths of the total delivery vehicles (or launchers) in the Soviet inventory; bombers accounted for only 8 percent of total launchers. The late 1970s and first half of the 1980s have seen a modest reversal of this trend toward heavy reliance on ICBMs. By 1984, the Soviets possessed the following inventory of nuclear forces (with percentages of the total force shown in parentheses):

Launchers			**Weapons** (Warheads)		
ICBMs	1,398	(52.8%)	ICBMs	6,420	(66.9%)
SLBMs	946	(35.7%)	SLBMs	2,122	(22.1%)
Bombers	303	(11.5%)	Bombers	1,052	(11.0%)
TOTAL	2,647	100.0%	TOTAL	9,594	100.0%

These figures show that the predominance of the ICBM has declined somewhat in the past decade, while the Soviet bomber force has made a small comeback, perhaps because the Soviet leadership wants to hedge against a projected increase in U.S. urgent hard-target kill capability. Due to the MIRVing of the Soviet ICBM force, however, the total percentage of Soviet nuclear weapons carried on ICBMs remains high (at roughly two-thirds of the total inventory). The MIRVing program, begun in 1975, has added nearly 4,500 warheads to the Soviet inventory in the past decade. The emphasis on heavy ICBMs with large throw-weight and high accuracy also gives the USSR a potential capability to simultaneously destroy almost the entire U.S. ICBM force in a single strike of SS-18 and SS-19 missiles.

The continuing Soviet emphasis on land-based ICBMs is also reflected in Soviet development of the SS-24 and SS-25 missiles, suitable for fixed or mobile deployment (and which would be in violation of the SALT II treaty). By concentrating its nuclear strike force in land-based ICBMs, the Soviet leadership has chosen the most politically potent nuclear instrument possible (due to both its visibility and its first-strike capability), as well as the leg of the nuclear triad that is most reliable and most easily controlled.

Soviet Nuclear Capabilities and Local Conflicts. At first glance, it may seem that nuclear balance between the superpowers is of little import for their rivalry in the Third World, where, after all, wars are fought with rifles, hand grenades, and occasionally tanks—but never with nuclear weapons. Neither superpower has come even close to employing nuclear weapons in a regional conflict. But the nuclear balance does influence the course of political and diplomatic events in the Third World in important, if subtle, ways. The achievement of nuclear parity was, in fact, a necessary precondition—though not a sufficient condition—for the USSR's major expansion into the Third World in the 1970s. The case for this is as follows.

From 1945 until roughly the mid-1960s, Washington maintained meaningful superiority over Moscow in strategic nuclear weapons. The key to this superiority was the U.S. capability to destroy with a first strike Soviet nuclear delivery vehicles in sufficient number to significantly blunt the effect of any all-out retaliatory strike. Although the Soviet Union, in such an eventuality, would have retained enough residual forces to make a serious counterattack against the United States, it could have retaliated only at the risk of inviting the wholesale destruction of its cities by a U.S. second strike. Any calculation of the ultimate outcome undoubtedly counselled prudence in the Kremlin. The risks and potential costs of conflict escalation to the nuclear level were clearly higher for the USSR than for the United States.

The nuclear superiority of the United States exerted a tacit but pervasive influence on diplomatic and military competition between the superpowers around the world. It offset the Soviet lead in conventional ground forces in Europe and it deterred Moscow from making its challenges to U.S. interests in the Third World too overt. The latter came about because of the risks of escalation implicit in any crisis or local conflict in which both the United States and the USSR were involved. Washington's nuclear advantage was by no means a tractable instrument—it could not prevent the USSR from putting pressure on Berlin, nor could it prevent the Soviets from indirectly and cautiously supporting revolutionary movements around the world. Above all, it was an insufficient factor in the total equation to guarantee diplomatic and political outcomes favorable to the West when certain other factors were missing. But, logically, it must have had a certain dampening effect on Soviet assertiveness and action in the Third World and elsewhere.

As the 1960s progressed, the political advantages enjoyed by the United States as a result of its nuclear superiority began to erode as a consequence of the USSR's buildup of its sea-based nuclear forces, the several-fold expansion of its ICBM forces, and the hardening of its missile silos. Robert McNamara, in January 1968, declared that the USSR "had achieved, and most likely will maintain over the foreseeable future, an actual and credible second strike capability."[1] That same year the Soviet Union deployed for the first time a medium-range ballistic missile (the SS-N-6) aboard a nuclear-powered submarine; that was followed by rapid deployment of nuclear-powered submarines with medium-range missiles and, in 1974, long-range missiles. The existence of this fleet made the Soviet second-strike force secure throughout the 1970s. Long before the U.S. Minuteman force became significantly vulnerable to a Soviet first strike with highly accurate, MIRVed systems, Soviet ICBM and SLBM invulnerability had radically altered the nuclear equation. By greatly reducing the utility of an American first strike, it lowered the threshold of risk for the USSR in local conflicts. In effect, the Soviet achievement of a secure and powerful second-strike force gave the USSR a kind of protective umbrella behind which it could exploit its advantage in conventional forces and its ties with revolutionary regimes and parties in the Third World.

Soviet theorists were well aware of the consequences of what was happening. One Soviet scholar, V. V. Zhurkin, in a work on U.S. behavior in local crises and conflicts, asserted that as a result of the Soviet attainment of nuclear parity, "The hopes of the U.S.A. for employing nuclear blackmail as a means of obtaining its goals in international crises were exploded."[2] This, in a word, was the Soviet leadership's belated answer to the notion of massive retaliation put forward by John Foster Dulles in the 1950s. Long before the Soviet Union had actually achieved nuclear parity, however (an achievement pegged by some Soviet writers as having occurred in 1970), the United States had begun to reevaluate its own nuclear doctrine and thinking. While many other factors were involved, it seems to be no accident that the USSR's more openly offensive approach toward conflict and revolution in the Third World after 1970 correlated with its achievement of effective nuclear parity. The shift from nuclear imbalance to approximate parity was not alone a sufficient cause for the Soviet Union's more activist role in global affairs during the 1970s, but it was a necessary condition. As such, it was also an important prerequisite to the rise of a Soviet global, rather than just European, empire in the 1970s.

The USSR as a Eurasian Land Power:
Defending Border Regions

The Soviet state, like the Russian state that preceded it, attaches an extremely high priority to the integrity of its territory and inviolability of its borders. While this is true to some degree of all modern nations, in the Soviet case the concern over territorial security is carried to an extreme—as witnessed, for example, in the shooting down of two Korean airline flights. The Soviet Union maintains the world's most extensive coastal defenses and the world's largest contingent of border troops (separate from the regular armed forces). Unlike the United States, it has chosen to deploy and maintain, at great expense, a highly efficient system of air defenses against intrusion by foreign aircraft. The Soviet armed forces are for the most part deployed as though the most likely theaters of conflict would be in or near the immediate borders of the Soviet Union. U.S. forces, by contrast, are deployed with the expectation that the most likely theaters of conflict will be far from U.S. borders.

Throughout its history, the Russian state suffered from a lack of natural geographical borders. Repeatedly invaded by foreign armies and culturally isolated from the European mainstream, the Russian people developed a deeply ingrained sense of territorial insecurity and vulnerability.

> Separated from the heretical Latins and the infidel Muslims, who surrounded Russia in the west and east, its rulers, clergy, and common people developed a sense of national-religious uniqueness rather than one of belonging to a broader, supranational community. This tended to produce in Russians a feeling of being isolated and under permanent siege.[3]

Some scholars have argued that this sense of insecurity was a driving factor in Russia's territorial expansion: the Russian state continually sought more natural borders, as well as the protection afforded by buffer zones of vast territorial expanse. Whether that was the case or not, the growing size of Russia did not, in fact, bring it a growing sense of security.

Coming as they did from a conspiratorial, revolutionary background, the Bolsheviks magnified this natural sense of insecurity into a deep-rooted paranoia. They regarded any person, state, or power beyond Soviet control as a potential enemy; viewed the "bourgeois, capitalist" world with hatred (and assumed it viewed them the same way); and suffered from a constant fear of attack and annihilation. In short, a combination of historical factors worked together to give the Soviet leadership an intense preoccupation with defending Soviet borders against any and all threats, real or imagined. Despite its expansionist tendencies and despite its achievement of superpower status, the Soviet leadership remains today fundamentally insecure. As a result, it has tended to use its conventional military forces in a particular way: *politically*, it has sought to gain maximum offensive advantage from its armed forces, using them as an instrument for intimidation; *militarily*, however, it has tended to deploy its conventional forces in a highly defensive manner. The one exception has been its efforts at power projection in the 1970s, which will be treated later; even those efforts, however, were generally quite cautious and involved only a tiny fraction of total Soviet forces.

While Soviet territorial sensitivity applies to all border regions, the central focus of Soviet concern is and always has been Europe. Not only is the greatest number of Soviet divisions stationed there, but the highest-quality divisions are there also. Soviet forces along the Chinese border, by comparison, are less well equipped and generally in a lower overall level of readiness.

What accounts for this fixation on Europe? The Soviets certainly recognize that China poses a major security problem, but there has never been a Sino-Russian war of any consequence, whereas Russia has suffered from European invasions throughout its history. Western Europe possesses the industrial base necessary for mounting a major conventional (and in theory, at least, nuclear) offensive against the USSR; China still does not, though the sheer size of its population is doubtless of concern to Soviet defense planners.

In Europe, the Soviets seek to accomplish four major objectives by the deployment of a large standing army in the western provinces of the Soviet Union and in certain Eastern European countries of the Warsaw Pact (Poland and East Germany, in particular). All of these objectives ultimately are related to the Soviet obsession with a buffer for its western borders.

1. *To maintain a stronghold on the Soviet empire in Eastern Europe.* The communist regimes of Eastern Europe put in place by Soviet power in the aftermath of World War II have given the USSR a buffer zone of security on its western frontier. Playing on fears of a threat from the West stimulates anti-German sentiment in Eastern Europe and makes it possible for the USSR to present itself as a defender against West German revanche; it also gives Moscow a plausible political justification for keeping standing forces in East Germany, Czechoslovakia, Poland, and Hungary.

2. *To prevent German reunification.* This remains the central objective of Soviet policy toward Western Europe and is a key reason the USSR maintains such a tight hold on East Germany. The presence of nearly 400,000 Soviet troops makes East Germany one of the most heavily militarized countries in the world (measured in troops per square unit of area). A divided Germany, from the Soviet point of view, is a Germany unlikely

to pose a serious security threat to the USSR or a challenge to its dominance of Central and Eastern Europe.

3. *To intimidate Western Europe.* The Soviet conventional buildup forced the Europeans to rely on U.S. nuclear protection (or commit to the high costs of an expensive conventional buildup). Intended or not, Soviet conventional preponderance thus forces Western Europe to rely on the politically most sensitive form of defense. This in turn has given the Soviets a tremendous source of political leverage in exploiting peace movements and anti-nuclear sentiment in Western Europe. Theater nuclear weapons also play an important intimidating role in the grand political strategy of the USSR. The deployment of the SS-20 intermediate-range nuclear missile beginning in 1977 was quite possibly a calculated step on the part of the Kremlin to create conditions that would further fuel anti-nuclear sentiment in Western Europe. Certainly, at a time when Soviet–Western European détente was in its heyday, there was no sound security justification for deploying against Europe a nuclear missile system of a wholly new character.

4. *To defend against an attack from the West.* The Soviets are politically astute enough to know that any such attack under present circumstances is unlikely, and politically paranoid enough to plan for meeting it anyway.

To accomplish these ends, the Soviet Union has committed a sizeable portion of its land forces to the Warsaw Pact. Over 100 Soviet combat divisions are deployed in Eastern Europe or in the western military districts of the Soviet Union, including 40 armored divisions. Among the equipment found in these divisions are 36,000 main battle tanks, over 13,000 artillery pieces (including multiple rocket launchers), and some 9,000 combat aircraft. These figures include only Soviet forces; they do not include the forces fielded by the Warsaw Pact allies of the USSR. The overall balance between the Warsaw Pact and NATO finds the Warsaw Pact enjoying a better than 2 to 1 advantage in tanks and a 2.6 to 1 advantage in combat aircraft. The Warsaw Pact also has an edge in terms of number of divisions and total uniformed manpower deployed.

The Rise of Soviet Power Projection Forces

Historical Perspective. A global empire cannot be acquired or maintained without the requisite military capabilities to support and sustain distant initiatives. Grouped under the rubric "mobility forces," such capabilities include naval combat power, sealift capacity, airlift capacity, and distant assault forces (both amphibious and airborne).

It is sometimes said that the USSR lacked the capability to project military power much beyond its borders prior to the 1970s. This is only partially correct. As early as the Spanish Civil War (1936–38), the Kremlin managed to muster sufficient sealift to furnish the Loyalist forces with large quantities of weaponry, and this capacity grew substantially in the 1950s and 1960s. What Moscow lacked was the airlift capacity required for rapid and versatile responses, assault forces adequate for direct military intervention outside the Soviet bloc, and the naval combat power essential for extending political influence overseas and for discouraging foreign interference in distant military operations.

The short reach of the Soviet Union was a direct consequence of the historical experience of the Russian empire. Until the middle of the nineteenth century, the Russian empire was able to expand with little external opposition to its east and south. While Napoleon sought to conquer Europe, and Britain acquired a vast overseas empire, the czars were content for Russia to be a relatively peaceful European nation with contiguous provinces only. However, periodically they would venture forth into the unknown of the non-European world. In the nineteenth century Russians were in North America (Alaska) and in Africa near Ethiopia.

But Russian military power was not well suited for the establishment or maintenance of overseas colonies and bases. Try as it might, Russia could not develop a navy anywhere equal to its army. Even buying ships and talent from abroad, the czars were not able to field a force able to go far from Russia and fight. Lacking warm-water ports, the Russians might be able to land parties in the New World, but they could not defend them against attack either from local natives or from forces organized by the other European powers. In sharp contrast, the Americans were engaged overseas, albeit to a very limited extent, not long after their War of Independence. From the beginning, U.S. leaders realized that they were part of an island state. Not so Russia. Russia was a Eurasian state, with an interior of enormous dimensions and dangers. Projecting power was a matter of assembling enough forces on a current border in order to engage in military action to extend that border.

A New Area of Soviet Power—Proactive, Not Reactive.   Soviet foreign and security policy in the first decade following World War II focused heavily on Europe and on relations with the United States. Only after Stalin's demise did the USSR begin serious efforts to advance its influence in the emerging nations of the Third World. It soon became evident that heavy conventional forces wedded to land lines of communication and support were of little use for advancing

Soviet influence. Nor did long-range nuclear weapons project force in meaningful ways (though the possession of a nuclear arsenal, as argued earlier, was a necessary condition to becoming a truly global power). In fact, a comparative study of the abilities of the United States and the Soviet Union to project power to the borders of the Soviet Union would have shown the powers to be about equal in the late 1940s and the 1950s. That is, it was about as easy for the United States to place and sustain a combat unit on one side of the border of the Soviet Union as it was for the Soviets to place and maintain a comparable unit on the other side. The lift potential of the United States following World War II was extraordinary. Further, U.S. commanders had ample experience operating large forces far away from home. The Soviets, on the other hand, had little strategic military lift and barely trusted their officers and enlisted soldiers.

Thus, the Soviets found that their only effective means of projecting their influence, if not power, was through assistance to "forces for national liberation." Support for coups, covert aid to revolutionary movements, and material assistance to radical regimes became the basic components of the Soviet capability. Lacking serious mobility forces, the Soviet leadership relied principally upon arms shipments to provide such support during the 1950s and 1960s. Whereas in the interwar period (1930 to 1939), the USSR had supplied less than 6 percent of world exports of combat aircraft and tanks, its percentage of the world market rose to roughly 37 percent of tanks and nearly 30 percent of combat aircraft during the first two decades of the postwar period. In more recent years, it has surpassed the United States as the predominant world supplier of arms. But in the early decades, whether in the Congo or Latin America or during the Cuban missile crisis, the Soviets had little choice but to back down in the face of a determined stance by the West. Their ambition far exceeded their true military reach. Their desire to influence events well beyond their borders, however, did not diminish. It took several decades for the USSR to acquire power projection forces worthy of the name.

The Achievement of Soviet Power Projection Forces.   A Soviet drive to develop effective mobility forces was in full swing by the end of Khrushchev's decade in power; it continued with accelerated momentum under Brezhnev. The growth in naval combat power was particularly dramatic: from 1961 to 1979 the USSR deployed three new classes of escort ships, five classes of destroyer or antisubmarine warfare (ASW) vessels, four classes of cruisers, and two classes of small carriers; the total number of new, large warships deployed was over 200. In effect, the Soviet Union constructed almost an entire blue-water navy in two decades, an achievement in some ways reminiscent of Imperial Germany's naval buildup prior to World War I. The USSR established a permanent, albeit small, naval presence in the Mediterranean and Indian oceans for the first time, and in 1964 inaugurated an extensive, ongoing program of port visits by Soviet warships to Third World countries. The Soviet fleet also began to play a significant diplomatic and deterrent role in local crises and conflicts. At present the Soviet fleets possess the beginnings of a major amphibious force, including long-range troop-carrying vessels, major tank transporters, and the necessary battle group combatants to allow the troops to be transported and landed in hostile territory. While the particular ship designs might not be exact copies of those the United States has built, the types of combatants needed for distant operations are just about the same and will include aircraft carriers capable of launching conventional as contrasted to vertical-or-short-takeoff-and-landing (VSTOL) aircraft, battle cruisers, and amphibious lift combatants.

In sealift, the Soviet maritime fleet grew from 590 ships with a combined capacity of 3.3 million deadweight tons in 1959 to an inventory of roughly 1,600 vessels carrying some 16 million deadweight tons in 1975. By 1985, there were nearly 1,700 ships in the Soviet merchant fleet, many of highly modern design, and publicized Soviet plans called for an annual increase of 250,000 deadweight tons until 1990. The Soviet Union has the world's largest inventory of the dual-purpose commercial vessels known as roll-on/roll-off (Ro-Ro) and roll-on/float-off ships. The Soviet inventory of the latter type of ship, largely attached to the Soviet merchant marine, now consists of 84 units with 28 additional ships on order, an addition of 7 to 8 ships each year since they first entered the Soviet inventory in 1974. The number of Soviet merchant ships and the deadweight tonnage of Soviet ships now surpasses that of the U.S. merchant marine, though the United States retains an operational lead provided that "Effective U.S. Control" vessels are counted (ships that are U.S. owned and operated, but registered under flags of convenience).

Moscow also made rapid strides in airlift: the aggregate lift capacity of the Soviet Military Transport Aviation (VTA) in millions of ton-miles grew from 11.4 in 1965 to 26.4 in 1977; it is still increasing steadily because of continuing deployment of the relatively new IL-76 long-range transport planes. Since 1980, the addition of 125 of these jet transports has nearly doubled the long-range military airlift of the Soviet Union; the total inventory of IL-76s is now over 250. Overall Soviet airlift capacity remains inferior to that of the United States, but the gap has lessened since 1975.

In the area of assault forces, the USSR further strengthened and refined its most potent strike force, namely the eight well-equipped airborne divisions placed under a special directorate in the Ministry of Defense. The range to which this force can be projected is still limited by available air transport, but within a roughly 2,000-mile radius of Soviet-controlled airfields, the USSR can probably match any airborne deployment by the United States, except in Europe. The utility of the airborne divisions for influencing the course of local conflicts or for intervening directly abroad has been demonstrated in the past. All seven divisions were placed on alert during the October 1973 War, a move that did much to influence U.S. decision-making during the crisis; the 105th Airborne Guards Division spearheaded the Soviet move into Afghanistan; and airborne forces also played a key role in the Soviet intervention in Czechoslovakia in 1968. Progress in amphibious assault capabilities has been much more moderate: the USSR reactivated the "naval infantry" (marines) in 1964, and by 1984 it had grown to about 16,000 troops (compared with 198,000 U.S. marines). Its role seems focused mainly on flanking moves in support of armies ashore. The USSR also procured three new classes of tank-landing ships between 1962 and 1979, including the modern and well-armed Ivan Rogov class, deployment of which continues. Soviet amphibious assault capability in terms of full-load displacement tonnage and amphibious troop capacity remains, however, far below that of the United States.

Though the Soviet Union in some respects might have been considered a superpower following its recovery from World War II, it did not become a truly global power until the 1970s, when these investments began to yield significant returns. The USSR's growing military "reach" greatly facilitated its massive interventions in the October 1973 War, the Angolan civil war, the Ogaden war, and the civil war in Afghanistan. While interventions on that order might have been conceivable in the 1960s, they would have taken place at relatively inhibited speeds, with much higher risk and more formidable logistical difficulties.

The USSR may next strive to attain a kind of "parity" in the area of power projection forces to match its earlier achievement of strategic parity. Admiral Gorshkov's announcement in December 1979 that the USSR's first nuclear-powered, large-deck attack carrier was under construction indicates the seriousness of the Soviet effort; some Western analysts had argued that the USSR would never build heavy carriers because of their high cost, increasing vulnerability, and low utility in defending a traditional land power. The principal value of the new carrier (or carriers), the first of which will be deployed around 1990, will be in projecting Soviet political influence and military power overseas. The new aircraft carrier is only the most dramatic product of an intensive ship-building program that seems to portend a future of increasing strength and assertiveness on the part of the Soviet fleet. As of 1980, the USSR was constructing four new classes of nuclear-powered cruisers, including a number of 32,000-ton battle cruisers with heavy guns for shore bombardment; such guns are of little utility against a modern, missile-equipped fleet, but they might have a telling impact in certain local crises, even if only passively deployed. The USSR is also constructing the new Berezina class of heavily-armed, 40,000-ton logistics craft apparently designed for replenishing warships on the high seas; this should reduce somewhat the navy's dependence on foreign port facilities.

Soviet air transport capabilities will also expand substantially during the coming decade, as a result of continuing deployments of the IL-76 long-range transport and of a new plane being developed, the An-40, expected to have a larger capacity than the American C-5. This growing airlift capacity will directly enhance the combat strength of the Soviet airborne division; amphibious assault capabilities will also improve as further deployments of the Kiev aircraft carrier, Kirov cruiser, and Ivan Rogov tank-landing ship continue.

The Soviet Style and Approach to Power Projection.   In examining the Soviet buildup of power projection forces, a certain pattern appears, suggesting the broad outlines of a Soviet strategy or approach to their problem. First, the Soviets made sure that they had power projection forces that were suited to operations on the periphery of the Soviet Union. This was merely an extension of their need to be able to "defend" their borders. Thus, they devoted considerable resources to the development of road, rail, and airport infrastructure along their borders to support the rapid introduction of material and follow-on forces. The same trucks that could move the second echelon in Europe were well suited to the invasion of a neighboring territory, as in the case in Afghanistan. This is also true for the development of armor and tactical aviation. It is interesting to note that even to this day the Soviets deploy most of their heavy tactical aviation in Afghanistan from airfields in the USSR just across the Afghan border. The same style of equipment evolution exists in the Soviet navy and their version of the marine corps, the naval infantry. The greatest amount of Soviet amphibious lift consists of very modern vessels, including a number of air-cushion or hover craft that are suitable for short-distance operations. These operations would include moves around the North Cape in Norway, against Jutland in the Baltic, and against the Japanese in the Pacific (or moves in support of existing Soviet forces on the disputed islands near the Kurile chain).

Second, as outlined in the past section, the Soviets have begun to field equipment suitable for distant operations. At present, the Soviet development of power projection forces seems to be lacking in only one very important area: the fielding of tactical aircraft that can be refueled in flight. This would enable quick movement to a distant location to support forces on the ground in combat. No doubt this feature will come in time, but for the present the Soviets are restricted to either making use of limited naval aircraft flown from their first-generation carriers, or employing an airfield currently in friendly hands where they can fly in tactical aircraft in crates for assembly and intermediate maintenance.

The most recent and dramatic changes in Soviet power projection capabilities have come in the evolution of tactical and command-and-control expertise. In the early days of the Angolan conflict, the Soviets acted more like the U.S. advisers in the Vietnam war. By the time the conflict in Ethiopia came along, the Soviets took over virtual command of the operation, but left actual combat to the Ethiopians and Cubans. In the case of Afghanistan, it became almost totally a Soviet show. While they certainly would like to leave the dirty work on the ground to the soldiers of the Kabul regime, providing only antiseptic air and logistics support, front-line Soviet troops have been required to keep the rebels down.

As noted earlier, the Soviet style and approach to power projection is changing over time. From support of coups and aid to rebels, to the transport and maintenance of combat forces overseas (whether their own or Cuban) and the development of military forces permitting them to fight their way into an area, their approach has had minimal risk to their own troops. Whereas the Soviets clearly would like to work against the interests of the West, undermine the overseas base structure of the United States, and generally enhance the geopolitical position of the Soviet Union, they have behaved patiently. They exploit situations where the chance for a payoff is high, avoiding those situations where there is a major chance of a direct U.S.-Soviet military confrontation, and have been willing to abandon an ally, temporarily if not altogether, if they believe it to be in their long-term interest to do so.

In the early years, the Soviets tended to do business with national leaders in the Third World who favored their positions, and whom they thought they could control. Experience proved that this strategy was often risky—as for instance when Sadat expelled them from Egypt. More recently, they have courted *potential* leaders, usually of similar ideology, whom they then aid in coming to power. This aid can take many forms, but the most dramatic is the use of Cuban allies in combat roles in support of a particular faction, as in Angola and Ethiopia (and Grenada). It is not that the Soviet Union forces Cuba to take actions it otherwise would not take, but that it encourages and supports the Cubans in their role as exporters of wars of national liberation.

The Soviets do not rely on good relations to harvest the political fruits of their labors. Instead, they begin early to consolidate their gains by installing people friendly to them in key positions; they also use the East Germans to provide organization and advice (and thereby control) over the internal security affairs of a country. It is not likely that the Soviets will be ingloriously thrown out of a Third World country again; they will act long before things reach that stage. It is possible they did just that in the case of Augustino Neto in Angola when they suspected he was thinking too seriously of warming up to the West.

How the Empire Advances Soviet Military Power.   Not only does Soviet military power help maintain the USSR's empire abroad, but the existence of the empire helps advance Soviet military power. Soviet satellite states in the Third World provide bases for forward operations and proxy forces to assist in those operations: Cuban troops, East German and Bulgarian security officers, and Czechoslovak pilots. Thus, while in some respects the empire may be a burden to the Soviet Union, it is also a boon to Soviet international power and status.

Cuba has been the principal power projection surrogate of the Soviet Union in recent times, with nearly 40,000 Cuban troops or advisers stationed overseas in the late 1970s (the number has gone down somewhat since then, but remains high). Cuban troops in the Angolan civil war and in the Ogaden conflict played the role of actual proxy combat forces; in other parts of the world they have helped advance Soviet diplomatic and political interests. A very good argument can be made that Vietnam is also a surrogate of the Soviet Union, but the situations are sufficiently different to distinguish between them. Vietnam is using Soviet assistance to do what it historically believed was its destiny to do: to control all of Indochina. And in doing so, the Vietnamese have incurred the hostility of their historical enemy, China. From the Soviet point of view, the situation fills their needs. On the one hand, China's attention is diverted to the south, which serves as a reminder that the Soviet Union has more than one way to create pressure on China; they don't have to rely only on incidents along the Sino-Soviet border. On the other hand, the Soviets are becoming a military factor in the Indochina region for the first time in history. While the Americans have withdrawn from Indochina, and are fretting over the situation in the Philippines, the Russians are establishing and using the infrastructure to support Soviet power projection operations in the South China Sea area.

The Soviets also use the "fraternal assistance" of some of their Eastern European allies. Besides the critical role the East Germans play in providing supervision and control of internal security machines in Soviet client states, the Soviets also make use of Bulgarians and other Eastern Europeans, especially in the area of logistical support to operations. In many ways, Soviet power projection operations are enviable. Their current action in Nicaragua is a good case in point. The Soviet Union has few of its people exposed in Nicaragua, thus minimizing any American public backlash that the Soviets are waging war on the United States in its own backyard. The Soviets also seem to understand the difference between winning and humiliating an opponent: if done well, an opponent may even try to convince himself that he has lost nothing; if done badly, the opponent might wake up and take revenge. Instead, the Soviets provide weaponry and logistics materiel. They leave it up to the Cubans to provide the more obvious assistance, an assistance that they probably are not as competent to deliver to a Latin audience as the Cubans. The Vietnamese join in by providing captured American weapons, and the PLO provides some military advisers. The East Germans are also known to provide internal security advisers.

In short, the Soviets have come a long way toward mastering the art of coalition warfare for low-level conflict. And while the same combination might be a disaster if used against a sophisticated opponent, it is well suited for many situations in the Third World.

The greatest advantage the Soviet Union reaps from its efforts to establish client and proxy states in the Third World is the possibility of gaining access to port facilities, airfields, and other strategically located base facilities. For decades, Soviet ideologists condemned bases as an instrument of imperialism, but this refrain has not been heard as often since the USSR has moved into the Third World itself. Interestingly enough, the Soviet Union no longer has access to its bases in Egypt and in Somalia—the largest it ever constructed abroad. The loss of those facilities, however, has been made up for in large measure by Soviet access to new facilities in Ethiopia, Syria, Angola, South Yemen, and Vietnam.

Concluding Thoughts

The Soviet Union is a manifest failure in most spheres of human endeavor: economic, social, ideological, cultural, and political. It has been dramatically successful, however, in building up raw military force and fairly successful in harnessing the scientific and engineering skills of its people toward that end. Without military power, the Soviet regime would not have endured to the present day or be the world power it is generally recognized to be.

From time immemorial power and prestige have been the principal reasons empires have been built and why one power after another has been willing to bear the high costs of sustaining them. The Soviet Union is engaged in empire building; it shows every sign of being perfectly prepared to continue.

Military power, alone, however, has rarely been a sufficient ingredient for the prosperity of any empire; the empires built largely on military power have historically been short-lived compared with those built on broader foundations. But while the eventual decline and dissolution of the Soviet Union may be virtually inevitable, it may well not come about before the entire world has paid a dear price for the militarism of the Bolshevik regime that has ruled in the Kremlin since 1917.

9

Charles Waterman

Resistance Movements in the Soviet Empire

President Reagan has urged joint U.S.-Soviet negotiations to aid in the resolution of conflicts in Afghanistan, Angola, Ethiopia, Kampuchea, and Nicaragua. The conflicts in these areas represent a phenomenon unique to the 1980s — that of a West-linked insurgency besieging a leftist regime that came to power in the 1970s. They signify that earlier leftist victories may yet prove inconclusive, and that outside assistance is now available to anti-communist resistance movements.

Accordingly, the president has promised that "America's moral and material support for struggling resistance forces must not and shall not cease." But this statement is suspect on grounds of historical precedent. Large democracies, in particular the United States, have proved too vulnerable to the cyclical vagaries of public opinion to be reliable supporters of insurgency in Third World conflicts.

The resistance movements themselves represent a very mixed political array. Ideologically, each contains major elements motivated by allegiances other than democratic, pro-Western sentiment:

- While varying in intensity from group to group, the essential driving force behind the Afghan Mujahideen is Islam—and in the case of certain organizations, fundamentalist Islam. While undoubtedly anti-communist, a future Mujahideen-dominated government would be both fractious and Islamic. And yet $250 million yearly is reportedly earmarked by the United States for the Mujahideen, supplemented by an extra $300 million during 1986 and 1987.

- Angola's National Union for the Total Independence of Angola (UNITA) has evolved in a moderate direction since its "anti-colonialist" line of the early 1970s. It has also attempted, with significant success, to broaden its political base beyond the Ovimbundu tribal origins of its leader, Jonas Savimbi. Should UNITA attain its goals, spokesman Jeremias Chitunda foresees including some elements of the present Marxist ruling party in a coalition government of between one and three years' duration. After many years of noninvolvement, in early 1986 the United States declared its intention to supply $15 million worth of anti-aircraft and anti-tank missiles to UNITA.

- The half-dozen or so Eritrean and Tigrean insurgent groups fighting the Marxist Ethiopian government are primarily motivated by separatist ethnic considerations. Ironically, several are themselves Marxist in political ideology—although not pro-Soviet. Should autonomy be wrested from the central Marxist government, a power struggle would undoubtedly ensue—with uncertain results. No significant U.S. assistance to Ethiopia's insurgencies has been reported.

- In Kampuchea, two noncommunist insurgent groups are linked in a loose coalition with the communist Khmer Rouge. The latter organization, responsible for killing up to 3 million persons while ruling the country between 1975 and 1979, is the most militarily effective of the coalition partners. Clearly, an ouster of the Vietnamese-supported regime by the rebel coalition would result in internecine strife over the nature of a new ruling structure. The United States has reportedly supplied as much as $5 million yearly in covert aid to the noncommunist factions, and in 1985 Congress moved to provide an additional $5 million in overt aid.

- The 15,000-strong Nicaraguan resistance movement also presents a varied political mix. The officer corps of the dominant Nicaraguan Democratic Force (FDN) is laced with right-wing followers of former Nicaraguan dictator Anastasio Somoza, despite efforts to present a more balanced image to the world. Two Miskito Indian groups are motivated primarily by ethnic considerations. American nonlethal aid of $27 million was authorized in 1985, with $100 million nonlethal and lethal assistance sought in 1986.

Finding universally applicable terminology for these movements is extraordinarily difficult. They are not "rightist," although some components are. They are by no means uniformly "democratic." To call them "freedom fighters" is propagandistic. Nor are they necessarily anti-leftist or anti-communist under all circumstances. We have settled on the phrases "anti-leftist" and "anti-communist," but with full cognizance of their inappropriateness for some factions and phases of the conflict.

In short, the major anti-leftist insurgencies around the world do not unanimously share Western political values. In fact, most probably do not in any profound sense.

But in the game of international strategy, this fact does not lessen the value of countering communist advances. The enemy of an enemy *is*, after all, often a friend.

The consequences of a leftist consolidation of power in these areas of contention have been the object of extensive debate. Generally speaking, the more alarmist interpretations fall into three categories:

1. Domino Effect Theories. Solid Vietnamese control of Kampuchea would lead to destabilizing efforts in Thailand; a Nicaragua free of internal concerns would resurface as an exporter of revolution to all of Central America and perhaps Mexico; a secure Marxist Angola would serve as a leftist revolutionary springboard in southern Africa; communist Ethiopia, if unthreatened, would destabilize the Horn of Africa — and perhaps act as a Soviet proxy elsewhere on the continent.

2. Southwest Asian Geopolitical Theories. Uncontested Soviet control and presence in Afghanistan would move the Soviets one step closer to warmwater access; place the strategic Gulf of Hormuz and Persian Gulf oil production facilities within operating range of more categories of Soviet aircraft than at present; facilitate possible ground military action in Iran and Pakistan; and generally upset the intricate network of power relationships in South Asia among India, Pakistan, the USSR, and China.

3. Power Projection Theories. Consolidated communist regimes would permit secure Soviet naval and air access for use in countering a U.S. military presence (as Camranh Bay in Vietnam does to U.S. bases in the Philippines); enable the Soviets to contest control of strategic sea and air choke-points (as Cuba does regarding American sea routes through the Florida Straits); and provide launch points for further power projection.

An opposing set of theories posits that the justification for pro-Western insurgencies is faulty because:

1. They force communist-dominated, but technically noncommunist, regimes such as Angola and Nicaragua into closer links with the Soviets.

2. They render unlikely the evolution of communist regimes towards a "neutral-communist" status — i.e., independent of Soviet/Cuban support.

3. Domino theories have not proved valid historically.

The Soviet Dilemma

Realistically, some governments resulting from current "pro-Western" insurgent victories would be a far cry from democracy as we know it. But, to appropriate a communist term, the "correlation of forces" would have shifted somewhat in the West's favor. And large indigenous populations would be freed from the repression of foreign-supported dictatorships.

To the Soviets, however, more than a modest power adjustment is at stake. Their deeply entrenched dogma holds that gains, once attained, should be irreversible, as the oft-used Soviet phrase "defense of the gains of socialism" conveys.

It is fairly recently that Third World communist states (Cuba, Vietnam, and later all of Indochina) emerged far from the Soviet community's borders. And during the 1970s, a number of prospective communist regimes also came into being — in Angola, Mozambique, Ethiopia, South Yemen, and Nicaragua.

While Soviet or other communist presence was welcomed by these countries, no defense commitment binds the Soviets to intervene in time of danger. Traditionally such intervention has occurred only in areas contiguous to the Soviet Union's own borders — as in Afghanistan. The 1978 Friendship Treaty with Vietnam, for instance, provides *only* for consultations against threats. And with Cuba, there is no military or political treaty at all. The effect of these "loose" treaties is to give the Soviets a greater option of intervening directly or by other means, as circumstances require.

Hence, counterrevolution in distant communist or prospective communist countries presents the Soviets with a dilemma. While loath to permit loss of these socialist gains, direct intervention in noncontiguous areas is neither inevitable nor compatible with normal Soviet defense policies.

The costly supply of enormous quantities of arms, technicians, and proxy forces — Cuba in Angola, Vietnam in Kampuchea — has thus far constituted the

Soviet response to this dilemma. But should the situation in these areas deteriorate badly, the Soviets would face the dilemma of a risky intervention or loss of previously attained socialist gains. At such times, the so-called "Brezhnev Doctrine"–which states that the Soviet Union and other members of the "Socialist Commonwealth" could send "military aid to a fraternal country to thwart the threat to the socialist order"–would be sorely tested.

Are Current Resistance Movements Viable?

An insurgency's long-term viability can be crippled by various problems. These are:

- Tribal or ethnic parochialism
- Ideological factionalism
- Unpopular allies or history
- Military weakness
- Unreliable external supporting states
- Unreliable contiguous supporting states
- Identification with a traditional foreign enemy
- Implausibility of compromise
- Potential of a Soviet-backed regime to escalate indefinitely

Applied here to Afghanistan, Angola, Kampuchea, and Nicaragua, the above issues provide a framework for analysis of the sustainability of these movements.

Tribal or Ethnic Parochialism. Is the insurgency's internal support base limited to only a particular ethnic portion of the populace – or can it legitimately claim to represent a majority? Are the operational areas in which popular support can be found limited or widespread?

In Afghanistan, popular support for the insurgency appears nearly universal, despite the country's division into twenty-three language groups and related dialects. It encompasses both Sunni and Shia religious sects, as well as Turkomans and Pathans. Although the main strength of the resistance derives from rural areas with a long tradition of independence from the capital, robust separatist resistance has occurred in most cities, including Kabul. Support for Afghanistan's communist regime originally came from both provincial and urban officers who had undergone training in the Soviet Union.

Angola's UNITA is primarily a rural-based organization, composed initially of Ovimbundu tribal elements from the southeastern third of the country. It is this area which forms UNITA's secure operational base. The organization has extended its breadth of operations beyond this area, and has consciously recruited individuals from other tribal backgrounds. Before the successful Angolan/Cuban offensive in the fall of 1985, UNITA claimed to control as much as 60 percent of the total population. In contrast, the ruling Movement for the Liberation of Angola (MPLA) is based primarily on the Kimbundu (some 22 percent of the populace) and urban dwellers of mixed blood (1 percent of the populace).

None of Kampuchea's resistance groups is distinguishable by ethnic criteria. Operations have primarily occurred in rural areas.

Nicaragua's two principal insurgency groups are not based on distinctive ethnic membership, with the exception of two smaller Miskito Indian organizations. The most hospitable operating areas for the resistance are in the far south, far north, and central areas where conservative peasants with middle-sized landholdings are common. In the Pacific and urban areas, operations have proved more difficult—but not for ethnic reasons.

Ideological Factionalism.   How politically cohesive are the various factions that comprise the insurgency? Is it likely to split, if subjected to extreme duress or, alternatively, success?

The Afghan resistance is notoriously divided among approximately ten major externally based factions—and many more internal groups. Factionalism based on personality conflicts, fundamentalist-secular strife, and degree of intimacy with Pakistan is rife. Nevertheless, a modest trend towards unification has occurred, with the emergence of a loose coalition known as the "Islamic Unity of Afghan Mujahideen." The inability of the various Mujahideen groups to coordinate operations has hindered the overall effort significantly. It also portends a major power struggle should the Soviets leave Afghanistan and the Mujahideen emerge victorious. Reportedly, tactical cooperation among internal fighting elements has been somewhat better than among external political groups.

Angola's UNITA is politically unified under the leadership of Jonas Savimbi. It does not appear prone to split as long as Savimbi is in control. It has long eclipsed the other major insurgency group opposing the central government—Holden Roberto's National Front for the Liberation of Angola (FNLA), based on the Bakongo tribe which comprises some 13 percent of the population. The challenge to UNITA is not to hold itself together, but rather to enlarge its membership base.

The most egregious case of political incompatibility within an insurgent coalition is in Kampuchea. Two noncommunist coalitions—one loyal to former head of state Prince Sihanouk, the other to ex–Prime Minister Son Sann—cooperate with the larger communist Khmer Rouge against the Vietnamese-imposed regime. Acts of violence between communist and noncommunist factions have occurred, even under shared battlefield conditions. It would present a nearly insurmountable problem should the insurgency be victorious.

The Unified Nicaraguan Opposition (UNO) is a 12,000-man umbrella resistance organization formed in June 1985. It includes all insurgency leaders except two, and membership in it is a prerequisite for receipt of U.S. aid. Nevertheless, Nicaragua's resistance remains badly split along political lines. The dominant FDN is plagued by the presence of right-wing ex–National Guard officers who supported former dictator Anastasio Somoza. At least one key liberal member in the UNO leadership has been reported on the verge of resignation because of the ultraconservative policies of his colleagues. This mistrust has hindered effective utilization of resources by the insurgency, and would undoubtedly lead to political strife in the case of a victory against the Sandinistas.

Unpopular Allies or History. Is the insurgency carrying political "baggage" that impedes its success?

The Afghan Mujahideen are remarkably free of damning alliances, and the lack of involvement by their leaders in previous regimes liberates the movement from lingering historical skeletons. None of the Mujahideen's external links imposes an embarrassing political burden.

Angola's UNITA has regularly accepted assistance from the politically isolated South African regime, particularly since the cutoff of United States assistance in 1976. The scope of this support has been limited in quantity, and in part composed of barter trade rather than gratis aid. UNITA's leadership acknowledges receiving South African support, points at the alternative of being defeated by Cuban or Soviet forces, and asserts that dealing with South Africa by no means implies acceptance of apartheid. The fact of this linkage, however, undoubtedly renders the garnering of Third World support more difficult for UNITA—and complicates political debate about Angola in the United States.

Nicaragua's FDN, as implied earlier, is identified by many as supporting a return of rightist, dictatorial policies of the Somoza era. This is probably unfair, given the disparate political tendencies within the FDN leadership, but ex–Somoza National Guard officers do occupy key policymaking positions, rendering the political appeal of the FDN less compelling. A number of well-documented human rights violations have reinforced this image. And the resistance's identification with the U.S. government, while adding to its credibility as a military force, does open it to the charge of being a tool of North American imperialism. To quote a liberal observer, "The Contras, and specifically the FDN, are perceived in Nicaragua as pro-Somozista, pro-Gringo, and pro-rich."

In Kampuchea, the entire coalition is hurt by memories of Khmer Rouge repression and outright genocide during its rule from 1975–78. Prince Sihanouk himself is unquestionably popular among the Kampuchean populace, and his involvement with the resistance serves to mitigate the Khmer Rouge taint somewhat. But even to those who understand the philosophical differences between the communist and noncommunist forces comprising the resistance, Khmer Rouge military predominance portends their dominance in any postvictory factional strife. Needless to say, the Khmer Rouge association renders Western states extremely wary of supporting this coalition.

Military Weakness.   What is the insurgency's military strength and quality?

The total number of Afghan Mujahideen is currently estimated as roughly 200,000, opposed to approximately 115,000 Soviet and 30,000 Afghan military troops. The quality of insurgent military activity has been mixed, although uniformly stubborn. Mujahideen leaders have generally complained about a lack of effective air-to-air weaponry, and a need for better anti-armor capabilities than the hand-held RPG7. Their utilization of mines and other personal weapons has been skillful. An early tendency to seize and defend territory in conventional-force fashion has been eradicated. Coordination between disparate Mujahideen groups is slight, minimizing the possibility for larger-scale actions. In general, Mujahideen activity has been sufficient to retain control of most rural areas, when not specifically challenged by a stronger Soviet/Afghan force. As with many nationalist groups enjoying the majority support of the populace, Mujahideen intelligence capacities have generally been excellent. One commonly cited figure sets Soviet casualties as of mid-1985 at 9,000 killed and 16,000 wounded. Total Afghan and Soviet casualties may be 60,000, according to Pakistani sources. Most military estimates place the number of Soviet troops required to pacify the entire country within a year or two at over 500,000. Present levels can only gradually wear down the population's will to resist over an undetermined period, perhaps decades.

UNITA, relying on relatively secure tribal-controlled base areas, holds a tenuous grip on a third of the country. It faces the conscripted 80,000-man Angolan army, its 35,000 Cuban protectors, and 1,500 Soviet advisers. UNITA's own strength is set at 2,000 regular troops, 18,000 semiregulars, 20,000 compact guerrillas, and 35,000 dispersed guerrillas. UNITA lists anti-aircraft guns and missiles, artillery, and anti-tank weapons as its most pressing material requirements—to be partially met by new U.S. assistance. With South African air support, the organization barely repulsed a 1985 Cuban/Angolan offensive into its territory. It now faces a strengthened government force with formidable air defense, C3I, air, and armor capabilities.

The Kampuchean resistance is composed of approximately 24,000 noncommunist guerrillas and 35,000 communist Khmer Rouge elements. It faces some 140,000 thinly spread Vietnamese occupation troops, and the weak, 20,000-man army of the Heng Samrin Kampuchean regime. The base camps of all resistance organizations located along the Kampuchean-Thai border are regularly attacked by the Vietnamese. The frequency of resistance operations deep inside the country has increased, however, aided by the reignition of anti-Vietnamese sentiment inherent in Khmer tradition. Ominously, the most effective and regular operations have been carried out by the Khmer Rouge, not the noncommunist elements.

The Nicaraguan resistance numbers up to 15,000 men and operates primarily in rural areas of the country. It faces a Nicaraguan army of 45,000, a popular militia of 60,000, and perhaps 2,000 Cuban military advisers. The insurgents have failed to build a significant apparatus in the urban, Pacific areas of the country. The quality of their operations has been mixed and has led many observers to feel the insurgents can harass, but not bring about the downfall of, the Sandinista regime. The introduction of Soviet helicopter gunships into the Sandinista inventory in 1985 became a source of concern to the resistance.

Unreliable External Supporting States. What is the scope, quality, source, and tenacity of the insurgency's external support? Is the main political thrust of the insurgency compatible over the long run with its source of support?

The Afghan Mujahideen have reportedly been supported by several Islamic states, including volunteer fighters. The Chinese and various Western countries have also figured heavily. As mentioned previously, public aid from the United States is $250 million per year as of 1985, with an additional $300 million authorized during 1986 and 1987. According to the Federation for American Afghan Action, $380 to 400 million had been funneled to the Afghans between 1979 and 1985. These figures, if accurate, are extremely high for this type of activity— even taking into account Mujahideen complaints that much foreign aid never reaches the fighting units. Western support for the Afghan insurgency has been remarkably free of the dissent that characterizes debate on similar activity in other parts of the world. Presumably, this state of affairs will continue as long as the Soviet presence remains at its present level. The robust form of Islam that underlies much of the resistance may not, in the case of a Soviet drawdown, produce a political system compatible with continued close Western support. And should the Soviets expand their scope of activities to include serious destabilizing activities in Pakistan, for instance, the West could well reconsider the wisdom of continued provocative activities in the Afghan quagmire. So far, political costs to the West resulting from involvement in Afghanistan have been small.

Although a variety of Middle Eastern countries, France, and communist

China have at one time or another aided UNITA, its most consistent external supporter has been South Africa. Shared requirements for survival should sustain this relationship. But UNITA's leaders attach great significance to the conspicuous resumption in 1986 of U.S. aid, halted by congressional action a decade earlier. They feel its mere reinstatement will have a weighty demoralizing effect on the current Angolan regime and its foreign supporters. According to UNITA's chief foreign spokesman, "$20 million supplied openly, with the United States clearly acting, would mean much, much more to us than $50 million covertly." It is difficult, however, to foresee a situation in which the United States could be trusted as a reliable, long-term supporter for a number of reasons: U.S. popular revulsion for South African internal policies; the probable harmful impact of continued Angolan hostilities on cherished regional peace efforts; the cyclical nature of the U.S. will to engage in controversial insurgency support operations that do not meet rapid success; and the presence of substantial private American interests that make Angola the United States' fourth largest trading partner in Africa. To cite one specific irritant, UNITA's leaders insist on their right to strike at Chevron facilities in Cabinda Province. "We are restrained only by operational limitations, not our links with the United States," says a senior spokesman with some acerbity.

The communist Khmer Rouge depends primarily on an estimated $60 to $100 million annual Chinese subsidy. Given the nature of the Chinese government, this assistance is probably stable. Additional Chinese support and support from the Association of Southeast Asian Nations (ASEAN) filters through to the two noncommunist coalitions. They reportedly have received covert aid from the United States since 1982, including $5 million in 1985. A move in Congress would grant them a further $5 million yearly in nonlethal assistance as of 1986. But the U.S. commitment is inherently unreliable, and in part designed for the limited objective of strengthening noncommunist elements against the Khmer Rouge. Not only will cyclical domestic changes in U.S. policy affect support to such activity, but inclusion of the discredited Khmer Rouge in the resistance coalition is a political burden for Western supporters. The likelihood that the Khmer Rouge would win any future power struggle with the conservative elements intensifies Western concerns about such support.

With a relatively small 1985 subsidy of $27 million in nonlethal aid and $100 million requested for 1986, the Nicaraguan resistance continues its tenuous hold on official support from the United States. Prior to a congressional aid cutoff in 1984, the United States had provided a total $80 million to the resistance. The continued presence of rightist supporters of ex-dictator Anastasio Somoza within the FDN leadership, inconsistent congressional attitude, the mixed image of the resistance with the American public—all militate against the consistency of the

United States as a stalwart backer. A liberal swing within the U.S. electorate could easily doom even the relatively small level of assistance now given.

Unreliable Contiguous Supporting States.   How dependable are countries that provide the insurgents with sanctuary, infiltration routes, and logistics transit capabilities?

Pakistan and, to some extent, Iran are essential to the Mujahideen. Soviet terror tactics against the civilian populace inside Afghanistan have rendered the 3 to 3.5 million refugees in Pakistan and 1.5 million in Iran the true "sea" in which these guerrillas "swim." The Pakistanis have a clear self-interest in ensuring that a Marxist regime does not consolidate in neighboring Afghanistan. And the confluence of Pakistani interests with Washington on this issue was a large factor in prompting the United States to grant a $3.2 billion force modernization program. But there are also substantial dangers to Pakistan resulting from its present course of action:

- Soviet threats have been made, and the possibility of future Soviet-Indian collusion to partition Pakistan cannot be totally ruled out.

- Air attacks on refugee camps are regularly made by Afghan/Soviet forces across Pakistan's borders.

- The large refugee population—related ethnically to part of Pakistan's own populace—could pose a latent threat to internal stability.

- Several internal ethnic groups, specifically Baluchis and Sindis, contain elements vulnerable to externally fueled separatist sentiment.

The Soviets probably assume the composite effect of the above elements will gradually induce the Pakistanis to reduce their services to the Mujahideen, and actively close off infiltration routes. This has not occurred.

UNITA, alone among the four insurgencies being considered, operates primarily within its own borders. It has not routinely depended on external sanctuaries, although it would retreat into South African–controlled Namibia if necessary. UNITA also relies on South Africa for logistics support, as well as periodic air intervention.

Thailand, backed by the remainder of ASEAN, the United States, and China, has its own self-interest in impeding the consolidation of the Vietnamese-controlled Kampuchean regime: first, largely ethnic Lao insurgency in Thailand could be inflamed; second, Thai borders are frequently crossed by the Vietnamese. The intensity of dangers resulting from Thailand's support to the Kampuchean insurgency is not comparable to that of Pakistan, however.

Honduras and, to a lesser extent, Costa Rica are essential to the Nicaraguan resistance. Honduras has materially benefited by the American military presence associated with the insurgency, despite charges that the United States has consistently backed ultraconservative political trends. Concerns about Nicaraguan cross-border military actions are real, but blunted by the U.S. military presence. Friction between the Nicaraguan guerrillas and reformist officers in the Honduran military establishment could portend serious future problems. And a fledgling, although repressed, anti-government insurrection has unsuccessfully attempted to infiltrate Honduras from time to time. As long as the U.S. military commitment is present, however, Honduras is not exposed to threats equivalent to those in Pakistan.

Identification with a Traditional Foreign Enemy. Besides the local leftist regime, who is the foreign enemy? Is this enemy playing a traditional hostile role, hence spurring nationalist emotions among the insurgents?

The Soviet Union is a state toward which the Afghan populace has a long history of suspicion and outright hostility. Added to the basic religious motivation of the Mujahideen, traditional nationalist emotion acts to the benefit of the insurgency.

In Angola, where the current foreign enemies are 35,000 Cubans and some 1,200 Soviet military advisers, traditional hostility towards a foreign power is not a major factor. There is no previous history of Cuban or Soviet involvement in Angolan affairs, and no historical scores to settle. A general anti-imperialist sentiment, originally directed at the Portugese during the struggle for independence, undoubtedly fuels UNITA's dedication—but the current foreign enemy does not arouse traditional hatreds.

In Kampuchea, the nationalist factor works on the side of the insurgents, in the form of traditional Khmer-Vietnamese enmity. Insurgent leaders claim to have minimized operations against the indigenous Kampuchean army in favor of direct actions against the Vietnamese. And as stated by a noncommunist resistance leader to a Belgian journalist in 1983, "our relations with the PRK [Heng Samrin] armed forces aren't bad, either. Most of Heng Samrin's soldiers are Khmer first. Many are still deeply faithful to Prince Sihanouk. In various instances they have given us food, intelligence, and ammunition. We don't want them to defect. They are much more useful where they are." A Vietnamese policy of resettling Vietnamese in fertile Kampuchea (an estimated 500,000 as of 1985) intensifies nationalist impulses to support the resistance.

The traditional perceived enemy of Nicaraguan nationalism is the United States—given a history of interference and outright military intervention since the early years of this century. Neither Cubans nor Russians have suppressed Nicaraguan nationalist movements in the past, and neither country inspires visceral nationalist hostility. Unlike other areas being considered, the resistance is identified with, not against, the state that most inspires nationalist enmity in Nicaragua. The perception of the FDN as Somozista-dominated intensifies this problem. The Sandinistas, of course, came to power in a wave of popular enthusiasm. While they have undoubtedly lost much support, this has not translated into commensurate increased enthusiasm for the resistance.

Implausibility of Compromise.   What are the minimum goals of the resistance? Is a political compromise between the insurgents and the regime realistic?

The maximalist goals of the Mujahideen are, of course, withdrawal of Soviet troops, overthrow of the communist regime, and installation of an Islamic or Islamic-oriented government. Implicit in such a victory would be return of refugees from Pakistan and Iran. The rebel groups are unimpressed with the prospects for any currently envisaged negotiations. As stated by Mujahideen leader Gulbadin Hekmatyar, "It is useless for us to sit down with the Russians. For what? They have invaded our country. The only solution is for them to withdraw their troops." Given Mujahideen military preponderance against the Afghan government alone, an initial agreement satisfactory to the resistance would have to include the following components: return of refugees, Soviet withdrawal, and the establishment of a coalition government including Mujahideen leaders. In their view, time would then bring about predominance of the anti-communist factions. While an understandable scenario, factionalism among the Mujahideen groups could hamper a unified approach to attaining power once the foreign military threat were removed. Soviet agreement to such a compromise is unlikely, unless political costs to them of continuing the struggle escalate considerably. Not only would it mean abandoning socialist gains in Afghanistan, it would set a politically undesirable example for the Moslem nationalities of Soviet Central Asia.

In Angola, the UNITA leadership envisages a mixed government after the exit of Cuban troops. UNITA leader Jonas Savimbi claimed in October 1985 that a growing movement within the ruling party (MPLA) favors negotiations with UNITA. Elements of the MPLA would be included in this coalition, and elections would occur after a transitional period of two to three years. UNITA leaders calculate that the MPLA's political appeal, narrowly based in any case, would diminish considerably during the transitional period. Much would depend on UNITA's ability to transcend its tribal character, and appeal on a nationwide basis.

A withdrawal of Vietnamese troops is sought by the Kampuchean resistance, along with overthrow of the Khmer People's Revolutionary Party regime. Were a coalition government and withdrawal to be offered by the Vietnamese — presumably as a result of intense Chinese pressure — it would be regarded by the insurgents as a stepping-stone towards a future victory. And as in previous cases, the insurgents are not politically compatible. It is difficult to envision a workable coalition between the noncommunist groups and the Khmer Rouge, once Vietnamese forces had withdrawn. Chinese promises to restrain the Khmer Rouge on this score cannot be considered conclusive.

The actual goals of the various insurgent factions in Nicaragua have been the subject of considerable discussion within the U.S. Congress. Clearly, they envisage an overthrow of the Sandinista regime, although a coalition could be seen as an intermediary step. As in the case of Afghanistan, factional strife between the various resistance groups would be an impediment to cohesive rule in the event of a Sandinista collapse. The extent of support enjoyed by the current Sandinista regime is also a subject of controversy. But even if a majority of the populace still supports the Sandinistas, they do not have effective, consistent control of most of the country's territory.

Potential of a Soviet-Backed Regime to Escalate Indefinitely.   What is the nature of the Soviet commitment to the beseiged regime, and what is the capacity of the counterinsurgency forces to absorb increased levels of assistance?

Experience since the Soviet invasion of Afghanistan seems to indicate the Soviets will tolerate modest losses for as long as it takes to subdue the resistance. They have the political will and capacity to escalate as necessary to sustain control of major centers and arteries. Their strategy of gradual pacification does not compel them to escalate further.

Many military analysts believe a process of escalation has been under way in Angola since the relatively successful government offensive in September 1985. These analysts point to a heavy use of Soviet air transports to move armor from the capital to front-line areas. They also point to implacement of air defense and C3I assets superior to anything the South African air force can muster. Some predict a Soviet/Cuban/Angolan attempt to rout Savimbi and pursue his retreating guerrillas into South African–controlled Namibia.

The Vietnamese in Kampuchea have the capacity to escalate as necessary, unless seriously constrained by Chinese threats. Soviet pressures, resulting from conditions made by the Chinese for improved relations, may have been responsible for a late 1985 reduction in forces deployed in Kampuchea — but the reduction was presumably on a temporary basis.

Given Nicaragua's exposed position vis-à-vis direct American intervention, the Soviet commitment to escalate in that country's conflict is not open-ended. However, the war has already witnessed a significant enhancement of Managua's counterinsurgency capabilities — most obviously by the supply of helicopter gunships.

Summary Comparative Observations

On the basis of the discussion above, we can draw the following comparative observations about these four insurgencies.

- Three of the four are primarily fighting foreign occupiers or communist forces invited in by a puppet regime—in Afghanistan, Angola, and Kampuchea. With the possible exception of Cubans in Angola, these foreign forces simply cannot be defeated by the insurgents alone—*if* the foreign troops remain in place. And the level of losses currently being suffered is not sufficient to cause their governments undue hardship. The key, then, is whether or not the occupier's political will to endure in a foreign conflict can be eroded over time. Unfortunately for these insurgencies, the tenacity of dictatorial, communist regimes has historically proved greater than the somewhat fickle cycles inherent in the democratic process. In the case of Nicaragua, the proximate enemy is the local leftist regime—albeit backed by Cuba and the Soviet Union. The task of the Nicaraguan resistance—quite different from the other conflicts—is politically and militarily to defeat the indigenous Sandinistas, not to raise the costs and erode the will of a foreign expeditionary force.

- In two cases—Afghanistan and Kampuchea—historic nationalist animosity is on the side of the insurgents; their traditional enemy is their current enemy. In Angola, UNITA's nationalist motivation, while present, is not rooted in anti-Cuban or anti-Soviet enmity. In Nicaragua, traditional animosities run against the insurgency.

- In all four conflicts, formal discussions occur between parties to the conflict—inevitably exclusive of the insurgents themselves. Under U.N. auspices, the Pakistanis hold proximity talks with the Afghan government. They report little progress as of early 1986. Vietnam has approached the People's Republic of China on several occasions with offers to permit the return of resistance fighters as individuals, but has met with no positive response. A U.S. Special Envoy for Central America meets sporadically with various Nicaraguan officials. And American intermediary activities between Angola and South Africa have sought a reduction and ultimate elimination of Cuban troops in Angola in exchange for South African withdrawal from Namibia and U.N.-supervised independence for that territory.

- Three of the movements—those in Afghanistan, Nicaragua, and Kampuchea—are plagued by internal factionalism that is barely submerged while the armed struggle is in progress. Were victory to occur, this factionalism would severely hamper the establishment of a viable regime. In Angola, the only significant anti-regime movement other than UNITA—Holden Roberto's FNLA—left the field in 1978. Factional fighting within UNITA appears minimal, and will probably remain so as long as the charismatic Jonas Savimbi remains alive.

- The Afghan and Kampuchean insurgencies face outright communist regimes. In Angola, Soviet-supported communists occupy key positions in a technically noncommunist Marxist regime. In Nicaragua, a leftist socialist regime with intense East bloc ties holds power. The formally noncommunist status of both Angola and Nicaragua theoretically renders a compromise solution slightly more realistic. Both latter countries, of course, charge that counterrevolutionary movements make it impossible for them to loosen dependence on their Cuban-Soviet backers—a primary goal of U.S. policy in both countries.

- Two of the resistance movements—those in Angola and Kampuchea— receive some support from quarters that can be considered reliable. Both South Africa and the Chinese see support to these two movements as integral to their own national security; added support received by these movements from the United States cannot be regarded as reliable. The Afghan Mujahideen also enjoy a level of Islamic and Chinese support that is likely to be sustained. And the reportedly large level of U.S. support to this cause has enjoyed surprising immunity from domestic political attack, in large part because the Soviet Union itself is directly engaged in Afghanistan. Should costs mount—in the form of a Soviet destabilization campaign in Pakistan, for example—pressures could develop in the West to minimize involvement in the conflict. In Nicaragua, official U.S. support demonstrably cannot be relied upon to continue from year to year. Whether more consistent private and third country assistance can be developed to a point of sufficiency is as yet unproven, and the resistance is resultantly vulnerable. One estimate places the current level of private aid at $25 million per year—a respectable figure if sustained.

- Of the four conflicts, the most ruthless counterinsurgency policies are being pursued by the Soviets in Afghanistan. Direct military action against the civilian populace, which is by and large supportive of the Mujahideen, is designed to force depopulation and deprive the guerrillas of food and other elemental support.

- One of the four groups, UNITA, was initially tribally based and requires further efforts to encompass other elements in the Angolan society—in particular urban population centers including the capital. The other three insurrections are broadly representative of their populations, although their operational base areas are primarily rural. With the uneven exception of the Afghan Mujahideen, clandestine organizational efforts by all groups in urban areas is insufficient. This is a particular failure of the Nicaraguan resistance.

Trends

The Main Battlefields.   In all four areas considered above, the insurgents are holding their own.

- The Mujahideen control most of Afghanistan—with the exception of cities where a large Soviet/Afghan military presence exists, major arteries, and any area where a Soviet offensive is under way.

- UNITA controls a third of Angola and has recently been promised limited U.S. aid. But it has been placed on the defensive by a massive Soviet/Cuban/Angolan buildup.

- The Kampuchean resistance is displaying an increasing capability to operate in the country's interior, in spite of the vulnerability of its bases along the Thai border.

- Nicaraguan resistance operations have probed deeper into the country than in the past.

Impediments to Success.   Despite its tribal and rural base, UNITA in early 1985 had appeared closer to attaining its objectives than other anti-leftist insurgencies. It had expanded its effective operations without unreliable superpower support, and was not plagued by the internecine strife that characterizes the other three organizations. The regime—even with Cuban support—was clearly on the defensive. But despite ten years of tenacious struggle, UNITA's base area is not secure in the face of overwhelming conventional forces buttressed by Soviet-supplied Angolan air power. Renewed U.S. assistance will help, but probably will not be sufficient, to solve UNITA's dilemma.

The Nicaraguan resistance, unless one considers outright U.S. military intervention a likely event, has different impediments to attaining its goal. The insurgents carry heavy political baggage in the form of the Somozista past of some leaders; they are on the wrong side of the nationalist issue; they rely to an unhealthy extent on unpredictable American support; and their urban infrastructure is very thin. On the other hand, there is no heavy contingent of foreign troops in the country, aside from some 2,000 Cuban advisory elements. And given consistent U.S. threats of intervention, there is unlikely to be any.

The Afghan and Kampuchean resistances, although easily the most effective indigenous forces in their countries, cannot win without breaking the political will of major *foreign* elements to sustain troops in their countries. Both movements are also ridden with factionalism, which would surface rapidly should success be attained.

The Soviet Response.   The Soviet response to these Western-backed insurgencies since Mikhail Gorbachev's assumption of power has been forceful. In most cases, counterinsurgency activity has markedly intensified, leading some commentators to refer to a "Gorbachev Test" of Western will. As of late 1985, counterinsurgency offensives had occurred in Afghanistan, Angola, Eritrea, Mozambique, and periodically in Kampuchea.

And statistics regarding quantities of Soviet military equipment given these regimes show a distinct increase during late 1985 and 1986.

These observations do not seem to portend any Soviet propensity to compromise readily on these Third World "socialist gains."

Other Vulnerable Communist States.   Were the West, nevertheless, to widen a strategy of offensive insurgency support beyond areas discussed in this report, two candidate countries come to mind: the first is Ethiopia where, as described previously, ethnically based insurgencies have fought the central government to a standoff for several years. But a substantial number of anticommunist, Amharic-speaking Ethiopians, some already organized in largely ineffective groups, would undertake anti-regime activities if support were available. No significant Western support to any of Ethiopia's dissident organizations has been reported, although periodic Saudi Arabian assistance to some Eritrean groups has occurred.

The second candidate is the People's Democratic Republic of Yemen (PRDY), Russia's volatile bastion in the southern tip of the Arabian Peninsula. Lacking resources, the PDRY economy is dependent on remittances from its citizens working in petroleum economies of Western-oriented Arab states. These workers form a large, vulnerable group constantly exposed to noncommunist influences. And the country itself includes provinces with historical linkages to Saudi Arabia and Oman. The PDRY communist hierarchy is severely split along tribal and ideological grounds—as exemplified by bloody strife in January 1986.

Conclusions

Six of the world's current insurgencies are anti-communist in orientation, several directly backed by the West and its allies. This is a direct reversal of the situation pertaining in the early 1970s, when almost all insurrections were leftist.

Of equal importance, all six current anti-communist insurgencies are in response to successful leftist insurrections or revolutions of the 1970s. Some of these new revolutionaries are dedicated democrats—while some are outright opportunists. But the message to Moscow is clear: if successful, today's counterrevolutions could demonstrate that socialist victories are reversible.

The long-term benefit to either East or West of this seesaw, cyclical warfare may prove limited. It does, however, have the immediate virtue of demonstrating to the Soviets that the Third World is not an open field for unopposed expansion.

The financial cost to the West of supporting these insurgencies is relatively minor. Economically, they are a bargain basement way of harassing the Soviet empire at its periphery. 1986 support figures from the United States ($250 million, Afghanistan; $100 million, Nicaragua; $15 million, Angola; $10 million, Kampuchea) total a relatively small outlay of $375 million. The political costs, however, can be excessively high in fractious Western societies.

The economic costs of Moscow's counterinsurgency efforts are fairly high, particularly if a proportion of military support to Vietnam and Cuba is figured alongside that to the beseiged countries themselves. The total value of arms transfers from the Soviets to affected areas between 1979 and 1983 gives some indication of the amounts involved: Afghanistan, $1.80 billion; Angola, $1.50 billion; Ethiopia, $1.80 billion; Kampuchea; $ .17 billion; Nicaragua; $ .10 billion. Total: $5.37 billion.

During the same period, Cuba received $3.1 billion and Vietnam $5.2 billion in arms transfers. If the arbitrary assumption is made that three-fourths of all arms transferred to the affected areas ($4.03 billion) and one-quarter of those transferred to Cuba and Vietnam ($2.08 billion) are used for counterinsurgency purposes—then a total of $6.11 billion for arms only between 1979 and 1983 is an order-of-magnitude figure of the amounts involved. This sum, of course, does not account for costs of the Soviet's own forces in Afghanistan; nonhardware costs such as training or advisers; or hard-currency payments made by Angola to the Soviets for arms received.

Current Soviet economic difficulties *could* render its leadership, in time, more compromising on peripheral arenas of conflict with the West. If so, the bargaining chips represented by these insurgencies would be significantly greater than at present.

Of equal importance for these revolutions is the political and economic health of Moscow's key proxies, Cuba and Vietnam. The former generally maintains some 43,600 troops outside of its borders (2,000, Nicaragua; 400, Congo; 35,000, Angola; 500, South Yemen; 5,000, Ethiopia; 700, Mozambique). Vietnam sustains approximately 140,000 troops in Kampuchea. The economic conditions of both countries depend on the Soviets, who supply $4.7 billion yearly to Cuba and $1 to 2 billion to Vietnam. Both are politically cohesive, despite some emerging North-South friction in Vietnam.

On balance, it is difficult to envisage an outright victory by the current movements in Afghanistan, Angola, Kampuchea, and Nicaragua. The very best that can be hoped for are compromises that dilute somewhat the Marxist complexion of the beseiged regimes.

What the anti-leftist revolutionaries realistically represent for the West, then, are the following:

- An inexpensive means of imposing economic and political costs on the Soviets.

- A modest possibility of forcing compromise political solutions in areas now dominated or heavily influenced by communist regimes.

- A statement to the Soviets that they have exceeded the high-water mark of their empire—and that further leftist revolutionary expansion will be opposed by the West.

- The building of Western bargaining chips for utilization across the spectrum of the East-West agenda.

Though limited, the above amounts to a lot. But an outright victory by any of the current anti-communist revolutions does not seem to be in the cards. And even the pragmatic expectations listed above demand a long-term consistency in Western support that has not been given in the past.

Part IV

Social Conditions in the Soviet Union and the Empire

10 *Mikhail S. Bernstam*

Trends in the Soviet Population

Demographically, the Soviet Union and the United States would be similar if the latter included Canada and Mexico—such is the relation between low fertile Soviet Slavic and Baltic people, or whites, and highly fertile Turkic peoples of Central Asia and Caucases, or nonwhites. The North American analogy would be closer still if Mexicans were better off and had no incentives to move to the north.

Like the United States and other welfare societies of the West, Soviet whites have experienced a protracted fertility depression. Also, like U.S. whites and blacks, out-of-wedlock fertility and single-parent households are on the rise among Soviet whites. The present low fertility levels are some 15 percent below the level of replacement of future generations. This implies a negative population growth in the near future. Combined, these trends portend a population shrinkage, a rise in the number of consumers relative to producers, declining human capital, an aging labor force, and a crisis of the social security system. In short, it suggests a stagnant economy with scarce capital and labor inputs and abundant social conflicts.

In addition, the quality of the Soviet population has deteriorated. The secular mortality decline has reversed and life expectancy has been decreasing. To

TABLE 10-1 **Population and Its Growth, USSR, 1959–2000**
(selected years)

	Population (in millions)			Growth (percent)		Annual Rate of Natural Increase (percent)		Share in the Total (percent)		
	1959	1979	2000	1959–78	1979–99	1959–78	1979–99	1959	1979	2000
USSR	208.8	262.4	299.0	25.7	13.9	1.14	0.62	100.0	100.0	100.0
Whites	181.6	215.1	224.7	18.5	4.5	0.85	0.21	86.9	81.9	75.2
Nonwhites	27.1	46.7	73.4	72.7	57.1	2.73	2.15	13.0	17.8	24.6

Sources: Data for 1959: *Itogi Vsesoiuznoi Perepisi Naseleniia 1970*, vol. 4 (Moscow, 1973), pp. 9–11 (without adjustment for ethnic reidentification); for 1979 for the USSR: *Chislennost i Sostav Naseleniia SSSR. Po Danrym Vsesoiuznoi Perepisi Naseleniia 1979 Goda* (Moscow, 1984), pp. 71–73; for 1979 whites and nonwhites (with adjustment for ethnic reidentification) and for 2000: Mikhail S. Bernstam, "The Demography of Soviet Ethnic Groups in World Perspective," in *The Last Empire: Nationalities and the Soviet Future* ed. Robert Conquest (Stanford, Calif.: Hoover Institution Press, 1986), tables 1 and 2.

be sure, a stagnation or an upturn in infant mortality can now be observed in populations with high illegitimate fertility, such as the United States[1] and the Soviet Union. An upturn in old age mortality can be found in countries where the elderly lack sufficient family care, such as Denmark[2] and the Soviet Union. However, only the USSR and Eastern Europe have experienced an increase in mortality at prime adult ages and a rise in industrial fatalities. The Soviet Union is also idiosyncratic in the very high morbidity of its female population and especially in high pathological secondary sterility due to work hazards and surgical abortions. This declining population quality complements the projected declining quantity of the Soviet white population.

At the same time, unlike the United States, the economic and demographic behaviors of white and nonwhite groups have diverged. There is a demographic split along racial and regional lines. Nonwhites now constitute about 20 percent of the USSR population; they form a separate and closed world of relative economic prosperity and concentrate in profitable agricultural market activities in their own region. Although they practice birth control, nonwhites retain very high fertility levels and thus experience high population growth. The population doubles each thirty years.

Table 1, based on the 1959 and 1979 Soviet censuses and my projection to the year 2000, summarizes the demographic split. The annual population growth between nonwhites and whites widens from 3:1 in the period 1959–78 to 10:1 in the period 1979–99. This is due to both white fertility depression and nonwhite fertility expansion. Nonwhites will have increased 2.7 times from 1959 to 2000 and their share in the USSR population will almost double from 13 percent to 25 percent. In another one hundred years, these population trends could split the country by half-and-half.

And given the nonwhite comparative economic advantage, their migration to the north is unlikely to substitute for the future depopulation of white areas. This case is opposite to that of Mexico and the United States.

This analysis focuses on the period to the year 2000 and considers the divergent fertility, declining life expectancy, and general quality of the population as well as their implications for the Soviet labor force given the white/nonwhite demographic split.[3]

The Quality of the Population and Human Capital

Mortality Trends. Is mortality really rising in the Soviet Union over years, across areas, at most ages, and among both males and females? If so, what causes these peacetime mortality increases in reverse of the secular trend? Is it God, weather, objective demographic and biological changes, self-inflicted bad habits (violence, drugs, heavy drinking), harmful polluting civilization? Or is it changing labor markets or working and living conditions deriving from specific government policies?

There are four independent sets of evidence and analyses of rising Soviet mortality. The first set is conventional demographic data. These have been officially reported but as yet have not been subjected to Western scrutiny. The second is econometric estimates of ultimate measures of the duration of life, that is, life expectancy at birth,[4] based on the unconventional procedure of pulling together demographic and economic variables. The third set is life expectancies at birth derived by conventional methods of mathematical demography. The fourth set is based on circumstantial evidence, which actually tells more about labor markets and social welfare than wages paid and welfare/social security rubles spent; this is the number of industrial invalids and family members who have lost their breadwinners. Finally, statistical analysis pulls these four sets of evidence together and offers an economic explanation of declining life expectancy of the Soviet population.

Values of life expectancy at birth among both Soviet whites and nonwhites are currently decades behind U.S. levels. My estimates for 1981–82 provide values of 60.80 years for Soviet males and 72.85 for Soviet females. This is the mid-1930s level of U.S. white males and the early 1950s level of U.S. white females. In the United States in 1983, the expectation of life at birth was 71.60 for white males, 67.10 for black males, 78.80 for white females, and 75.30 for black females.[5]

The evidence points to a trend of declining life expectancy in the USSR across regions since the second half of the 1960s, with one short-term interruption in 1981–82. By official estimates, life expectancy at birth dropped among males from 66 years in 1965–66 to 65 in 1970–71 to 64 in 1971–72 due to mortality increases after age 15. In the same period, life expectancy also decreased by about one year among females aged over 35.[6] The data then disappeared, but the later trend can be discerned without interruption from other indicators. Various total and regional data suggest that the survivorship ratios from birth to ages 25 to 30 have been consistently declining among females since the beginning of the 1970s.[7] The lowering of survivorship indicates a downward trend in female life expectancy at birth since the early 1970s.

Less scanty and more convincing and comprehensive evidence comes from cross-sectional series (by fifteen union republics and the USSR as a whole) on age-standardized death rates.[8] A steady increase in these rates in most republics is equivalent to a trend of declining life expectancy at birth since the mid-1960s through 1980.

TABLE 10-2   **Crude Death Rates per 1,000 and Death Rates per 1,000 Directly Standardized for Age with the 1970 USSR Age Distribution as the Standard, USSR and Union Republics, 1958/59–1984** *(selected years)*

Republic	1958/59	1969/70	1980	1984
USSR	7.4	8.2	10.3	10.8
	7.8	*8.2*	*8.9*	*NA*
Russian	7.6	8.6	11.0	11.6
	7.6	*8.6*	*9.9*	*NA*
Ukrainian	7.2	8.8	11.4	12.0
	7.5	*7.7*	*8.3*	*NA*
Byelorussian	7.2	7.5	9.9	10.5
	7.2	*6.9*	*7.7*	*NA*
Latvian	10.4	11.2	12.7	12.9
	8.2	*8.2*	*8.8*	*NA*
Armenian	8.0	5.2	5.5	5.8
	7.4	*NA*	*6.2*	*NA*
Uzbek	6.1	5.8	7.4	7.4
	NA	*6.8*	*8.5*	*NA*
Tadzhik	5.7	6.3	8.0	7.4
	NA	*NA*	*8.6*	*NA*
Kazakh	7.1	6.0	8.0	8.2
	NA	*NA*	*9.0*	*NA*
Azerbaidzhan	7.2	6.9	7.0	6.8
	6.7	*NA*	*8.4*	*NA*

Note: First line of each row denotes crude death rates. Second line (italic) denotes age-standardized death rates.

NA = Not available.

Sources: Crude death rates: *Narkhoz*, various years; age-standardized death rates: see footnote 8 in text.

Table 2 presents the time series of these age-standardized as well as non-standardized — or crude — death rates. Table 3 presents estimates of life expectancy at birth for both sexes combined for the period 1959–84. Table 4 provides the values of life expectancy for males and females for three five-year periods, 1970–74, 1975–79, 1979–83, for fifteen republics and the USSR as a whole. Although life expectancy values in Table 4 are lower than those in Table 3, three independently and differently derived sets of data show a good match in terms of trends. We can derive the following seven conclusions from them:

TABLE 10-3   **Expectancy of Life at Birth, Both Sexes, USSR and Union Republics, 1958/59–1984** *(selected years)*

Republic	1958/59	1969/70	1980	1984
USSR	68.98	69.26	68.81	68.86
Russian	68.82	68.68	68.02	68.05
Ukrainian	70.35	70.12	69.64	69.67
Byelorussian	70.49	71.47	71.53	71.34
Latvian	69.20	69.21	68.99	69.03
Armenian	67.58	74.63	74.58	74.69
Uzbek	70.32	71.32	68.50	69.73
Tadzhik	71.63	70.25	68.90	70.58
Kazakh	68.67	71.89	68.96	68.81
Azerbaidzhan	69.17	69.54	69.25	70.82

Methodology and Sources: See Appendix 1.

1. Mortality has indeed increased since the second half of the 1960s in many Soviet areas and since the early 1970s in most republics. The increase continued steadily in most white and some nonwhite republics through the early 1980s with an interruption in 1981–82.

2. The mortality rise was due not only to the aging of the population, but also to an increase in age-specific death schedules and decline in life expectancies across many ages. Mortality increases at ages 20 to 40 in the last twenty years can be explained to an extent by the fact that cohorts born after wars and famines gradually replaced the decimated cohorts born earlier. These earlier-born cohorts had already lost their weakest members during previous calamities and were thus better off and more homogeneous in terms of health and vitality than regular heterogeneous cohorts.[9] High life expectancy in Byelorussia relative to other white republics serves as an illustration.[10] But this effect can better explain the past than the present. It can explain why Soviet mortality was so low before the mid-1960s and why it then began to increase as the proportion of persons with normal health distribution increased in the population. It cannot explain mortality increases at most ages through all of the 1970s, within clusters of cohorts born both before and after 1945.[11] At any rate, the argument that heterogeneity of the population has been restored applies only to one lexicographic stripe and cannot be used recursively. Thus the normal cohorts, joining age group 20–24 in 1970 and moving to 25–29 in 1975

TABLE 10-4 **Expectancy of Life at Birth, USSR and Union Republics, 1970–1983** *(selected years)*

Republic	1970–74		1975–79		1979–83		
	Fem	Male	Fem	Male	Fem	Male	Both
USSR	74.01	63.43	72.85	62.11	72.85	60.80	67.22
Russian	73.46	61.54	72.45	60.95	72.74	59.34	66.55
Ukrainian	75.17	64.67	74.46	62.23	73.33	62.25	68.26
Byelorussian	76.30	67.74	77.57	67.75	NA	NA	NA
Lithuanian	75.55	65.28	74.73	64.12	NA	NA	NA
Latvian	74.26	62.89	75.36	62.41	72.50	61.65	67.50
Estonian	73.55	64.04	73.93	62.36	NA	NA	NA
Moldavian	71.43	64.99	68.63	62.58	NA	NA	NA
Georgian	76.90	67.95	76.56	66.38	NA	NA	NA
Armenian	77.84	68.33	75.63	64.85	NA	NA	NA
Uzbek	73.48	68.04	73.77	63.10	71.05	64.40	67.78
Tadzhik	71.21	65.10	68.71	60.32	NA	NA	NA
Kazakh	75.02	64.54	72.99	64.41	NA	NA	NA
Azerbaidzhan	73.53	65.04	70.85	62.93	NA	NA	NA
Kirgiz	72.57	63.83	70.49	63.82	NA	NA	NA
Turkmen	70.54	64.42	69.08	62.31	NA	NA	NA

NA = Not available.
Methodology and Sources: See Appendix 1.

and 30–35 in 1980, cannot be blamed for the continuous decline in life expectancy at ages 20–24 throughout the entire period.

3. There is currently no white/nonwhite mortality differential. Neither racial, nor regional, nor cultural factors contribute to differences in mortality and life expectancy levels.

4. Mortality has increased at a faster rate among nonwhites than among whites. Given the current clustering of both white and nonwhite life expectancies within the same narrow range, earlier low nonwhite mortality rates were probably due to some underreporting of deaths. The rapid recent increase is thus partly due to an improved registration of deaths.

5. Life expectancy in the Russian Soviet Federated Socialist Republic (RSFSR) for both sexes is one of the lowest in the country, and male life expectancy is the lowest. In the first half of the 1980s, an estimated male life expectancy fell to 59.3 years—slightly lower than in Colombia, Ecua-

dor, the Philippines, and Thailand, and slightly higher than in Algeria, Jordan, and Pakistan. [12]

6. Mortality is very sensitive to economic factors beyond general trends in medical advances. For instance, a short-term mortality decline and corresponding slight rise in life expectancy can be observed in 1981–82. This must have been due to a temporary weakening of the influence of the factors determining the longer-term mortality increase, including its resumption in 1983. In 1981, Soviet females were relieved from a number of hard and hazardous occupations, a paid leave of absence was established for nursing mothers, and minimum social security payments were increased for the handicapped and families who lost their breadwinners. [13] These measures should have reduced industrial injuries among working women and infant mortality among illegitimate children of working mothers; they also should have improved living standards of the poor. The mortality-reducing effect could last until females found other hard jobs, since these are better-paying. The general trend has consistently been that women substitute for men in hard and hazardous occupations when men switch to equally well-paying but more mechanized jobs. Also, many lighter industrial occupations to which women were transferred after each consecutive decree appeared to be no less hazardous. [14]

7. The most startling finding is the steepness of the decline in life expectancy within the last twenty years. By the mid-1980s, the advances of the late 1950s and 1960s have completely vanished. According to Table 3, the USSR life expectancy for both sexes returned to the level of the late 1950s, i.e., 68.5 to 69.0 years. According to Table 4, it fell to 67.2 in the early 1980s, to the level of the mid-1950s. The USSR male life expectancy seems to have fallen some time in 1981–82 even below the mid-1950s level of 63 years, [15] to a remarkably low level of 60.8 years. This is apparently the level of the early 1950s. It seems that the demographic result of the twenty-year period of Brezhnev-Andropov-Chernenko rule — during which an income transfer society expanded — was a return to the immediate post-Stalin or pre-Khrushchev years. These were the years of a relatively primitive health care system, with incomes less than half present amounts, when the middle class lived in overcrowded, shared flats and blue-collar workers lived in barracks, and when the majority of urban dwellers were malnourished and peasants were starving. After the dramatic welfare improvements of the last three decades, a heavy demographic price is being paid. Arguably, the costs offset the gains.

The Causes of Heightened Mortality. The comprehensive theory of mortality causes was formulated by Hamlet, the Prince of Denmark. He found that individuals die of two basic causes: of life and of death. This means that at a given level of medical technology (itself a result of human development) a corresponding level of mortality is influenced by living and working conditions. Mortality analysis should thus go beyond health care. Differences in death rates from the same structure of diseases (Hamlet's "death of death") are influenced by economic conditions (Hamlet's "death of life").

For example, in the United States, one can observe higher mortality rates from heart diseases in states with high industrial and urban concentration (e.g., Pennsylvania, New York, New Jersey, Massachusetts) relative to less industrialized areas. Nonetheless, mortality from direct impacts, such as accidents, is higher in states with lower levels of industrialization.[16] Apparently, the latter areas have lower work safety due to both a less advanced technological mix and a competitive pressure to reduce production costs. Generally, as industrialization further advances, work conditions improve without a lag. More efficient labor and insurance markets promote safety. In addition, an abundant supply of urban, and especially suburban, housing improves life expectancy. And free labor brings amenities. As a combined effect of these factors, along with medical advances, life expectancy has been increasing in all states.

The USSR has been strikingly different. Until recently, improved sanitary conditions and medical advances increased life expectancy. In the last two decades this was offset and reversed by negative impacts, such as deteriorating safety, increasing work hazards, and lagging or unequally distributed sanitary improvements in rapidly growing cities. Still, housing gains and more advanced industrial conditions in the cities led rural life expectancy to decline relative to urban life expectancy in the 1970s. (Both declined, but rural life expectancies decreased more.) As industrialization continued, urban housing construction did not offset the impact of increased industrial injuries and crowdedness, especially among young workers and recent migrants to the cities. Mortality from cardiovascular diseases has increased from 3.85 per 1,000 in 1970 to 5.54 per 1,000 in 1983, thus exceeding that in the highest industrial American states with relatively older population.[17] At the same time, industrial injuries, accidents, and hazards as a cause of death increased their share of all causes by 50 percent. They became the second major cause of death in many industrialized areas (both urban and rural); the second cause of death at all working ages in all areas; and the main cause of death among males of prime working ages.[18]

Appendix 2 presents the econometric test of fundamental economic causes of Soviet mortality, using data by republics for various years in the period 1959–80.

TABLE 10-5   **Social Security Recipients by Categories, USSR,
1941–1984** *(selected years)*

	Number (millions)			Proportion of Population		
	Total Recipients	Old Age Retirees	Handicapped and Families Who Lost Breadwinner	Total Recipients	Old Age Retirees	Handicapped and Families Who Lost Breadwinner
1941	4.0	0.2	3.4	2.03	0.10	1.73
1961	21.9	5.4	10.5	10.12	2.50	4.85
1966	32.0	16.0	11.1	13.78	6.89	4.78
1970	40.1	23.7	12.0	16.59	9.81	4.96
1975	44.4	28.8	11.9	17.53	11.39	4.71
1980	48.7	33.1	12.6	18.42	12.51	4.76
1984	53.6	37.2	13.7	19.56	13.58	4.97

Note: There are only three categories of social security recipients: 1) old age retirees,
2) handicapped military veterans of past wars, and 3) other handicapped and members of the
families who lost breadwinners. For years after 1975, only a) total number of social security
recipients and b) old age retirees are directly available. We calculated the residual and then
calculated the number of military handicapped as depleted at 3% per anum (that is, their
mortality rate in previous years). From these, the second residual was derived, which is the
number of other handicapped and members of the families who lost breadwinners.
Sources: *Narkhoz* 1974, p. 614; 1979, p. 439; 1984, p. 465.

To my knowledge, this is the first such test in the literature. The analysis demonstrates that rising industrial injuries have been the main cause of declining life
expectancy in the USSR, offsetting the gains from improved housing.

This conclusion is also supported by circumstantial evidence. Table 5 presents
the data on the numbers and proportions of social security recipients in the USSR
distributed by two major categories: old age retirees and the handicapped and
members of the families who lost their breadwinners.[19]

Both handicapped and family members who lost their breadwinners are
mostly victims of injuries, accidents, etc., related one way or another to working and living conditions. One can observe a sustained trend of increasing numbers as well as continuing high proportions of the handicapped and persons who
lost the family breadwinner. Since the eligibility did not change in the period
under study, no new categories of recipients qualified. The handicapped and
orphans increased their numbers at the same rate as the entire population, about
1 percent per annum. This is why their proportion in the population did not decline
in the Soviet Union and remains high, at about 5 percent of the total population.[20]

At least two conclusions can be drawn on the causes of declining life expectancies in the USSR. First, declining Soviet life expectancy is not a health problem. It is an economic problem of living and working conditions and of the state of labor, assets, and amenities markets. Second, Soviet industrialization and urbanization are different from their modern Western counterparts. In terms of demographic responses, the Soviet Union is behind its stage of industrial development and in many respects is similar to Europe in the early industrial era.[21]

Let us consider a stylized scheme of effects. There are two types or stages of urbanization, U-1 and U-2, and two types or stages of industrialization, I-1 and I-2. U-2 develops housing markets, improves living conditions, and positively influences life expectancy.[22] In U-1, sanitary conditions in overcrowded settlements are inferior to those in the countryside and negatively influence life expectancy. I-2 produces new, safer technology, makes labor superior to alternative types, and increases life expectancy. I-1 creates work hazards, increases fatal and damaging injuries, and reduces life expectancy. Together with advancing medical technologies and nutrition, U-2 and I-2 compete against U-1 and I-1. The net effect—i.e., whether life expectancy increases—depends on the relative impacts of these factors.

In the USSR before the mid-1960s, rapid medical advances, better nutrition, fast housing growth, and industrial improvements produced significant increases in life expectancy. Since that date, however, medical advances slowed while impacts of U-1 and I-1 prevailed over U-2 and I-2. Urbanization of the countryside and industrialization put the country in an especially disadvantageous position, without impacts of U-2 and I-2. Industrialization seems not to have translated its technological progress into improved conditions in the USSR in the last two decades. It has instead increased the negative human impacts. While U-2 improved in terms of growing per capita urban living space, urban conditions in terms of housing units per young and middle-aged working family have deteriorated. Each year about 3 million new families have been formed, whereas the number of new housing units built per annum has declined from 2.5 million before 1965 to 2.0 million thereafter.[23] Of course, units are inherited from deceased residents, but housing shortages have continued. Per capita urban living space increased due to the significantly improved living conditions of persons with seniority claims for housing; these were priorities of age, position, income, length of time in the labor force, or merely length of time in the housing queue. But the comparative disadvantage of young and middle-aged workers, especially rural immigrants who crowd into the workers' dormitories, has increased. Correspondingly, at the bottom of economic distribution in the cities, sanitary conditions have deteriorated.

In short, one can conclude that the welfare gains of the recent stage of socialist industrialization are negative. Improvements in housing, sanitation, and other living conditions have lagged behind progress in urbanization; industrial safety and other working conditions lagged behind technological progress, rising wages, and incomes.

One has to emphasize that these gaps have been widening precisely in the two decades of expansion of the social transfer society during the Brezhnev regime. Rising wages, incomes, and social transfer programs were achieved at the expense of reduced safety, increased industrial injuries, and the growing number of the handicapped and orphans, especially within the subpopulation of young workers, migrants, and other relatively disadvantaged segments of the population. From a worker or consumer welfare perspective, the growth in real income was in part illusory: it was offset by worsened work and social environments. This was not a public management error but a matter of policy.

Fertility Trends, Population Growth, Labor Force, and Demographic Split

Divergent Markets and Demographic Split.   Many countries have sub-populations with vastly different levels of natural increase, fertility, and economic mobility. The differences may be along many lines—racial, ethnic, regional, social, urban/rural, etc. However, the general trend in any country is towards convergence unless government policies successfully separate individual economic mobility from demographic mix. In the United States, for example, Mexican immigrants in the second generation adopt the average U.S. demographic behavior in terms of the number of children per couple and expenditure per child.[24] But countries such as South Africa and Israel retain divergent subpopulations because opportunities for economic mobility are closed for some population segments.

It is not a matter of discrimination and racial quotas but rather of economic separation. Discrimination and quotas restrict labor market entries for the disadvantaged, which subjects them to tougher competition. It thus induces individuals in those segments to lower their fertility relative to more advantaged segments in order to increase parental expenditures per child so that children become effectively competitive despite the discrimination. This is one reason why Jewish urban fertility—as well as fertility of other middlemen minorities—has been lower than that of their host populations. For a similar reason, black *marital* fertility in the United States is lower than white marital fertility.[25] Only when *all*, not some, opportunities on the outside labor markets are closed do the disadvantaged segments concentrate in their homelands. In such a noncompetitive environment they do not have to increase expenditures per child and thus reduce fertility. The standard for their children's future is fixed at the parents' level of

TABLE 10-6 **Educational Level of Employed Males, Soviet Union Republics, 1970 and 1979** *(percentages)*

	1970			*1979*		
	Higher	*Secondary*	*Secondary & Higher*	*Higher*	*Secondary*	*Secondary & Higher*
RSFSR						
Total	17.3	13.2	30.5	24.3	24.5	48.8
Rural	8.1	8.1	16.2	12.9	19.3	32.2
Collective farmers	3.3	5.3	8.6	6.8	17.3	24.1
Uzbek SSR						
Total	17.4	24.5	41.9	25.1	42.6	67.7
Rural	12.8	26.3	39.1	20.3	47.7	68.0
Collective farmers	3.9	25.4	29.3	7.6	50.4	58.0
Tadzhik SSR						
Total	15.4	18.3	33.7	23.6	33.1	56.7
Rural	11.2	17.9	29.1	18.8	36.0	54.8
Collective farmers	2.5	14.0	16.5	7.3	35.0	42.3
Turkmen SSR						
Total	17.6	19.0	36.6	25.0	34.6	59.6
Rural	12.4	19.6	32.0	18.5	40.2	58.7
Collective farmers	4.3	17.4	21.7	7.6	42.4	50.0

Source: *Chislennost' i Sostav Naseleniia SSSR. Po Dannym Vsesoiuznoi Perepisi Naseleniia 1979 Goda* (Moscow, 1984), pp. 158, 161, 168, 169, 171.

well-being.[26] High fertility and high natural increase of the population follows. The Soviet Union is unique in the sense that its white/nonwhite demographic differentials do not correspond to any of the above model situations. The government has been consistently working towards economic convergence, not divergence. There are no major economic markets closed for nonwhites fully or even partially (except some caste occupations such as the high military corps and Christian clergy). Quite the contrary, the government implemented nonwhite preferential policies and quotas from which nonwhites greatly benefited, especially in rapidly rising educational levels.[27] The economic mobility of nonwhites is a success story. Nor has there been religious or other conservative resistance by nonwhites to the consumption of goods of economic development, such as health

TABLE 10-7   **Educational Level of Employed Males by Selected Manual Labor Occupations, 1970 and 1979, and by Selected Industries, 1979, Russian and Uzbek Republics** *(percentages)*

	1970				1979			
	RSFSR Education		Uzbek Education		RSFSR Education		Uzbek Education	
	H	S	H	S	H	S	H	S
Manual Labor Occupations								
Machine-tool and metal workers	5.2	22.6	8.1	28.7	11.9	37.4	16.2	47.3
Food production workers	2.6	11.6	3.7	21.4	7.4	27.9	8.6	52.4
Trade and food service workers	6.5	18.0	10.8	32.8	13.4	34.9	19.4	51.9
Shipping and storage workers	4.7	16.5	8.1	26.8	10.5	29.6	14.6	43.7
Utilities	1.1	4.3	1.6	9.0	3.9	13.3	3.6	30.5
Agricultural workers	0.5	3.3	1.0	17.4	2.1	12.7	2.7	47.6
Industries								
Supplies	NA	NA	NA	NA	7.6	24.1	11.6	36.9
Trade and food	NA	NA	NA	NA	3.7	28.2	6.1	43.9
Procurements	NA	NA	NA	NA	3.2	18.7	6.0	40.7
Utilities	NA	NA	NA	NA	3.1	25.3	4.7	41.8
Agricultural	NA	NA	NA	NA	2.5	15.3	1.5	47.3

NA = Not available.   H = Higher;   S = Secondary.

Source: *Chislennost' i Sostav Naseleniia SSSR. Po Dannym Vsesoiuznoi Perepisi Naselennia 1979 Goda* (Moscow, 1984), pp. 173, 175, 184–85, 188.

care, low mortality, income increases, accumulation of capital, secondary and higher education, luxuries and assets (brick houses, furniture, automobiles), etc.

Nevertheless, neither demographic nor behavioral economic convergence has occurred. Actually, divergencies in fertility, occupational selection, household strategies of resources allocation, etc., have widened — to such an extent that one can observe a demographic split and a voluntary separation of nonwhites on their internal markets in nonwhite republics.[28]

Tables 6 and 7 show that educational levels of employed males in nonwhite republics are generally higher than in the Russian Republic (which, containing half of the USSR population, stands here for whites at large). Significant increases

TABLE 10-8   **Comparative Trends in Urbanization, USSR Nationalities and Republics, 1959–85**

Republic	Percent Nationality Urban	Percent of Population of Republic Urban				
	1970	1959	1970	1979	1984	1985
Russian	68.0	52.4	62.3	69.3	72.2	72.6
Ukrainian	48.5	45.7	54.5	61.3	64.7	65.4
Byelorussian	43.7	30.8	43.4	55.1	60.9	62.0
Latvian	52.7	56.1	62.5	68.5	70.3	70.5
Armenian	64.8	50.0	59.5	65.8	67.3	67.6
Uzbek	24.9	33.6	36.6	41.2	42.3	41.9
Tadzhik	26.0	32.6	37.1	34.9	33.7	33.6
Kazakh	26.7	43.8	50.3	53.9	56.6	57.1
Turkmen	31.0	46.2	47.9	48.0	47.4	47.4

Sources: Column 1: *Itogi Vsesoiuznoi Perepisi Naseleniia 1970*, vol. 4 (Moscow, 1973), pp. 20–42; Columns 2–6: *Narkhoz*, various years.

occurred in both regions in the 1970s but the nonwhite educational advantage remained stable. The tables demonstrate, however, a remarkable concentration of educated males in nonwhite republics in activities that presumably require the least human capital. Among RSFSR male collective farmers, 24.1 percent had higher and secondary education in 1979; in the same year their counterparts in the Uzbek SSR had 58.0 percent with college degrees and high school diplomas. Urban employed males in the RSFSR were more highly educated than rural; in all Central Asian republics there was little urban/rural difference for men with college degrees, while there were actually proportionally *more* males with high school diplomas among rural workers, and among collective farmers of all peoples, than among urban employed males. On this score significant progress was made between 1970 and 1979, so that seemingly much of the increment in educated males was absorbed by collective farms.[29]

Both Tables 6 and 7 clearly indicate that most of the advances in education in Central Asian republics were made by individuals who perform the most menial jobs, mostly in agriculture and activities related to its products.

Table 8 demonstrates not only a low level of urbanization of nonwhites relative to whites (roughly half on the average) but also a remarkable recent pattern of de-urbanization, or ruralization, in three nonwhite republics: Uzbek, Tadzhik, and Turkmen.

These three republics are the most homogeneous nonwhite republics, which

TABLE 10-9   **Migration Patterns, USSR Republics, 1959–69, 1970–74, 1975–78, and 1979–83**

Republics	Net Migration (in thousands)			
	1959–69	1970–74	1975–78	1979–83
Russian	−1745	−408	+695	+735
Ukrainian	+429	+228	+39	−7
Byelorussian	−319	−51	−85	−5
Latvian	+122	+76	+27	+42
Estonian	+72	+41	+19	+24
Armenian	+124	+66	+50	−41
Uzbek	+364	+118	+123	−163
Tadzhik	+129	+27	−1	−53
Kazakh	+703	−16	−469	−269
Azerbaidzhan	−44	−48	−7	−109
Kirgiz	+134	0	−78	−83
Turkmen	+20	+27	−30	−31

Methodology and Sources: See Appendix 1.

implies that slightly increasing urbanization in other nonwhite areas is probably due to white migration to the cities. This unique pattern of "ruralization"[30] conforms to the above pattern of occupational distribution and the nonwhite preference for agriculture. (The ruralization statistics may seem to be due partly to high population growth in rural relative to urban areas, but this did not prevent net urbanization in the past.) Two other major trends fostered this ruralization. One is that rural migration to the cities is not for work but for education. This is temporary; after graduation rural youths return home with college degrees to take menial agricultural jobs. The numbers of urban immigrants and outmigrants thus cancel each other.[31] The second trend is de-urbanization resulting from the fact that whites in nonwhite areas, who are mostly urban, have been leaving these regions.[32] This reduces the population growth of nonwhite cities and leads to the decline of their share in their republics' population.

Thus nonwhite areas have become even more ethnically homogeneous and the demographic split of the USSR has widened. Table 9 presents migration patterns in the USSR for the last twenty-five years.

The table shows that since the mid-1970s in the Kazakh and Kirgiz republics and since the late 1970s in the rest of the nonwhite areas, the literal territorial separation between the two segments of the USSR population has become a major trend.

Its causes lie in the expansion of nonwhite private agricultural markets and concomitant improvements in the economic status of nonwhites relative to whites.[33] Reliable estimates of relative standards of living are notoriously difficult to make; some Soviet sources place nonwhite living standards at 25 to 35 percent above those of whites.[34] Contrary to that, the consensus in Western literature is that white living standards are higher than those of nonwhites by 25 to 35 percent on a per capita basis.[35] But Western estimates are made using uniform state retail prices.

Of course, participation in socialized agriculture is a uniform condition for having the privileges of private plots. But private farming ("personal subsidiary plots") was explicitly established along ethnic lines with special preferences to nonwhite populations.[36] As a result, of all Soviet peoples, nonwhites in their republics gained unique opportunities: the acquisition of unrestricted land *entitlements* without having to save for lands purchase; an opportunity to invest funds in virtually unrestricted livestock accumulation; the production of highly priced output; and the accumulation of household wealth without real competition. Whereas in most white areas both the possession of land and livestock ownership on the private plots declined steadily in the 1960s, 1970s, and 1980s, it significantly expanded in Central Asia and Kazakhstan.[37]

One has to emphasize the impact of private plots specifically in the household *wealth-generating* strategy and in fertility decision making. Private plot entitlements are important in one respect because they generate higher flows of household income and allow higher child expenditures relative to other households within the same area. This is the case in all Soviet regions,[38] and private plots by themselves do not make nonwhites in their republics behave in any special way. Of much more importance is the emergence of a self-contained economic system in Central Asia and other nonwhite republics, where private farming has become the prevailing labor market for nonwhite offspring. The internal abundance of inputs and the nonparticipation of outsiders in this process has secured the transmission of unique advantages and of accumulated assets from parents to children.

The stock of inheritable wealth rather than income flows is the main advantage of this system in a country where most property rights are banned. With or without education and other opportunity-creating inputs, children in this case do not have to compete on outside markets. Young nonwhite households are entitled to what in Soviet conditions is an estate. This multigenerational wealth, based on entitlements, does not dilute with high fertility because the grown-up children receive their own private plots from socialized sources. Under those conditions, education comes as a free good and parents do not have to spend more per child to ensure better education for a more competitive future. Annual per capita income flows may still be lower in nonwhite areas than in industrial white regions (depending on the estimate of market prices of agricultural produce), but parents can secure their children's economic mobility not via income but via wealth.[39]

High nonwhite fertility, low use of educational gains in urban occupations, high concentration in small-scale agriculture, de-urbanization, etc., are not signs of "backwardness," "underdevelopment," "lack of modernization," etc. Rather these are well-calculated "un-modernization"– the substitution of a superior wealth-generating primary economic activity (family farm) for the income/consumption economic mode of industrial wage labor, which produces an inferior life under Soviet conditions.

Demographic Expansion and Demographic Depression. I argued that in voluntarily separated spheres, a small price needs to be paid to make children competitive and successful while high opportunities are provided for them. Very high fertility of nonwhites in their republics should follow from these conditions, and it does. But changes in positions of young parents and their children relative to those of older parents and their children should also affect terms of competition and thus influence fertility trends.

Of various intergenerational income transfer programs, such as seniority wage scales and housing distribution, public education, etc., the social security system is the most obvious example. Public pensions not only transfer income from the working age population and the children to the elderly, but, more significantly for fertility effects, make interfamily transfers from young parents to older parents. Under undistorted life cycle conditions, individuals aged over 40 would support their retired parents. Under the social security system, individuals aged 16 to 40 relieve individuals aged over 40 from this burden and thus allow the latter to invest more in their adolescent children.[40] In order to secure their own small children's competitiveness, younger actual and potential parents aged 20 to 40 have to catch up with the per child investment of the middle-aged parents. To achieve this, younger parents inevitably have to reduce the number of their children. This produces a reversed pyramid of cohorts of parents and children. Under these conditions fertility can indeed decline significantly below the level of replacement of current generations, i.e., below 2.1 to 2.2 children born per average woman.[41]

This microeconomic system, common to the USSR and Western industrial countries, is in my view the most important factor of fertility decline below replacement among the majority of Soviet whites. Table 10 demonstrates that the RSFSR, the Ukraine, and Latvia now have had at least fifteen years of implied negative growth rates; other white republics either have entered this stage since the late 1970s or are approaching it.

Russian fertility is the lowest, fluctuating between 1.7 and 1.9 births per woman and 0.8 and 0.9 Net Reproduction Rates (NRRs). This implies highly negative growth in the near future, and the fear of the forthcoming Russian depopulation is widespread in the Soviet demographic literature.[42] Actually, in the core areas of Central Russia, population has been already "dying out" for some fifteen years[43] as it has been recently in West Germany, Austria, Denmark, Belgium, Iceland, Hungary, and northern and central Italy. This simply means that the number of deaths in the aging and low fertility population exceeded the number of births. And this is not a short-term anomaly, but the forthcoming trend for all populations with a sufficiently long record of below replacement fertility.

Interfamily transfer programs influenced the new trends among the nonwhite populations of Central Asia and Caucasus. Table 10 shows that Kazakh ethnic fertility began to decline rapidly from very high levels after the late 1950s whereas among Central Asian whites it continued to increase until the mid-1970s.[44] There are no cultural and religious differences between Kazakhs and other Central Asians. A naive notion that whites who moved to the Kazakh Republic in the 1950s taught nonwhites to use birth control devices (while Uzbeks were left uneducated in their homogeneous republic) can be rejected outright. First, birth control is a matter of individual choice based on economic incentives. The demand for information is high when decision to control is made; if costs of search are high and supplies of contraceptives are low, irregular, and of poor quality as in the Soviet Union, abortion serves as a substitute. Second, whites themselves have a poor knowledge of contraceptives and substitute abortions for them.[45] Third, traditional Islamic populations have used folk birth control methods since the Middle Ages.[46]

A serious explanation comes from an analysis of economic changes. After the Virgin Lands Program started in the Kazakh Republic in 1954, many collective farms were transformed into state farms. State farms differed from collective farms in three crucial respects: the members' income was higher, state farm children were registered as workers and thus had advantages in attaining higher education, and state farmers received social security. The combination of these inputs not only reduced the fertility of *young* state farm parents as they were taxed to transfer income to middle-aged parents, but also reduced even more the fertility of young *collective* farmers because their children were at a competitive disadvantage relative to state farm children.[47]

When in 1964 the social security system was expanded to the collective farm population, fertility control began to be practiced and fertility reduction started

TABLE 10-10   **Total Fertility Rates, Net Reproduction Rates, and Intrinsic Growth Rates (per 1,000), USSR, Republics and Nationalities, 1958/59–1982/83**

	Republic			Nationality		
	1958/59	*1974/75*	*1982/83*	*1958/59*	*1974/75*	*1982/83*
USSR						
TFR	2.810	2.407	2.367	2.810	2.407	2.367
NRR	1.271	1.110	1.080	1.271	1.110	1.080
IGR	8.9	3.9	2.8	8.9	3.9	2.8
Russian						
TFR	2.626	1.993	2.050	2.637	1.891	1.886
NRR	1.187	0.919	0.935	0.192	0.873	0.860
IGR	6.4	−3.1	−2.5	6.5	−5.1	−5.6
Ukrainian						
TFR	2.296	2.044	2.037	2.714	2.011	2.087
NRR	1.038	0.943	0.929	1.227	0.928	0.952
IGR	1.4	−2.2	−2.7	7.6	−2.8	−1.8
Byelorussian						
TFR	2.795	2.198	2.092	2.717	2.307	2.196
NRR	1.264	1.014	0.954	1.228	1.064	1.002
IGR	8.7	0.5	−1.7	7.6	2.3	0.1
Latvian						
TFR	1.938	1.981	2.028	2.019	2.179	2.231
NRR	0.876	0.914	0.925	0.913	1.005	1.017
IGR	−4.9	−3.3	−2.9	−3.4	0.2	0.6
Armenian						
TFR	4.730	2.819	2.352	6.059	3.382	2.822
NRR	2.139	1.300	1.073	2.740	1.560	1.287
IGR	28.2	9.7	2.6	37.3	16.5	9.4

among *young* Central Asian nonwhites due to the same incentives.[48] Table 10 captures an extremely rapid fertility decline, by almost 20 percent within eight years, among Uzbeks from 7.4 births per woman in 1975 to 6.1 in 1983. Similar trends can be observed among other Central Asian nonwhites. Social security is a very effective contraceptive indeed, especially if assisted by abortions on demand.[49]

However, fertility is still very high among Soviet nonwhites, and the high concentration of private plots is the main influencing variable for this. The positive effect of reduced competition for children's economic mobility offsets the fertility-depressing effects of involuntary intergenerational transfers. As a net result, one can find in Table 10 Total Fertility Rates (TFRs) such as 6.1 among

TABLE 10-10 **continued**

	Republic			Nationality		
	1958/59	*1974/75*	*1982/83*	*1958/59*	*1974/75*	*1982/83*
Uzbek						
TFR	5.044	5.678	4.650	5.745	7.439	6.091
NRR	2.280	2.620	2.121	2.597	3.432	2.778
IGR	30.5	35.7	27.8	35.4	45.7	37.8
Tadzhik						
TFR	3.926	6.265	5.473	4.683	7.975	7.114
NRR	1.775	2.890	2.496	2.118	3.679	3.245
IGR	21.3	39.3	33.9	27.8	48.2	43.6
Kazakh						
TFR	4.462	3.299	2.927	7.228	5.077	4.492
NRR	2.018	1.522	1.315	3.268	2.342	2.049
IGR	26.0	15.6	10.7	43.9	31.5	26.6
Azerbaidzhan						
TFR	5.005	3.949	3.009	6.537	5.133	3.912
NRR	2.263	1.821	1.372	2.956	2.368	1.784
IGR	30.2	22.2	11.7	40.1	31.9	21.4
Turkmen						
TFR	5.123	5.769	4.755	6.071	7.938	6.656
NRR	2.316	2.661	2.168	2.745	3.662	3.036
IGR	31.1	36.3	28.7	37.4	48.1	41.1

Sources: TFR by republics: *Vestnik Statistiki*, various years; TFR by nationalities: author's estimates based on various sources described in the text; NRR: calculated on the basis of survivorship ratios to the mean age of childbearing found in Soviet sources (see, e.g., footnote 7); IGR: calculated as log (NRR)/mean age of childbearing.

Uzbeks and Kirgiz, 6.6 among Turkmen, and 7.1 among Tadzhiks in 1982–83. NRRs were 2.8, 3.0, and 3.2, respectively, which is exactly the population increase in each generation (that is, in this case, each twenty-eight to twenty-nine years) under conditions of age stability. If one compares these numbers with 0.9 among Russians and Ukrainians, the demographic split and the country's demographic future is displayed. Indeed, implied growth rates of Central Asian nonwhites are about 4 percent per annum. This means doubling each seventeen years. Even if nonwhite fertility declines steeply to 4.0 births per woman in the 1990s as we predict, the *implied* growth rate would still mean doubling each thirty-two years after stabilization.

The growth implications of simultaneous white demographic depression and nonwhite demographic expansion are presented in Tables 11 and 12.

These tables also lead us from simple population distributions by racial and

TABLE 10-11   USSR Population by Ethnic Groups, Adjusted for Nationality Reidentification, 1959–2100 *(in thousands)*

	1959	1970	1979	1984	2000	2050	2100
Whites	181554	202758	213991	219338	224738	190657	136326
Slavs	161023	179054	188793	193185	196273	159021	106810
Main Slavs	159279	177054	186907	191260	194332	157303	105440
Russians	114113	126363	133487	136749	138828	107233	64881
Ukrainians	37252	41541	43564	44470	45215	40417	32669
Byelorussians	7913	9328	9855	10040	10287	9651	7890
Baltic People	4714	5259	5531	5667	5901	5775	5057
Ugro-Finns	3277	3683	3791	3817	3815	3351	2633
Southern Whites	8521	10536	11885	12696	14866	19091	18909
Armenians	2786	3607	4314	4813	6446	10286	10805
Other Whites	3887	4072	3830	3812	3714	3251	2765
Jews	2267	2150	1810	1765	1624	1250	949
Nonwhites	27062	38596	47663	53704	73418	141202	157727
Uzbeks	6015	9212	12452	14098	24464	64198	75784
Tadzhiks	1396	2181	2972	3605	6043	18831	22473
Kazakhs	3621	5372	6583	7294	8850	11020	10597
Azeri	2939	4368	5385	5963	7284	9128	8785
Kirgiz	968	1502	1939	2248	3239	5588	6253
Turkmen	1001	1530	2029	2389	3629	7683	9573
Tatars	4967	6171	6838	7211	7848	8371	7724
Misc.	209	365	780	811	883	919	837
Total:	208826	241720	262436	273854	299041	332780	294892

Note: Data is derived from the 1970 and 1979 censuses (ethnic distribution by all territorial units) and adjusted for ethnic reidentification.

Sources: 1959: *Itogi Vsesoiuznoi Perepisi Naseleniia 1970*, vol. 4 (Moscow, 1973), pp. 9–11 (without adjustment for ethnic reidentification); 1970–2100: Mikhail S. Bernstam, "The Demography of Soviet Ethnic Groups in World Perspective", *The Last Empire: Nationalities and the Soviet Future*, ed. Robert Conquest (Stanford, Calif.: Hoover Institution Press, 1986), tables 1 and 2.

TABLE 10-12 Ethnic Groups as Shares of the Total USSR Population, 1917–2100 (percentages)

	1917	1959 Reported	1970 Reported	1979 Reported	1979 Adjusted	1984 Projected	2000 Projected	2050 Projected	2100 Projected
Whites	87.94	86.94	84.19	81.95	81.54	80.10	75.15	57.30	46.23
Slavs	74.51	77.11	74.62	72.68	71.94	70.54	65.63	47.79	36.22
Main Slavs	67.75	76.27	73.98	72.10	71.22	69.84	64.99	47.27	35.76
Russians	45.38	54.65	53.37	52.35	50.86	49.94	46.42	32.22	22.00
Ukrainians	18.36	17.84	16.86	16.14	16.60	16.24	15.12	12.15	11.08
Byelorussians	4.01	3.79	3.74	3.61	3.76	3.66	3.44	2.90	2.68
Baltic People	2.71	2.26	2.11	2.02	2.11	2.07	1.97	1.74	1.71
Southern Whites	3.23	4.08	4.32	4.46	4.53	4.64	4.97	5.74	6.41
Nonwhites	11.44	12.96	15.69	17.81	18.16	19.61	24.55	42.43	53.49
Main Nonwhites	6.13	7.72	10.02	12.05	12.07	13.44	18.12	35.93	46.64
Uzbeks	1.16	2.88	3.80	4.75	4.74	5.44	8.18	19.29	25.70
Tadzhiks	0.29	0.67	0.88	1.10	1.13	1.32	2.02	5.66	7.62
Kazakhs	2.78	1.73	2.19	2.50	2.51	2.66	2.96	3.31	3.59

Sources: Data for 1917: Mikhail S. Bernstam, "The Demography of Soviet Ethnic Groups in World Perspective," in *The Last Empire: Nationalities and the Soviet Future*, ed. Robert Conquest (Stanford, Calif.: Hoover Institution Press, 1986), tables 1 and 2; for 1959 and 1970: *Itogi Vsesoiuznoi Perepisi Naseleniia 1970*, vol. 4 (Moscow, 1973), pp. 9–11 (without adjustment for ethnic reidentification); for 1979 (reported): *Chislennost i Sostav Naseleniia SSR. Po Dannym Vsesoiuznoi Perepisi Naseleniia 1979 Goda* (Moscow, 1984), pp. 71–73; for 1979 (adjusted) and 1984–2100: Bernstam.

FIGURE 10-1   **Population of the USSR by Major Ethnic Groups, 1917–2100** *(in millions)*

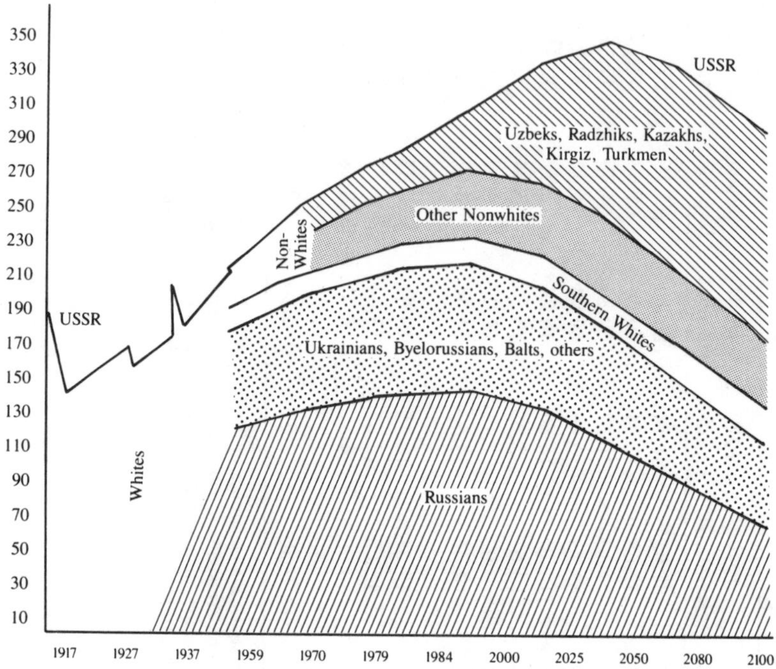

Sources: Tables 10-13 and 10-14.

ethnic groups to the murky waters of population projections. Although demographic projections are somewhat safer than economic ones (fewer variables are involved), they still are no more than mechanical exercises under given assumptions. If we assume that every single Soviet ethnic group will experience a decline in its rates of natural increase at the same speed as it had in the 1960s and 1970s, then Tables 11 and 12 show what may happen in the years 2000, 2050, and 2100. In seven words: the USSR will be a different country.

It will be a country with rapidly declining white population from the mid-1990s on (that is, very soon) and a continuously growing nonwhite population, albeit one gradually losing its growth momentum. It will be a country that will increase from 279 million in 1986 to 299 million in 2000, reach 333 million in 2050, and drop to 295 million in 2100. A country in which the whites' share will decline from 80 percent in 1984 to 46 percent in 2100 while the nonwhites' share will increase from 20 percent in 1984 to 53 percent in 2100. In the year 2100, the largest nationality will not be the Russians; it will be the Uzbeks, constituting 26 percent of the total population. More importantly, already in the early twenty-first century the country will be transformed from the "one majority/many minorities" structure to the "many minorities" structure. This may or may not provide a ground for increased competition of special interest groups. At any rate, the split in demographic and economic trends between whites and nonwhites will materialize in the numerical ethnic split of the country by the middle of the twenty-first century.

The word "majority" was used in quotation marks because the Russians, if adjusted for assimilation (nationality reidentification from one census to another), are no longer the arithmetic majority in the Soviet Union. In the 1979 census the Russians constituted 137.4 million or 52.4 percent of the USSR population. Since some members of minority nationalities residing in the RSFSR listed themselves as Russians, an adjustment from the natural increase data yields 133.5 million or 50.9 percent of the total.[50] In 1984, by my calculations, the Russians ceased to remain the majority and became a plurality at 136.7 million or 49.9 percent. They will begin a natural decline in the mid-1990s, reaching 138.8 million in 2000, that is, 46.4 percent of the total; then decline to 107.2 million in 2050 and to 64.9 million in 2100, that is, 32.2 percent and 22.0 percent of the USSR population, respectively. (Again, one must repeat, these are only projections. Their only advantages over mere guesswork are their internal consistency in complying with a set of assumptions and their reliance on the analysis of past trends.) Figure 1 illustrates the derived and projected long-term trends in the USSR population distribution by ethnic groups.

Labor Supply Depression. As Tables 5 and 11 show, the fastest growing population of the USSR has not been the Tadzhiks. It has been the old age social security recipients who increased from 16.0 million in 1966 (after extension of the system to collective farmers) to 37.2 million in 1984, that is, by 4.7 percent a year. Their growth slowed down in the 1980s, but, as the population will be aging, the ratio of retirees to workers will be steadily on the rise. This is a social security phenomenon familiar to all Western countries. According to our projections in Tables 13 and 14, based on the derived Soviet mortality schedules, the number of "old age persons" (defined for the USSR as males aged 60 and over, and females aged 55 and over) will increase by almost 40 percent in twenty years.

Within the same period, the proportion of the old age persons will increase from 15.5 percent to 19.1 percent in the USSR and from 16.4 percent to 21.4 percent in the RSFSR. A more relevant measure of dependency is the number of persons of working ages (16 to 59 for males and 16 to 54 for females) per old

TABLE 10-13 USSR Age Composition and Labor Force, 1979, 1984, 1989, 1994, and 1999

Age Group	1979			1984 – Model Three			1984 – Model Five		
	Total	Males	Females	Total	Males	Females	Total	Males	Females
0–14	64926.8	32929.7	31997.1	67668.8	34035.1	33633.6	67963.1	34342.8	33620.2
Labor force (16–59, males; 16–54, females)	151611.2	75902.2	75709.0	157665.7	81550.6	76115.1	156730.0	80921.1	75808.9
Old age persons (60+, males; 55+, females)	40599.6	10496.0	30103.6	44329.6	10605.0	33724.6	44982.1	10936.3	34045.8
Workers per old age person	3.73			3.56			3.48		

Age Group	1989 – Model Five			1994 – Model Five			1999 – Model Five		
	Total	Males	Females	Total	Males	Females	Total	Males	Females
0–14	70283.9	35329.6	34954.4	70523.7	35301.0	35222.6	68300.8	34159.9	34140.9
Labor force (16–59, males; 16–54, females)	159299.1	82233.7	77065.4	161793.2	83881.6	77911.6	166631.9	85360.1	81271.8
Old age persons (60+, males; 55+, females)	49716.8	13751.7	35965.1	54179.5	15994.7	38184.8	56569.1	18381.1	38188.0
Workers per old age person	3.20			2.99			2.95		

Methodology and Sources: See Appendix 1. Numbers may not add to totals due to rounding.

TABLE 10-14 **RSFSR Age Composition and Labor Force, 1979, 1984, 1989, 1994, and 1999**

Age Group	1979 – Model Five			1984 – Model Five			1989 – Model Five		
	Total	Males	Females	Total	Males	Females	Total	Males	Females
0–14	29741.7	15098.2	14643.5	31220.1	15769.9	15450.1	31814.8	15953.7	15861.0
Labor force (16–59, males; 16–54, females)	82713.8	41432.4	41281.4	83872.0	43508.1	40363.9	82956.6	43055.3	39901.3
Old age persons (60+, males; 55+, females)	22477.5	5404.8	17072.7	25124.9	5678.0	19446.9	27910.6	7370.5	20540.1
Workers per old age person	3.68			3.33			2.97		

Age Group	1994 – Model Five			1999 – Model Five		
	Total	Males	Females	Total	Males	Females
0–14	31209.1	15559.7	15649.5	29723.2	14803.0	14920.1
Labor force (16–59, males; 16–54, females)	82282.2	42867.5	39414.7	82883.8	42562.9	40320.9
Old age persons (60+, males; 55+, females)	30325.7	8703.4	21622.3	31307.4	9961.7	21345.7
Workers per old age person	2.71			2.65		

Methodology and Sources: See Appendix 1. Number may not add to totals due to rounding.

age persons. This will decline from 3.73 in 1979 to 2.95 in 1999 in the USSR and from 3.68 in 1979 to 2.65 in 1999 in the RSFSR.

This is a very high dependency burden compared to the United States. In the latter, according to the middle series of official projections, the number of persons of working ages (18 to 64) per old age person (aged 65 and over) will decline from 5.40 in 1985 to 4.96 in 2000.[51] There will be almost twice as many working age persons to support a retiree in the United States as in the USSR by the end of the century, yet even this is considered to be a high burden.[52]

To be sure, many Soviet persons of pension ages continue to work, but they still receive their retirement benefits. Also, the age of retirement is lower in the USSR relative to the United States but so is life expectancy, especially among males.

The main Soviet labor supply problem will come from the increasing scarcity of the working age population in white areas where the bulk of Soviet GNP is now produced. The problem, however, is not numerical manpower shortages per se but the scarcity of workers relative to industrial capacity in many white areas. This has already led to the abandonment of unfinished construction and unused machinery worth billions of rubles.[53] The problem is intensified by the low quality and productivity of labor. According to the USSR Central Statistical Administration, manual labor has recently performed 40.1 percent of total work in manufacturing, 57.5 percent in construction, and 46.0 percent in mining.[54] Moreover, in 1984, turnover constituted 19.3 percent of the total labor force[55] or, if one makes an adjustment for agriculture, over 23.5 percent of the non-agricultural labor force and at least 25 percent of industrial manpower. One can appreciate the dependence of Soviet economy on demographic trends in numerical manpower.

The decline in the growth of labor happened by the early 1980s, and the manpower increments continue to decline.[56] My projections in Table 13 show that only 2.6 million more workers can be expected in the period 1984–88 relative to 5.1 million in 1979–83. Another increase of 2.5 million is projected for 1989–93, and a seeming recovery in terms of the 4.8 million worker increment in 1994–98. All these increases are, in a sense, illusory. In reality, labor-intensive Soviet industry has entered a protracted period of labor supply depression with immense economic consequences.

The increases are illusory because the entire source of additional manpower is from the nonwhite republics. At best, these additions will be largely absorbed by the service sector, trade, and various branches not involved in manufacturing industries. It is even more likely that labor increments will concentrate in nonwhite agriculture and private plots. One cannot reasonably expect any nonwhite labor immigration to the labor-demanding white areas, although white outmigration from Central Asia and Kazakhstan will continue on a small scale.

Table 14 shows that the RSFSR will suffer an absolute labor force decline throughout the rest of the century without a recovery. Due to the combination of high mortality and two decades of low fertility, the number of new entrants will be smaller than the number of workers of large cohorts departing via death or retirement.[57] The total number of persons of working ages will decline in the RSFSR by 0.8 million in 1984–88, and by 0.7 million in 1989–93, and increase by 0.6 million in 1994–98. The number of working males will decline by 0.4 million in 1984–88, by 0.2 million in 1989–93, and by 0.3 million in 1994–98. The changes are small but the ending of labor force increases should, under Soviet labor market conditions, portend the stagnation of the entire Soviet industrial growth that for decades has been based largely on the growth of labor inputs.

Finally, it appears that the new Soviet policy of technological innovation is a response to the forthcoming manpower crisis. For Soviet leaders technology has become a magic wand that will compensate for depleting supplies of labor. A recent Soviet estimate is that new technology will relieve from manufacturing and retrain 13 to 19 million Soviet workers, that is, 10 to 15 percent of the Soviet labor force.[58] Yet if labor intensity is not reduced quickly, the Soviet Union may soon face a "supply-side" industrial depression and economic stagnation.

Some Unscientific Policy-Related Remarks

Western observers of Soviet demographic trends, searching for U.S. policy avenues, have concentrated on the phenomenon of the demographic expansion of the nonwhite population. The expansion has been analyzed assuming that this region is like a part of the Third World, with high fertility and little economic development. There has also been interest in the fundamentalist religious customs and the possible spillover from this fundamentalism to political activity. Correspondingly, a claim of the growing South on the wealth of the industrial North has been usually envisaged. Nonwhites have been seen as future destructors of the Soviet empire and thus as a target of Western opportunity. Our analysis suggests that such a strategy is implausible. Nonwhites, of all people, are the chief benefactors of the status quo. Their demographic expansion, while eventually changing the ethnic makeup of the Soviet Union, cannot be immediately—or perhaps ever—translated into political outcomes. The implications for the empire's sustenance will depend on the changes in relative economic positions of white and nonwhite populations. Some members of the political elite, intellectuals and students, urban middle class, etc., may, from their group interest perspective, dream about socialism with a local face. For the populace, the opportunity costs of sedition would be too high. Nonwhites have established their separate economic markets on which they have found a satisfactory mode of development. Their fertility will be further reduced and their highly educated offspring will become a sophisticated managerial stratum on family farms. Islamic religious practice will be an income-elastic luxury good. In search for policy options, one should not waste opportunities looking in that direction.[59]

The forgotten whites, the Russians above all, are experiencing a protracted demographic depression with declining life expectancy and below replacement fertility. Not only are some of the intellectual elite extremely sensitive to this trend, but this is a prime issue of the populist agenda that can unite intellectuals with the populace. It may give intellectuals a chance to contribute something good and relevant to their poor country for the first time in history. Also, the rising new generation of the military is likely to embrace the issue of demographic depression. The labor supply depression and a stagnating industrial development provide motives for the military to challenge the ideological and political leadership. There are also some scattered indications that the military is sensitive to the forthcoming depopulation of their kind. The demographic agenda might even become the basis for a coup.

As far as Western policymakers are concerned, they can obtain large political gains at very low cost. They can establish a symbolic alliance with the victims of Soviet demographic development. One cannot imagine a stronger political position vis-à-vis another nation than taking a stand in defense of those literally dying of the industrial and economic policies of their government. There is nothing on earth that the Soviet government could successfully argue in response to such a Western stance. It would find such a situation unbearable in dealing with its population.

Appendix 1

Estimates of Life Expectancies and Projections of the Current Age Groups

We explored two possibilities of making estimates of life expectancy in the absence of the direct official data. We shall use what is available: cross-sectional data on crude and age-standardized mortality, age and sex composition, the number of births, migration, indicators of living standards, and general population data.

The first possibility is to predict the unknown values of life expectancies. This can be done by regressing the known values of life expectancies for both sexes against crude death rates, age-standardized death rates, sex ratios, and various economic variables reflecting living standards. This method will simultaneously provide an analysis of exogenous factors influencing the mortality changes.[1]

We estimated the following long-form and short-form relationships for twenty-four observations (republics and the USSR) for 1958–59, 1969–70, 1974–75, and 1978–79, for which we could derive the values of life expectancies:

1. $oe_0 = -58.468 + 263.74 \exp(1/m_s^2) + 145.40 \exp(1/m_c^2) + 0.28278 \ W$

$-318.38 \exp(1/H^2) - 3.0807 \log N + 1.6110 \log B + 5.7230 \log T$

$$R^2 = 0.921 \qquad \text{standard error is 0.283 years}$$

2. $\log oe_0 = 0.29670 + 3.9398 \exp(1/m_c^2) - 6.5394/H^2$

$$R^2 = 0.605 \qquad \text{standard error is 0.009,}$$

where oe_0 is life expectancy at birth, m_c is crude death rate, m_s is age-standardized death rate, W is the proportion of females in the population, H is urban living space per capita urban population, N is the number of nurses per 10,000 population, B is the number of hospital beds per 10,000 population, and T is the time variable (59, 70, etc.). The data on economic variables was derived from *Narkhoz*, various years.

The short-form equation, despite its high standard error (high, that is, as a difference of two exponents), was necessary for years after 1980 for which we do not have the data on age-standardized death rates. Actually, the equation is not deficient if one considers that only crude death rates and urban living space per capita could determine 60.5 percent of the variation in life expectancies. In Table 3 the values of e_0 derived by the short-form equation are adjusted to correspond to the values derived by the better-fitted long form.

The second possibility is to create tentative model life tables that would yield, among other things, expectancies of life at birth. The mathematical rule is that once we know the age composition for the initial year, the number of births for all years under observation, the total number of the population in the final year adjusted for migration, and assume the fixed model mortality schedule (the model life table), only one life table level would yield the given final population number with the only possible age composition.

Since none of the four Coale-Demeny regional model life tables[2] that demographers usually employ in such exercises matches Soviet mortality schedules and life tables, we had to create Model Five (Model USSR). We smoothed the survivorship schedules between five-year intervals for sex-specific age groups (implied by the above referred actual age compositions). This was done in order to create the model survivorship schedules.

$$5P_x = 5L_{x+5}/5L_x$$

where $5P_x$ is the proportion of persons in a given five-year age group in the life table population who are alive five years later, $5L_x$ is the number of persons of the original cohort of 500,000 alive between ages x and $x+5$, and $5L_x +5$ is the number of the same persons alive between ages $x+5$ and $x+10$. Naturally, more refined techniques described in Coale-Demeny were employed for ages 0–1, 1–4, and over 75.

Relative to the same mortality levels in the Coale-Demeny regional models, the Soviet population has higher mortality at prime adult ages, probably due to industrial injuries, and, correspondingly, lower infant and old age mortality. The remarkably low old age mortality at the current levels of life expectancy is probably due to the anti-adverse selection by famines within the current old age cohorts.

After model $5P_x$ schedules were available, we employed the following procedures. First, the specific five-year age group survivorship schedule (life table $5P_x$) was derived for any given population by sex. This unique schedule had to fit the initial age composition at the beginning of the five-year interval (including five birth cohorts of the interim period) and the total population number at the end of the five-year interval.[3] That is, the fit was made so that

$$\text{Population}(t+5) = \Sigma 5Nx(t+5) = \Sigma 5Nx(t) \; 5Px$$

where $5Nx$ is the actual number of persons of a given sex in each five-year age group in the year (t) and five years later (t+5) including the number of births within the interval.[4] We repeat that only one $5Px$ schedule within a fixed model life table and only one $5Nx(t+5)$ distribution could satisfy these conditions. And only one level of life expectancy at birth exists for the given population under these conditions.

For the period 1979–83 we used for testing purposes both the Coale-Demeny Model Three (Model East) and our Model Five (Model USSR) deriving unique $5Px$ schedules in both.

Second, the stationary numbers of survivors (life table $5Lx$) and the numbers of person-years lived at age x and over (life table Tx) were derived by sequentially multiplying 500,000 by the $5Px$ schedule and by integrating the resulting $5Lx$ schedule into the Tx schedule. That is,

$$5L_0 = 500{,}000 \; 5P_0 \; ,$$
$$5L_5 = 5L_0 \; 5P^{(0-4)} \; ,$$
$$5L_{x+5} = 5L_x \; 5P_x \; , \; x=5, 10, \ldots, 100 \; ,$$
$$T_x = \Sigma 5L_x \; ,$$
$$T_0 = 5L_0 + \Sigma 5L_x .$$

Third, the values of life expectancy at birth were derived since

$$oe_0 = T_0/100000.$$

For the period 1979–83, Model Three yielded life expectancies at birth for the entire USSR population of 60.68 years for males and 74.22 for females; Model Five yielded 60.80 and 72.85 years, respectively. For the RSFSR in 1979–83 Model Three yielded 58.52 for males and 74.09 for females; Model Five yielded 59.34 for males and 72.74 for females. Male life expectancies at birth were lower and female higher according to the Coale-Demeny Model East relative to our Model USSR.

Note that all these results, including estimates of life expectancies and age compositions, are extremely sensitive to migration assumptions with regard to sex. We assumed proportional sex distribution of migrants. In reality there was a higher share of males among migrants.[5] Correspondingly, republics with positive net migration, such as the RSFSR, should in reality have somewhat lower male and somewhat higher female life expectancy than we estimated because we eliminated more females and did not eliminate enough males when we subtracted migrants. The opposite is the case for republics with negative net migration such as nonwhite republics.

After the 1979–83 5^Px schedules and the 1984 age composition by republics and the USSR were estimated, the conservative assumption was made that life expectancy will not decline further and that the constant 1979–83 5^Px schedules can be applied to project the population into 1989. The number of births was arbitrarily assumed to decline slightly. The assumption could not affect the labor force projections because all workers of the year 2000 have been born before 1984. Finally, simple five-year sex-specific age group projections were lexicographically made from 1984 to 1989, from 1989 to 1994, and from 1994 to 1999. Again,

$$\text{Population}(t+5) = \Sigma 5^Nx(t+5) = \Sigma 5^Nx(t) \, 5^Px.$$

Appendix 2

An Analysis of Mortality Determinants

Table A2.1 presents the econometric test of fundamental economic causes of Soviet mortality, using data by republics for various years in the period 1959–80.

The dependent variables are either life expectancy or the inverse value of crude death rate per 1,000. The latter is a proxy for the cross section of life expectancies in nonstationary populations. The test demonstrates an ambiguous influence of such widely discussed direct health inputs as the number of doctors, nurses, and hospital beds per capita. Doctors and nurses are collinear and substitutable. Soviet progress in expanding medical personnel and facilities did not make much difference in mortality trends. The analysis is reasonably complete because the "nesting" test with additional independent variables, such as per capita income, wages, social welfare expenditures, etc., did not produce changes in general statistics. The only independent variables that consistently influenced life expectancies in a predicted direction and with high statistical significance (always at the 1 percent level) were proxies for living and working conditions.[1] Theoretically, these were proxies for the current stages in urbanization and industrialization in the USSR. The proxy variable for living conditions is urban living space per capita urban population. The proxy variable for working conditions is the proportion of the population handicapped and belonging to families who lost their breadwinners. This proxy indirectly represents regional distribution and time increments of victims of industrial injuries.

As predicted, life expectancy is positively related to per capita urban living space,[2] and the proxy for life expectancy (inverse crude death rate) is negatively related to the proxy for working conditions and industrial injuries. Housing construction was thus a major factor in either increasing life expectancies or keeping them from falling even lower than they have. When elasticities are evaluated and recalculated into real values, we find that each additional square meter of per capita urban living space increases life expectancy at birth for both sexes for all population by 0.7 years. Per capita urban living space increased in the USSR from 9.9 sq. m. in 1966 to 13.8 sq. m. in 1985.[3] All other things being equal, life expectancy could have declined in the same period by another 2.7 years without urban housing construction. This is an additional contribution to life expectancy decline by negative factors such as adverse working conditions.

TABLE A2.1   **Determinants of Life Expectancy and Mortality, USSR and Union Republics, 1959–1980** *(selected years)*

	Dependent Variables		
	1	*2*	*3*
	Life Expectancy at Birth	*Inverse Crude Death Rate*	
Independent Variables			
Constant	−58.468	−0.068	0.808*
	(0.756)	(0.209)	(2.886)
Inverse crude death rate	145.400*		
	(4.390)		
Inverse standard death rate	263.740*	0.777*	0.815*
	(9.052)	(7.977)	(8.133)
Prop. females	0.283*	0.315	0.420*
	(2.820)	(1.200)	(3.058)
Prop. retirees		−0.711*	−0.916*
		(−8.020)	(−9.279)
Prop. handicapped and lost breadwinners		−1.300*	−1.539*
		(−4.116)	(−4.196)
Urban living space (inverse)	−318.380*		
	(−4.173)		
Doctors			0.063*
			(4.649)
Nurses	−3.081*	0.087*	
	(−2.579)	(5.091)	
Beds	1.611	−0.035**	0.023
	(1.644)	(−2.290)	(1.303)
Time	5.723*	0.040	0.025
	(2.709)	(0.895)	(0.513)
R̄²	0.921	0.935	0.931
N	24	48	48
Years	1959, 70, 79	1975, 78, 80	1975, 78, 80

Sources: See Section "The Quality of the Population" and Appendix 1.

  *Significant at the 1% level.
**Significant at the 5% level.

11

Nick Eberstadt

Health of an Empire:
Poverty and Social Progress
in the CMEA Bloc

The problem of human poverty is of considerable rhetorical and practical concern to contemporary Marxist-Leninist governments. Indeed, to no small degree, these states have defined their political and economic programs, their mode of social organization, and even their justification for existence in terms of their conception of the issue of poverty. The diverse writings of Marx are animated and unified by their attention to material deprivation and social injustices, and by their insistence that these failings were systemic — remediable only by the utter transformation of the system that had generated them. Lenin and his successors, who built upon the rubble of the Russian empire the first of the many state apparatuses explicitly committed to the interpretation and application of Marxism, made it their stated goal to construct and promote a system of governance that would serve human needs. The eradication of material poverty was professed to be integral to both the revolutionary struggle and the quest for "scientific" socialist construction. That sentiment informs Stalin's dictum that "human beings are the most important and decisive capital in the world," a statement that has been repeated with only slight modifications by Marxist-Leninist leaders around the globe for the past half-century.

The performance of Marxist-Leninist states in alleviating and overcoming mass poverty in the territories under their administration was understood, in some formulations of Marxist-Leninist thinking, to affect directly the "correlation of forces" between the "socialist" and "capitalist" camps, insofar as it would alter the confidence, the support, and ultimately the legitimacy of existing noncommunist states in the eyes of their own workers and voters. No less importantly, the elimination of undernutrition, ill health, illiteracy, and other manifestations of physical poverty would enhance national production and thereby accelerate socialist construction, as well as augment the resources the state might harness in either domestic campaigns or "international struggle."

Western nations have offered their own responses to the problem of poverty; these include the tradition of private and voluntarily supported charities, the evolution of the "welfare state," and the invention of a form of government-to-government resource transfers known as "foreign aid." Though there are similarities between Western and Marxist-Leninist strategies to alleviate poverty—not least because certain programs, actions, and approaches in the West have taken their cue from the Marxist-Leninist attacks on mass poverty—efforts in the two systems are governed by distinct and even incompatible conceptions of what "poverty" actually is. The attenuation of poverty, from the liberal Western standpoint, is linked to the extension of human choice. Planned progress in a socialist command economy, by contrast, is meant to occur precisely by subordinating these many individual choices to a single "social preference function" according to which resources are allocated and prices set.

Insofar as the liberal humanist and the Marxist-Leninist traditions express antithetical attitudes about the relationships between the individual, the society, and the state, it would seem unrealistic to expect from them a unanimity on what "progress against poverty" actually means.

These irresolvable philosophic differences do not vitiate the need for an understanding of the comparative performances of Marxist-Leninist states and noncommunist societies in their respective efforts to deal with poverty. For better or worse, this understanding is of operational significance because of the enduring contest between Marxism-Leninism and the political philosophies to which it is hostile. Intellectually, attempts to further such an understanding need not be doomed to complete frustration, for despite profound differences in their outlook on poverty, there are aspects of poverty that both communist and noncommunist states take to be meaningful—aspects, moreover, that are subject to unambiguous measurement and quantification.

Reliability and Usefulness of the Economic and Social Data Pertaining to Poverty

In theory, if not always in practice, central economic planning requires data. To meet the claims of efficacy made for them by their proponents, centrally planned economic systems actually require *more* and *better* data than market-oriented systems. This is because the political authorities of such a command economy assume direct responsibility for disseminating economic information and managing economic adjustments throughout society—functions that markets perform spontaneously and impersonally through the price mechanism. Soviet-style economies generate considerable amounts of data on economic and social conditions, some of which are published with regularity. Table 1 displays some of the indicators of macroeconomic performance for the 1970s and 1980s released by the USSR and some of its allies.

In an economy whose governance is explicitly predicated on and ideologically justified by the quest to meet human needs, one might expect that macroeconomic indicators would provide an especially accurate measure of the material prospects for the populations in question. In reality, such numbers provide at best an opaque lens through which to divine the material welfare of local populations. A number of problems come into play. Morris Bornstein has summarized some of them:

> First, statistics are not published on many internal and external economic activities of interest. Second, the statistical concepts used may give an incomplete picture of economic activity; for example, figures for national income in terms of net material product (NMP) exclude most services. Third, statistical methodologies—and changes in them—often are not fully explained. Fourth, administratively set non-scarcity prices are used to aggregate physical output series. Also, the uneven incidence of indirect taxes and subsidies on different categories of goods and services distorts the relative shares of different end-uses of national product. Commonly, the share of consumption is higher, and the shares of investment and defense are lower, at the officially established than at factor cost excluding indirect taxes and subsidies.[1]

Some other important limitations may also be noted. Soviet-style statistical systems are typically ill-equipped to measure activity in the informal or private sectors

TABLE 11.1   **Estimates and Indices Pertaining to Economic Performance for Certain Soviet Bloc Countries, 1971–83**

Country	1971–75	1976–80	1981–83
A) *Official Estimates of Changes in Net Material Product (percent per annum)*			
Bulgaria	7.8	6.1	4.0
Czechoslovakia	5.7	3.7	0.6
East Germany	5.4	4.1	3.2
Hungary	6.2	3.2	1.7
Poland	9.8	1.2	−4.3
Rumania	11.2	7.3	2.7
Unweighted average	7.1	4.3	1.3
USSR	5.6	4.2	3.7
B) *Official Estimates of Changes in Material Product Used for Consumption (percent per annum)*			
Bulgaria	7.0	4.0	4.2
Czechoslovakia	5.3	2.5	1.3
East Germany	5.3	2.5	1.6
Hungary	4.7	3.1	1.3
Poland	8.7	4.5	−4.7
Rumania	NA	7.1	0.7
Unweighted average	NA	4.2	0.7
USSR	5.8	4.7	2.6
C) *Official Estimates of Changes in Net Material Product Used for Net Investment (percent per annum)*			
Bulgaria	12.9	0.1	1.7
Czechoslovakia	8.4	1.4	−10.4
East Germany	2.9	3.0	−4.2
Hungary	8.1	−2.0	−11.1
Poland	18.1	−11.8	−9.8
Rumania	NA	6.6	−10.3
Unweighted average	NA	−0.5	−7.4
USSR	3.3	3.2	5.3

of the economy, even though such activity may be considerable and may bear directly on the material well-being of substantial fractions of the local population. Accounting procedures for the socialist sector of the planned economy are problematic when it comes to assessing net value added through economic activity rather than gross output, and tend to bias statistical series upwards as an economy becomes more complex. Time series data for a socialist planned economy are further affected by the problem of intertemporal indexation; the political

TABLE 11.1 **continued**

Country	1971–75	1976–80	1981–83

D) *Official Indices of Economic Change for Selected Soviet Bloc Countries (1970=100)*

	Net Social Product		Gross Industrial Output		Gross Turnover In Foreign Trade	
	1980	1984	1980	1984	1980	1984
Bulgaria	194	229	206	247	383	576
Czechoslovakia	159	169	124	191	300	423
East Germany	162	180	174	204	303	439
Hungary	159	174	159	169	386	570
Poland	169	157	207	202	385	415
Rumania	230	262	290	336	481	467
USSR	167	192	178	206	426	633
Cuba (1975=100)	125	186	176	245	364	537
Mongolia	195	259	234	359	345	600
Vietnam (1975=100)	114	154	113	199	160	233

Sources: Panels A–C: Jan Vanous, "Macroeconomic Adjustment in Eastern Europe in 1981–83: Response to Western Credit Squeeze and Deteriorating Terms of Trade with the Soviet Union," in *East European Economist: Slow Growth in the 1980s*, ed. JEC, U.S. Congress, vol. 2 (Washington, D.C.: U.S. Government Printing Office, 1985). Panel D: Sovet Economocheskoi Vzaimopomoshchi, *Statisticheskii Ezhegodnik Stran-1985* (Moscow: Finansy i Statistika, 1985).

administration of prices severely compromises any efforts to use price series to derive "real" changes in economic activity. Finally, as Charles Wolf has noted, the statistical publications of Soviet-style economic systems are often construed by leadership as an instrument of policy. Hence, they are subject to political "adjustments," as well as to concealments. Release of data, therefore, need not necessarily imply accuracy.[2]

In and of themselves, these problems greatly complicate any attempt by independent observers to understand the economic changes represented in statistics produced by Soviet-style economies. The degree of such difficulties may be suggested from situations in which Soviet bloc authorities and noncommunist agencies have access to roughly the same data, and employ the same theoretical constructs. Hungary, for example, is a member of the International Monetary Fund (IMF), and is obligated by its membership to share a wide array of financial and economic data with the Fund to which foreign agencies customarily have no access. By the reckoning of Hungarian authorities, "net material product" rose at a rate of 3.2 percent per year in the 1976–80 period. IMF data, however, indicate the rate of growth in "net material product" to have been 1.9 percent—two-fifths lower than Budapest's computation. By the same token, Hungarian accounts put the real rate of change in gross fixed investment over those same years at 2.4 percent while the IMF data suggest it was –0.2 percent—a difference not only in magnitude, but also in a sign![3]

Thus, while the official economic data in Table 1 are suggestive of economic slowdown in the Soviet bloc between the 1960s and the 1980s—a phenomenon accorded much discussion and analysis—they are not fully capable of portraying its dimensions accurately. Neither are they comparable with purportedly comparable economic statistics from noncommunist nations. They are still less useful in suggesting the impact that economic changes in these Marxist-Leninist countries have had on the material well-being of local populations.

This does not mean, however, that there are no data by which we can reliably assess changes in the material well-being of these populations. Alternative measures do exist.

The most important of these is arguably the health of the population. There are a number of reasons for using health conditions to compare poverty among nations. First, all modern states profess to champion improved health for their populations. Second, better health comes close to being a universally desired personal attribute; indifference to one's own health, or to the health of family and friends, is considered pathological in a wide array of cultures with little else in common. Third, various health characteristics may be objectively and precisely measured. As Oskar Morgenstern noted more than a generation ago, economic statistics are subject to an irreducible margin of uncertainty, owing to the specificities of the valuation process.[4] Demographic statistics circumvent that problem: in principle, there is no difficulty in determining whether a person is born, alive, or dead. The meaning of such determinations, moreover, is quite independent of the ideology or social system of the society such numbers depict. Fourth, health conditions are directly shaped by the social, economic, and political factors that prescribe the material limits of daily life, and thus reflect indirectly upon such things as nutrition, sanitation, public hygiene, education, housing, and the varieties of social stratification. Fifth, improved health, and the conditions that make it possible, are widely thought to be integral to the process of modern economic growth. Finally, good health is considered valuable by those who enjoy it. On the basis of some arbitrary but nonetheless plausible assumptions, Dan Usher calculated that the early postwar economic growth rate for Sri Lanka would be doubled by an imputation to account for the increased utility to consumers of their own extended lifespans.[5] (Indeed, it is almost tautological to assert that good health is an important component of one's quality of life or standard of living.)

To begin the measurement of poverty in the Soviet empire, we examine levels and trends in the national health of the Soviet bloc countries and compare these results with those achieved in noncommunist nations. This will include health conditions in the member states of the Council for Mutual Economic Assistance (CMEA, also known as COMECON). Full and active CMEA membership currently extends to Warsaw Pact Europe, Mongolia, Vietnam, and Cuba. This definition of the Soviet empire excludes many states dominated by, dependent upon, or apparently sympathetic to Soviet power: Afghanistan, Angola, Cambodia, Ethiopia, Laos, Libya, Mozambique, Nicaragua, North Korea, South Yemen, and Syria. There are several reasons for excluding these countries from our surveys. This diverse group includes governments of dubious Marxist-Leninist credentials, states with Marxist-Leninist aspirations that have yet to achieve mastery over the society and economy within their claimed territory, and regimes with minimal ability or inclination to release statistics pertaining to the lives of the peoples they rule. By contrast, full and active CMEA membership implies acceptance in Moscow of the state's interpretation of Marxism-Leninism, and requires, at least officially, the compilation and exchange of accurate data on economic and social conditions.

Eastern Europe and the USSR

The phenomenon of secular deterioration of health conditions in the Soviet Union is examined in detail in Mikhail Bernstam's chapter in this volume.[6] This deterioration is remarkable and anomalous for an industrial country during peacetime. Industrial development and conscious social policy have typically been expected to stabilize the death rate and to reduce it.

But the Soviet experience may no longer be unique. Mortality data from the USSR's Eastern European allies indicate that improvements in overall life expectancy came to a halt in many of these societies during the 1970s. In several, overall life expectancy has declined slightly in recent years. Although their patterns of mortality change are still distinct from the Soviet Union's in important ways, Warsaw Pact Europe is now evincing certain health trends that would be exceptional among Western nations, but that appear quite familiar in the Soviet context.

Like the USSR, Eastern Europe enjoyed rapid health improvements in the 1950s and early 1960s. During this period, the unweighted life expectancy at birth for the six Warsaw Pact nations (Bulgaria, Czechoslovakia, East Germany, Hungary, Poland, Romania) rose by nearly six years; in contrast, the life expectancy of the twelve European NATO states rose by less than three and a half years.[7] In the early 1950s, lifespans were nearly six years shorter in Warsaw Pact Europe than in NATO Europe; by the second half of the 1960s, that gap had been narrowed to two and a half years. Since that time, however, the gap has once again

TABLE 11-2   **Declines in Life Expectancy at Birth in Eastern Europe,**
              1964–84

Country	Period	Change in E_o (Years)	Change in Male E_o	Change in Female E_o
Bulgaria	1970–80	−0.2	−0.7	+0.3
Czechoslovakia	1964–83	−0.1	−0.9	+0.7
Hungary	1972–83	−0.1	−1.8	+0.4
Poland	1975/78–84	−0.3	−0.5	0
Rumania	1976/78–81	−0.2	−0.6	+0.2

Sources: Bulgaria: United Nations, *World Population Trends, Population and Development Interrelation and Population Policies: 1983 Monitoring Report Volume 1* (New York: United Nations, 1985). Czechoslovakia: United Nations, *Demographic Yearbook 1969* (New York: United Nations, 1970); *Statisticka Rocenka 1985* (Prague: Federalny Statisticky Urad, 1985). Hungary: *Demografia Evkonyv 1983* (Budapest: Kozponti: Statisztikai Hivatal, 1984). Poland: *Rocznik Statystyczny 1985* (Warsaw: Glowny Urzad Statystyczny, 1985). Rumania: United Nations, *Demographic Yearbook 1983* (New York: United Nations, 1985). World Health Organization, *World Health Statistics Annual 1983* (Geneva: WHO, 1983).

widened so that by the early 1980s lifespans were nearly five years longer in NATO Europe. In part, this reflected changes in the West; while Western Europe's health improvements had slowed in the late 1950s and early 1960s, they sped up, for a variety of reasons, in the 1970s and early 1980s. But the rapidly growing gap also reflected Eastern European health trends. After rapid strides, health improvements suddenly came to a halt. Indeed, for the region as a whole, life expectancy may have dropped slightly in recent years. As Table 2 points out, five out of six Warsaw Pact countries have registered a decline in national life expectancy in their most recent life tables. Only East Germany has continued to record steady gains in life expectancy, but in recent years even these have been modest. Over the course of the 1970s, for example, life expectation at birth in the German Democratic Republic (GDR) rose by less than a year.[8]

Eastern Europe's stagnation, and even decline, in health can be better understood by decomposing the problem. Life expectancy at birth may be considered the product of survival chances during the first year of life and survival chances thereafter. Table 3 depicts infant mortality patterns in Eastern Europe. In contrast to the Soviet Union, there has been no recorded rise in infant mortality for the region as a whole (although registered rates increased slightly in Czechoslovakia in the early 1960s); rather, measured infant mortality rates in the region fell by nearly two-thirds between 1960 and 1983. Even so, such measured improvements do not compare favorably with achievements in Western Europe during the same period. Although infant mortality in Eastern Europe in 1960 was almost

TABLE 11-3 **Recorded Infant Mortality in Warsaw Pact Europe and NATO Europe, 1960–83** *(deaths per 1,000 births)*

	1960	1965	1980	1983
Bulgaria	45	31	20	17
Czechoslovakia	24	26	18	16
German Democratic Republic	39	25	12	11
Hungary	48	39	23	19
Poland	55	42	26	23
Rumania	75	44	29	24
Unweighted average, Warsaw Pact Europe	51	35	22	18
Unweighted average, 9 NATO Europe countries	1.89	1.48	1.65	1.78

	Percentage Decline in Recorded Mortality Rates		
	1960–65	*1965–80*	*1965–85*
Unweighted mean Warsaw Pact Europe	−33	−38	−47
Unweighted mean 9 NATO Europe countries	−19	−44	−55

Note: Figures presented only to two places, thus may not add or average due to rounding.

9 NATO Europe countries: Belgium, Denmark, Federal Republic of Germany, France, Greece, Italy, Netherlands, Norway, United Kingdom.

Sources: World Bank, *World Development Report* (New York: Oxford University Press), various years.

twice as high as in Western Europe — and thus presumably easier to reduce — the decline recorded between 1960 and 1983 was only slightly higher in Warsaw Pact Europe than in NATO Europe (65 percent vs. 64 percent). Moreover, NATO Europe's drop in infant mortality has been the more rapid since 1965 (a 56 percent decline between 1965 and 1983, versus 47 percent in Warsaw Pact Europe).

Table 4 shows the expectation of life at 1 year of age for European countries between 1960 and 1981. By this measure, Eastern Europe was slightly worse off in 1980 and 1981 than it had been in the mid-1960s. For the region as a whole, life expectancy at age 1 was more than half a year lower in 1980–81 than 1964–66. Only East Germany registered improvement by this measure, and it was marginal (0.06 years between 1964–66 and 1980–81). All other countries experienced declines; Hungary lost nearly two years. In contrast, Western European nations

TABLE 11-4 **Expectation of Life at Age 1, 1960–81**

	1960	1964	1965	1966	1970	1975	1980	1981
Bulgaria	71.7	72.4	72.2	72.3	72.3	71.7	71.7	71.7
Czechoslovakia	71.2	71.2	71.0	71.1	70.2	70.9	70.7	71.0
German Democratic Republic	70.7	71.3	71.3	71.4	71.0	71.4	71.2	71.6
Hungary	70.9	71.8	71.4	72.2	71.2	71.1	70.2	69.9
Poland	70.6	71.1	71.5	71.9	71.7	71.9	70.7	71.5
Rumania	70.3	70.8	71.0	71.3	70.6	71.3	70.4	70.6
Mean, Eastern Europe	70.9	71.5	71.5	71.7	71.1	71.4	70.7	71.1
USSR	71.4	72.1	71.4	71.6	70.0	69.5	69.3	69.3
Mean, Northern Europe	72.1	71.9	72.2	72.0	72.3	72.9	73.7	74.4
Mean, Southern Europe	70.5	71.1	70.9	71.4	71.9	72.2	72.7	73.7
Mean, Western Europe	71.3	71.2	72.0	71.6	71.8	72.7	73.7	73.7

Source: Jean Bourgeois-Pichat, "Mortality Trends in Industrialized Countries," in *Mortality and Health Policy*, ed. United Nations (New York: United Nations, 1984).

during this period are estimated to have gained about two years in life expectancy above the age of 1.

Eastern Europe's current health problem is principally an adult problem, as can be seen in Table 5. Between the mid-1960s and the early 1980s, life expectancy for those men 35 and older decreased throughout Eastern Europe, including East Germany, while that for women registered only slight improvement. These changes may be contrasted with the record of NATO Europe, where 35-year-old men gained over a year, and women almost two and a half years, during the same period.

Health trends among Eastern European adults are further decomposed in Table 6. Between the mid-1960s and the early 1980s death rates for men over 30 not only rose overall in each of these nations, but also rose for nearly every five-year age group in each country. For the region as a whole, death rates for men in their forties jumped by over two-fifths, and by over a third for men in their fifties. For Eastern European women, stagnation—and reversal of health progress—was evident in some age groups in some countries in the 1960s, and became more widespread in the 1970s. Health trends for adults in Eastern and Western Europe contrast starkly. Taken as a group, the decline in five-year cohort death rates for Western women in the countries in Table 6 range from 31 percent (early thirties) to 17 percent (over 85). Thus, the least age-specific mortality improvement for this Western European group is more than the greatest of Eastern

TABLE 11-5 **Life Expectancy at Age 35 for Eastern and Western European Populations, Mid 1960s and Early 1980s**

	Mid 1960s	*Early 1980s*	*Change*
Eastern Europe			
Bulgaria			
Male	38.39	37.3	−1.1
Female	41.2	41.8	+0.6
Czechoslovakia			
Male	36.3	35.07	−1.2
Female	41.15	41.46	+0.3
German Democratic Republic			
Male	37.58	36.76	−0.8
Female	41.45	NA	NA
Hungary			
Male	37.1	34.36	−2.7
Female	40.67	40.89	+0.2
Poland			
Male	37.11	35.77	−1.3
Female	41.69	42.49	+0.8
Rumania			
Male	38.08	36.3	−1.7
Female	40.94	40.9	0
Western Europe Selected Countries			
Italy			
Male	37.66	38.4	+1.7
Female	41.67	44.3	+2.7
UK (England & Wales)			
Male	36.6	38.3	+1.7
Female	42.1	43.7	+1.6
West Germany			
Male	36.48	37.7	+1.2
Female	41.27	43.7	+2.4
Norway			
Male	39.22	39.6	+0.4
Female	43.01	45.9	+2.9
Netherlands			
Male	38.9	39.6	+0.7
Female	43.4	45.9	+2.5
Greece			
Male	38.73	41.2	+2.5
Female	41.38	45.0	+3.6

NA = Not available.

Sources: United Nations, *Demographic Yearbook* (New York: United Nations, various issues); World Health Organization, *World Health Statistics Annual* 1983 (Geneva: WHO, 1983).

TABLE 11-6 Mortality Change for Adults in Eastern and Western Europe Between the Mid 1960s and the Early 1980s
(percentage changes)

Eastern Europe	Females — Age Group										
	30/34	35/39	40/44	45/49	50/54	55/59	60/64	65/69	70/74	75/79	80/85
Bulgaria (1961–83)	−11	−31	−19	0	2	−3	−5	4	−6	−4	4
(1972–83)	−11	−25	−10	−7	4	−4	−11	−11	−2	−3	−6
Czechoslovakia (1965–83)	−13	−15	−10	0	2	5	3	3	−3	−3	0
(1972–83)	−13	−15	−5	−6	−6	2	0	7	0	1	1
GDR (1965–81)	−27	−31	−17	−9	−8	−6	−8	−5	−7	−7	−7
(1972–81)	−11	−21	−5	−6	−4	−6	−9	−4	−6	−7	−8
Hungary (1966–82)	22	20	17	27	17	21	10	7	−1	−3	−2
(1972–82)	22	20	12	11	11	11	1	3	−7	−10	−7
Poland (1965–82)	−28	−25	−14	−9	−2	−3	−8	−16	−18	−9	−10
(1972–82)	−11	−8	−5	0	2	1	3	−3	−8	−9	−3
Rumania (1966–83)	−15	0	0	0	2	1	−4	6	−3	NA	NA
(1972–83)	−11	−6	4	9	6	2	1	3	−5	−3	0
Unweighted average											
Mid 1960s–early 1980s	−12	−14	−7	2	3	3	−1	−3	−4	(−6)	(−3)
Mid 1972–early 1980s	−5	−9	−2	0	2	1	−3	−1	−5	−2	−4
Western Europe — Selected NATO Countries											
England/Wales (1966–82)	−25	−31	−29	−29	−17	−6	−8	−14	−18	−20	−19
Greece (1966–81)	−25	−30	−25	−28	−18	−22	−11	−23	−11	−16	−6
Italy (1966–79)	−33	−36	−33	−26	−19	−24	−28	−31	−28	−18	−14
Netherlands (1966–81)	−20	−20	−22	−12	−12	−17	−20	−24	−29	−28	−27
Norway (1965–82)	−64	−44	−45	−47	−41	−35	−34	−41	−42	−37	−33
West Germany (1965–82)	−20	−27	−26	−24	−21	−22	−27	−27	−29	−24	−22
Unweighted average	−31	−31	−30	−26	−21	−20	−21	−26	−27	−26	−19

TABLE 11-6 continued

	Males—Age Group										
Eastern Europe	*30/34*	*35/39*	*40/44*	*45/49*	*50/54*	*55/59*	*60/64*	*65/69*	*70/74*	*75/79*	*80/85*
Bulgaria (1966–83)	13	27	56	41	35	37	15	17	27	21	14
Czechoslovakia (1965–83)	–5	12	27	44	35	29	13	11	7	13	9
GDR (1965–81)	–11	5	16	27	10	–1	–7	–5	3	7	1
Hungary (1966–82)	39	56	85	102	74	54	31	23	22	18	12
Poland (1965–82)	5	10	28	33	33	23	6	2	0	2	–3
Rumania (1966–83)	16	24	49	55	37	27	10	7	–	14	–
Unweighted average	10	22	44	50	37	28	11	9	(11)	(13)	(9)
Western Europe—Selected NATO Countries											
England/Wales (1966–82)	–17	–28	–23	–21	–18	–16	–21	–18	–15	–12	–11
Greece (1966–81)	–27	–13	–19	–22	–12	–8	–6	–7	–7	–5	–5
Italy (1966–79)	–31	–33	–23	–9	–3	–8	–13	–14	–12	–12	–7
Netherlands (1966–79)	–18	–19	–23	–14	–13	–13	–10	2	3	2	–3
Norway (1965–82)	–33	–21	–16	0	–5	–3	–6	–5	0	–1	–5
West Germany (1965–82)	–22	–9	–6	–2	–7	–18	–22	–18	–12	–7	–8
Unweighted average	–25	–21	–18	–11	–10	–11	–13	–10	–7	–8	–5

Sources: United Nations, *Demographic Yearbook* (New York: United Nations, various issues); World Health Organization, *World Health Statistics Annual 1983* (Geneva: WHO, 1983); *Statisticka Ročenka Ceskoslovenskoe Socialisticke Republiky 1985* (Prague: Federalny Urad, 1985); *Anarul Statistic al Republicii Socialiste Romania 1984* (Bucharest: Directia Centrala De Statistica, 1984).

TABLE 11-7 Mortality Change for Adults in the USSR, Eastern Europe, and Selected Western European NATO Countries *(percentages)*

	Age Group										
	30/34	35/39	40/44	45/49	50/54	55/59	60/64	65/69	70/74	75/79	80/84
Males											
USSR (early 1960s–1974)	19	20	37	29	26	22	20	25	–	27	–
Eastern Europe (mid 1960s–early 1980s)	10	22	44	50	37	28	11	9	11	13	9
Western Europe, 6 countries (mid 1960s–early 1980s)	–25	–21	–18	–11	–10	–11	–13	–10	–7	–8	–5
Females											
USSR (early 1960s–1974)	–6	–5	5	6	13	15	4	12	–	11	–
Eastern Europe (mid 1960s–early 1980s)	–12	–14	–7	2	3	3	–1	–3	–4	–6	–3
Eastern Europe (1972–early 1980s)	–5	–9	–2	0	2	1	–3	–1	–5	–2	–4
Western Europe, 6 countries (mid 1960s–early 1980s)	–31	–31	–30	–26	–21	–20	–21	–26	–27	–26	–19

Sources: For Eastern and Western Europe: see Table 6. For USSR: Murray Feshbach, *A Compendium of Soviet Health Statistics* (Washington, D.C.: U.S. Bureau of the Census for International Research, 1985).

Europe's. The same is true for men, where the Western group's most modest performance (a decline in mortality of 5 percent for men over 80) is distinctly superior to the Eastern European group's best (a rise in mortality of 9 percent for men in their late sixties).

It is true that health improvements for adults were modest in certain Western nations between the mid-1960s and the early 1980s; Norway offers a case in point. For certain specific cohorts in the West, death rates may actually have risen slightly (for example, Dutch men between the ages of 65 and 79). Even so, the downward trend in mortality among Western European adults has been unmistakable, as has been the upward trend among the Warsaw Pact states in the East. Indeed, performance has been so distinct that there are only a few five-year age cohorts for either women or men in which the "best" health results of any of the Warsaw Pact states is better than the "worst" of the six NATO nations selected in Table 6.

Table 7 compares the Eastern European health decline with the Soviet Union's earlier decline, and with contemporary changes in some of the countries of NATO Europe. Though decline in adult health occurred earlier and more rapidly in the USSR, Eastern Europe's experience seems largely faithful to the pattern. The correspondence is closer for men. Eastern Europe's women have not, at least to date, suffered the same broad-based reversal in health that Soviet women experienced in the 1960s and early 1970s. Even so, the Eastern European pattern for women mirrors the Soviet experience, albeit more faintly: health progress in both cases is greatest for women in their thirties, and setbacks are most pronounced for women in their fifties. Against a Western European backdrop, the health problem of Eastern Europe's adult population looks like a less virulent, but distinctly recognizable, strain of the "Soviet malaise."

How is this pattern of broad health reversal to be explained? Some analysts have suggested that rising adult mortality may be a delayed after-effect of war. Rainer Dinkel, for example, has argued that male cohorts that have passed through a major war may be expected to have unusually high mortality rates in their later years, since the healthiest portion of the cohort will have been initially selected for active combat, and since the group surviving the war will include the wounded, the disabled, and those whose health may have been permanently damaged.[9] Shiro Horiuchi, in an examination of mortality patterns for the generation that passed through World War I, noted that death rates in later life seemed to be increased for men, but not for women. Boys who were in their early teens during World War I, he wrote, seemed to have the greatest health troubles in later life; he suspected that they were particularly affected by the stress of wartime conditions, especially by the nutritional shocks of reduced availability of foods.[10]

Are today's health problems in Eastern Europe and the USSR a consequence

TABLE 11-8 **Adult Mortality Change in East and West Germany, 1965–Early 1980s** *(percentage changes)*

| | Age Group | | | | | | | | | | | |
	30/34	35/39	40/44	45/49	50/54	55/59	60/64	65/69	70/74	75/79	80/84
Males											
East Germany (1965–81)	–11	5	16	27	16	–1	–7	–5	3	7	1
West Germany (1965–82)	–22	–9	–6	–2	–1	–18	–22	–18	–12	–7	–8
Females											
East Germany (1965–81)	–27	–31	–17	–9	–8	–6	–8	–5	–7	–7	–7
West Germany (1965–81)	–20	–27	–26	–24	–21	–22	–27	–27	–29	–24	–22
Differences, East Germany minus West Germany											
Males	11	14	22	29	17	17	15	13	15	14	9
Females	–7	–4	9	15	13	16	19	22	22	17	15

Source: See Table 6.

TABLE 11-9   **Estimated Annual Cigarette Consumption per Person 15 Years of Age or Older, Selected Eastern and Western European Nations**

Country	1960	1965	1970	1975	1980	1985 (or latest year)
Poland	2252	2458	2897	3245	3489	3157
Hungary	2117	2371	2745	3070	3389	3189
German Democratic Republic	1360	1473	1574	2039	2291	2390
Federal Republic of Germany	1637	2147	2531	2608	2588	2419
United Kingdom	2756	2767	3066	3124	2746	2141
Sweden	1186	1361	1724	1902	1956	1781

Source: U.S. Department of Agriculture Databank; United Nations, *Demographic Indicators of Countries: Estimates and Projections as Assessed for 1980* (New York: United Nations, 1982).

of shocks sustained during World War II? It is certainly true that both civilian and military casualties were higher on Nazi Germany's eastern front than on its western front. Nutritional distress was also more pronounced in Eastern Europe, not only during the war but in the years following the National Socialist Army's surrender. Consequential though these differences may have been, they can provide only limited assistance in explaining the differences in health patterns in Eastern and Western Europe today. For one thing, Horiuchi's studies indicated that mortality in later life was largely unaffected by wartime stresses for the women who survived them, yet rising female mortality has been an integral part of the recent Soviet and Eastern European pattern of health problems. For another, the timing of the rising death rates in the Warsaw Pact is inconsistent with the European pattern after World War I, or the Western experience after World War II. Whereas increases in male mortality in Western Europe were specific to the cohorts that passed through a great war as teenagers, recent increases in Soviet and Eastern European mortality have beset those who would have been middle-aged at the end of World War II, and those who were not yet born. Finally, a difference in adult health trends is apparent among the East and West Germans, even though they experienced World War II as a single nation. As can be seen in Table 8, adult male mortality has fallen in West Germany since the mid-1960s, even as it has risen for certain age groups in East Germany. The gap in mortality performance between East and West Germany, moreover, is roughly the same for both men and women over 40 — the adults in the early 1980s who would have been alive during the Second World War.

TABLE 11-10   **Estimated Per Capita Consumption of Distilled Spirits, Eastern European Nations, 1960–80** *(liters of pure alcohol)*

Country	1960	1970	1980
Bulgaria	0.8	1.9	2.0
Czechoslovakia	1.1	2.5	3.5
German Democratic Republic	1.4	2.5	4.3
Hungary	1.4	2.8	4.3
Poland	2.4	3.1	5.9
Rumania	1.1	2.4	2.2
Unweighted average, Eastern Europe	1.4	2.5	3.7
Index (1960=100)	100	183	271*
USSR	4.7	6.2	6.8
Index	100	131	144
Unweighted average, 8 NATO Europe countries	1.2	1.8	2.2
Index	100	153	187

*1979.

Sources: M. Harvey Brenner, "International Trends In Alcohol Consumption and Related Pathologies," in *Alcohol and Health Monograph No. 1*, ed. National Institute on Alcohol and Alcoholism (Washington, D.C.: Department of Health and Human Services, 1981); Werner K. Lebach, "Continental Europe," in *Alcoholic Liver Disease: Pathology, Epidemiology and Clinical Aspects*, ed., Pauline Hall (New York: John Wiley and Sons, 1985); Vladimir G. Treml, *Alcohol in the USSR: A Statistical Study* (Durham, N.C.: Duke Press Policy Studies, 1982).

Eastern Europe's health problems are to be understood less in terms of past stresses than in terms of the stresses of the present. Certain predictably injurious habits, for example, have been broadly embraced by adult populations of the Warsaw Pact countries. One of these is smoking. Table 9 shows that cigarette smoking rose sharply in Eastern Europe between the mid-1960s and the early 1980s. Between 1965 and 1985, cigarette consumption per adult rose by nearly a third in Poland, by more than a third in Hungary, and by more than 50 percent in East Germany. By contrast, it rose by about 20 percent in Sweden and by almost 15 percent in West Germany, and actually fell by more than 20 percent in the United Kingdom. In Western Europe, moreover, the nicotine content of cigarettes was falling during those two decades. By the mid-1980s over 150 packs of cigarettes a year were consumed per adult in both Poland and Hungary; this was nearly half again as many as in the United Kingdom, and well over half again as many

TABLE 11-11 **European Countries Where Distilled Spirits Account for More than One-Third of Total Consumption of Alcohol**

Country	1980
Poland	69.0
Soviet Union*	59.7
Iceland	57.7
Sweden	48.2
East Germany	46.4
Finland	43.6
Hungary	39.1
Czechoslovakia	36.4

*1979.

Sources: In Europe: Werner K. Lebach, "Continental Europe," in *Alcoholic Liver Disease: Pathology, Epidemiology and Clinical Aspects* (New York: John Wiley and Sons, 1985); in USSR: Valadimir G. Treml, *Alcohol in the USSR: A Statistical Study* (Durham, N.C.: Duke Press Policy Studies 1982).

as in Sweden. In most of Western Europe, cigarette consumption per adult began to decline in the 1960s or early 1970s. No such trend has been evident for Eastern Europe. Dips in consumption in Poland and Hungary in the early 1980s were synchronous with economic difficulties, and thus may represent changes in purchasing power or availability rather than changes in attitude or preference.

As Table 10 indicates, the use of hard liquor also rose sharply in Eastern Europe during the 1960s and 1970s. The increase in hard liquor consumption was particularly pronounced in the Northern Warsaw Pact countries: Czechoslovakia, Hungary, East Germany, and Poland. In those countries, per capita consumption of alcoholic spirits was two and a half times the Western European level in 1980. There appears, moreover, to be some convergence between the Northern Warsaw Pact nations and the USSR. In 1960, while these four Eastern European countries consumed about a third more liquor per capita than Western Europe, intake levels were closer to other European patterns rather than to that of the Soviets. Today their intake level stands almost exactly halfway between Western Europe's and that of the USSR. Moreover, hard liquor has emerged as the alcohol of choice throughout the Northern Warsaw Pact, as Table 11 demonstrates.

Just as in the Soviet Union, heavy drinking of hard liquor has become an accepted and chosen feature of daily life for a substantial and growing fraction of the national populations of Warsaw Pact Europe. In Hungary, recent studies have suggested that over 10 percent of the typical household's disposable income is spent on alcohol.[11] By contrast, alcoholic beverages in 1980 accounted for

TABLE 11-12   **Medical and Health Resources in Eastern Europe and the USSR, 1960–83**

A) Doctors, Including Stomatalogists, per 10,000 Population

	1960	1970	1980	1983
Bulgaria	17.0	22.2	30.0	32.9
Czechoslovakia	17.5	22.2	30.0	32.9
German Democratic Republic	12.1	20.3	26.1	28.2
Hungary	15.3	22.1	28.1	30.0
Poland	12.7	19.3	22.5	23.5
Rumania	13.5	14.7	17.9	19.7
Unweighted average, Eastern Europe	14.7	20.3	26.2	28.2
USSR	20.0	27.4	37.5	40.4
Ratio, Eastern Europe to USSR (USSR = 100)	74	73	70	70
Index, Eastern Europe (1960 = 100)	100	138	178	192

B) Percentage of Public Consumption Funds Allocated to Free Public Health and Physical Education

	1960	1965	1970	1980	1983
Bulgaria	15.6	14.1	13.4	15.0	16.7
Czechoslovakia	15.3	14.7	15.0	15.2	15.8
German Democratic Republic	19.0	17.7	15.3	17.9	19.0
Hungary	22.9	22.9	16.7	14.7	14.8
Poland	NA	25.1	25.3	25.7	19.3
Rumania	(182)	(174)	(151)	(157)	(166)
Unweighted average		(18.9)	(17.1)	(17.7)	(17.1)
USSR	18.4	16.5	15.6	14.6	14.2

NA = Not available.

Sources: Council for Mutual Economic Assistance Secretariat, *Statistical Yearbook 1979* (Moscow: Statistika, 1979); Soviet Ekonomicheskoi Vzaimoposhci, *Statisticheski Ezhegodnik Stran 1984* (Moscow: Finansi i Statistika, 1984).

about 4 percent of private consumption in Sweden, something like 2.2 percent in France and the United Kingdom, and under 2 percent in the United States.[12] In Poland, it has been estimated that 1979 expenditures on alcohol accounted for a third of all expenditures on "food" and equaled the sums spent on clothing;[13] around the same time, French and Portuguese households spent three times as much on clothing as on drink, Americans spent four times as much, and in Spain the ratio was nine to one.[14] (Such comparisons, of course, are limited by the problematic relationship between nominal incomes, prices, and household purchasing power in a system where markets are neither necessarily in equilibrium, or even approaching equilibrium.) Poland's Ministry of Labor Wages and Social Affairs estimated that, in the late 1970s, one employee out of thirty-nine "is drunk while working"; even more interesting was the suggestion that "one professional driver out of every twenty-six in public transportation enterprises operates his vehicle while drunk."[15] Dangerous drinking may be considered a male predilection, but Eastern European data detail a progressive "feminization" of alcohol abuse since the mid-1960s. In Hungary, the Eastern European nation with the most comprehensive data on causes of death, the incidence of mortality from cirrhosis was higher for women in 1980 than it had been for men only fifteen years earlier. For the entire adult female population, the death rate from cirrhosis more than tripled between 1964–66 and 1980; for women in their late thirties and their forties, the cirrhosis death rate jumped by a factor of five.[16]

Eastern Europe's adult population today may well be more susceptible to serious health threats — many of them lifestyle-related — than they were two decades ago. Increased health risks, however, do not inevitably lead to a deterioration in national health conditions. Properly framed and implemented, state social policies and other government-led interventions can prevent health deterioration even during periods of seriously increased health risks. Indeed, the most basic of the stated objectives of social policy, from the nineteenth century to the present day, typically has been to protect and maintain the physical well-being of the national population. Eastern Europe's secular increase in adult mortality over the past twenty years argues incontestably that the measures undertaken by Eastern European states have not been adequate to this task.

A government's first line of defense against illness and disease is its health policy. Eastern Europe's public health systems are, in varying degree, replicas and interpretations of the Soviet public health system. Health care systems in all Warsaw Pact nations are characterized by relatively high ratios of medical personnel and hospital beds to population, and provide extensive services that are nominally free of charge. As Table 12 illustrates, however, there is a striking dissonance between inputs in the public health system and the resulting health of the Warsaw Pact populations. The relationship between the availability of medical personnel and the health level of the national population, in fact, appears to be broadly *negative*: countries with greater numbers of medical personnel per 10,000 population generally seem to have lower levels of adult life expectancy.

TABLE 11-13 Mortality Change for Five Eastern European Nations' Adult Populations During the Economic Slowdown of the Early 1980s *(percentage changes)*

	30/34	35/39	40/44	45/49	50/54	55/59	60/64	65/69	70/74	75/79	80/85
Males											
Bulgaria (1980–83)	+6	+8	+14	+8	+2	+5	+3	+4	+7	+2	−7
Czechoslovakia (1981–83)	−5	+3	+2	+7	+5	+2	+5	+8	+1	+1	−4
Hungary (1980–82)	+14	0	+2	+5	+4	+6	+2	+2	+2	−1	−5
Poland (1978–80)	−4	+5	+9	+5	+8	+8	+2	+4	0	+6	+8
Rumania (1980–83)	+5	−6	+2	+3	+6	+2	0	+5	−5	−4	−8
Unweighted average	+3	+2	+6	+6	+5	+5	+2	+5	+1	+1	−1
Females											
Bulgaria (1980–83)	0	0	0	−7	0	−1	−2	−4	0	0	−10
Czechoslovakia (1981–83)	0	–	+12	0	−2	0	+4	+8	+2	+2	+2
Hungary (1980–82)	+10	+6	−4	−5	−3	0	−4	+2	−3	+1	−4
Poland (1978–80)	0	0	+5	+6	+2	+4	+2	+3	+1	+2	+4
Rumania (1980–83)	0	−6	0	−3	−2	−3	−1	+2	−6	−4	−13
Unweighted average	+2	0	+3	−2	−1	0	0	+2	−1	0	+4

Sources: United Nations, *Demographic Yearbook* (New York: United Nations, various years); *Statischeski Godoschnik na Naroda Republik Bulariya 1984* (Sofia: Komitet po Edinna Systema za Sotsialna Informatsiya Pri Ministerskiya S'vet, 1984); *Statisticka Rocenka Ceskoslovenskoe Socialisticke Republiky 1985* (Prague: Federalny Statistiky, Urad, 1985); *Anarul Statistic al Repubicic Socialiste Romania 1984* (Bucharest: Directia Centrala De Statistica, 1984); *Rocznik Statistyczny 1985* (Warsaw: Gtowny Urzad Statystyczny, 1985).

This seems to be true not only among Warsaw Pact countries at any given point in time, but also within any given Warsaw Pact state during the period in question. The anomalous correlation suggested by Table 12 should not necessarily be taken to mean that Eastern Europe's medical personnel have contributed to health decline within the region; it does offer evidence, however, that the Warsaw Pact's labor-intensive health care strategy, in which priority accords to the quantity of "doctors" fielded rather than to the quality of training or equipment for those people designated to be medical professionals, is ineffective in meeting the health needs of the local populations.

In the command economies of the Warsaw Pact, where prices need not respond to scarcities and where income does not necessarily provide access to goods, patterns of state expenditures do not always give a reliable measure of the quality, or even the quantity, of resources allocated by government to its subsidiary services. To the extent that recorded state expenditures reflect the actual allocation of public resources, it appears that the share of resources devoted to health care in the Warsaw Pact countries fell between 1960 and 1980, even as the overall health level of various national populations was stagnating or declining. As Table 12 illustrates, percentage of public consumption funds allocated to free medical care and physical education in the four Eastern European nations for which continuous data were given dropped from 18.2 percent in 1960 to 15.7 percent in 1980. By 1983, that fraction had risen to 16.8 percent; even so, it was lower than the figure twenty-three years earlier. Among all nations for which such data can be found, the Warsaw Pact is the only large region in which a smaller share of national resources appears to be devoted to health care in the 1980s than in the early 1960s. It is noteworthy that the two countries in which the fractional share of public consumption funds earmarked for health care dropped most sharply—Hungary and the USSR—also suffered the sharpest reversal in adult health conditions.[17] In Eastern Europe, as in the Soviet system, the labor-intensive health care strategy promoted over the past two decades was not a focus for increased health care allocations; rather, in some significant sense, it was an alternative to them. This strategic choice is all the more consequential in a system of socialized medicine. Soviet and Eastern European medical care is, in principle, financed directly and virtually entirely by the state; thus, the quantity, quality, and composition of national health care resources are determined, in principle, not by the consumers of these services but by their leaders.

Since the mid-1960s, Eastern Europe's social policies have failed, in broad measure, to protect adults against lifestyle-related stresses. It also appears that they have failed to protect adult populations against health stresses attendant on fluctuations in, or shocks to, the local economy. Table 13 highlights the problem. The early 1980s (or, in the case of Poland, the late 1970s and early 1980s)

TABLE 11-14   **Statistics Pertaining to Health, Mongolian People's Republic**

A) *Medical Personnel (including stomatologists) per 10,000 population*

1960	1970	1980	1983
9.7	17.9	21.9	23.3

B) *Percent of Public Consumption Funds Allocated to Free Medical Care and Physical Education*

1960	1970	1975	1980	1983
NA	NA	25.5	18.6	19.2

C) *Most Recent Official Estimate of Life Expectancy at Birth*

Year	Male	Female	Total
1964/65	64	66	65

D) *United Nations Estimates of Mongolian People's Birth Rate, Death Rate, and Expectation of Life at Birth for Comparison with CMEA Data*

	Birth Rate*	Death Rate*	Total (years)
United Nations, c. 1970	40.4	10.3	59.5
CMEA, 1970	40.2	12.3	NA
United Nations, 1980–85	34.4	7.2	64.6
CMEA	36.2	9.8	NA

NA=Not available.

*Per 1,000 population.

Sources: Council for Mutual Economic Assistance Secretariat, *Statistical Yearbook 1979* (Moscow: Statistika, 1979); Soviet Ekonomicheskoi Vzaimoposhci, *Statisticheski Ezhegodnik Stran 1984* (Moscow, Finansi i Statistika, 1984); United Nations, *Demographic Indicators of Countries: Estimates and Projections as Assessed for 1980* (New York: United Nations, 1982).

was a period of economic difficulty for all Warsaw Pact states. While the interpretation of statistics concerning the volume and quantity of goods and services in centrally planned, command-oriented economies is necessarily a tricky and ambiguous business, there is little doubt that the pace of economic growth dropped significantly during those years;[18] in at least some of those states, the actual level of aggregate production may have dropped as well. Social policy, as it is understood in the West, is supposed to provide support and protection for those elements within a society who find themselves endangered by the consequences of economic slowdowns or contracts. With the exception of the German Democratic Republic (where adult mortality in the early 1980s fell for both men and women), Eastern Europe's Warsaw Pact states evidently failed to mitigate the vulnerability of their adult populations to life-imperiling risks during a period of economic trouble. In Western Europe, social policies are in large measure independent of economic trends, or consciously designed to operate countercyclically against them; thus, since the end of World War II, health conditions in Western Europe have tended to improve regardless of the current state of the local economy. However social policies may be designed in Eastern Europe, mortality rates suggest that the vulnerable and the exposed have not acquired the additional protection needed simply to keep death rates stable during a period of economic turbulence. The "business cycle" may no longer affect the health of the general populace in Western countries, but adult Eastern European populations, as a whole, do not appear to enjoy that same good fortune.

Mongolia

Outer Mongolia was the first country in which a Marxist-Leninist government was brought to power with Soviet assistance.

Since the establishment of the Mongolian People's Republic in 1924, the USSR has remained intimately involved in Mongolian affairs. The USSR currently stations a Red Army garrison in Mongolia equivalent in size to the number of households in that country, and provides its capital Ulan Bator with credits and subsidies that may account for as much as half of all consumption in the socialized portion of the Mongolian economy.[19] Soviet advisers and technicians have played an important role in building the sinews of government in Mongolia, and in helping to set both the priorities of government and the procedures of local administration. It is, therefore, particularly interesting to note the difficulties in obtaining general information on health conditions in Mongolia today—more than sixty years after the victory of "Mongolian Socialism."

Mongolia does not lack information on its government's efforts to improve the health of the local population, as Table 14 details. Yet the CMEA's *Statistical Yearbook* has routinely omitted Mongolia from its tables on infant mortality in the member states. (Mongolia's own *Statistical Yearbook on the People's Economy* provides no information on infant mortality, even though it has chapters devoted to both population and public health.) Equally interesting, the 1984 edition of the CMEA *Statistical Yearbook* gives a figure for life expectancy in Mongolia—but for the mid-1960s! In the years since 1964–65, the period of the estimate, Mongolia has conducted two full national censuses: one in 1969, the second in 1979. Under ordinary circumstances, one would expect such exercises to provide a basis for updating life expectancy estimates.

What accounts for the paucity of data on the health of the Mongolian people? Such sins of statistical omission would be consistent with the Soviet approach to dealing with bad news, and the Mongolian People's Republic is perhaps more completely under Soviet tutelage than any other state in the contemporary world. But the most uncharitable interpretation is not always the most correct. It is possible that an increasingly complete registration of vital events has resulted in computations that now appear embarrassing next to the seemingly salutary numbers from earlier decades, and that Mongolian authorities are waiting for reality to catch up with and exceed the unrealistic estimates of past performance.

Between 1960 and 1970 Mongolia's recorded death rate rose sharply: from 10.5 deaths per thousand to 12.4 deaths per thousand, or by more than a sixth. The change suggests improvements in statistical coverage, not a health crisis; such increases in measured death rates have been witnessed in the demographic accounts of many less-developed countries as they improved their enumerative capacities. The United Nations has offered estimates for birth rates, death rates, and expectation of life at birth for Mongolia for the period since 1950.[20] For the years 1980–85, it gives an estimate of life expectancy of 64.6 years—almost as high as the figure Mongolia offered for itself two decades before. But there is reason to expect this U.N. estimate to overstate contemporary health levels in Mongolia. Mongolia's own estimate of its current crude death rate is about a third higher than the projection the U.N. offers (see Table 14, panel D). The U.N.'s estimate of Mongolia's crude death rate for about 1970 is much closer to Mongolia's own figure for 1983; they would be consistent with a life expectancy at birth for Mongolia in the early 1980s of about 60, or perhaps slightly less.

In comparison with some nearby states,[21] a life expectancy in the high fifties or low sixties would seem like a considerable achievement.[22] The U.N., for example, has placed Afghanistan's life expectancy just before the Soviet invasion at about 40 years (although those projections were based on extremely scant information). Even so, a life expectancy in the high fifties or low sixties (and the living standard that would presumably accompany such health conditions) would hardly rank as a triumph. The U.N.'s *Demographic Yearbook*'s life tables indicate that expectation of life at birth in Iran in the period 1973–76 was about 57 years. Fifty years and more of socialist development in Mongolia may have done slightly more for the health of the Mongolian people than seems to have been done by two decades of rule by the Shah in Iran.

Vietnam

While there is little doubt that the Socialist Republic of Vietnam is today impoverished, the limited capabilities of the Vietnamese statistical system present difficulties to any analyst who wishes to carry beyond generality the discussion of poverty in contemporary Vietnam. Despite the ostensible importance of timely and reliable data to the process of scientific socialist planning, Vietnam's statistical organs are still underdeveloped. Ten years after victory in the South and thirty years after the establishment of socialist power in the North, Vietnam has yet to achieve near-complete registration of births and deaths. A recent analysis by the U.S. Bureau of the Census suggested that one-tenth of all births, one-third of all deaths, and more than half of all infant deaths may have gone unregistered in the years immediately following Vietnam's 1979 census.[23] Under those circumstances, it should not be surprising that Vietnam, though a member of the World Health Organization, provides no information to that institution on either the incidence of infectious and communicable disease or the causes of death for the general population: there is presently in all likelihood no way that such things can be known. These limitations, of course, speak to conditions of poverty in the nation as a whole. They should also chasten us against the exacting use of other Vietnamese statistics presuming to measure social or economic results.

Hanoi's own assessment is that the national life expectancy was nearly 66 years in 1979: about 64 for men and 68 for women. These numbers, which are reprinted without qualification in the CMEA *Statistical Yearbook 1984*, significantly overstate Vietnam's average length of life, since they have been calculated on the assumption that the registration of deaths is essentially complete. A U.S. Bureau of the Census investigation of recent demographic trends in Vietnam uses a model that implies that life expectancy in Vietnam would have been about 58 in 1979.[24] Other organizations have made lower guesses. The World Health Organization, for example, gives a figure (derivation unexplained) of 55 years for Vietnam's overall life expectancy for the years 1980–84;[25] the United Nations' Department of International Economic and Social Affairs gives 53.5 as the life expectancy in Vietnam for 1980 to 1985.[26]

If Vietnam's life expectancy in the early 1980s were approximate to the WHO and U.N. figures, contemporary Vietnam's overall health levels would be roughly comparable to those of Bangladesh or India. On the other hand, if the Bureau of the Census' assumptions were closer to the truth, Vietnam's life expectancy might not be far different from Mongolia's, and somewhat lower than those of the Philippines or Thailand. Current figures, in short, do not afford much precision in assessing material well-being in Vietnam, for there is a world of difference between the Bengali and the Filipino standards of living. It is worth noting, however, that Vietnam's life expectancy estimates would fall short of Sri Lanka's, a poor nation that has been able to achieve good health for its populace largely through its social welfare policies—and at a comparatively low financial cost. Moreover, it would bring Vietnam's putative life expectancy only slightly above the level independent analysts have ascribed to contemporary China.

Cuba

When the Castro forces came to power in 1959, Cuba was perhaps the healthiest Latin nation in tropical America;[27] its statistical system was one of the Caribbean's best. In the years since the consolidation of communist power, Cuba has gained the reputation of an exemplar of health progress. The notion that Cuba's performance has been exceptional is by no means limited to sympathizers with or publicists for Havana. A study prepared by President Reagan's Commerce Department in 1982, for example, stated that Cuba's health care system "rivals that of most developed nations."[28] Under these circumstances, it might be assumed that a solid body of statistical evidence can be found by which to document a broad-based and unambiguous improvement in health conditions in Cuba since the Castro revolution. Surprisingly, this does not seem to be the case. While Cuba does appear to have experienced health advances since the late 1950s, its pace of progress does not seem extraordinary in comparison with those nations and areas against which it might most fairly be judged. Moreover, since the early 1970s Cuba's health statistics have been beset by peculiar and puzzling inconsistencies. While no foreign observer can interpret these inconsistencies with absolute confidence, the simplest explanation would be that certain key health figures had been deliberately falsified.

Between 1960 and 1974, according to official Cuban life tables, life expectation at birth rose by about six years, from about 64 to about 70. This was a rapid rate of improvement; on the other hand, it was not unprecedented in Latin America or the Caribbean. Life expectancy in Honduras, for example, rose by over a decade between 1961 and 1974, although from a much lower base. Among countries and territories with life expectancies closer to Cuba's own, Guyana's lifespan increased by nearly seven years in a nine-year period (1950–52 to 1959–61); Barbados' rose by over seven years in the same period; Costa Rica's rose by over seven years in the course of a decade (1962–64 to 1972–74); and Puerto Rico's jumped by nearly seven years in a five-year period following Operation Bootstrap (1949–51 to 1954–56).

The rapid increases in life expectancy in Cuba in the early 1960s do not seem to have carried over into the early 1970s. According to the official life tables, expectation of life at birth for Cuban women rose by 0.3 years between 1970 and 1974; for Cuban men it rose by only 0.1 years. By the early 1970s the pace of overall life expectancy improvement, by these official estimates, appeared to be less than one-tenth of what it had been in the 1960s.

One of the principal reasons for the slow pace of overall health progress in the early 1970s, as reflected in these life expectancy estimates, was the trend in infant mortality. According to Havana's life tables, infant mortality did not decline in the early 1970s. To the contrary: according to these official life tables, infant mortality rose by over 20 percent between 1970 and 1974. A rise in death rates in properly constructed life tables would not be a statistical artifact, insofar as reliable life tables are expected to represent the actual level of mortality for each age group for the period in question.

In point of fact, there is reason to expect Cuba's 1970 life tables to have been fairly reliable. Registration of births and deaths seems to have been nearly universal by 1970. The indirect estimate of infant mortality in Cuba's 1970 life tables, for example, and the official infant mortality tally from the vital registration system were within 2 percent of each other. By 1974, however, the life table estimate for infant mortality was 55 percent higher than the figure from the vital registration system. It appears in just four years as if the Cuban vital registration system had gone from missing less than 2 percent of the nation's infant deaths, to missing over 35 percent. One might think that an apparent breakdown in the vital registration system would augur poorly for the government's capacity to cope with problems of infant health. During these years, however, Cuba's *Statistical Yearbooks* have steadily claimed that infant mortality fell by more than a quarter; the *Yearbooks* use the official figures from the vital registration system.

The opening of a gap between the indirect (life table) and direct (vital registration) estimates of Cuban infant mortality coincided with other changes in the processing of infant mortality statistics in the early 1970s. Responsibility for verification of the infant mortality rate from vital registration statistics had previously resided with JUCEPLAN, the economic planning organ; during 1972 — the year of a big drop in registered infant mortality — responsibility was transferred to the Ministry of Health. From then on, the Ministry of Health was in the position of producing and checking those numbers that would be used to evaluate its own effectiveness. At the same time, infant mortality data were designated as henceforth "provisional"; they could thereafter be changed long after the infancy of the cohort in question, and frequently were. Cuba's 1977 and 1982 *Statistical Yearbooks*, for example, both give figures for infant mortality in the region of Isla de Juventud for 1974, but the 1977 estimate is over half again as high as the estimate that appears in the 1982 edition.

TABLE 11-15 Reported Incidence of Selected Infectious and Parasitic Diseases in Cuba, 1959–1983 *(per 100,000)*

Year	Acute Diarrhea	Acute Respiratory Infections	Chicken Pox	Diphtheria	Hepatitis	Malaria	Measles	Polio	Syphilis	Tetanus	Tuberculosis	Typhoid
1959	NA	NA	NA	4.7	NA	2.1	2.9	1.6	0.7	NA	18.0	5.1
1960	NA	NA	NA	8.1	NA	19.0	10.3	4.3	0.7	4.1	27.6	13.0
1965	5,707	—	118.6	8.2	115.8	1.7	121.6	—	30.4	6.7	65.0	3.1
1970	7,694	10,162	150.1	0.1	102.6	—	105.2	—	7.8	2.6	30.8	5.0
1975	6,874	15,520	161.7	—	217.0	0.9	113.4	—	47.6	0.7	14.2	4.0
1980	6,839	21,980	200.7	—	208.3	3.1	39.1	—	44.7	0.3	11.6	1.0
1981	7,836	27,596	425.1	—	147.2	5.9	190.1	—	36.9	0.2	8.6	1.8
1982	8,732	27,441	191.5	—	208.4	3.4	238.8	—	38.5	0.2	8.3	1.3
1983	8,527	33,001	291.1	—	101.2	3.0	33.2	—	44.3	0.2	7.7	0.6
					Index (1970 = 100)							
1959	NA	NA	NA	4700	NA	124	3	NA	9	NA	58	102
1960	NA	NA	NA	8100	NA	1118	10	NA	9	158	90	260
1965	74	NA	79	8200	113	100	116	—	390	258	211	62
1970	100	100	100	100	100	—	100	—	100	100	100	100
1975	89	153	108	—	212	52	108	—	610	27	46	80
1980	89	216	134	—	203	182	37	—	573	12	38	20
1981	102	272	283	—	143	347	180	—	473	8	28	38
1982	113	270	128	—	203	200	227	—	494	8	27	26
1983	111	325	194	—	99	176	32	—	568	8	25	12

NA = Not Available. — = less than .1 per 100,000.

Sources: Republic of Cuba, *Anuaria Estadistico de Cuba* (Havana: Comite Estatal de Estadistica, various issues).

A recent National Academy of Sciences study examined Cuba's demographic data for reliability. On the whole, the study concluded, the data were internally consistent and probably reliable. The sole exception, the author noted, was the infant mortality rate after 1970:

> From the early 1970s on, the consistency between the indirect and the official rates disappears; indirect estimates indicate constant or even rising child mortality, while the official figures show a continued rapid decline. . . . The sharp drop (in infant mortality) from the mid-1970s to 1980 is not supported by the available child survivorship data . . . in the absence of evidence that registration has deteriorated, the official sequence is accepted, with the qualification that it is not independently supported and requires final confirmation from surveys in the early 1980s.[29]

Unfortunately, few of the data that might verify or correct the official infant mortality series since the early 1970s have yet been released in the 1980s. The returns from the 1981 census, for example, have yet to be disseminated publicly. Interestingly, preliminary reports on the census did not provide standard information on the distribution of population by age and sex, but instead lumped men and women together in a new and unusual set of age categories (including a single category for all boys and girls under sixteen years of age). While one may speculate on the reasons for this novel mode of demographic classification, it is worth remembering that these adjustments have had the effect of frustrating efforts of outside observers to ascertain independently the level of child mortality in Cuba between the 1970 and 1981 censuses.

Other puzzles and paradoxes have appeared in Cuba's health statistics for the period since 1970. High levels of infant mortality are typically associated with a high prevalence of infectious and parasitic disease. Cuba's infant mortality rate is said to have fallen from 38.7 per thousand in 1970 to 19.6 per thousand in 1980, or by almost half in a decade. It is said to have fallen still further since then. Yet there has been no corresponding drop in the reported incidence of infectious and parasitic disease. This may be seen in Table 15. Between 1970 and 1980, the reported incidence of certain diseases did decline: typhoid, tuberculosis, and tetanus fell significantly; no new cases of diphtheria were reported; and the cases of measles fell dramatically (only to rise very sharply the next year). On the other hand, the reported incidence of syphilis, malaria, hepatitis, chicken pox, and acute respiratory infection was substantially higher in 1980 than it had been in 1970. The reported incidence of acute diarrhea was slightly lower in 1980 than it had been in 1970, but it then rose in the early 1980s to the highest levels yet registered. It is possible that increases in the reported incidence of certain dis-

TABLE 11-16   **Reported Incidence of Selected Communicable**
or Infectious Diseases: Cuba 1982 and USSR 1974
(or most recent previous year) *(incidence per 100,000 population)*

Disease	Cuba, 1982	USSR, 1974	Ratio, USSR=100
Acute diarrhea	8,732	(409) *(1966)*	NA
Acute respiratory infection	27,441	18,623	147
Brucellosis	0.6	5.6 *(1966)*	11
Chicken Pox	191.5	419.4	46
Diphtheria	–	–	NA
Hepatitis	208.4	223.6	93
Malaria	3.4	.1 *(1969)*	2830
Measles	239	149	160
Meningococcol infections	8.2	6.2	122
Mumps	261	247 *(1966)*	106
Polio	–	–	NA
Scarlet Fever	2.3	146.2	2
Tetanus	0.2	0.2	100
Typhoid	1.3	6.6	20

– = Less than .1 per 100,000.
NA = Not applicable; parenthetical figure for USSR for acute diarrhea refers to incidence of
    bacterial dysentery.
Sources: Republic of Cuba, *Anuario Estadistico de Cuba 1983* (HavaNA: Comite Estatal de
Estadisticas, 1984); Murray Feshbach, *A Compendium of Soviet Health Statistics* (Washington:
US Bureau of the Census Center for International Research, January 1985).

eases reflect improvements in diagnostics and greater outreach of medical personnel, rather than an actual increase in illness for the general population. Even
accepting this as a possibility, it would be surprising to witness such a high level
of poverty-related diseases in tandem with such a low level of infant mortality.

Table 16 sharpens the paradox. It compares the reported incidence of certain infectious and parasitic diseases in the USSR in 1974 (the last year for which
infant mortality figures have been released) and Cuba in 1982. Cuba's reported
infant mortality rate in 1982 was 17.4, just over half of the USSR's adjusted rate
of 31.9 for 1974.[30] Yet the reported incidence of poverty-related diseases is not
correspondingly lower in Cuba. On the contrary, while Cuba's reported incidence
of certain diseases is lower than the USSR's, it is in Cuba that the prevalence of
a number of major diseases appears higher, including acute respiratory infection, malaria, measles, meningococcal infections, mumps, and possibly acute

diarrhea. Completeness of morbidity reporting may differ in Cuba and the USSR, even though the two countries engage in numerous exchange programs, assistance schemes, and coordination projects in the area of health, both within the confines of the CMEA and bilaterally. It would seem counterintuitive to find the greater prevalence of infection and parasitic disease in the nation with the dramatically lower infant mortality rate.

With the important and perennial exception of defense-related numbers, the Soviet statistical system — and the statistical systems of the Warsaw Pact states — are thought seldom to resort to the falsification of inconvenient data at the central level. While other data may be suppressed, or released in misleading comparisons, comparatively few instances of seemingly deliberate alterations have been uncovered by Western observers in the period since World War II.[31] The attitude toward numbers accorded political import may be different in Havana. In the 1960s Cuba altered and deleted reports on the then all-important sugar harvest "to impede the enemies of the revolution," as President Castro explained at the time. And in 1983, documents uncovered in the invasion of Grenada show Maurice Bishop, the late prime minister, praising "the Cuban experience of keeping two different sets of records in the banks," and recommending that "comrades from Cuba . . . visit Grenada to train comrades in the readjustment of the books."

According to Cuba's own life tables, infant mortality fell about 32 percent between 1960 and 1974. Over roughly the same period, according to their life tables, infant mortality fell 40 percent in Panama, 46 percent in Puerto Rico, 47 percent in Chile, 47 percent in Barbados, and 55 percent in Costa Rica.[32] If the National Academy of Sciences' reconstructions are correct, infant mortality in Cuba fell by only 25 percent in the nearly two decades between 1960 and 1978. If those estimates are reliable, the revolutionary Cuban experience would represent not the most rapid, but instead one of the slowest measured rates of progress against infant mortality in all of Latin America and the Caribbean for that period.

Conclusion

A few cautionary comments are in order after this brief review of social and economic conditions within the CMEA bloc.

First, although today it is commonplace to talk of an economic slowdown in the Soviet Union and Eastern Europe between the mid-1960s and the mid-1980s, the dimensions of this slowdown can be only tentatively assessed in the West. The slowdown itself, for reasons already discussed, is not accurately represented in the data the CMEA countries publish. All independent attempts to interpret the slowdown are based upon, and therefore limited by, these data. Adjustment factors may be applied to these data in an attempt to bring them into line with Western conceptions of national income or economic output, and such efforts will reflect the care and competence of the assessor. But it is unrealistic, and indeed unreasonable, to expect a single and reliable derivation of trends to be adduced from the CMEA data. Assessment of economic trends in the CMEA bloc is further complicated by the obvious but often neglected fact that command economies and market-oriented economies are geared to perform very different sorts of tasks. Changes in aggregate output, for example, may have very different consequences with respect to the capacity to mobilize for and prosecute a war in a market-oriented economy, on the one hand, and in a centrally planned economy on the other. Economic data from centrally planned societies, as it happens, provide comparatively little assistance to the independent observer who wishes to assess the material condition of the local population. Ironically, the economic data from these socialist countries may be of intrinsically less use in assessing the material well-being of their populations than are comparable economic data from more market-oriented societies not guided by Leninist political parties.

Second, for the period since 1960 there is little convincing evidence of exceptional improvements in health conditions in any of the CMEA countries under consideration. In both the Soviet Union and much of Eastern Europe, health progress (as measured by mortality decline) has apparently ceased for broad portions of the local population and serious reversals in health conditions, affecting major population groups, have been recorded over the past twenty-five years. Mongolia's health situation, as best it can be determined, is not distinctly superior to that of the nearby countries with which it might most easily be compared, sixty years and more of "Mongolian Socialism" notwithstanding. The dimensions of health progress in Vietnam are uncertain, for the statistical authorities in that nation are as yet apparently unable to compile, process, and analyze timely and reliable data on basic social and demographic trends. In Cuba, measured health progress was rapid though not unparalleled in the 1960s, but inconsistencies and discrepancies in subsequent data have raised as yet unanswered questions about statistical claims for the 1970s and the early 1980s.

Third, data on health conditions in the CMEA bloc provide an insight into the interpretation of social and economic data from Soviet allied states that is not widely appreciated by students of communist systems. It is significant that health trends in the USSR and Eastern Europe are today broadly inconsistent with measured trends in net material product, educational advance, housing conditions, and other indicators typically taken to signify social progress. The dissonance should encourage reflection on the reliability of these basic social and economic data, and on their meaning. Moreover, it may raise questions about the very nature of material poverty itself, as experienced by individuals in centrally planned command economies. The questions surrounding the infant mortality rate in Cuba emphasize the possibilities of "important" numbers, unrelated in the Western way of thinking to defense or security considerations, under Marxist-Leninist rule. It should be remembered that the data pertaining to poverty are unavoidably fraught with political significance under Marxist-Leninist rule.

Finally, it should be remembered that poor performance against domestic poverty may only marginally constrain a mobilized country in its attempts to project power abroad. Strategy and will, often the decisive factors in contests between nations, need not be affected by performance in meeting the physical needs of a general population, or by local and international sentiments concerning such performance. Failure to alleviate material poverty more expeditiously can constrain to some extent a command society in its efforts to mobilize economic and military might. But it will have little impact on the ability or inclination of command states or Marxist-Leninist leaders to take advantage of the mistakes, the weaknesses, the lack of cohesion, or the irresoluteness of their chosen opponents.

Part V

The Future of the Empire

12

Dennis Ross

Where Is the Soviet Union Heading?

The Soviet Union has answered the late Andrei Amalrik's question: It has survived beyond 1984. While alive and clearly the world's other superpower, the Soviet Union presently appears to be struggling. Will it right itself? Will the challenge it poses to us diminish or increase? Will Soviet internal stresses create opportunities or dangers for the United States? Can we do much to affect the shape of Soviet development over the next ten to twenty years?

If we are to answer these questions, we must first understand something about the nature of current Soviet problems, the solutions Soviet leaders are likely to consider, and the responses they are likely to make given Soviet tradition and the ethos of the Soviet system. My general sense is that the steps the Soviets will take to deal with the problem that seems to cut across all others – declining economic growth – will seem inadequate to most Western observers. I also suspect that the Soviets may be satisfied simply to reverse an image of decline. Still, the constraints on Soviet choices and the reluctance to tighten the screws on their consumers will give the Soviets a strong stake in improving relations with the

United States and the West. That may provide us the potential for leverage with the Soviets, but it does not mean that we will be able to translate the potential into political gain.

The Current Soviet Situation

The problems the Gorbachev leadership confronts domestically have been well catalogued elsewhere.[1] It is sufficient for my purposes here to summarize them. Put simply, the Soviet polity began showing clear signs of distress in the early 1980s. Corruption was rampant in official circles; the second economy was thriving, frequently with the use of stolen state materials; alcoholism was reaching epidemic proportions; life expectancy among Soviet males showed a sharp decline; infant mortality was rising; ethnic tensions between Russians and non-Russians appeared more politically salient at a time when the non-Russian population was growing twice as fast as the Russian; plentiful sources of labor were drying up at a time when the main new increments in the labor force were going to be coming from the Moslem areas of Central Asia; and the Soviet reservoir of raw materials—while still abundant—was becoming far more expensive to extract.

Superimposed on these problems were clear-cut signs of political and economic stagnation. Politically, the ossification of the Brezhnev years had set in, with officials throughout the Party and State apparatuses guaranteed lifetime job tenure regardless of their performance and despite their resistance to Brezhnev's calls for an end to bureaucratic inertia and action on reform efforts to deal with burgeoning economic problems.[2]

Fed by the declining growth in labor and material resource availability and plagued by perennially low levels of factor (labor and capital) productivity, Soviet economic growth rates began to decline in the 1970s. In the early Brezhnev years, Soviet gross national product (GNP) grew by more than 5 percent; by the late 1970s it had dropped to 3 percent; and in the early 1980s it was around 2 percent. Per capita consumption growth rates fared worse, declining to around 1 percent in the early 1980s and projected to stagnate throughout the latter part of the 1980s.

For a regime whose whole ethos is grounded in delivering economic growth and in promising a better future, this spelled trouble. At the very least, the "contract" of the Brezhnev period that existed both among the Soviet elite and between the elite and the Soviet masses could not be sustained with declining (and potentially very low) economic growth rates. That contract provided for a quasi-corporate pluralism with no serious deprivation of elite interests or material needs, job and physical security, a continuing military buildup, and an incrementally improving situation for Soviet consumers in the form of diet, housing, durable and nondurable goods, and the like. To sustain the contract in the 1970s, the Brezhnev regime cut capital investment, and in effect began a process of mortgaging future economic growth for the sake of the Soviet military buildup and the Food Program.

As one observer noted, the consequences of the Brezhnev approach and the signs of economic stagnation were clear: "Declining growth in the productivity of capital, labor, or land, increasing obsolescence of production techniques, technological stagnation, shortages of consumer goods, and a decline in the quality of industrial products."[3]

Brezhnev's successors have begun the task of facing up to his legacy and the socioeconomic difficulties bequeathed to them. Beginning with Andropov and dramatically accelerated under Gorbachev, the Soviet leadership has certainly addressed some of the symptoms of societal malaise. Law and order have been reemphasized with a crackdown on corruption and with a discipline campaign geared to the workplace. Strong steps have been taken to reduce alcoholism—raising the price of alcohol, limiting the hours of its sale, and increasing the penalties for being drunk in public and at work. More than this, a fundamental precept of the Brezhnev contract—and certainly the symbol of stagnation—has been dropped: the guarantee of job security for members of the elite. Personnel turnover throughout the State and Party machineries has been extensive, reflecting a major reversal from the Brezhnev years where stability and "trust in cadres" were the hallmark of his rule. (More on this below.)

All these steps indicate the commitment of the post-Brezhnev (and particularly the Gorbachev) leadership to get the country moving again. Whether they will do more than treat the symptoms of malaise is hard to say. By themselves, they may for a time enhance labor productivity and inspire a greater degree of hope among the Soviet public. For them to change the Soviet policy, however, they must act as a spur to economic growth.

It is the decline of economic growth that makes all other social problems more severe—making the values of the regime less compelling; undercutting morale; exacerbating ethnic tensions by forcing investment choices that benefit some groups or regions over others; increasing cynicism as the gaps between regime rhetoric and achievement and between performance and expectations widen; limiting the resources available for correcting the serious deficiencies in Soviet health care; and so on. The anti-corruption and discipline campaigns may help along the margins, but the Soviet leadership must find the resources to retool and/or replace aging capital stock in manufacturing and transport.

Investment in these areas has lagged because of the decisions made in the

1970s. Now, as Gorbachev has noted and as the draft of the 12th Five Year Program reveals, capital investment is being targeted, and there is a high priority on high-technology industries, machine building, and the re-equipping of existing plants.[4] Gorbachev has said 4 percent growth in national income is needed to meet capital investment, defense, and consumption needs. According to one observer, to reach a 4 percent annual rate of growth in national income

> without changing the present system of economic management and raising productivity would require the labor force to grow by eight to ten million over the next five years, fuel and raw materials by 10 to 15 percent and capital investment by 30 to 40 percent. But such resources are simply not available.[5]

Whether or not these precise figures are correct, there can be little debate that changes in the Soviet system are needed to address the problems of the economy. Will the needed changes or reforms be made?

Prospects for Reform

Many observers of the Soviet scene are dubious about the prospects for reform in the system. They see a political culture that regards reform as anathema. They see bureaucratic resistance in the central ministries and at lower levels of management that is deep and entrenched. They see an economic structure that serves to maintain the power and privilege of the Party and State elite. And, most fundamentally, they see the Party as being committed, above all else, to the maintenance of its primacy—something that requires the safeguarding of Leninist ideology, the single-party system, the State-owned economy, and the unimpeded right to intervene throughout the system and the economy.

Indeed, some observers see the introduction of market mechanisms—the *sine qua non* of reforming the Soviet economy—as a fundamental blow to the primacy of regional Party secretaries, the backbone of the Party apparatus. As Alexander Yanov put it, in the absence of market mechanisms to regulate the relationship of supply and demand, the local Party secretaries bring order to the chaos of the provincial economy by assuming the role of super-arbiter—i.e., the distributor of supplies to industrial enterprises and associations on the basis of perceived political need or value.[6] Being denied this role means being denied much of their power.

Those who highlight the role of tradition and the Party's determination to preserve a broad structure (which assures Party intervention, maintains collectivization of agriculture, and guarantees central planning and a material-technical supply network) that has meant so much to Party dominance, see little or no prospect of serious change or reform in the Soviet Union. Milovan Djilas, Tito's former close associate, goes so far as to say:

> In my opinion, changes in the Soviet system are least likely. One reason is that this system is more than other systems permeated, one might say, with *imperialist class privileges.* I believe that the Soviet system has no internal potential for change . . .[7]

Does the Soviet system have no prospect for change? Djilas admits that a national crisis (a military or revolutionary crisis) might induce change, but he sees little prospect short of that. But, perhaps, Djilas and others who are pessimistic about the prospects for change in the Soviet system envision only far-reaching change—and do not consider the prospects for more limited reform. (Something they may discount because they see it as having limited effect). Perhaps they also disregard the possibility that leaderships can respond to events or national needs before they create national crises.

What are the chances for more limited reform? While the obstacles to change or reform in the system are immense, there may be several factors favoring reform on at least a limited basis. The most important in this regard is the seemingly broad-based consensus to get the system moving again.

Having a consensus generate change in a Soviet succession period is not unusual. Following Stalin's death, there was a broad consensus on the need to relax the more onerous features of the Stalinist system of rule, which threatened the masses and elite alike, and kept all living in fear. The result was that the massive terror apparatus and the power of the KGB were whittled down in size; pressure on Soviet citizens was reduced; the image of an intensifying class struggle—something justifying total isolation from the outside world and constant purges to wipe out insidious class enemies—was dropped.

Following Khrushchev's demise, the consensus was driven by a desire for bureaucratic and organizational peace. The Soviet elite sought relief from Khrushchev-like campaigns to reorganize the Party and State apparatus, to restructure the economy and seek radical changes in investment targets and priorities, to pressure members of the broad nomenclature by calling for a "circulation of elites," and to appeal, seemingly, over the heads of the bureaucracy to the Soviet public. The result of the post-Khrushchev consensus was that the theme "trust in cadres" replaced that of "circulation of elites" as the hallmark of the new regime. Bureaucratic stability replaced bureaucratic reorganization. Lifetime job security replaced the personnel upheaval and shifts of the Khrushchev period.

The very success of the Brezhnev period in translating the post-Khrushchev consensus into what I have referred to elsewhere as a "coalition maintenance" style of rule[8] — and its consequences for the ossification of the system — has contributed to the post-Brezhnev consensus. This is a consensus that reflects a broad desire to get the system and the country moving again. Whether this consensus will succeed and overcome the sense of stagnation, the signs of societal malaise, and the pressing problems of economic growth remains to be seen. But the consensus is a factor that favors the introduction of at least limited change or reform in the system.

The change may not all be progressive — i.e., the consensus has certainly favored the introduction of the discipline and anti-corruption campaigns. These may make for improvement and greater efficiency in the economy — particularly given reduced waste and loss of resources — but they are obviously not "liberalizing" responses to the current maladies of the Soviet system. (That they seem to have generated a positive response among the Soviet public reflects the broader yearning to get the country moving again and perhaps also the deeper cultural predisposition among Soviet citizens that makes such responses seem appropriate.)

Nonetheless, these campaigns are indicators that the post-Brezhnev leadership has recognized that it confronts serious problems that require responses. That recognition seems to have been crystallized by the events in Poland in 1981. While understanding that Poland was not the Soviet Union, the rise of Solidarity, the appearance of a proletarian or workers' revolution in a socialist country, the obvious failure of the Polish Communist Party, and the unavoidable need for Polish military and security organs to step in to take over for the Party must have shaken the Soviet elite about the consequences of longer-term stagnation in the Soviet Union — particularly at a time when an aged and infirm leadership presided over the Communist Party of the Soviet Union (CPSU), was fraught with corruption, and appeared incapable of addressing the building socioeconomic problems within the Soviet Union.

Even Konstantin Chernenko, who was so dependent on Brezhnev and who had the greatest stake in perpetuating the Brezhnev style of rule, understood the danger of not reversing the adverse trends in the USSR. Indeed, with the specter of Poland seemingly very much in mind, he called in 1981 for the Party to recognize the importance of serving the "proper interests" of all segments of society and warned that disregarding broad mass and class interests was "fraught with the danger of social tension, of political and socio-economic crisis."[9] Andropov seemed to have Lech Walesa in mind when he said in 1983: "If the Party's bond with the people is lost, into the resultant vacuum come self-styled pretenders to the role of spokesman for the interests of the working people."[10]

Poland made it clear to a broad segment of the Soviet elite that continuing to muddle along was potentially dangerous. Andropov pulled few punches in speaking of the need to face up to the real situation in the Soviet Union and the importance of turning things around. He said the Party must "see the facts as they are," must "soberly realize where we find ourselves," and must perceive in "our society its real dynamic, with all its possibilities and needs." He laid particular stress on the economy and made it clear that these problems had to be approached differently and with a new sense of urgency:

> We cannot be satisfied with our pace in shifting the economy into the rails of intensive development. . . . It is obvious that in looking for ways to resolve new tasks we were not energetic enough, that not infrequently we resorted to half measures and could not overcome the accumulated inertia quickly enough. Now we must make up for our neglect.[11]

Gorbachev has clearly picked up the Andropov mantle. He has persistently stressed the need to face up to problems; he has been extremely blunt about failures in leadership; he has repeatedly stated that the acceleration of economic growth is of "paramount political, economic, and social importance."

Gorbachev has also made it clear that he understands the essence of the challenge the Soviets face economically—namely one of converting the Soviet system from an extensive pattern of growth (where the Soviets simply needed to mobilize their vast labor and raw material resources) to an intensive pattern (where technological innovation and high productivity become the motors of growth). As he put it:

> The . . . special feature of the plan for 1986 is its orientation toward implementing a practical transfer to intensive methods of management. This is dictated by life, itself, by the complicated situation which is developing with labor and material resources, and by the exhaustion of primarily extensive factors in economic growth.[12]

But as he has also observed, converting to an intensive pattern requires new approaches that are still being resisted by some:

> Now we have to realize it [a new approach], both in the process of further studying the plan in industries, republics, krays, oblasts, associations, and enterprises and of course in concrete, practical work. This aspect must be stressed also because many workers at the center, in localities, *including economic planning bodies, have not completely understood the importance of evaluating and solving the economic, social, and financial problems of the country in the new way.*[13] (Emphasis added.)

The watchword of the Gorbachev regime has been "exactingness" in judging citizens and officials alike—as the replacement of such a senior official as Baibaykov, the longtime head of GOSPLAN (centralized state planning), demonstrates. The implication for those who do not shape up and adhere to the "new way" is that they will be shipped out. That threat of removal is new; the rhetoric is not new.

The exhortation from the center, the need to implement economic experiments, the importance of accelerating innovation and factor productivity, and the calls for less petty interference with the work of enterprises are not new. One heard similar calls even during the Brezhnev period. To be sure, there was a much more upbeat assessment of the country's situation and there was not the same sense of urgency or recognition of the nature of the problems confronting the country.

But the rhetorical prescriptions for restoring economic growth were not all that different from what we are hearing now. What is different is that far-reaching personnel turnover is taking place throughout the Party and State apparatuses. Note, for example, that by 1986, 40 to 50 percent of the Obkom Party secretaries were replaced since the last Party Congress in 1981; half of the ministers in the State apparatus also were replaced. As many as 40 to 50 percent of the Central Committee members were new. There is a new head of the GOSPLAN; eight new all-union ministers; a new head of the defense industries. (Indeed, the military has not been immune from the changes—with new heads of the Main Political Administration, the Strategic Rocket Forces, and the navy, and a new editor of the military paper, *Kraznaia Zvezda*, all being appointed since Gorbachev has become General Secretary.)[14]

Some of the changes have come naturally as advanced age throughout the Soviet elite is finally taking its toll, with vacancies created by deaths. But an increasing percentage of the personnel changes—certainly during Gorbachev's brief tenure—have resulted from forced retirements, and that is significant. The speed with which Gorbachev is moving on the personnel front means that there is sufficient consensus and support among the elite to permit him to make these sweeping changes. If nothing else, this is an indicator of both the desire for change and the belief in its necessity—factors that would seem to militate in favor of at least limited reform of the system.

The personnel changes could, of course, betoken greater efforts at reform. They could be a precursor to more fundamental structural reform. In this sense, it could be argued that Gorbachev is first taking advantage of the consensus to get the country moving again, to put his people or personnel appointments in place throughout the system. Once in place, and once his own position of power is thus cemented, he may be prepared to make the radical changes he often says will be necessary. One could also argue that having been able to put his people in place and to sweep aside the deadwood in the system, he will be much more on the spot to show clear-cut improvements. That, too, could build pressures to make more sweeping structural changes in the system of Soviet economic management.

Among other things, what argues against more than limited reforms may be Gorbachev himself. His career suggests that he is a tough, dynamic, opportunistic, and lucky political operative—not a reformer. He could change, but there is little to suggest that he is a Khrushchev-type who is willing to alienate several major institutional constituencies at the same time. In this regard, while he may be riding a consensus to get the country moving again and to deal with some of the visible signs of malaise (corruption, alcoholism), it is not clear that the consensus goes farther than that. In fact, it may be believed that replacing "fossilized" officials with younger, energetic, and less self-satisfied planners and managers is the key to putting the country back on the right track.

Regardless of whether it is, Gorbachev by dint of his interests and inclination is not likely to push precipitously beyond the bounds of elite consensus—at least not until lesser approaches to economic reform have been tried and found wanting. That makes much more sense than taking steps that cross certain ideological divides and thus run the risk of coalescing opposition to Gorbachev.

What is the likely Gorbachev program of limited changes or reforms? He and others have previewed much of it. In essence, it will be a mixed program: one that includes greater centralization for macroplanning of the economy as a whole, but also greater decentralization for more macroplanning at the enterprise level. The former is reflected in the consolidation of six government ministries into one agri-industrial administration to improve planning and coordination in the countrywide agribusiness sector. The latter is manifested by increased calls for greater autonomy for individual managers and enterprise directors, giving them greater financial and planning autonomy to determine the type of products they make. Along with providing local managers with greater autonomy in deciding what they produce and with whom they shall make contracts, Gorbachev has also hinted that there will be greater accountability. Note, for example, Gorbachev's comment, "The problem is that you squander countless resources in every industry, but nobody is going broke, comrades."[15]

Reaching planned output targets—regardless of the most inefficient use of resources to do so—has always been rewarded. Gorbachev is suggesting that this will no longer be the case. Greater accountability and responsibility at the local level is one factor in changing that norm. Another is greater oversight from a more streamlined and efficient center, which will also concentrate capital resources in priority areas. And still another factor in introducing greater efficiency and responsibility is the appointment of younger and more dynamic managers who have a record of getting the job done.

The combination of macroplanning, greater micro responsibility and autonomy, and more effective management from the younger generation—coupled with the greater use of material incentives to boost productivity and the much wider application of agricultural and industrial "experiments" that have been tried in at least a limited way before[16]—probably represents the general recipe Gorbachev has in mind for turning the economy around. It is a recipe that represents another effort to rationalize the present system and structure, but not to overhaul it. The Gorbachev recipe constitutes change insofar as it denies job security—or, at least for managers and members of the elite, ties it to performance. It also constitutes change insofar as it probably reverses the commitment and trend toward wage egalitarianism as a way to reward workers for performance and thus to motivate them to produce more.[17]

One suspects that the key to success of the Gorbachev plan—in the minds of its creators—rests less on these changes and much more on personnel changes and the appointment of a younger generation of planners and managers. The younger generation is certainly better educated and more competent. And their determination to reverse current trends, to make changes, to produce improvements, to enjoy the good life, and to create a sense of internal dynamism seems to be what Gorbachev is counting on.

Is he right to do so? Will the combination of better planners and managers and the rationalizing—but not restructuring—of the current system be the proper catalyst to overcome Soviet problems and reverse the downward trends in economic growth? It is difficult to find any economist specializing in the Soviet economy who believes that such piecemeal and noneconomic responses to the problems of the Soviet economy are likely to have much effect. Radical restructuring along the lines of what one sees in Hungary or China is seen as a necessary *first step* toward economic regeneration. Without this and without a redirection of Soviet investment priorities—which would include a significant reduction in capital investment in defense—the Soviets will be unable to introduce greater innovation into the system, raise productivity, and modernize their transportation infrastructure, their metallurgy, construction, and light industries—or so Western specialists on the Soviet economy seem to think.

Given the nature of the needs and the character of the bottlenecks in the Soviet economy, these Western specialists are probably right about the effect of the more limited approach I believe Gorbachev will adopt. While not being an economist and having no competence to challenge the assessment of Western economists (or for that matter some Soviet economists who have called for more wide-ranging reform in the Soviet economy), I think a note of caution is in order. After all, economic forecasting is not an exact science. Moreover, it is difficult to estimate just what effect noneconomic changes will have on economic performance. Replacing a generation of administrative planners and managers that are old, tired, fearful of change, opposed to taking chances, and satisfied to do things the way they have always done them with a younger, less risk-averse, more determined elite not satisfied with traditional ways of doing business ought to have some effect. Perhaps not as much as Gorbachev wants. But perhaps more than we in the West think is likely.

At a minimum, I think the Gorbachev style, his refining of the current system of economic management, and his wholesale replacement of much of the elite responsible for planning and administering the Soviet economy could well produce some improvement in the economy. Any such improvement would probably buy Gorbachev time and defer the need to consider more fundamental reform until perhaps the early 1990s or later. If, as some believe, the younger generation of Soviet leaders will not be content to muddle along and will see the inability to overcome economic stagnation as threatening to their power and privilege (and their ability to pass on the good life to their children),[18] they may be more likely to accept more radical approaches to economic reform at that point. Such a sentiment would surely be given greater impetus at that time if Chinese growth rates continued at their present rate and created the specter of China overtaking the Soviet economy within a twenty-five to thirty year period. (That would undoubtedly have a shock effect on the Soviet leadership.)

This latter point reminds us that the choices the Soviets make internally may be affected by their external environment. It is also the case that the Soviets' internal situation is likely to have an effect on their external behavior.

Before discussing how the Soviets' internal needs might affect their behavior toward us, it is useful to consider some of the alternative futures we might see in the Soviet Union if the Gorbachev approach to reenergizing the Soviet system does not work. The alternative future possibilities are not likely to emerge before the 1990s—though some of the indicators of different futures may emerge before then and give us a hint of future direction.

Alternative Futures in the Soviet Union

There are a number of alternative possibilities for future internal Soviet organization and orientation. For the purposes of this essay, I will briefly outline several of these, although I will make no effort to be exhaustive. I will be presenting pictures of the Soviet future that will, undoubtedly, be drawn more sharply and distinctly than is likely to be the case. Indeed, the actual Soviet future is likely to be marked by elements from each of the three possibilities described below.[19]

The "Liberal" Future. This is the future that most in the West would like to see, but the one that is hardest to square with Soviet tradition. It would involve sweeping reforms in Soviet economic and political institutions. One would see a significant opening of the Soviet system, with much freer flows of information, greatly decentralized decision making, an end to the centralized material-technical supply network, the use of market mechanisms, and a redirection of internal priorities to generate investment, to retool the Soviet economy, and to fuel labor productivity.

These are the kinds of changes Western specialists on the Soviet economy have always claimed were needed to overcome the structural defects in the system and generate dynamism and growth. They continue to seem farfetched in the Soviet Union we know today.

Perhaps a sense of desperation could produce them. Before discounting this possibility, several developments or possible indicators of potentially sweeping changes are worth noting.

First, one has seen the emergence of a group of economists in the Novosibirsk Academy of Sciences who seem to have Gorbachev's support and who are challenging many of the holy of holies in the Soviet system—e.g., arguing that enterprises should be allowed to fail; making it clear that unemployment will have to be allowed to increase and, in some cases, encouraged if the economy is to undergo its necessary transition; and emphasizing that there is nothing wrong with using market mechanisms to determine prices, profits, and relationships between enterprises and production runs. Second, one has seen such a senior Party secretary as Boris Yeltsin—presumably acting for Gorbachev—not only insisting on the need for much greater openness but also challenging many of the perquisites and specialized privileges of the *nomenklatura* that set its members apart from the rest of the society.

Third, one has seen the passing of an extraordinary seventeen-page document (purportedly prepared by senior Soviet officials) to Western journalists.[20] The document says the Soviet economy is dragging fifteen years behind the Western economies and is likely to increase its debt to the West sixfold within the next fifteen years unless drastic changes are made—changes that require not just economic but political reforms permitting the full and free flow of information.[21] Perhaps the document is not authentic. Or perhaps those officials who passed it had ulterior motives—e.g., highlight how bad things are and how far some might be prepared to go in responding to the situation as a way of frightening the leadership into accepting more limited but previously unthinkable reforms. (Or more cynically, highlight how far things had already gone in terms of discussion to frighten the elite into taking steps to preempt further such discussion.) Whether or not the document is authentic or there were hidden agendas in passing it, it is no longer inconceivable that it could have come from members of the elite — something that indicates the extent of ferment and the yearning for change among at least a part of the broad Soviet elite.

Does that mean the liberal future is likely? By itself, probably not. Those who yearn for change have yet to demonstrate that they can break through the barrier to achieve it. Moreover, the straws in the wind that suggest the potential for change are probably consistent with a more limited "liberal" future. By this I mean a future that creates greater liberalization and autonomy for the technocrats in the system. They might be granted greater authority in economic decision making; provided more information and the ability to exchange it with other economic managers; permitted to use more of their own criteria to shape economic growth; allowed to extend more experiments beyond narrow sectors of industry or agriculture to the economy as a whole. Technocratic weight in the system would thus increase, but there would be no real or immediate changes in political institutions. In other words, economic managers and specialists would gain great autonomy, rights, and influence in the realm of decision making for the economy, but not an increase in their political role or political rights.

What would indicate that the "liberal, technocratic" future was beginning to take shape in the Soviet Union? At a minimum, we should look at recruitment and promotion patterns and the type of people going into the leading positions in the apparat. Are we seeing increasing evidence of specialists and technocrats in the *nomenklatura* generally? Are they going into the critical positions? How are they faring? Are they bringing in people with similar backgrounds and are they really supplanting more traditional, less skilled types? Besides looking at the profile of the elite — and whether it is changing in the technocratic direction — we should be watching whether limited experiments with pricing, profit, and new success mechanisms and indicators are being extended from limited sectoral or regional areas.

While one might argue that we are beginning to see signs that the Gorbachev leadership is moving in the direction of the liberal, technocratic future, it is worth noting that the picture is not all that clear-cut. Apart from Gorbachev's increasing harangues about bureaucratic resistance, there is the sobering possibility that as much as a quarter of those forced out of their positions by Gorbachev may be back in either their previous or similar jobs.[22] That would suggest that the weight of resistance Gorbachev now faces is becoming stronger — and it may betoken alternative futures representing either a Stalinist retreat or more muddling along.

A Stalinist Retreat to Austerity, Autarky. Soviet desperation triggered by fear of where the country is heading might not breed a more enlightened future.

On the contrary, it could breed a retreat toward the Stalinist past to save the system as the Soviet leaders know it and to protect its ideological underpinnings. Greater savings exacted from the Soviet people would be used to generate the resources needed to compete militarily with the West during this period of decline.

For some in the Soviet leadership, a Stalinist retreat may be a more acceptable way to deal with burgeoning Soviet problems than turning to more "liberal" alternatives that could undermine the Party's role and change its character. Such a retreat would require imposing severe austerity on the Soviet people; further, a general tightening of the screws on Soviet citizens, requiring additional restrictions and perhaps permitting the Soviet government to forcibly move people to meet labor needs in different republics, could also be expected.

To justify a return to draconian measures and a major enforced reduction in the standard of living, the Soviet leadership would have to paint the picture of a serious deterioration in East-West relations that threatened a mortal danger of war. Under these circumstances, extraordinary sacrifices would be called for and imposed on the population. Externally, one could expect Soviet actions either reflecting or designed to trigger a severe souring of relations with the United States, Soviet restrictions on East-West contacts, and a severe crackdown on Eastern and Western European economic and trade relations. Internally, one could expect the weight and role of the security organs to be increased visibly, particularly at a time when stricter internal controls would be enforced.

Will any of this happen? Not likely; while the weight of the security organs has been increased, the Gorbachev leadership shows no interest in turning the clock back; moreover, the ease with which Gorbachev removed Romanov from the Politburo—the one leader perhaps most inclined to use and reemphasize the Stalinist legacy—suggests that the rest of the leadership may not be willing to do so either.

Perhaps current Soviet leaders fear that the Soviet public simply will not tolerate austerity on the levels of the Stalin period, particularly after having its base needs incrementally met and expectations raised over the last twenty years. Perhaps the leaders fear the dangers inherent in a severely deteriorating international environment—and are not prepared to face those consequences. Perhaps they fear the consequences for themselves of possibly unleashing another Stalin; or, perhaps, they recognize that a Stalinist approach is good for mobilizing resources but not for generating growth in societies moving into the postindustrial age.

Whatever the reason or reasons, Soviet leaders are not likely to retreat to a Stalinist past to deal with present or future systemic problems. Muddling through—where they continue to avoid basic choices—is still another option that is likely to be more appealing.

More of the Same—The "Muddling Through" Option. This option would basically continue the current Soviet course. There would be some concessions to economic rationality, but no structural change in the management of the economy. The tinkering or refining of the past would continue, but the Party predominance and the restriction of the use of market mechanisms to only limited sectoral experiments would not be altered.

The inability to make basic choices, the imposing weight of traditional vested interests, and the inability to break through bureaucratic constraints all might explain why the "muddling through" option will win out in the end. One demonstration of movement in that direction is Gorbachev's increasing frustration with the bureaucracy along with the indication—as noted above—that as many as 25 percent of those removed from positions in Gorbachev's first year may now be back in place.

If I were to bet on the future path the Soviet Union will take, I would bet on some mix between the "liberal, technocratic" and "muddling through" options. One may see the weight of the technocrats increase without liberalization of political structure. Whether that would prevent the gradual deterioration in the Soviet system and psyche that would probably result from the "muddling through" option, I cannot say. I can say that for now and for the next few years I expect no great changes—though I do expect some modest improvements in economic performance.

Moreover, whether or not Gorbachev succeeds in buying time, he is going to have a strong stake in good relations with the West. This is true regardless of one's assessment of how much the Gorbachev program will improve the performance of the Soviet economy. Even if one accepts the unconventional view that the Gorbachev recipe for economic growth may have more effect than Western observers believe, Gorbachev must still come up with resources to meet broad capital investment needs. That will prove difficult in circumstances where the military competition with the United States is becoming more intense and focused on areas that play to U.S. strengths—i.e., high-technology areas such as SDI and Stealth where the Soviets find themselves either lagging behind or having to devote an inordinate share of resources to compete.

This is not a time when Gorbachev will want to be putting increased resources into defense. But that may be hard to avoid if he is unable to constrain American military developments. The fact that developments such as SDI and related emerging technologies may be difficult to counter and potentially capable of devaluing much of the Soviet military investment over the last twenty years only adds to Gorbachev's interest in improving relations with us and cutting an arms control agreement.

Apart from trying to head off or restrict our military developments, Gor-

bachev's interest in gaining Western help in the form of trade, technology transfer, investments, and credits also gives him a strong incentive to improve ties
with us. By itself, such an improvement will make the Europeans and Japanese
far more able and willing to expand the scope of their commercial dealings with
the Soviets. Certainly, more expansive European and Japanese technology transfer
to the USSR is likely in an improved atmosphere of U.S-Soviet relations and not
nearly so likely otherwise.

I would argue also that Gorbachev does not discount the possibility that
improved U.S.-Soviet relations could additionally lead to a significant expansion
of U.S. commercial activity and investment in the Soviet Union. Such an eventuality would, undoubtedly, depend on a repeal of the Jackson-Vanik and Steven-
son amendments, but that may not be so farfetched if U.S-Soviet relations show
marked improvement and Jewish emigration from the Soviet Union increases — as
it may for reasons related to their interests in good relations not only with us but
also with the Middle East.[23]

In short, Gorbachev has a strong stake in improving relations with us. He
probably also has significant fears about us and about the consequences of not
getting the Soviet Union moving again. He wants to engage us and give us a stake
in having good relations with the Soviet Union, without appearing weak in the
process. The traditional Soviet fear that we will exploit any sign of weakness will
limit the character of and the pace at which the Soviets will make concessions.
It will continue to make the Soviets very difficult negotiating partners. It will
also trigger Soviet impulses to show that they can compete effectively with us
and that they can make life difficult for us if we behave in a way that suggests
we are intent on making it hard for them.

Both sets of impulses — demonstrating their ability to compete and demonstrating their ability to put pressure on us — should be taken seriously and, in fact,
are already in evidence at this time. An example of the former is current Soviet
behavior in the Middle East. The Soviets have been actively cultivating Western-
oriented regimes and over the last few months have been putting out feelers to
the Israelis designed to indicate their presence in the area and that they are now
more flexible under Gorbachev. All their activity has been geared toward the Middle East peace process and ending the past twelve years of Soviet exclusion and
American dominance as the potential peacemaker or arbiter in the area. The Soviets hope that their apparent flexibility, the pressures of Jordan and Egypt for an
international conference, and the Israeli interest in restoring bilateral relations
and increasing Jewish emigration from the Soviet Union will lead us to acquiesce
in Soviet reentrance in the peace process.[24]

That, of course, would be a major boon for Gorbachev, being the equivalent
today of Khrushchev's leapfrogging of containment in the 1950s. More than just

competing now in the Middle East, however, the Soviet surge of support for the Sandinistas in Nicaragua, more aggressive posture in Afghanistan, and pressure on the Pakistanis are presently demonstrating the Soviets' determination to hold onto what they have and the options they have for putting pressure on us. Apart from trying to signal that they are not weak, they may also be trying to convince us that we may not like the consequences of souring relations with the Soviets; hence we, as much as they, have an interest in improving relations—or so they want us to think.

Any such behavior does not change the reality of the Soviet position. Rather, it reflects the Soviet style and reminds us of what we are likely to confront as we try to take advantage of current and future Soviet needs.

What to Aim for in Our Relations with the Soviets

There is no mistaking the fact that we currently have the makings of a strategic opportunity for shaping U.S.-Soviet relations in the years ahead. To take advantage of this opportunity, we have to know what it is we want; what is possible; and how well we can sustain certain postures (e.g., continued pursuit of SDI, high levels of military spending, absence of arms control agreements, and support for insurgencies against Soviet clients in the face of pressures from Congress and our allies). While Soviet needs are not likely to change soon, our leverage could decline under the weight of our own economic and political pressures, particularly if it looks like our policies are preventing deals with the Soviets. In light of that, it makes sense to keep a number of points in mind about what we can achieve and what we should push for now and over time:

On Arms Control. While the Soviets are not going to disarm or easily give up the strategic weapons we regard as most threatening, they are moving them out of their silos. That means, as indicated by their proposal at Geneva, that they will surrender some of their heavy ICBMs. To the extent that they go beyond their current proposal, one can assume that they will insist on comparable cuts in U.S. offensive forces and an operational freeze on SDI. Indeed, this is the "grand compromise" that Western critics of the Reagan administration hope will be struck—i.e., 50 percent cut in offensive forces, in return for a U.S. pledge to limit its work on SDI to research in the laboratory.

SDI is surely a symbol to the Soviets and its development is what they are determined to restrict. However, the Reagan administration is equally determined to pursue SDI as a research program to see if it can reach fruition and change the basis on which our security rests. If we are to strike a deal, it might be one in which we inform the Soviets that we are prepared to accept some limited restrictions on defense as part of the overall reduction in offensive forces to cut their ICBMs and IRBMs well beyond their proposal at Geneva, and both sides would have to accept specific restrictions on and means for verifying the numbers and deployment patterns of mobile missiles. We would accept some limitations on the point at which elements of SDI might be deployed—ten to twelve years—and would also agree to certain restrictions on the character of SDI technologies and the pace at which operational tests on them could be conducted. While being prepared to work out a regime that linked offense and defense, defined the particular components that would be tested, and regulated the timing at which such tests would be conducted, the Soviets would have to accept that some SDI research and testing would be permitted outside the laboratory.

The Soviets will not favor such a deal but may be prepared to accept it if they see it is the only way to slow the pace of SDI development.

On Third World Activism.   The Soviets are not going to give up their creed of supporting wars of national liberation—and they certainly will not surrender positions in countries in which they have invested a great deal. On the other hand, the Soviet economic situation and generally lowered expectations about "socialist" prospects in the Third World are such that the Soviet leadership does not seem to be in an expansionist mood in the developing world. Gorbachev conveyed this in his initial speech as General Secretary when he offered not aid but rather "sympathy" to those in Asia, Africa, and Latin America struggling for "liberation from colonial oppression."[25] That does not rule out competition in regions judged to be particularly important, like the Middle East, but it does imply a generally lower level of Soviet activity throughout the Third World as a whole.

We have an interest in fostering that sentiment, and certainly the Soviets must think the prospects for improved relations with us depend on lowered levels of Third World activity on their part. But we should seek more—not just a general lessening of the scope of Soviet activity, which will occur anyway, but rather a set of understandings and positive, cooperative behaviors on specific areas. I have three in mind: Iran, North Korea, and Libya.

With regard to Iran, I am thinking specifically in terms of Soviet behavior after Khomeini dies. There is almost certain to be a struggle for power in Iran; the more violent it is, the greater the scope for Soviet involvement. The Soviets must be put on notice now about how seriously we will regard any meddling in Iran—and about how any such meddling is likely to draw us in. Making Iran a special "target" for good Soviet behavior is important not simply to head off a possible confrontation there but to let the Soviets know that if they are seriously interested in an improvement in relations with us they must be prepared to exercise restraint in the face of possible opportunities. Nowhere is this more true than in Iran, given our stake in the power there. A Soviet willingness to work out and abide by an understanding on post-Khomeini Iran would not only be a useful form of crisis prevention but also an excellent measure of Soviet earnest.

The same could be said of North Korea. Here I am referring not just to possible threats to the South or disruption of the Olympic Games in 1988, but particularly to North Korean nuclear developments. Few countries flout international norms and prohibitions more than the North Koreans. Nuclear weapons in their hands are simply unacceptable. Though the Soviets do not control the North Koreans, they have been providing them an increasing amount of military assistance and it is difficult to believe that the North Koreans could go nuclear without some degree of Soviet assistance or knowledge. We should approach the Soviets privately and make the point that we don't have a nonproliferation policy toward North Korea, we have an *anti-proliferation policy*. If the Soviets are serious about broader cooperation with us, they will commit themselves to an anti-proliferation policy vis-à-vis North Korea and act both with us and unilaterally in ways that demonstrate this.

I raise Libya as another area to target with the Soviets. In this regard, Soviet support for Libya directly and indirectly is a kind of symbol of the Soviet willingness to aid and train radical groups to threaten moderate regimes and oppose efforts toward peace in a region like the Middle East. Historically, the Soviets have sought to maintain a double-track policy: one of normal state-to-state relations and one of party-to-party or clandestine relations with those who threaten the very regimes with which the Soviets maintain normal ties. If the Soviets want a normal relationship with us, they have to be prepared to change the character of their dual-track policy. Reducing material support for a regime like the Libyan one—which supports radical, rejectionist, and nihilist groups internationally— would be a useful measure of such a change.

On Internal Change in the Soviet Union. We are not going to be able to force significant political change in the Soviet system; the Soviets will remain highly sensitive to any attempts to intrude in their internal affairs—and will respond in a disproportionate way to deter such "effrontery" on our part. Still, current Soviet needs create certain important opportunities even on domestic Soviet issues. The most obvious is emigration and treatment of refuseniks and dissidents. Public harangues by the U.S. government will get us nowhere. However, mass protests sponsored by private organizations are useful—not only because they create a political context that makes private entreaties from the U.S. government more credible, but because they keep the pressure on, and make it clear to the Soviets that an easing of emigration policies is essential to achieving the commercial activity they seek with the West.

Besides the emigration issue, those in the West who think about doing business with the Soviets might gear their commercial activity to limited reforms in the Soviet style of management. For example, as Alexander Yanov has argued, Western firms should demand the right to deal directly with managers of factories rather than having to work through the Ministry of Foreign Trade.[26] They could legitimately claim that this will make their dealings far more efficient and more likely to produce profitable investments in the Soviet Union. Given Gorbachev's desire to increase the autonomy of managers and decrease the power of some of the ministries, such an approach—depending on how it is made—might not be unacceptable.

The virtue of linking commercial activity or Western investments to such limited reform is that it gives the managers and enterprise directors more of a stake in doing business differently; it might, thus, set an important precedent and build the weight of those who favor reform—or at least more of a decisive approach to dealing with Soviet domestic problems.

Anything that moves the Soviets in that direction is in our interest. From our standpoint, the most favorable *realistic* change that can take place in the Soviet Union is the growth of a sociology (which seems more likely in the Gorbachev generation) that seeks to deal with domestic problems and that is not satisfied with external successes as substitutes for internal progress.

We want to see a Soviet Union that is inward looking, that seeks to create a sense of internal dynamism fuelled by *internal* and not *external* expansion. The emergence of a new generation in power may make that more likely, provided they face a United States that is determined to make outside adventures expensive; that is determined to compete aggressively in the economic and high-tech spheres; and that is prepared to cooperate in military and commercial areas once the Soviets demonstrate in deeds — not simply words — their commitment to such cooperation.

Henry S. Rowen and Charles Wolf, Jr.

The Future of the Soviet Empire: The Correlation of Forces and Implications for Western Policy

In attempting to assess the future of the Soviet empire, we will first assemble a balance sheet covering the strengths and weaknesses of the system. In the two succeeding sections, we consider trends of these strengths and weaknesses and make a general assessment of the empire's future prospects. These sections provide background for concluding sections on options and implications for U.S. and Western policy toward the Soviet Union.

The Empire's Strengths and Weaknesses: A Balance Sheet

Attempting a "bottom line" assessment of the Soviet empire's strengths and weaknesses is challenging and risky. Not only is such an assessment inherently difficult, but the empire's future also depends on factors other than its strengths and weaknesses. For example, its future may be significantly affected by random, or at least unpredictable, events occurring outside as well as inside the empire. Such possibilities include nuclear accidents graver even than Chernobyl; significantly worse (or better) drought conditions and crop shortfalls or windfalls; repercussions from the possible dramatic success of China's economic liberalization; and, perhaps, the emergence of more innovative and effective policies by the United States and the West.

In any event, a "bottom line" assessment can be made only if we know the intervening lines, which essentially relate to the specific components of the ledger and their respective trends.[1]

Constructing a balance sheet of strengths and weaknesses, at a given point in time, and then evaluating their prospective trends over time, is analogous to what Marxist-Leninist rhetoric refers to as the "correlation of forces." "Correlation" suggests a close association and interdependence among the elements under consideration.[2] In fact, the operative political, economic, military, and social elements or forces are often disparate, independent, and unrelated or, at best, only partly related. The "balance sheet" idea allows for independence, as well as interdependence; it is more accurate because it is less pretentious.

The Empire's Strengths.   The quintessential strength of the Soviet imperial system lies in the priority and the reality of power possessed and exercised by the ruling class — the *nomenklatura* — within the Soviet Union itself, and by its counterpart ruling elites in the Marxist-Leninist "fraternal" or "vanguard" states that constitute the contiguous and extended empires. As described in Vladimir Bukovsky's discussion in chapter 2, "The Political Condition of the Soviet Union," the ruling elite within the Soviet Union and its counterparts without exhibit a high degree of cohesion. This cohesion is grounded in their common interests, reinforced by the dominant role of the Communist Party of the Soviet Union (CPSU) and its closely symbiotic relationship with the Soviet military establishment and with the security organs of the State — the KGB and the MVD internal security forces.

In its seven decades of experience, the *nomenklatura* has demonstrated an increasing ability to transfer leadership smoothly. It has also developed and perfected a pervasive system of internal controls whose surveillance capabilities and well-grounded reputation for ruthless coercion enable its mastery to be exercised with much less visible force — violence and terror — than was employed in prior decades. This system of internal controls enables the Soviet ruling class to spot and to disrupt dissidence before it crystallizes, providing a model for emulation by the ruling elites in other parts of the empire, with assistance provided by the Soviet Union as necessary.

The system, although not capable of efficiently managing a large, complex society, is capable of commanding a few high-priority activities. These include the maintenance of power internally and the creation of military might. The military might of the world's second superpower is summarized by Bruce Porter and James Roche in chapter 8, "The Expanding Military Power of the Soviet Union." The Soviet military apparatus, encompassing nuclear and conventional forces and ground, air, and naval projection forces, is in turn supported by the world's third largest industrial base and by the large population of the Soviet Union. Moreover, the empire draws additional support from the military power of the Warsaw Pact countries of Eastern Europe and, selectively, of Cuba, Vietnam, and North Korea—countries that possess significant concentrations of military power in their own respective spheres.

These instruments of power are legitimized by another of the empire's strengths, albeit a declining one: the appeal and the rhetoric of Marxist-Leninist ideology justifies and nurtures the power of the *nomenklatura* by the utopian purposes that it ostensibly serves. This ideology still retains attraction for aspiring elites in some of the developing countries as a promising means of acquiring and maintaining political power, as described by Herbert Ellison in chapter 5, "Marxism-Leninism in the Third World." But it is still more important that this ideology provides for the creation of a strong party structure, which then becomes the instrument for achieving and maintaining political control.

Another Soviet asset (one that also entails elements of weakness and vulnerability) is the 270 million, relatively well-educated population (the percentage of the Soviet population with a high school education has increased five-fold since the 1930s), consisting of multiple nationalities concentrated in 15 national republics, and over 60 separate ethnic groups. Within this heterogeneous population, a dominant position is exercised by the largest and strongest nationality— the Russians—concentrated in the Russian Soviet Federated Socialist Republic. Most of this multinational population has a long history of passivity and inertia under conditions of coercive rule and material deprivation, which has instilled a pervasive fear of disorder and chaos—and given power to the rulers. The Soviet population, especially the Russians, are intensely nationalistic, proud of their achievements in history, in the Great Patriotic War, in literature, ballet, and chess, but not proud of their role in the creation of the Soviet state. They are both sensitive to and strongly cohesive in the face of perceived external dangers and threats.

The strengths of the Soviet empire include the development of an effective system for extending and defending both the contiguous empire in Eastern Europe and Afghanistan and the more remote empire abroad. The external empire extends from Cuba to Vietnam and encompasses a diversity of Marxist-Leninist and "fraternal" states including Angola, Ethiopia, South Yemen, Nicaragua, and

Mozambique, as well as other cooperative and supportive countries. The Soviet imperial system is supported by a combination of sheer military power in Eastern Europe and Afghanistan, as well as more subtle political, economic, security, and propaganda instruments. These instruments are coordinated in what has been referred to as the "Red Orchestra," under the management of the International Department of the CPSU (as elaborated elsewhere in this volume; see chapters 4, 5, and 7). The Red Orchestra is a means of conducting an indirect, multifaceted war—short of the direct combat involvement of the Red Army.[3] In addition to the Soviet Union itself, prominent players in the orchestra include Cuba, the German Democratic Republic (GDR), and, in some instances, Czechoslovakia, as well as other Eastern European countries and North Korea.

Finally, the strengths of the Soviet empire are enhanced by the frequent disunity among its adversaries in the United States, Western Europe, Japan, and China—a disunity that can often be counted on and galvanized within and among these countries. Notwithstanding the divergencies that exist within the Soviet empire itself, the centripetal organizational, ideological, and coercive forces that bind the empire together often contrast sharply with the vocal and policy disunity prevailing among the empire's adversaries, especially with respect to Soviet advances in the Third World.

The Empire's Weaknesses.   The foregoing elements of strength are substantial. Nevertheless, the debit side of the empire's ledger also includes significant entries. Most salient among them, as discussed by Richard Ericson in chapter 6, "The Soviet Economic Predicament," is the stagnation of the Soviet economy. The economy has experienced a low rate of real overall economic growth since the mid-1970s, a nearly flat and perhaps declining level of real per capita consumption, a decline in factor productivity, and, recently, severely reduced hard currency earnings due to the decline in the world price of oil. These economic failings are intrinsic to a system in which incentives are collective rather than individual. Such a system can develop rapidly for a limited period through the intensive exploitation of human and raw materials, but these sources are exhausted sooner or later. In the Soviet case, the human material is already much "depleted," as described by Bukovsky in chapter 2 and Mikhail Bernstam in chapter 10, "Trends in the Soviet Population." This is happening also to such valuable resources as oil due to overly rapid development. Moreover, the progress of technology (with the exception of weapons) is weak in such a system. Similar stringencies beset the economic and social performance of much of the empire outside the Soviet Union itself, as Nick Eberstadt has shown in chapter 11, "Health of an Empire: Poverty and Social Progress in the CMEA Bloc."

These economic stringencies lower the military potential of the Soviet Union, limit its capacity to incur the costs of expanding and defending the empire, and erode the legitimacy of the communist system. It is becoming increasingly clear to people inside and outside of the empire that the Soviet Union, in its present configuration, will never be able to catch up with the West economically.

An important inhibitor of economic performance is the large share of total output going to what can be called the "security sector." This comprises 1) the military establishment (estimated recently by the U.S. intelligence community at 15–17 percent of gross national product [GNP] in 1982 rubles);[4] 2) activities such as civil defense and various impacts of the military on the civilian economy (such as the military functions of the Soviet merchant marine, Aeroflot, and the priority accorded the military in its access to high-quality inputs); and 3) the cost of the external empire, estimated in chapter 7 to be about 4 percent of GNP in 1983. Altogether, the share of GNP going to this security sector is roughly 25 percent. By comparison, the equivalent share for the United States for this same definition is about 8 percent of GNP.

Although economic inefficiency and a large defense allocation are heavy burdens, it would be a mistake to conclude that these factors will soon cause Soviet military power to erode or cause Mr. Gorbachev to be a supplicant in arms control or other East-West bargaining arenas. The processes at work are long-term ones and Soviet military power will pose grave dangers for the West for a long time to come.

As noted earlier, the Soviet population is, in some respects, a source of strength to the system; yet its diversity, internal frictions, and antagonisms are also a source of current and potential weakness. Dissidence and activism by nationality groups outside the Soviet Union—especially from the Islamic world and Eastern Europe—carry the potential threat of contagion to related ethnic groups within the Soviet Union. Demographic changes in the Soviet population are likely to place increasing stresses upon the system, as the proportion of Moslems and other non-Slavs rises in relation to that of the Great Russians and other Slavs, particularly in the context of long-standing resentment of Russian-Soviet domination, position, and privilege that pervades the entire system. The Russians, for their part, resent the disproportionate burdens they feel that they bear. These trends and tensions are reflected especially by Bukovsky and Bernstam in their respective chapters.

Discussions by Bernstam and Eberstadt call attention to the remarkable deterioration of health conditions, shortened life expectancy, and other social problems plaguing the Soviet system. These social ills contribute significantly to absenteeism and lower productivity. Moreover, if resources are to be devoted to alleviating the causes of social deterioration, resources now available for the military, for meeting the costs of the empire, and for the investment and technological demands of Soviet industry will be further constrained. Beyond these economic consequences, social deterioration exacts a moral toll and exercises a corrosive effect on the system's legitimacy and durability.

Outside the borders of the Soviet Union itself, the permanent irreconcilability of Eastern Europe to Soviet domination and the impulse of the Eastern Europeans toward greater autonomy and closer involvement with Western Europe add to the vulnerabilities of the empire, as seen in Charles Gati's chapter, "The Unsettled Condition of Eastern Europe." The weaknesses and fragility of parts of the extended empire abroad and their vulnerability to domestic and foreign challenges and reversals are underscored by Charles Waterman's account in chapter 9, "Resistance Movements in the Soviet Empire." These and other potential resistance movements and the costs of maintaining, let alone expanding, the empire add further to the stresses confronting the Soviet imperium.

Pervading the Soviet system, and the empire as a whole, are its multiple and fundamental contradictions, as suggested in Bukovsky's and other chapters of this book. These contradictions include an ideology that preaches a doctrine of classlessness while the reality consists of a class system with special privileges for the *nomenklatura*; an essentially imperial system that proclaims its opposition to imperialism; an official stance that extols the dignity of work, social consciousness, and personal sacrifice in the midst of widespread corruption, cynicism, and popular alienation from the system; a system that depends for political control on a centralized, multilayered, and frequently unresponsive bureaucracy while the demands of the economy plainly require decentralized incentives, initiatives, and innovations; a security apparatus that tries to preserve a near monopoly of informational access, while the trend of technology plainly requires broad and decentralized access to information; a system that has enclaves of technological modernity (in the military) that coexist with a pervasive backwardness in much of the economy, which is akin to conditions in the Third World; and a system that preaches the eventual dictatorship of the proletariat, while in practice ruthlessly dictating *to* the proletariat. In terms of Hegelian dialectic, these inherent contradictions lead to the antithesis that jeopardizes the basic thesis of the Soviet system and its empire.

Finally, in the world outside the extended Soviet empire, the system confronts other forces that may aggravate its weaknesses: for example, the reemergence of the United States as a more vigorous competitor. Probably more important in the longer term is the great and growing economic, technological, and potential military strength of the noncommunist industrial world as a whole, as well as the systemic challenge posed by the economic reforms of China—a challenge that may provide an alternative economic model as well as a more formidable military threat to the Soviet Union itself.

Trends in the Empire's Strengths and Weaknesses

Trends in the empire's balance sheet can be compared to changes in the balance sheet of a large corporate conglomerate's ledger. Whether the firm prospers or declines will be reflected in the growth of its assets relative to its liabilities, and hence in changes in its net worth. Similarly, the future of the Soviet empire will be reflected in, as well as affected by, trends in its balance sheet of strengths and weaknesses.

Are the Empire's Strengths Growing or Receding? Some of the empire's strengths may wax, while most will probably wane over the next decade and beyond.

There is no compelling evidence of a decline in either the capabilities or desire of the Soviet ruling class to maintain and exercise power. But there may be serious disagreements about the means. For example, one insightful observer, Professor Shlapentokh, has commented on the contrasts between the speech by Gorbachev and the speeches by other Politburo members at the 27th Party Congress in 1986. The General Secretary stressed the need for reform, incentives, and decentralization, while the pronouncements of the other Politburo members emphasized the opposite themes of centralized Party control, continuity, and strengthening of the existing structure. In the past, Party Congresses in the Soviet Union have been occasions for tedious repetitions of the Party line enunciated by the General Secretary and endorsed by other speakers, rather than occasions for expressing such conflicting views.[5]

Another experienced observer has developed several different scenarios in which the *nomenklatura*'s power and control might be eroded and contested. Professor Alexander Shtromas introduces the concept of a "second pivot" or "counter-elite"– namely, a faction within the ruling elite that is prepared to cooperate, if not collude, with outside elements pressing for change. He has suggested that such fissiparous tendencies may arise among the more technical and efficiency-oriented members of the Party or the military.[6]

The views and questions raised by Shlapentokh and Shtromas are both provocative and worthy of continued attention. However, they should probably be interpreted as ripples in a continued wave of firm, relentless, centralized power possessed and exercised by the Soviet structure, rather than a perceptible trend toward the weakening of the *nomenklatura*'s capability and appetite for wielding unchallenged power.

Nor does the military power of the Soviet Union show any signs of significant weakening. There are probably serious arguments and differences within the Soviet Defense Council – chaired by the General Secretary – concerning the relative emphasis to be placed on strategic nuclear offense and defense forces, or on the modernization of conventional ground and projection forces. However, the most serious pressure constraining the competitive growth of Soviet military power is likely to come from the lagging performance of the Soviet economy, rather than from frictions within the leadership. But this is probably a long-term concern rather than an acute present one.

The appeal of Marxist-Leninist ideology—another of the empire's putative strengths—has already declined, as noted earlier, and seems likely to wane in the future. In Europe, the ideology's low and declining stature has been particularly evident. Its decline has been most visible in those parts of Europe where communist parties in the past have had significant residual strength: Italy, France, Spain, and Portugal. Most important is its status in the Soviet Union itself, where Marxist-Leninist ideology increasingly is seen primarily as a rationalization for the rule of a privileged class.

Despite its loss of appeal as a model for economic development, the ideology continues to attract aspiring elites in the Third World as a means of securing and maintaining political power. Consequently, Marxist-Leninist manifestations in the Third World will continue, usually in combination with hypernationalist rhetoric and emotion.

Although the extended Soviet empire is under anti-communist insurgent pressure—in Afghanistan, Angola, Ethiopia, Nicaragua, Cambodia, and Mozambique—these attacks may be successfully repelled by the Red Orchestra. Moreover, in considering the Soviet empire's strengths, it would not be prudent to ignore the opportunities that remain for adding to them by further imperial extensions in Central America, Southwest Asia, and Southern Africa.

A major factor adding to the strength of the Soviet empire is the trend towards growing differences in the Western Alliance, especially the disputes between the United States and Western Europe, and those between the U.S. and Japan. In Western Europe, these differences relate especially to the Strategic Defense Initiative, the pursuit of nuclear arms agreements, and the so-called Reagan Doctrine on U.S. Third World Policy. More broadly, the view seems to be taking hold in Northern Europe that "European" interests are diverging from American ones, along with a perceptible edging toward a middle ground between American and Soviet positions. Yet the Western Alliance has a long history of frictions and divergencies, including the deployment of Intermediate Nuclear Forces in 1983–85, the proposed neutron bomb deployment in 1977, U.S. policy in Vietnam in 1970–75, and the aborted proposals for the European Defense Community in the 1950s and 1960s. Nonetheless, the growth of anti-Americanism, especially in Britain and Germany, largely among elites, may represent a basic new division. If so, and if the current differences grow, they may lead to reduced U.S. involvement in Europe's defense. It is possible that such a reduced U.S. role might stimulate a more vigorous, cohesive, and self-reliant European security effort. It seems more likely that such a development would give the Soviet Union greater scope for dividing and coercing Western Europeans, moving them toward a "Finlandized" status.

The recurring and serious frictions between the United States and Japan, and the possibility (which now seems unlikely) of a significant rapprochement between the Soviet Union and China, might strengthen the empire's position in Asia in the future compared to its current, not very strong position.

Are the Empire's Weaknesses Growing or Receding?　If the trends in the empire's strengths present a mixed and ambiguous picture, those of the weaknesses seem to be clear: all of them seem to be intensifying.

Most important is the economic weakness. The most likely prospect is for a permanent lag in Soviet per capita output behind that of the West by about a generation (around twenty-five years). To be sure, slight improvement in the Soviet economy has been reported for 1985–86, in response to Gorbachev's specific restrictions on the production and distribution of alcohol and insistence on reduced absenteeism.[7] However, this is likely to be as short-lived as the response that ensued to Andropov's corresponding efforts in 1983–84.

The secular lag in Soviet economic performance will permit only slow growth in the resources available to meet the competing resource demands of the military, investment in industry and new technology, the empire, and the living standards of the Soviet public. The prospect of such a large and permanent lag will generate growing pressure on Moscow to achieve improved performance. This might eventually take the form of moving economic decision making either toward lower levels of the Party and the government bureaucracy or toward enterprise managers. Whether the system moves toward either form of decentralization, and, in particular, to marketized rather than bureaucratized decentralization, is surely one of the fundamental policy choices confronting the Soviet leadership.

In contrast to the Chinese, who have adopted both forms of decentralization, the Soviets thus far have adopted little of either. If genuine decentralization is pushed by Gorbachev, and there is no compelling evidence that he is doing so, it will be strongly resisted by the *nomenklatura*. In this domain, the Soviet leadership confronts a fundamental dilemma. Without pervasive marketized reform, the system's performance will lag and stagnate. But if the regime does adopt significant market-oriented reform, the ensuing repercussions are likely to be far-reaching and significant: the distribution of income will be altered; repressed inflation is likely to be replaced by open inflation; entrepreneurs and professional people are likely to benefit at the expense of bureaucrats and wage earners; and labor strife may well emerge. In time, the scope and intensity of Party control would be jeopardized.

However, in the absence of basic systemic change, the economic capacity of the regime to support the military establishment, to extend the empire, and even to maintain it, is likely to diminish. The political significance of a permanent economic lag could be even greater than simply presenting harder choices in allocating scarce resources. After all, the United States and Western Europe have also been experiencing slow growth since the early 1970s and their prospects are not brilliant. But from the beginning, the Soviet state has held out the promise of outdoing the West in economic performance and, for many years after World War II, it made some progress toward that goal. Now it is clear that this will not happen. Continued poor performance of the system will sharpen the question of why the Soviet people should be saddled with such an unproductive system.

Soviet economic stagnation appears in stark contrast to the much greater economic growth of the Soviet empire's adversaries, especially in Asia. The aggregate GNP of the NATO countries today is three times that of the Warsaw Pact countries. Although annual percentage growth in these countries may not be much more rapid than in the Warsaw Pact countries, NATO's much larger economic base will create correspondingly larger absolute increments of output in the years ahead. Japan's GNP will soon surpass that of the USSR (measured on a purchasing power parity basis) if it has not already done so, and will be far ahead of it by the year 2000. Assuming that China remains on its present course, Chinese GNP, currently about $900 billion—approximately half that of the Soviet Union—will probably be almost equal to that of the USSR by the year 2000.

Demographic trends are also against the Soviets. The Russians increasingly will be a minority among the multinational and multiethnic Soviet population. This would not be of great importance were it not for the decline in the ideology's appeal and the dominant, as well as resented, role of the Russians in the system, especially in the military. The demographic trend could slowly undermine one of the main cohesive forces in Soviet society. Non-Slavs have fared relatively well under communism in the past, and there is little reason to expect significant political dissension from them in the near future. But most of the Moslem peoples have not been assimilated into the Russian culture. The potential for trouble exists and probably is growing.

Indicators of social ills show a worsening situation with no sign of improvement, as noted by Bernstam in chapter 10. In turn, these social ills contribute to lowered economic performance (e.g., through industrial accidents, lower morale, and reduced physical vigor in the labor force), and to the demographic stresses described above. Beyond these effects it is difficult to assess the longer-term significance. At the least, more resources will have to be devoted to limiting pollution (e.g., preventing further "Chernobyls") and improving health care.

The empire's weaknesses in Eastern Europe are also likely to grow. The Eastern Europeans may resist being held down economically by being locked – through the Council for Mutual Economic Assistance (CMEA) – into the lagging Soviet system. Continued poor economic performance may well increase dissidence, resistance, and outbreaks of violence. Soviet weakness might, in time, force Moscow to allow the Eastern Europeans greater latitude to make internal system changes and to have more extensive dealings with the West.

Uncertainties about the outlook for the anti-communist resistance movements in the extended Soviet empire are substantial. Although, as noted above, these resistances may be successfully quelled, other outcomes are also possible. One may assume that the Soviet Union and its Marxist-Leninist associates have a strong chance of quelling these "freedom fighters" in each individual instance, and still one may conclude that the chances of their doing so in all of the six current cases – in Afghanistan, Angola, Nicaragua, Ethiopia, Mozambique, and Cambodia – are quite small. For example, if the Soviet empire's prospects of retaining control for the rest of this decade are, say, two-to-one in each of these six instances, the prospect that control will be maintained in all of them is only one in ten! The conclusion follows that it is likely that the Soviets will experience a significant setback in perhaps one or two instances. (We discuss the significance of such possible setbacks below.)

Finally, the systemic "contradictions"– so dear to the hearts, minds, and rhetoric of communist theorists in expounding upon the weaknesses of capitalist democracies – seem likely to deepen and widen in the years ahead, thereby undermining the belief, even among confirmed ideologues, about an inevitable historical trend toward Marxism-Leninism. The history of the last several decades seems to have disposed of the Leninist view that imperialism is the "highest and last stage of capitalism." It remains to be seen whether imperialism turns out to be the highest and final stage of communism.

Some Futures for the Soviet Empire

It is tempting, but probably misguided, to apply one or more of the numerous theories of broad historical change to assess the future of the Soviet empire. Each of them – for example, the theories of Aristotle, Gibbon, Hegel, Spengler, Toynbee – might have something to contribute to such an assessment. However, their contributions are more likely to be discernible retrospectively than prospectively. Theories about the rise, decline, and fall of empires – and especially about the duration of each stage – are uniformly tidier and more convincing when looking backward than forward.

Empires of the past have often seemed at the time to be flowing forward while in retrospect they actually were ebbing. For example, the Roman, Ottoman, Russian, British, and French empires appeared to be gaining externally when, viewed retrospectively, they were actually decaying from within. Some of the failing empires lost everything rapidly through war, as in the case of Japan and Germany. Some were acutely destabilized as a result of war, as in the case of the Russian empire following World War I, or their fall was hastened, as in the empires of Britain and France following World War II.

In most instances, the burdens or costs associated with empires seem to have traversed four phases: an initial phase in which empire costs rose as the imperial power acquired its foothold and thereafter its hegemony; a second phase of declining costs, resulting from establishing unquestioned dominance and the extinction of opposition to the imperial power; a third phase in which empire costs rose as a result of emergence of opposition and resistance from internal or external sources; and, finally, a concluding phase in which the empire fell, and the associated economic burdens, as well as political and military benefits, were removed.[8]

If there is a general theory on the ending of empires, it is that a combination of internal weaknesses and external forces contributes to their decline and fall. Absent defeat in a major war or a convulsive internal revolution, empires are not likely to end (or their termination is likely to stretch over a long period) unless external forces and internal weaknesses exercise mutually reinforcing pressures to produce an early collapse.

It has often and correctly been said that the Soviet empire is the last of the European or world empires. We earlier considered a number of criteria according to which the Soviet empire qualifies as a member of that genre.[9] No other world empire still endures. Only the merest vestiges of the British and French empires remain; there are no German, Japanese, Portuguese, Spanish, Italian, or Dutch remnants. China rules over some non-Han peoples, including those in Tibet, but 90 percent of its inhabitants are Han.

To be sure, the Soviet Union and the international communist party machinery, as well as certain circles in Latin America, Europe, and Japan, sometimes refer to American imperialism.[10] However, application of the term to the United States bespeaks propaganda, rather than description. The U.S. "empire" simply doesn't pass the tests referred to earlier.[11] For example, there is no place outside the United States where U.S. military forces would not rapidly withdraw if they were requested to do so. The United States has Puerto Rico, but that island can have independence whenever 51 percent of its electorate votes for it. Moreover, the texture of the U.S. relationship with its allies, especially in Europe and Japan, differs fundamentally from that which characterized empires of the past, as well as the Soviet empire of the present.

In any case, the semantics are not as important as the prospects. What then can be said about the outlook for the various parts of the Soviet empire: the overseas empire; the contiguous empire of Eastern Europe and Afghanistan; and the inner empire within the multinational, multiethnic state of the Soviet Union itself?

Concerning the overseas empire, none of the Marxist-Leninist states within it is secure: Cuba faces the enduring hostility of the United States; Vietnam remains in jeopardy from China as long as it pursues its campaign in Kampuchea and maintains close military and political cooperation with Moscow; Ethiopia is faced with resistance from the Eritreans and from internal national opposition; Angola is under challenge from within; Nicaragua faces resistance from the Contras; the South Yemen People's Republic is subject to disruption both from within and from North Yemen.

While none of these states—especially those at the end of the preceding list—is important to the Soviets in a material sense, the network that they are part of is highly important to the Soviet leadership. Cuba is especially useful, as is Vietnam, although their loss would not directly impair the security of the Soviet homeland. However, both are members of the inner "family" of the CMEA, and the Soviet Union's potential for extending its empire through adroit and indirect application of power would be drastically impaired by an adverse change in their status. As emphasized by Bukovsky, the extended empire is one of the few major accomplishments of the system—one that helps to sustain the belief of its adherents in the future triumph of Marxist-Leninism. Thus, erosion of the extended empire would be an enormous setback. This is not to say that the loss of some parts cannot be contemplated without erosion of the whole. After all, in the 1970s Egypt and Somalia passed from the status of being a part of the extended empire to being separated from it. One can certainly contemplate such possibilities in South Yemen, Mozambique, Angola, Ethiopia, or Nicaragua, and perhaps in several of these instances. In contrast, a reversal in Cuba would be a serious matter, one likely to have wider ramifications throughout the empire.

Although the extended empire presents prospects for adverse changes, significant opportunities may also arise for future extensions of the empire. Opportunities may emerge or be created in Central America, perhaps elsewhere in Latin America, and in Southern Africa. Soviet leadership, faced with the accumulating evidence of slow decline, might decide to step up challenges in this area. It has the means to do so, and expansionist moves in the Third World, using mostly indirect instruments, are much less dangerous than moves along the periphery in Europe or Asia. In sum, we can discern no clear trend in the size and strength of the overseas empire for the next decade or two.

More vital to the Soviet empire's future is the maintenance of Soviet dominance and control in the contiguous part of the empire, Eastern Europe and

Afghanistan. Eastern Europe's high importance to the Soviet Union derives from the fact that it provides a symbol of the effective political use of the Soviet Union's military capabilities, a presumed contribution to forward defense of the Soviet homeland, and the area from which a politically useful coercive threat to Western Europe is made tangible and visible. It also provides a base from which military operations could be launched against Western Europe. From a negative standpoint, the loss of control over this region would very likely have profound repercussions for the internal stability of the Soviet Union.

Despite Soviet controls, further upheavals and threatened or actual Soviet interventions may occur in Eastern Europe. They may recur in Poland, in post-Ceausescu Rumania, and elsewhere in the region—with the lowest likelihood in Hungary and East Germany.

To a lesser extent, Afghanistan possesses some of these same valued attributes: the removal of a potential source of internal instability within the Soviet Union, a coercive threat to Pakistan, and a military base flanking Iran and measurably adding to Soviet striking power against Iran and the Straits of Hormuz.

Of course, other, quite different scenarios might ensue. For example, some degree of "Finlandization" might occur in Eastern Europe, although this is harder to envision than the "Finlandization" of Western Europe. One possible end point in this direction would be the reunification of Germany—a prospect that neither the Soviet Union nor its allies in Eastern Europe, nor most of the allies of the United States in NATO, are eager to contemplate. Nonetheless, the long-term weakening of the Soviet Union may oblige them to do just that. In sum, trends in the Eastern European portion of the contiguous Soviet empire are unfavorable; they are more promising, from the Soviet point of view, in the southward direction toward the Persian Gulf.

With respect to the empire inside the Soviet Union—the inner empire—increased alienation and disaffection, rather than substantially increased active dissidence, seem in store. The demographic changes and pressures alluded to earlier could provide a growing source of tension between Moslems and non-Moslems, and between the dominant Great Russians and the many ungrateful non-Slavs.

Economic stagnation is unlikely to be a source of active resistance in itself. But together with other factors, it is likely to contribute to a growing belief that change—and radical change—is needed. Movement toward change is most likely to arise within the leadership itself. The empire's fundamental flaws and troubles, externally as well as internally, are surely a source of policy differences at the apex. Whether, and to what extent, possible moves toward liberalization of the economy should be undertaken, is only one among many likely policy differences among the inner circle. Yet, to paraphrase Benjamin Franklin, the Soviet leadership has a powerful incentive to hang together because of the greater fear of hanging separately. If Gorbachev's still ambiguously expressed inclination toward genuine change does not produce effective results, or if their very effectiveness engenders opposition among other elements in the Party leadership and bureaucracy, then Gorbachev's own tenure may be more limited than his relatively young age would suggest.

In the short run, very likely nothing much of real importance will change: no major economic liberalization and no return to Stalinist terror. But looking ahead, the odds gradually mount that *something* consequential will happen. We sketch six possible developments. These six by no means exhaust the possibilities, nor should they be considered as completely independent paths; interactions among some of them would be likely.

More of the Same. We suppose that the most likely course to the year 2000 is no fundamental change in the system, with very slow economic growth (and possibly periods of negative growth) — no marked change in the structure of power, the workings of Soviet institutions, or the characteristic behavior of the population. This would continue to be an extraordinarily static, not to say stagnant, society. There may be enough change at the margin, in agriculture, in the provision of services, or in trade with the West to keep the gap with the West from widening further, but this path precludes any real catching up.

This is the most likely path because of the extreme conservatism of the ruling elite, the high effectiveness of its organs of internal control, the probable avoidance of major internal and external disasters, the record of apathy of the Soviet peoples, and the regime's continued ability to co-opt and control potentially restive elements. This, in short, is the "muddling through" path that most Western Sovietologists presage.

However, the odds are growing of a major change occurring by the end of the century. This might be through deliberate choice by the leadership, possibly led by Gorbachev (or his successor), or through uncontrolled events. That is, changes of a "top-down" or a "bottom-up" character are both possible — although the former seems much more likely. Clearly, the possibilities are beyond anyone's capacity to predict. But there are several candidates, and while each seems improbable taken alone, the occurrence of one or a combination of them seems moderately probable.

A Shift to Market Socialism. As in the case of China, this would entail privatizing much or all agriculture (recreating the family farm); legitimizing a wide range of service functions; and freeing up labor, capital, and goods markets to a considerable extent — but presumably retaining state ownership of major industrial enterprises. In many ways this would amount to a modern-day "New Economic Policy," one similar to the limited – and temporary – return to capitalism in 1921. Efforts to improve individual motivation through the use of market incentives, along lines that China is following, would improve economic performance and contribute to greater efficiency, but at the considerable risks that we have noted. The gravity of these risks, as they are likely to appear to the *nomenklatura*, suggests why this course of action is resisted. Still, at some point the risks of not changing the system could come to look worse than those of changing it. This path assumes that Gorbachev, or a successor, wants to do more than the equivalent of rearranging the deck chairs on the Titanic.

A substantially changed system would eventually be more pluralistic than the present one. (In between, it could be less so; the period of détente and increased contacts with the West in the 1970s was accompanied by a harsher domestic political climate.) But although this vision does not produce democracy – at least not for a long time to come – it would be an important step away from a totalitarian system. People who have greater economic independence are likely to have greater personal independence, which implies greater political independence. Of course, it is true that the country has neither a tradition of civil liberty, nor laws binding on rulers, nor independent corporate bodies as a counterweight to central authority. [12] Most people in the West would continue to find much that they disliked about such a polity. Moreover, a regime that improved economic performance and gave people more personal liberties could become more popular; if it survived the transition, this shift could stabilize what is now a latently unstable system. In time it would have a much larger economic base. Such a regime might still be imperialist in character – although arguably less Marxist-Leninist in ideology. After all, a pre-Soviet Russia vastly expanded its territory and a post-Soviet Russia might continue the tradition.

A Military Takeover.   Although the military now, as in the past, seems thoroughly under Party control, the army is the only group with the means to overthrow the regime. Its leadership might be motivated to do so to save the country from military inferiority, the danger of internal decline, and the eventual loss of control over Eastern Europe. Such a move might also be strongly motivated by the feeling among the Russian-dominated military that Russian culture and the Russian people are being destroyed by socialism.

One cannot say much about the nature of a possible military government. Conceivably, it could have a "Bonapartist" character and launch foreign military adventures, but there is no reason to think that this would be likely. A military government is more likely to be concerned with keeping the country together. It could also have a strong "Russian" character and seek to improve the poor condition of the Russian people. Moreover, the military might not seek to rule, but simply carry out a palace revolution as the guards' officers did on several occasions in the eighteenth century. If they were motivated by a desire to escape economic stagnation, they might put someone in place who would adopt market socialism.

One thing would clearly follow from any such development: whatever residual credibility the Soviet brand of Marxism-Leninism has in the world would practically disappear—just as Maoism has disappeared (except for such an exotic movement as the Shining Path in Peru).

Centrifugal Movement of the Nationalities. Economic stagnation, demographic changes, and the growing perception of the failure of the Soviet model will strengthen the nationalities at the expense of the Center. The ideological goal of the creation of the "Soviet Man" would have seen Russians, Uzbeks, Latvians, etc., disappear. This goal was never universally popular (to say the least) and it has receded. The entire experience with Soviet socialism has led to a powerful—if restrained—resistance and countermovement by Russian and other nationalities to the universal Soviet model.

By themselves, behavior changes motivated by nationality will probably not have a marked political effect in the next decade or two. However, if a major setback to the system occurs, or even if it just continues to stagnate, there could be increased agitation for more power to be given to the republics. Most Russians would welcome a change in which their identity would not be submerged, and in which more deference would be accorded to their traditions, to the Church, and to the preservation of their culture, monuments, and countryside.[13] For many Russians, despite the fact that they are the dominant national group, the price of the present system is too high. However, the Balts, the Western Ukrainians, and others have latent separatist tendencies. The Moslems are gaining in numbers and have a sound basis for believing that they will play a more important role—and have greater independence—in the future than in the past. Their prospects for political influence would be much heightened if a sense of wider Moslem consciousness were to emerge as against separate Uzbek, Tadzhik, Azeri, etc., consciousness.[14] If such movements were to generate momentum, where would they stop?

Foreign Expansion. The incentives for the leadership to avoid a major military conflict are large. These followers of Lenin surely understand the importance of avoiding risky adventures. But the combination of great military strength and poor prospects might be enough, under some circumstances, to tip the balance inside the Politburo towards making a large expansionist move. If Soviet leadership were to make such a move, assuming that it retains elementary prudence, it would try hard to avoid a substantial risk of nuclear war—or of any war—with the United States. It would probably try to exploit circumstances in which the United States might reasonably be deterred from responding, say through a move in an area of Soviet strategic strength and American strategic weakness, such as Southwest Asia.[15] In any case, unless it throws all caution to the wind, its approach would be to use military force to achieve a victory without engaging (it would hope) in a major war. Of course, its expectations could be wrong.

Serious and Prolonged Internal Disarray. The possible causes described so far assume that someone is always dominant in Moscow, that power will continue to be passed on to successors—even by way of a coup by a Party faction or the military—without continuing political turbulence. In contrast, this path assumes that the Soviet Union enters into a period in which power would be divided among contesting groups without one of them becoming quickly dominant. Such a situation would be marked by shifting coalitions, paralysis of governmental functions, and perhaps violence. In some respects, its condition could become similar to China's at the height of the Cultural Revolution. Russia experienced such a period in the seventeenth century (1604–13), the "Time of Troubles," during which control of the throne was competed for by various pretenders, revolts and famines occurred, and confusion reigned.

There are, of course, strong incentives to avoid such a situation, including the fear that foreign enemies will take advantage of any disarray and the danger of losing control over parts of the empire. Probably the emergence of any such chaos would be rapidly quelled by the military which, on form, would likely remain cohesive. (Still, one should recall that more than a few disaffected Russians joined General Vlasov to fight on the German side during World War II.)

Implications for U.S. Policy

What Is in the U.S. Interest? The overriding American interest is the survival of our own country, as well as the democracies of Western Europe and Japan as free and secure societies. Construed more broadly, our interests extend to the furtherance of pluralistic and open political systems elsewhere in the world, including the Soviet empire. Because the Soviet Union poses, by far, the most important threat to these interests, the effect of various futures for the Soviet empire on our security should be our paramount concern.

The overriding interest in security almost certainly will require a major military effort on our part for the indefinite future—although that future might see major changes in alliance relations and American forces. Only if and when there is a marked reduction in the military threat from the Soviet Union would a large and sustained reduction in our military efforts be prudent.

It is banal to observe that we would like to see the Soviet empire quietly decline and to see the Soviet system transformed from a militarized, aggressive, coercive, Leninist regime into one more conducive to peace and progress. In this optimistic vision, Moscow would withdraw support from its overseas positions, in time restore the freedoms of the East Europeans, and give the peoples of the inner empire liberties they have never had. Such a political transformation almost certainly would be led by a significant economic transformation: it would begin with a gradual lessening of central control over the economy and with a greater use of markets for products, labor, and capital. It might also be associated with the decentralization of power to the various republics. In the process, many people outside the ruling class—farmers, entrepreneurs, professionals—would gain wealth and status. Such a diffusion of economic power probably would bring about a diffusion of political power. Although it is not an iron law that market systems and pluralist political systems always go together—the counterexamples of Nazi Germany and a number of Third World countries come to mind—the record suggests that there is a strong correlation between the two.

There are five difficulties with this vision. First, it seems utopian. Why should one contemplate so remote a prospect, recognizing that the present Soviet system—even though chronically ailing—retains considerable resilience, as well as substantial human and material resources to sustain itself? And there is no tradition of Soviet pluralism. One answer is that a look backward in time reveals extraordinary and unforeseen developments in other societies, ones that also were or seemed powerful and resilient, changes so extraordinary as to suggest that a dramatic shift for the Soviet Union is not beyond possibility. Within only two decades after the mid-1930s, the British and French empires virtually disappeared, Germany and Japan were radically transformed, and China became a communist state. Now China is experiencing an equally extraordinary change of course— one of uncertain destination—that was predicted by no one a decade ago. Moreover, the Soviet system is doomed to permanent inferiority—and decline relative to such rapidly growing neighbors as China and Japan—unless it is abandoned or at least substantially modified. Unlikely as it seems now, we might wake up some morning and find that extraordinary events are taking place in that country.

A second possible difficulty entails an application of what might be called the First Law of International Politics, that every significant action causes significant reactions. Its most obvious application in this instance is that the relaxation of the Soviet grip on Eastern Europe could result in the reunification of Germany. Such a prospect—which seems remote today—evokes expressions of concern in Eastern Europe and to some extent in Western Europe (some for political effect and others, no doubt, sincere). We believe that the profound changes that have taken place in West German society make these worries unwarranted, but some neighbors hold a different view. In any case, we do not hold the reunification of Germany to be against American interests—depending on the nature of the successor regime.

A third objection is that the Soviet system might succeed in adjusting its command economy at the margins enough to improve economic efficiency without a serious weakening of Party control. Military programs might be scaled back somewhat, parts of the "second" economy might be legitimized, and family agricultural plots might be expanded, without fundamentally altering the system. The expected resulting improvement in economic welfare could help the regime to muddle along. A "reform" that marginally improves a hostile system is not in our interests. We observe, however, that interested parties much closer to the scene than ourselves—namely, some in the Politburo and many in the *nomenklatura*—evidently believe that even modest changes are too risky or will accomplish little.[16] Whatever the present situation, when the regime has to face up to its predicament with seriousness, presumably no sooner than the likely failure of the current Five-Year Plan and perhaps later, some minimal shifts might be adopted. But it is doubtful that minimal ones will be enough to save the system.

The fourth difficulty is that the path toward the desired condition described above—or for that matter, any radical change in the Soviet system—might not be peaceful. Indeed, it might be dangerous to the West. We take this last objection to be the most serious. At least it is often voiced by members of the European elite and some Americans as well.

A familiar theme is that we should try to strengthen the position of the putative reformers, the dissenters, the closet liberals in the Kremlin. According to this view, this faction is opposed by the neo-Stalinists, members of the *nomenklatura* who feel threatened and who feel that the old ways are the best ways. The reformers and their ostensible allies, the dissidents, need outside support against the forces of reaction.[17] The conclusion is drawn that the West should help them through arms agreements and economic support.

An extension of this view is the position that the present Soviet regime should be propped up by the West not only to help its "doves" and to persuade it to be more civil, but also to avoid any possibility of its calamitous collapse. Some in the West worry—although few specialists think this at all likely—that the Soviet Union will fall into a state of chaos as described earlier. This might take the form of a violent contest for control of the state; for example, a military takeover, as in Poland, might occur. This, in itself, would not necessarily be a bad thing, but the worry is that the resulting regime could have a "Bonapartist" character. Or a "Solidarity" type of movement might arise with the Russian version behaving without the prudence and circumspection of the Polish original; the result could be violent popular upheavals, repressions, and, eventually, a disintegration of government authority and control. Or this control might be lost as the consequence of some nationalities breaking away if Moscow appears sufficiently weak; civil war might even occur. Although these possibilities seem remote to almost all Western observers, perhaps they seem less remote to the rulers of that country.

While the emergence of violence would be deplorable, none of these possibilities would be of grave concern to the rest of the world—indeed, it would benefit from the weakening and distraction of Soviet power—if the Soviet Union did not possess tens of thousands of nuclear warheads and an ability to send many of them great distances. But it does have these weapons, and the possible weakening and dispersion of control over them is a legitimate concern to the rest of us.

This line of argument, and the policy prescription it leads to, fits the old Irish saying, "Better the devil you know than the devil you don't know." The argument—a familiar Western European one—is that the Soviet system has evolved from a revolutionary movement to a conservative oligarchy more intent on preserving its privileges than advancing the cause of world revolution or, especially, risking war with the West. Its backwardness is a necessary consequence of the centralized control over the economy and political life. The oligarchs know they are in trouble, but they are not disposed to do things that risk mobilizing the superior resources of the West against them, or to chance a large-scale upheaval in Eastern Europe, in which the peoples of that region might turn to the West for help en masse. Nor would the leadership chance major dissidence inside the Soviet Union. Soviet activities in the Third World do not threaten vital Western (or at least European) interests. In short, the present system may not be the best of all imaginable worlds, but it is the best of all feasible ones and should therefore be preserved, with Western help if necessary.

Although this position merits thought, if for no other reason than that it seems to be held in influential circles, it assumes that living with the devil we know does *not* entail large risks. But the hazards are comparative. What we know of the Soviet system suggests that the present regime poses large risks to us through its compulsive expansionism, the invention and manipulation of external and internal "threats" against its system as a means of justifying the rulers' coercion, its declared aim to defeat the West and to bury and supplant capitalism, and its extraordinary and sustained military buildup. On the other hand, it has repeatedly demonstrated a capacity to retreat when weak and pressed; it did so in 1921 when under great strain, in 1946 in Iran, in 1948 with regard to Tito's defection, and in Cuba in 1962, to cite a few examples.

In light of these intrinsic and repeatedly demonstrated characteristics of the

Soviet system, an accommodative and even supportive policy prescription is most unconvincing. Soviet leaders, now under growing pressure to change the system, would be (marginally) relieved from having to make such changes. The Soviet system would remain highly militarized, driven to expand wherever possible. We would continue to have to defend ourselves against it—and therefore to live with the ever-present danger of war. Moreover, under such a policy, the risk would still remain of a political upheaval in Eastern Europe, or within the Soviet Union, which might result in violent spillovers elsewhere.

Clearly, we cannot assert with certainty that a successor regime worse than the present one is impossible. An ordering of American (and presumably that of other peoples') preferences would no doubt place the status quo, unpleasant as it is, ahead of war with a politically destabilized Soviet Union. But to argue that the West should help the "good guys" in the Soviet Union—the closet liberals—in order to help the dissidents in the society lacks adequate basis in history or current developments. The "liberals" in the Politburo are largely a figment of Western imagination and wish. Andropov was portrayed as one and Gorbachev has been similarly portrayed. Indeed, Gorbachev does advocate, some of the time, such steps as decentralization of authority. But the net effect of actual policy changes since his coming to power is a kind of neo-Stalinist tilt, not only at home but in the rest of the empire; the current "discipline" campaign even echoes the Stakhanovite movement under Stalin. He also recently has been reported as supporting the rolling back of the tentative market liberalizing moves made in Cuba since 1976. And the empire's campaigns in the Third World are being pursued with more vigor under Gorbachev than under his immediate predecessors.

The final objection is that Western policies are irrelevant to change in the Soviet domestic system or to its foreign policies.[18] This view would have more force were it not for the fact that the Soviet system is in grave trouble, with a highly uncertain future. In plausible future circumstances, outside forces might come to play a substantial role, as they have at periods in the past.

In short, 1) the Party will continue powerfully to resist any basic change to the system; 2) declining health of the Soviet masses, lower economic consumption, or the erosion of support for communism in the world are not likely to be enough to bring about basic system change soon; 3) the system will change only when the rulers' status and power are threatened—a circumstance that is likely to create strong pressures for radical changes in the long run; and 4) what would impel the *nomenklatura* is the faltering of the control system over the inner empire and over Eastern Europe, the clear failure of overseas activities (which would raise the question of its future at home), the erosion of military power, the threat of a military takeover, and economic decline to a point that would cause serious outbreaks of worker violence. Some developments such as these may happen by the year 2000, and perhaps sooner. Sooner or later – and probably later rather than sooner – the oligarchs in Moscow may be obliged to follow the Chinese down the road to the market and to some form of capitalism.

What Does This Mean for Western Actions?

The strategy of containment of Soviet power, conceived in 1947, was viewed as a holding action until internal changes occurred in the Soviet Union. George Kennan supposed then that a Western policy of containment would, within ten or fifteen years, promote tendencies to moderate or break up Soviet power. The weaknesses he discerned were its economic backwardness, the disillusion and exhaustion of its people, the uncertainties associated with the transfer of power from Stalin, and the inevitable emergence of strains within the Party structure; in time the system would mellow.

The Soviets managed well the transition from Stalin, and later ones, and have sustained themselves well beyond Kennan's forecasted period. The Western policy of containment eventually broke down. In one respect the system *has* mellowed: the incidence of terror is much reduced. Where Kennan erred was in not realizing that the central control apparatus in the Soviet Union could be so improved in power and effectiveness that the *nomenklatura* could become even more solidly entrenched without fundamental systemic change and with a diminished need to employ the gruesome methods of the postrevolutionary Cheka. In fact, the capabilities of the Soviet security organs – KGB and MVD – have been strengthened, so much so that they can exercise more stringent control with less use of naked force. Moreover, Soviet military power has burgeoned, the Soviet empire has made substantial geopolitical advances, and the incidence of international terror has mounted with direct and indirect Soviet complicity.

If we assume, for the moment, that the West could adopt a unified strategy towards the Soviet empire, what strategy now would be most likely to promote the aims we have proposed? There are three arenas of action: the overseas, contiguous (Eastern European and Afghanistan), and inner parts of the Soviet empire. In addressing these, four types of instruments can be distinguished: military, diplomatic, economic, and actions towards the peoples (as distinct from governments) of the empire.

The present Western stance towards the Soviet empire is complex, indeed contradictory, in part because there is no unified Western strategy. This is not only a matter of national differences within the alliance. There is clear disagreement within the United States, for instance, on whether or not to contest parts of the Soviet overseas empire. Until recently the Clark Amendment precluded support for the opposition to the Movement for the Liberation of Angola (MPLA) in Angola, and public and congressional opinion remains divided on the issue of supporting the Contras' opposition to the Sandinistas in Nicaragua.

There *is* general agreement in the United States, and to a lesser degree elsewhere in the West, on the importance of competing militarily (with the United States doing the most and Japan the least). In this endeavor, advances in military technology are a central part of the West's strategy. This is its principal offset to the Soviet—and Warsaw Pact—superiority in many types of forces. (There is a contrary strand of Western opinion, however, that holds that improvements in Western technology help to feed the so-called—but imaginary and counterfactual—"ever-escalating" arms competition with the Soviet Union; therefore mutually agreed, or unilateral, restrictions on Western technology development should be imposed. Some of the domestic opposition to the Strategic Defense Initiative, a program that poses a severe set of technical and resource challenges to Moscow, is motivated by this view.) The United States and its allies also agree on restricting the flow of certain military technologies through the mechanism of the Coordinating Committee on East-West trade (COCOM).

Diplomatic relations with the Soviet Union are more or less formally correct, but these relations inevitably reflect the fundamental hostility between the two camps. The frequent expulsion of embassy personnel on both sides and Soviet harassment of Western journalists are manifestations of this hostility. Instances of cooperation occur in arms agreements, cultural exchanges, and scientific visits and projects. Here, as in other dimensions of East-West relations, there is a difference within the West: Europe, and Northern Europe especially, has gradually moved towards closer relations with Moscow.

Economic relations are modest in scale. In 1984, U.S. exports to the Soviet Union were $3.5 billion and imports were $376 million; the corresponding trade figures for West Germany were $4.0 billion and $5.2 billion, respectively. This amounts to a tiny fraction of the trade of these Western countries. (In contrast, it is a large part of total Soviet trade.) Interestingly and perhaps surprisingly, the West heavily subsidizes trade with the Soviet empire; in 1981 alone subsidies to the communist countries altogether came to about $3.0 billion, roughly 20 percent of the total value of new loans to these countries granted that year with government support.[19] One-fourth of the subsidies went to the Soviet Union, and another 60 percent to Eastern Europe. Most, but not all, of the subsidies came from the Western European nations. Recently, the United States offered further subsidies to induce the Soviets to buy grain in accord with the formal 1983 agreement between the two governments.

With respect to the overseas empire, the West is sharply divided. The United States, despite internal divisions, supports several anti-communist insurgencies and France helps to defend Francophone Africa. But most Europeans are indifferent to the expansion of the overseas empire and many are actively opposed to American efforts to support those who are resisting (as in Nicaragua and El Salvador).

As for policies affecting the peoples of the empire, the West (Japan excepted) tries to supply them with information on internal and external events, is generally open to accepting them if they can get out, and sometimes tries to help some of them do so. An example is the American Jackson-Vanik legislation, which links U.S. granting of most-favored nation (MFN) trade benefits to Moscow with the relaxation of Soviet restrictions on the emigration of Jews and other peoples.

This summary suggests the difficulty of formulating a coherent Western strategy. Still, in the interest of helping to understand the logic of our basic choices, the following broad policy alternatives are worth distinguishing: to increase pressure on Moscow; to reduce pressure on, or even help, Moscow; and to continue present, but modified, policies.

Increase Pressure. This course would entail eliminating the current trade subsidies to the Soviet Union (and also, more doubtfully, to Eastern Europe) and restricting trade, reducing or ending Western lending, intensifying efforts to stem the transfer of technology usable for economic as well as military purposes, competing more vigorously in the military arenas, and increasing support for non-communists fighting to reverse the empire's 1970s expansion.

The justification for this policy rests on the fact that the Soviet Union is the self-declared enemy of the Western democracies. Its rulers see the contest between Marxism-Leninism and the capitalist democracies as permitting no final compromise: one side or the other will win. It is only prudent that the West, and all non-Marxist-Leninist societies, do what they can to weaken this self-declared mortal and irreconcilable enemy. Moreover, only when forced to do so will the system changes we desire be made. This argument is recognized and accepted to a considerable degree in our military and alliance activities and in American efforts to contest the overseas empire, but it is not much reflected in other respects.

We have previously presented the arguments that are offered against such a strategy: that a sick bear may become a more dangerous one and lash out militarily, or it might fall into domestic disorder that would be dangerous for us as well as the Soviet peoples. Critics of this strategy equate this position with trying to "spend the Soviet Union into bankruptcy," and contend further that, "of course the Soviets will spend whatever is needed to maintain their position."

Gorbachev says it directly:

> The United States wants to economically tire the Soviet Union, to exhaust the Soviet Union economically by encouraging the arms race.

> They want to create all kinds of difficulties for the Soviet leader-
> ship. . . . They are trying to create a situation where only the
> U.S.S.R. will reduce its weapons. . . . This is completely in error.
> And the . . . sooner they realize it's erroneous . . . the better it will
> be for everybody.[20]

Reality suggests otherwise.

The United States and the West are already depicted persistently by Soviet propaganda activities as a relentless and threatening foe to justify the Soviets' huge military efforts; and Leninists are among the least likely people in the world to "lash out" if pressed. The concept of "bankruptcy" is not meaningful in this context, but that of extreme pressure on resources is. The fact is that the Soviets spend about 25 percent of GNP on security efforts, and the costs of the empire do not preclude a further increase in these categories; but any such increase would further hurt investment or cut into already constricted consumption.

A more telling objection is that, whatever the merits of this strategy, the West is not united; this stance would not be accepted by the Germans, other Europeans, and the Japanese. They will continue to spend a modest share (or less in Japan) on defense; they will continue to subsidize trade with Moscow (providing loan guarantees at subsidized rates or other forms of subsidization); they will persist in adopting only minimal restrictions on transfers of militarily useful technology; and they will remain largely indifferent to Soviet advances in the Third World. Moreover, it is doubtful that this strategy of increased pressure would command necessary support in the United States.

This is a realistic prediction from today's perspective, although it might change if the Soviets were to move against the Western position in Berlin, try to bring Yugoslavia back into the empire, invade Iran, or act in some other way to heighten the perceived threat to Western Europe or Japan.

On balance, this line of policy has much to recommend it because the nature of the Soviet system is such that only domestic failure and determined foreign resistance will bring about the system changes we desire. Nevertheless, despite the strong case that can be made in its behalf, it is not now politically feasible as an overall guideline for strategy.

Reduce Pressure — and Perhaps Provide Help to the Soviets.   This course of action, which is at the other policy extreme, is supported by worries concerning the decline of the Soviet empire, and its internal and external consequences: once again, unless the sick bear recovers, he may become a more dangerous one. (An extension of this line of thought suggests that the Soviets might someday use the threat of internal chaos to evoke Western help.) Various arguments are advanced to support this position — some familiar from the 1970s détente period when the Soviet empire was not perceived to be in deep trouble. In addition to the above argument on preventing a dangerous destabilization, it is sometimes held that pressure on Moscow should be reduced—or help provided—because:

- *Tangible benefits would thereby be gained:* for example, more Jews or ethnic Germans would be allowed to emigrate; concessions might be made to Japan concerning the northern islands held by Moscow; other concessions might be granted on Afghanistan or in arms negotiation.

- *Intangible benefits would be gained*; e.g., strengthening the web of convergent interests between East and West—as promised but not realized in the 1970s—would produce restrained Soviet behavior.

- *Moderation of the most repressive aspects of the regime would be achieved.* This familiar argument lost much force during the Brezhnev regime as it became evident that external relaxation was—and perhaps had to be, given the character of the system—accompanied by greater internal repression.

Conceivably, one way to try to shrink the overseas empire is to link Soviet concessions there to benefits elsewhere. Kissinger and Nixon tried this approach in the early 1970s vis-à-vis Soviet support for Vietnam by trying to link reductions in the support to the prospect of détente. They failed but went ahead with the détente policy anyway. One difficulty in pursuing this policy is that the overseas empire is not highly costly to the Soviets, although they are probably reluctant to take on new members as costly to support as Cuba and Vietnam.[21] Moreover, these ventures are highly valued in Moscow. They provide military facilities and sources of logistic support for Marxist-Leninist liberation struggles. They distract the Americans, divide the West, and probably provide satisfaction to the rulers of the last great world empire and some support for the belief that the future belongs to communism. They enable the Soviets to play on the world scene in a way that is gratifying, particularly in contrast to the limited satisfactions derived from dealing with drunkenness and slack effort in the factories or handling the "irresponsible" Poles.

Given the Soviet leadership's notions about the attributes of a great power, prospects for obtaining a genuine retrenchment of Soviet imperial behavior are not good unless the regime is *in extremis*. That possibility cannot be ruled out for the future but it does not seem promising soon. It should be noted that Gorbachev might initiate a countermove by proposing the creation of "spheres of influence," conceding primacy of U.S. interest in Central America for Soviet primacy in Afghanistan and Southwest Asia. Given the West's (once again) growing dependence on Persian Gulf oil, as well as the importance of sustaining the resistance in Afghanistan and the implications of such a deal for the future of

TABLE 13-1   **Directions for Western Policy Toward the Soviet Empire**

Western Policy Instruments	Parts of the Empire		
	Inner	E. European	Overseas
Track 1			
Military	Compete— especially with advanced technology; selective coop.	Promote neutrality stance; in event of hostilities, plan conditional Western restraint.	Resist extension and support anti-communist resistance.
Track 2			
Economic	Unsubsidized trade; business contacts at enterprise level.	Normal trade (plus?); promote decentralized ties.	Economic restrictions.
Diplomatic	Formal (minus).	Formal.	Support anti-communists.
Track 3			
People-Oriented	Support autonomous capacities; expand information access and bilateral exchanges.	Promote cultural, religious, profes-sional, etc. ties.	Support anti-communists.

Pakistan, and therefore access to the oil of the Persian Gulf, we should reject such a proposed trade.

The central flaw of this and similar transactions is that the principal danger to the West lies in the nature and essential aims of the Moscow regime. As long as such a regime remains in power we will remain in danger. So the alternatives are not a troublesome but basically prudent system versus one that in its decline might lash out suicidally against us. Instead, the main choice is between a profoundly antagonistic and expansionist (albeit cautious) system, which, if it retains its present character, could eventually come into serious conflict with us, versus one that may find it necessary to change its character or be overthrown. No one can guarantee a graceful decline and fall of the Soviet empire, but the attempted preservation of the status quo offers no guarantee of safety either. We reject this strategy because it derives from a profound and wishful misconstruction of the Soviet system.

The Preferred Strategy: Modifying Present Policies

When one examines what is arguably most in our interest and is, or might be, feasible, one contemplates a set of aims and actions that are portrayed in Table 1: along one axis are the three parts of the empire towards which our strategy needs to be addressed; along the other, the four main instruments or modes of action.

As Table 1 shows, the policy approach summarized in each cell is not identical across parts of the empire or across instruments. Indeed, there is a strong case for a good deal of variation.

The resulting policy vector can neither reasonably be described as a "pressure" one (although many people in Moscow might see it that way) nor as a "relaxation" or "supportive" one. It entails basically a significant modification of the present strategy.

This general approach amounts to what can be described as a three-track strategy toward the empire.

Track 1: *Vigorous competition on the security fronts* — competitive against the overseas empire, against threats to U.S. allies on the Soviet periphery, and against threats to the continental United States.

Track 2: *More or less formal relations on the diplomatic front and predominantly nonsubsidized relations on the economic front.*

Track 3: *Supportive actions regarding the peoples of the empire.*

The main case for this three-track course is that it does not entail undesirable or perhaps unrealistic modifications of existing strategy. The current disparate policy mix is the result of forces pulling in different directions, and the resultant vector is not easily shifted. Nonetheless, the present — admittedly inconsistent — position of the West has at least not prevented the Soviet Union from entering into its troubled condition, and its continuation is not likely to keep the Soviet sickness from deepening. Consequently, a modified version of the present Western stance towards the Soviet Union has much to recommend it.

This policy line is basically a mix of serious competition where it is essential (in the military area as well as in the Third World, including the extended Soviet empire), mostly normal relations in diplomatic and economic terms, and watchful waiting. It is important to be aware that, left to itself, the bear's condition will likely worsen.

This strategy can be best described by examining its application to the three parts of the empire.

Containing and Shrinking the Overseas Empire.   During the détente of the 1970s, Moscow made large leaps forward in Angola, Ethiopia, and elsewhere in the Third World by exploiting America's paralysis and Europe's indifference. It seems to have assumed that this behavior would not endanger the economic and military benefits of détente. (If the resulting collapse of détente was predicted in Moscow, the prospective gains from extending the empire were evidently judged to be worth more than the costs.) From the American perspective, it would not be difficult to draw up a list of places from which we would like to see the Soviets withdraw. Cuba would be high on such a list, for instance, for the removal of Soviet forces – thus rectifying a flaw in the deal on the removal of missiles in 1962 – and Cuban forces from Nicaragua and Africa.

The central issue is not the appeal of communism to the masses of the Third World. Although the ideological component of the competition is more important in the Third World than in the developed one, the dominant phenomenon at work is the willingness of local aspiring rulers or oligarchies, or those already in power, to "contract" with the Soviet Union for protection and support in exchange for services rendered. This is clearly so in Cuba, Nicaragua, Ethiopia, Angola, South Yemen, and Afghanistan. Such deals now follow a standard formula (as described in chapter 4 by Francis Fukuyama): the creation of a vanguard Marxist-Leninist party, with the programmed security organs and control apparatus that are essential ingredients of such a regime, backed by Soviet weapons, often Cuban troops, and help of various kinds from other members of the empire. To lubricate the process, the formula calls for capitalizing on internal sources of disaffection – namely, the exploitation, inequities, poverty, nationalism, and resentment that are endemic in much of the Third World.

Where the contract is effectively implemented, the result is usually a robust position of centralized power. It is also one that, by its nature, leads to further expansion, with the formula used and adapted to particular circumstances – as we observe in conflicts on three continents. Each "node" of the empire generates internal and external enemies and seeks to support local friends (e.g., in El Salvador by the Sandinistas, SWAPO by the MPLA in Angola). Also, as noted earlier, the empire is a mutual help organization: the Soviets help them all; Soviet gains in Africa have been crucially assisted by Cuba; the Sandinistas have depended on Cuban help; East Germans provide expertise in internal security; North Korea often provides arms; and Gadhafi supplies money and arms. Training camps and the supply of arms link the Soviet Union, several Eastern European countries, the PLO, the Red Brigade, and the Red Army Faction, among other groups.

In our view, it is crucial that the West continue and strengthen its efforts in this contest. Not to do so will allow Soviet military power to be directly installed (as in Vietnam, Afghanistan, and Cuba) in more and more places. Among other effects, this could not help but reduce the American ability—and motivation—to help to defend Europe and Japan.

One means of strengthening these efforts is by enlisting the cooperation and participation of some Third World countries, as well as legitimate freedom-seeking movements within other Third World countries, in the development of cooperative forces for joint undertakings to contain and reverse the overseas Soviet empire.[22] This objective requires the sustained use of diverse political, economic, military, and paramilitary elements. Cooperative forces developed in concert with selected Third World countries and movements can be a valuable element in this part of the preferred strategy.

We should try harder to persuade our allies, as well as other like-minded countries who are not formal allies, at least to stop objecting to efforts to contain and erode the overseas empire or, better, to join in these efforts. There are three good reasons for doing so: 1) when people are willing to fight against communism, there is a general political and moral argument that the democracies should help them; 2) the extension of the overseas empire implies the extension of Soviet military power to the detriment of our overall security—and that of Europe and Japan; and 3) the expansion of the empire can have serious regional consequences—for instance, in Central America, especially if Mexico were to become destabilized through a combination of internal problems and external influences.

Reversing the Soviet empire in the Third World can be of enormous significance in its effect on the actual and perceived "correlation of forces." It is conceivable that a path to Moscow—that is, to the substantial transformation of the Soviet system—may lie in a "long march" through Luanda, Phnom Penh, Aden, Managua, and Havana.

The Eastern European Part of the Empire. Although the overseas empire is valuable to the Soviets, the Eastern European part is of especially high strategic importance to Moscow. The division of Germany, the creation of a defensive glacis, the incorporation of parts of the area occupied in World War II into the Soviet Union, and the continued domination of the rest (with the exception of Yugoslavia and a portion of Austria) were accomplishments of the highest order. These will be strongly defended.

However, the peoples of this area remain deeply unreconciled to Soviet domination and to the imposition of communist rule. There can be no doubt that if Soviet power were withdrawn, the present regimes would be quickly overthrown. The Eastern Europeans overwhelmingly see themselves as Europeans (indeed, the term *Eastern* European is not a favored one in the area, *Central* European is preferred), not as members of the great Soviet empire; they are pulled culturally and through economic interest to the West. It is to be expected that they will seek every opportunity to gain more latitude vis-à-vis Moscow, and also that, as a consequence, serious trouble will continue to erupt there from time to time.

The decline of Soviet power will be seen as offering them the possibility of more freedom. Of course, Moscow and the entrenched ruling party elites in these countries will continue to regard popular movements in this area (such as the Prague Spring and Solidarity) as grave threats, not only to control of this zone but also to the Soviet Union itself. But, as its failure to stamp out Solidarity for sixteen months demonstrated, even if the suppression was finally executed adroitly if perhaps not permanently, Moscow's dominance by the early 1980s had weakened. And the continued near-total alienation of the Polish people from the regime shows that the suppression of December 1981 was far from complete. By the 1990s, Moscow's ability to control Eastern Europe may be still weaker, not because it will be unable through force to suppress popular dissidence but because the price of doing so may look increasingly high.

There is much at stake for the West. For about a decade after World War II, the United States actively contested the complete consolidation of Soviet rule over the region. But when the Hungarian revolt was suppressed without any Western response, it became evident to all that Soviet rule there would no longer be seriously challenged by the West (although Yalta has never been accepted in the West as giving the Soviets *de jure* rights). With some handwringing over oppressions and occasional Soviet invasions, the West has conceded the region to Moscow. The American policy towards the area—which carries the label "differentiation," implying the use of "carrots" and "sticks" adjusted to the behavior of the region's governments—has modest content. For instance, under this policy the most Stalinist of the region's regimes, that of Rumania, is accorded preferred status because of its somewhat independent foreign policy stances vis-à-vis Moscow.

In contrast is the Federal Republic of Germany's (FRG) policy toward the area. Under former Chancellor Willy Brandt, who was profoundly shaken by the failure of the United States to challenge the building of the Berlin Wall in 1961, the FRG took the lead in the West to improve relations with Moscow and the countries of Eastern Europe, especially the German Democratic Republic. This *Ostpolitik* consists of an accommodating line towards the East on many issues, a forward-leaning stance on arms control, and economic subsidies— especially to the GDR in return for limited emigration to the West and other tangible and hoped-for intangible benefits. It goes along with a cool attitude toward such manifestations of the human struggle for freedom as Solidarity. *Ostpolitik*'s sources seem to be the resultant vector of a set of forces: tangible benefits from East Germany, as well as shared cultural values with it; fears deriving from the rise in Soviet strength and lowered confidence in American power and wisdom; hopes about the mellowing of the Soviet system; and long-term strategic advantage in coming step-by-step closer to the East Germans. There are obvious dangers in a line that causes the Federal Republic to edge toward a more neutral stance between the United States and the Soviet Union, to subsidize the Warsaw Pact, and to undermine support for sustaining its own defenses. Indeed, the final position of such a line could be the ending of the Western Alliance and perhaps a divided Western Europe. But there are also potential strategic benefits in a policy that builds on the evident attraction of the East Europeans toward the West. As the Soviet Union gradually weakens, the attractions of this line are likely to become increasingly evident.

From this perspective, it is remarkable that the West's assessment of the military threat from the Warsaw Pact against Western Europe, the core problem of Western security, has invariably assumed that the Eastern European allies of the Soviet Union would unquestioningly and promptly follow Moscow's orders in a conflict with the West. To say the least, this assumption is doubtful, especially if the Eastern Europeans were to be offered an alternative. It is often observed that NATO, like many alliances that have preceded it, is a potentially frangible alliance. The Soviets certainly are working hard to fragment it. Yet it has been rarely observed that the Warsaw Pact, whose non-Soviet peoples hate and despise their Soviet masters, have much less of a shared interest in following Moscow's commands than the West Europeans have in defending themselves. Because the Eastern Europeans comprise 30 percent of the active-duty manpower in the Northern Tier of Eastern Europe and about one-half of the air and ground units, their behavior in the early days of a conflict with NATO could be crucial in determining the outcome. Even after reinforcement by ready Soviet forces sent from the Soviet Union, the East Europeans would still make up a large part of the Warsaw Pact forces opposite those of NATO. Only after a long period of mobilization and reinforcement could Soviet forces be so large as to make relatively insignificant those of its allies. But if such a Soviet mobilization were to occur, NATO would also have a long time to mobilize and reinforce as well. An equally important fact is that the Soviet lines of supply run for 1,000 kilometers through potentially hostile Polish, Czechoslovakian, and German territory.

Given the importance of the role of the Eastern Europeans in the balance in Europe, it would seem a matter of the highest importance that the members of the Soviet General Staff have their existing doubts maximized that the Eastern Europeans are not to be relied on. In effect, there should be a competition, in the event of a grave crisis or conflict, for the support of the Eastern Europeans. On their side of this contest, the Soviets would have local instruments of control over the military forces of their Pact allies and peoples; the West would have strong common interests with these same peoples, including their soldiers, as well as the ability to promise sparing them pain and damage.[23] In the end, if the Eastern Europeans – and for that matter the Baltic peoples and those of the Ukraine – were not to support Moscow in a conflict with NATO, any attack by Moscow on the West would be in jeopardy. At least the resulting balance of instruments and influence would be closer than has usually been assumed.

The main implications for Western policy toward Eastern Europe are these: 1) Actions that reinforce the essential unity of Europe from the Atlantic to the Bug (the river marking the Eastern border of Poland) should be promoted, not only for reasons of common culture and human rights but also because the security interests of the West will thereby be strengthened. *Ostpolitik*, in this respect, if pursued appropriately, has the potential for contributing to Western security. 2) The Eastern Europeans should be encouraged in the view that their ability to act independently and in their own interest could enable them to prevent Moscow's taking them to war against the West. 3) In the unlikely circumstance that a crisis or conflict comes, NATO should then do all in its power to persuade the Eastern Europeans to drag their feet on compliance with Moscow, to stand aside, and to sabotage the Soviet war effort. To strengthen Eastern European incentives toward such behavior, NATO should apply the leverage of offering to mitigate the destruction that NATO forces would inevitably inflict on Eastern Europe in a war with the Warsaw Pact. (It is important to note that the increased precision of weapons delivery supports such a political strategy.) And without Eastern European support, the prospect for a successful NATO counterattack into Warsaw Pact territory would greatly improve, a factor that should help to encourage the Eastern Europeans not to cooperate with Moscow – and Moscow never to make a move against the West.

Such a policy line will not, in the foreseeable future, undo Yalta and bring about the freedom of these peoples. The West has no stomach for trying. But tangible measures to emphasize the unity of Europe can benefit those in its Eastern half as well as reinforce the security of the West.

Probably the most effective help to the peoples of Eastern Europe has been through the broadcasting activities of Radio Free Europe, West German radio and television, the BBC, and other Western electronic media. These broadcasts play a crucial role in informing the Eastern Europeans about developments within their countries as well as in the outside world. Recently, they were the primary source of early information on the Soviet reactor fire at Chernobyl. Changes in communications technology are rapidly increasing the capacity of these peoples to get information. For example, direct broadcast television to Western Europe has a "footprint" that spills into Eastern Europe. Also, the rapidly shrinking size of the antennas required for receiving satellite transmission will add further to the ability of the Eastern Europeans to access information from the West. Already, there are reports of hundreds of satellite dishes in Eastern Europe (and in the Soviet Union as well) trained on Western communications satellites.[24] As these technologies develop, all of the peoples of Eastern Europe (and of the Soviet Union) will be increasingly able to maintain closer connections with the West and with each other.

In this spirit, what should be the West's economic policy toward Eastern Europe? Trade with Eastern Europe and the Soviet Union makes up a very small part of the total trade of the West, of Western Europe, and even of the Federal Republic of Germany.[25] Despite recurring hopes among Western businessmen of large, untapped markets in the CMEA area, the fact is that the system-imposed slow growth of the area makes fantasies of these hopes. Normal, unsubsidized trade will remain small because Eastern Europe's economic performance is greatly depressed by the command system imposed on the CMEA countries. As a rough estimate, the Eastern European economies produce about one-half the output and much less than half the trade they could were they allowed to have a free-market system.

As we have seen, Western governments, predominantly those of Western Europe, subsidize much of their trade with the region. These subsidies stem from a mercantilist, export-oriented policy bolstered by internal and external political motivations. This is especially true of the Federal Republic of Germany, which transfers large sums of money to the GDR. The main problem with these subsidies, beyond the largely hidden but real costs they impose on Western taxpayers, is that they support oppressive regimes. They also reduce the burden on Moscow, which has been subsidizing them to a modest but not negligible extent (about 2 percent of the Soviet GNP in 1983), an amount the Soviets are eager to reduce; Western subsidization makes it easier for them to do so.[26] On the other hand, there are the direct and indirect benefits to the West from such subsidies as mentioned above.

A potential resolution of these conflicting pulls is for the West to try to support activities in these countries designed to circumvent the central bureaucracies. An example is Western efforts to support Polish agriculture through the Catholic Church, rather than through the government. (Of course, as the recent setback to this venture illustrates, these governments do not embrace Western efforts to circumvent them.) Looking ahead, the Eastern European governments are under great pressure to give more scope to private enterprises and to free markets. There are thus likely to be increased opportunities for the promotion of and direct contact with private enterprises and markets. The West might be able to reinforce this pressure through joint ventures or through loans or equity investments in various enterprises. It is a matter of careful judgment for Western governments as to whether and how such arrangements should be promoted.[27]

The Inner Empire.   The core need in dealing with the Soviet Union proper is a militarily strong West. Under Track 1, this is an area for vigorous competition. The U.S. military buildup of the 1980s, designed to close the gap that opened up with the Soviets over the preceding decade and before, has not been accompanied by parallel efforts on the part of our European allies or the Japanese. As a result, the military balances between NATO and Warsaw Pact forces in Europe, and between free world forces and those of its adversaries in other parts of the world, are far from satisfactory. The Soviet nuclear buildup has effectively negated the U.S. threat to defend allies through the use of nuclear weapons; indeed, the Soviets have increased and protected their own theater nuclear forces. There has also been a steady improvement in Soviet conventional forces to the point where—especially if its Eastern European allies support them—a successful blow against Western Europe might be manageable. More worrisome, because a move in this direction is more likely, is the fact that Soviet forces have a clearly superior position in the direction toward the Persian Gulf. Only in the Far East do the Soviets have clear weaknesses with their long, thin line of communication through Siberia, and the potential difficulty of naval access to the Pacific. Even there, a large buildup has occurred in Soviet naval and air power, measurably assisted by the Soviet base at Camranh Bay (itself an ironic legacy of the U.S. military investment in Vietnam in the 1970s).

Looking ahead, Soviet prospects look much less promising because the growth in resources available for the military has slowed and trends in technology—centering on electronics—disfavor the Soviet system. The Soviet military is also rightly concerned about its technical lags—just as Gorbachev is about its overall technical failings. These lags in weapons technology especially impact on conventional weapons. The ongoing revolutions in sensors, communications, stealth, and precision delivery are definitely not originating in the Soviet Union. Its command economy is notoriously poor at creating and applying these technologies, and its military leaders fear that it will fall further behind the West in this area.

It is true that, even if their military resources don't grow appreciably, even if they remain near present levels, the Soviets would still be able to continue a large program of military modernization. Soviet military spending, measured in dollars, is about as much as that of the United States, around $300 billion a year. Nonetheless, the prospect of a military growth slowdown is hardly something to be viewed with equanimity by a system that has shown an enormous appetite for military power. Furthermore, exigencies might cause military spending to be cut—a contingency likely to evoke great resistance within the Soviet military. There is already grumbling by the military directed at the Party over its recent defense policies, and part of the cause doubtless has to do with money. Things will probably get worse. Lagging productivity, the primacy apparently being given by Gorbachev to modernizing factory capital equipment, and his declared intent to improve the level of consumption imply that something must give, and it is hard to see how this could not affect the military sector. One sure way to get a boost in machinery output—a high priority for Gorbachev—is to switch some military production lines to making such equipment. On balance, probably the best bet is that Soviet defense spending will continue through the rest of the 1980s at the equivalent of around $300 billion a year, with perhaps slight growth, and with well over one-half of this amount spent on new equipment. But the pressure to cut costs is growing.

In sum, the Soviet Union is on a path that will very likely cause its relative military power slowly to decline. But the present level of the Soviet military effort is so high that there is no warrant in this prediction for a slacking off of Western defense efforts.

Of course, this assessment depends on the Soviets' continuing to face at least a moderately cohesive West. If the Western alliances erode or fall apart, this relative decline prediction is definitely not applicable. Also, the Soviet leadership must be gratified by the prospect that growth in U.S. military spending is also probably ended, at least for a time. Budgetary pressure, together with a belief that the Soviet Union isn't looking for a major confrontation with the West, has produced a substantial shift in congressional attitudes. If the U.S. defense budget is constant or grows only slowly for the next several years, what might we do within this total?

Most useful would be an expansion of our efforts to counter and reverse the overseas empire. Most obviously underfunded is support for those resisting its expansion in the Third World. Here incremental dollars can have a large effect. This means funds for security assistance, as well as improvement in the management of such assistance, and associated training and logistics support by our own forces. After deducting the large share of such assistance earmarked by Congress for Israel and Egypt, these funds come to around one percent of our total national security expenditures, a far smaller proportion than is warranted by their strategic significance. Congress has been especially stingy with these funds because of the controversies surrounding some of the contests at issue (e.g., in Nicaragua and Angola), and the anxiety that such efforts in support of the emerging "Reagan Doctrine" might increase, rather than reduce, the likelihood of U.S. forces being drawn into such conflicts. And, of course, there is always more political support for money for our military services than for programs that have the label "assistance." The strategic needs strongly argue otherwise.

The core American strategic interest, beyond the security of the United States itself, has been the protection of Western Europe. The continued increase and modernization of Soviet forces calls for sustained effort on the part of NATO to improve its conventional forces. Here a distinction is needed between what should be done and who should pay for it. As to the former, the key elements of a modernization program include increased investment in much more accurate air-delivered and ground-launched missiles with improved warheads, improved air defenses (and perhaps defenses against conventionally armed ballistic missiles), and improved sensors and command and control. The cost of such a program could be met if NATO were to manage a sustained 3 percent a year real growth in defense spending—a rate that is not being implemented. Here the United States faces a dilemma: the Europeans have the resources to do much more to defend themselves, but the more the United States does the stronger is the European's incentive to do less. Moreover, we have interests elsewhere that are not being adequately met, especially in the Persian Gulf region. This fact raises the question as to whether it makes sense for such a large proportion of our defense resources and our forces to be based in, or committed to, Europe. We would certainly have to draw on these forces if serious trouble broke out in the Middle East, Eastern Asia, or elsewhere. They have played a key role in the security and political stabilization of Europe, but it is also evident that the presence of American forces in Europe for nearly half a century has weakened the Europeans' incentive to do more for their own defense. One big question is whether or not a shift of U.S. forces away from Europe would accelerate the creeping trend of neutralism (a trend all too evident in Northern Europe) or would reverse it. Another is what the Soviet Union might do if the U.S. presence and perceived commitment to Europe's defense were markedly reduced.

Reflection on these questions leads us to conclude that there should be no large change in our current European commitments. Clearly, the United States should not, and will not, withdraw from Europe unilaterally. The incentives such a move might create for greater defense effort by the Europeans, or the heightened risk of a move by the Soviets, are too uncertain to gamble. But what the United States should consider, and probably should implement, is a change in our deployments. At least, we should make more explicit that many U.S. forces in Central Europe are a reserve for use elsewhere, and perhaps some should be shifted elsewhere, e.g., to the southern flank of NATO where they could move directly and be brought rapidly to bear on the most threatened area, the Persian Gulf.

A future, obviously not imminent, in which both great powers remove themselves from the two halves of Europe is one that has much to commend it, especially from an American perspective. But that implies that the Soviets would relinquish the gains secured by the Red Army in World War II, and, very probably, also implies the reunification of Germany. That is not a negotiable proposition in the foreseeable future, although it must be said that the future can't be foreseen.

Another area for policy change is our ballistic missile defense program. The rebuilding of American military forces since the late 1970s has seen no significant change in U.S. strategy, with the important exception of the Strategic Defense Initiative. The technical possibilities for defense against a considerable variety of attacks are significant, although there are serious reasons to doubt whether political support for SDI can be sustained if the administration persists in the position that no defense should be built until it can be a multilayered, largely space-based one premised on providing wide protection to the American people. It would take decades of research and development with an uncertain outcome. The best position substantively and politically is to build ABM defenses in stages beginning with ground-based interceptors that could be available soon. Such a defense could guard against a precursor attack against our command-and-control system, among other missions. It would strengthen deterrence of a Soviet nuclear atttack, help to stabilize the nuclear balance, and add to the credibility of an appropriate U.S. response to a Soviet attack on Western Europe. There are also technically and potentially promising possibilities for a ballistic missile defense of military forces in Europe against nonnuclear as well as nuclear attack.

Another related area is nuclear arms negotiation. Clearly, little has been accomplished by earlier arms agreements; indeed, most of them arguably have been dysfunctional. We sought and did not get "linkage" to more restrained Soviet behavior in the Third World; we failed to win a scaling back of Soviet efforts on long-range nuclear forces (to parallel our own unilateral and large budget reductions in offensive and defensive forces during the 1960s and 1970s); and we failed to get the sought-for reduction in the growing threat to our silo-based ICBMs. The vaunted ABM Treaty—which was supposed to signify agreement not to try to defend one's cities against nuclear attack—was followed by a sustained modernization of Soviet air defenses, continued development of Moscow ABM defenses, and a vigorous program of ABM research, including testing of anti-tactical ballistic missile defenses. This happened during a period when we deployed no new ICBMs, lost interest in ballistic missile defense (until President Reagan's revival of this topic in 1983), and scaled back even further our spending on offensive arms. As a result, the Soviet nuclear threat to the West was greatly heightened during this period of arms agreements.

Looking ahead, no fundamental improvement is likely if we continue pursuing agreements based on the concept of mutual assured destruction (a concept which, among its other defects, is inconsistent with our interest in protecting allies because it calls for us to commit national suicide on their behalf, something that is neither rational nor credible to carry out). Moreover, the Soviets have been violating the spirit and the letter of these agreements. They have learned that these negotiations and agreements are an effective way to bolster opposition to the U.S. technical advances they fear (e.g., the Safeguard anti-missile program in the early 1970s and the Strategic Defense Initiative today), and to create divisions within the West (e.g., the Euro-missile issue), so far without accepting significant constraints on themselves.

It is striking how little a difference the current negotiations on nuclear arms—those on intermediate-range missiles and intercontinental-range ones—if successful, would make to our principal concerns: the vulnerability of forces in Europe to sudden nuclear attack; the vulnerability of our land-based ICBM force and, more generally, the conditions that make for preemptive instability stemming from the vulnerability of many of these forces on both sides; reducing the potential for destructiveness of the offensive forces on both sides; the imbalance between the conventional forces of NATO and the Warsaw Pact; or saving much of the money spent on nuclear forces. This admitted, as it sometimes is by arms control advocates, one is then told that the *real* goal is reaching agreements, building confidence, laying the groundwork for the next step, and so on. This line of argument was unpersuasive when advanced after the signing of SALT I in 1972, and it has come to look progressively less convincing in succeeding years. The root cause of its lack of credibility should by now be obvious: although the Soviet leadership has strong reasons to avoid nuclear war, it also has a strong compulsion to manipulate these instruments of power for its hostile and unceasing campaign to divide and neutralize the West.

This analysis applies to an agreement eliminating intermediate (and perhaps some short-range) U.S. and Soviet missiles from Europe: the nuclear threat to Western Europe would be reduced by very little (given the many thousands of weapons based in the Soviet Union and at sea that could be quickly delivered against Europe), and the number of NATO weapons deliverable against the Soviet Union would not be much reduced. The main significance of such an agreement would be symbolic; it would be a major step towards the "denuclearization" of Germany. Defenders of such an agreement correctly observe that it would restore the *status quo ante* militarily to the situation before the deployment of both SS-20s and NATO intermediate-range missiles. But one cannot so easily undo a political process in which Western governments declared that these missiles were needed to link Europe's security to that of the United States. Now the strategy for the defense of Europe, a strategy that has depended substantially on nuclear weapons in Europe, needs to be reconsidered. This in itself is not necessarily bad, but it creates a good deal of uncertainty about the future of Europe's defense.

Abandoning the main arms control strategy that has been so unsuccessfully pursued does not imply dropping efforts to limit certain dangers of nuclear forces through cooperation with an adversary, nor, still less, does it require spending more money on these arms. Indeed, it can reasonably be argued that the nuclear arms control process, by focusing attention on maintaining parity with the growing numbers of Soviet forces, has caused us to play a "matching" game (for example, in large ICBMs), rather than to concentrate on the nuclear forces we really need. If the latter course were pursued, we would probably evolve a smaller, better controlled, and more precise and discriminate nuclear force than we now have or are likely to get if we remain locked in to the concepts that dominate the current negotiating process.

The arms control negotiations that have taken place in recent years provide no basis for changing these judgments. The Soviets are still trying to weaken the U.S. nuclear tie to Europe and to kill the Strategic Defense Initiative. What is new is more vigorous and bolder Soviet leadership and recognition of a grave Soviet economic situation. So there is a stronger Soviet need than before for arms control agreements as a step toward a revival of détente. This would ease Soviet access to Western technology and capital *and* promote reduced Western military efforts. From the Soviet standpoint, all the vectors point toward getting a major agreement. Our analysis suggests that it may not be in the U.S. — and arguably the Western — interest to do so.[28]

Useful agreements *have* been reached in some areas such as the atmospheric test ban and limiting the spread of nuclear weapons, and some other areas of mutual interest might be found (such as the proposal by Albert Wohlstetter and Brian Chow for self-defense "keep-out" zones against space mines threatening space satellites).[29] To put it differently, most of those things that most need doing with nuclear forces — improvements in command and control, protection of forces, reducing the capacity for indiscriminate destruction — must be done by each side essentially on its own, not through negotiated agreements.

Moreover, there would be more profit in focusing less on nuclear forces and more on Soviet general purpose forces. After all, it is the Soviet ground, air, and naval forces that pose the greatest danger to Europe and other of our allies and friends. Significant reductions in these forces and the return of some of them to the Soviet homeland could make an important contribution to Western security, but not through "balanced" reduction with the West as in the negotiations for Mutual Balanced Force Reductions (MBFR) in Europe. The MBFR negotiation so far has had the principal effect of legitimizing the Soviet military presence in Eastern Europe. What Western Europe needs for its security is "unbalanced" force reductions; specifically, the reduction of Soviet forces in Eastern Europe to a level that would allow them to retain their hold on that area (for they clearly would not go below *that* level), but that would markedly reduce the threat to Western Europe. Such unbalanced reductions would have a stabilizing effect on European security, whereas "balanced" reductions would be destabilizing because American weapons and troops would retreat across the Atlantic, while those of the Soviet Union would retreat—at most—across the Bug. The goal of unbalanced reductions in the East is a goal worthy of negotiation. Of course, if such an arrangement were to be pursued, its implementation would have to guard against an asymmetrical weakness: the relatively greater difficulty for the West to end the subventions that might be offered on our side once interest group pressures have been created to support them, compared to the ease with which the Soviets could reverse or blur their force reductions or rapidly move forces back into Eastern Europe.

Of course, it will be said that because the Soviets will try to preserve their military superiority over Western Europe, such an effort would fail. This overlooks both the growing Soviet weakness and the value of staking out a position truly in the Western interest. In any case, such an arrangement is more relevant to events that might happen in the real world than trying to prevent nuclear war through the types of nuclear arms and MBFR discussions that have been pursued.

Diplomatic and economic relations are in Track 2, the domain of more or less normal, unsubsidized relations. Unsubsidized trade with the Soviet Union will be small. Much of what the Soviets both export and import are homogeneous, primary commodities (oil, natural gas, and gold among the exports; grains among the imports). Such widely produced and consumed commodities are exceptionally difficult to control. Moreover, Soviet noncommodity trade outside the COMECON (CMEA) bloc is largely with Western Europe, and to a limited extent with Japan, China, and other less-developed countries. These nations normally will not agree to restrictions on trade with the Soviet Union; indeed, as we have seen, many of them (and the United States, as well) subsidize it through below market-rate loans and by "dumping" food (e.g., the United States offers subsidized grain and the European Economic Community (EEC) exports portions of its surplus butter mountain).

For these and other reasons the current U.S. policy (sometimes violated) of engaging in normal trade and lending practices with the Soviet Union and urging a similar position on its allies is the best one could hope for. This implies no subsidization in any form, direct or indirect, including no government export or loan guarantees, export rebates, or below-market interest rates. Lending by commercial banks should be fully exposed to the financial and other risks attendant to lending to the Soviets, without any explicit or implicit safety net provided by governments. Formal trade controls through COCOM would continue to be limited to military-related technology (recognizing the myriad complications that inevitably arise in connection with dual-use technologies). Economic advantages should be granted to Moscow only for clear and substantial benefits in return, such as returning to the Soviet Union many of the Soviet forces in Eastern Europe.

The diplomatic and economic strategy toward Eastern Europe should be differentiated from that toward the Soviet Union. *This* should be the main "difference" in our policy toward the Warsaw Pact. The principal aim of this strategy, as described above, should be to reinforce ties with the West; this implies formal or normal diplomatic relations and the promotion of cultural ties and contacts with various groups in these countries. On economic relations, Western governments might especially encourage the types of activities discussed earlier that show promise of furthering larger strategic goals.

There would continue to be, along this track, the pursuit of joint interests with the Soviet Union and parts of the empire in selected areas—e.g., protection of the environment, allocation of geosynchronous satellite slots, fishing matters, and sports, including the Olympics—as aspects of formal relations.

Track 3 focuses on supportive actions regarding the peoples of the Soviet empire. The United States and other Western countries long have pursued policies directed toward reaching the peoples of the Soviet Union and the external empire. These policies have sought to provide information via radio broadcasts about the external world and about the Soviet system. They have assisted in the emigration of some groups, especially Jews and ethnic Germans, and have (with fluctuating interest) supported dissidents who are working for a less repressive Soviet system.

Western efforts should continually emphasize the distinction between the Soviet ruling class and the peoples of the Soviet Union and its empire. The West can advance these and related themes along Track 3 in two ways: through unilateral actions (e.g., broadcasting and other modes of transmitting information), and by using the economic power of the West, along with Soviet economic weakness, to promote the interests of, and contacts with, these people. Soviet bureaucrats obviously want all dealings to be channelled through them. However, because of the troubled circumstances the system faces, the West is well-situated to attach conditions to economic and other relations with Moscow to circumvent, to a degree, the power of these officials. The Soviet predicament makes it likely that some of these conditions would be met if the West bargained with a reasonable degree of firmness and dexterity.

What might these conditions be in regard to information? It is evident from the magnitude of the Soviet broadcast jamming efforts, and other activities to suppress the flow of information, that the authorities see the suppression of Western information as highly important. Of even greater importance is the control of internal communications. For example, the shutting down of the telephone exchanges was an important move by the Polish authorities in the crackdown on Solidarity on December 13, 1981.

Advances in technology are making it more difficult for the regime to control access to information from the West, as well as control internal communications. In the future, the proliferation of the technologies of copying and storing information, communications, and computation will open up many paths by which the peoples of communist societies will be able to communicate among themselves and with the outside world. Relevant technologies include transistor radios, audio cassettes, copying machines, typewriters with memory disks, video recorders, digital communications, fiber optics, direct TV broadcasting, computers and computer disks, memories, printers, and the shrinking size of satellite receivers. The cost to the Soviet system of rejecting the use of these technologies and the burden on the authorities of monitoring their use will become impossibly great. Although the regime will continue to try to limit access to them (as it does now by restricting numbers of copying machines and access to them), it will be a losing battle. These technologies are increasingly essential for economic development. Moreover, as internal conditions in the Soviet Union worsen, the political salience of freer internal communications will rise.

For the West, it is important to put information access high on the agenda both in unilateral actions and in negotiations with Moscow. Information supplied by the West should encompass factual material about the economies, living standards, health conditions, social and political freedoms and mobility, and other attributes of open, free, and pluralistic political and economic systems contrasted with those of the Soviet empire. Expanded efforts in this field should cover a broad spectrum: for example, seeking resumption of direct dialing to those countries where it has been cut off; expanded transmissions throughout the Soviet Union and empire by the Voice of America, Radio Liberty, Deutsche Welle, Radio Free Europe, and the BBC; improvements in anti-jamming capabilities through increased multifrequency operation, increased power and antenna gain, and satellite transmission,[30] combined with seeking agreement from the Soviet Union to end jamming efforts (as in the mid-1970s); transmission at multiple and shifting frequencies directed throughout the empire; extensions of periodic and equal television time on Soviet and U.S. networks to the leaderships of the two countries, thus enabling them to communicate more extensively with publics of the other country; similar exchanges of "op ed" articles in the Soviet print media (*Pravda, Izvestia, Trud*) and in the major U.S. news media (the TV networks, *New York Times, Wall Street Journal, Washington Post, Los Angeles Times, Boston Globe*, etc.); removal of the Soviet prohibition on sending parcels to people from outside; invitations to Soviet citizens from diverse fields, professions, and occupations in Soviet society, insofar as possible outside the *nomenklatura* (for example, environmentalists, youth groups, architects, women's groups, teachers, farmers, machinists, writers, artists, soil scientists, and petroleum engineers). We should also reconsider restrictions on supplying the Soviets with modest capacity personal computers. (The negative aspect of such supply is that the Soviets would use some of them for military purposes; the positive aspect is that they may help transform the system.)

In economic relations, emphasis should be placed on trade and investment transactions that maximize Western visibility and provide opportunities for wider contact between Western businessmen and Soviet enterprise management and workers. This approach can serve several purposes, including making more visible the vast superiority of Western products and providing more direct exposure to the results of free, competitive markets and democratic political systems. We should negotiate for having clearly identified Western products sold and distributed in the Soviet Union and Eastern Europe. We should also encourage undertakings in which Western engineers and businessmen would work in various parts of the Soviet Union itself, especially outside the Moscow area. Although doing this would be a natural part of the business of some Western firms (e.g., McDonald's, Marks and Spencer, and other retail chains), many Western firms, in the absence of countervailing influence, naturally conform to the wishes of the Soviet bureaucratic "gatekeepers," and work entirely through them.[31] These firms should be encouraged to insist on activities that bring them into direct contact with consumers, and Western governments should develop and use various techniques for doing this.

Being Attentive to Developments Within the Empire.   While keeping up our guard and pursuing the proposed three-track strategy, we need to be exceptionally attentive to developments inside the empire that could offer opportunities as well as dangers. We believe that a major turning point is unlikely to come before the 1990s; it might not come until late in the 1990s, and perhaps not then. The kinds of opportunities to look for and promote include a significant retrenchment and reversal of the overseas empire; a gradual extension of some freedoms for the Eastern Europeans, in the direction of enlarging their autonomy and liberties (their possible "Finlandization"); a slowing of Soviet military modernization and perhaps a marked reduction in the Soviet forces deployed as a threat to Western Europe; and, most importantly, some movement toward enlarging the liberties open to the peoples of the Soviet Union. Cautions are also in order: on the threat side are possible Soviet efforts to extend the overseas empire and, especially, further forward moves in Southwest Asia or elsewhere around the Soviet periphery.

The West should fix its sights on the goal of encouraging the transformation of the Soviet empire from a bureaucratically hidebound, expansionist oligarchy toward becoming a more pluralist society. Admittedly, this is a tall, if not fanciful, order that can be attained only gradually and in the long run, if then.

Some may be reluctant to embrace the combination of activism with prudence reflected in our three-track strategy. Indeed, it may be argued that the prospective economic and eventual military decline of the Soviet empire relative to the free world implies that we need only wait. History will be on our side. There are two reasons why such a position is unwarranted and dangerous.

First, the Soviets retain impressive capabilities for expansion and aggression. They may be motivated to use these capabilities to offset and mask the reality of decline. This observation has implications for Western military programs, alliance policy, security assistance, and cooperative forces that we addressed above.

Second, we should be concerned not only with the decline of the Soviet empire but also with its transformation in forms and directions away from secrecy, coercion, and violations of human rights and toward freedom, peace, and progress. Without exaggerating the efficacy of external influences, a policy of normal economic transactions without subsidization and intensified efforts to reach the people within the Soviet Union and its empire should be pursued to further the aim of systemic transformation.

Notes

2. Vladimir Bukovsky, "The Political Condition of the Soviet Union"

1. Richard Pipes, *Survival Is Not Enough* (New York: Simon & Schuster, 1984), p. 199. This is a corollary of Plato's assertion that changes in any constitution originated in the ruling class itself (*Republic of Plato* 545D). Cited in Alexander Shtromas, *The Fall of the Soviet Empire*, Second International Congress of the Professors' Peace Academy, 1985.

2. Vladimir Ilyich Ulyanov Lenin, "Left-wing Communism—An Infantile Disorder," 1920, in *The Lenin Anthology* (New York: Norton, 1975).

3. *Pravda*, April 24, 1985.

4. *Arkhiv Samizdata*, No. 5042, pp. 3–4, 16, 18.

5. *Pravda*, April 24, 1985.

6. V. Lenin, "Polnoe Sobranie Sochinenii," 37, pp. 299–300. Quoted in Bertram D. Wolfe, *Lenin and the Twentieth Century* (Stanford, Calif.: Hoover Institution Press, 1984), p. 144.

7. Wolfe, p. 142.

8. Wolfe, p. 147.

9. Wolfe, p. 144.

10. Wolfe, p. 155.

11. Wolfe, p. 155.

12. Wolfe, p. 146.

13. Wolfe, p. 150.

14. Wolfe, p. 153.

15. These figures vary in different years. Thus, in 1919, 250,000 members; in 1923, 485,500; in 1928, 1,304,471. See Leonard Schapiro, *Communist Party of the Soviet Union* (New York: Random House, 1970).

16. This expression was used by A. Avterkhanov.

17. Charles Wolf, Jr., K. C. Yeh, Edmund Brunner, Jr., Aaron Gurwitz, and Marilee Lawrence, *The Costs of the Soviet Empire* (Santa Monica, Calif.: the RAND Corporation, 1983).

18. Lenin, "Polnoe Sobranie Sochinenii," 42, pp. 95–96.

19.   Anthony Sutton, *Western Technology and Soviet Economic Development* (Stanford, Calif.: Hoover Institution Press, 1968–73).

20.   Lenin, "Polnoe Sobranie Sochinenii," 42, p. 116.

21.   Schapiro, pp. 331, 443.

22.   Schapiro, p. 465.

23.   Schapiro, p. 458.

24.   12 S'ezd RKP(b), *Stenograficheskii Otchet*, 1923.

25.   12 S'ezd RKP(b), pp. 56–57.

26.   Schapiro, pp. 452, 621.

27.   Schapiro, pp. 609–10.

28.   I. Stalin, *Sochineniia* 5: 71.

29.   S. G. Strumilin, *Planovoe Khoziaistvo* 7 (1927) 11.

30.   Schapiro, pp. 628–29.

31.   See Kudenko case, *Khronika Tekushchich Sobytii* 35 (1975) 56–58.

32.   Michael Voslensky, *Nomenklatura* (New York: Doubleday and Co., 1984), p. 95.

33.   Shtromas.

34.   Dusko Doder, "Andropov Rushed Renewal into Motion," *Washington Post*, July 28, 1985.

35.   *Pravda*, April 24, 1985; June 12, 1985.

36.   O. Bogomolov. "Soglasovanie Ekonomicheskikh Interesov i Politiki pri Sotsializme," *Kommunist* 11, 1985.

37.   *Pravda*, April 24, 1985.

38.   12 S'ezd RKP(b), p. 29.

39.   Leonard E. Hubbard, *Soviet Labor and Industry* (London, 1942), pp. 280–81.

40.   Ilya Ilf, Evgenii Petrov, *Zolotoy Telenok*.

41.   Donald Hodgman, *Soviet Industrial Production, 1928–1951* (Cambridge, MA: Harvard University Press, 1954).

42.   Schapiro.

43.   *Kommunist* 11, 1985, p. 62.

44.   Schapiro, p. 640.

45.   Boris Komarov, *The Destruction of Nature in the Soviet Union* (White Plains, N.Y.: Sharpe, 1980).

46.   Komarov.

47.   David Tolmazin, "Soviet System and Environment: Degradation of Water Supplies," *Kontinent* 44.

48.   Grani, No. 133, 134, 1984.

49.   Komarov.

50.   Prof. Yuzhakov, ed., *Bolshaya Encyclopedia, 1900–1907.*

51.   *Russkaya Mysl*, February 7, 1985, p. 435.

52.   *Arkhiv Samizdata*, No. 5042, p. 26.

53.   Konstantin Simis, *USSR: The Corrupt Society* (New York: Simon & Schuster, 1982).

54.   Andrei Babich, "What Is Concealed Behind Gorbachev's 'Reform?'" *Russkaya Mysl*, August 16, 1985, pp. 1, 4.

4.   Francis Fukuyama, "The Political Character of the Overseas Empire"

1.   I am using the term "overseas" synonymously with "Third World," with the understanding that some parts of the empire like Afghanistan and North Korea are part of the Eurasian landmass and contiguous with the Soviet Union. Eastern Europe is excluded from this definition, since its level of social and political development and relationship to the USSR are quite distinct from those of Moscow's Third World allies.

2. The term "client" will be used to signify a state associated with Moscow that is significantly weaker and therefore dependent on the Soviet Union for various types of support, but that also performs services for the USSR in return, in the sense of "patron and client."

3. No state (including the Soviet Union) is, of course, considered genuinely communist.

4. Although the Cuban Communist Party did not start out as one.

5. For example, North Korea is listed as a socialist state in Leonid Brezhnev's report to the 25th CPSU Congress but not in the 26th Congress report.

6. For example, the slogans issued on May Day and on the anniversary of the Revolution.

7. This is not for lack of trying on the client's part; Mozambique, for instance, applied to CMEA for membership and was rejected.

8. The dividing line between left-wing national democracies, such as Egypt under Nasser, and a non-Marxist-Leninist socialist-oriented state, such as Algeria, is a very fine one. Soviet rankings reflect their desire to accord clients differing degrees of prestige and therefore do not necessarily correspond to the exact ideological character of the regime in question.

9. The communists came to power in China in this period as well.

10. Stephen Sestanovich, "The Place of the Third World in Overall Soviet Foreign Policy," unpublished paper presented in Bellagio, Italy, November 1985, p. 5.

11. According to Abraham Becker in an unpublished paper delivered at Bellagio, 61 percent of Soviet economic aid in the Khrushchev period was concentrated in three countries: Egypt, Afghanistan, and India.

12. The South Yemeni National Liberation Front took over power from the British in 1969, but its descendant, the Yemeni Socialist Party (which absorbed the small Yemeni Communist Party), constituted itself as a formal Marxist-Leninist vanguard party only in 1978.

13. Vadim Zagladin, ed., *The World Communist Movement* (JPRS UPS-84–034-L, August 29, 1984).

14. Rostislav Ul'yanovskii, "O natsional'noi i revolyutsionnoi demokratii: puty evolyutsii," *Narody Azii i Afriki*, no. 2 (March-April 1984): p. 16.

15. Thomas H. Henriksen, "Angola, Mozambique, and the Soviet Union: Liberation and the Quest for Influence," in Warren Wainstein and Thomas Henriksen, eds., *Soviet and Chinese Aid to African Nations* (New York: Praeger, 1980), pp. 61–63.

16. A brief description of Cabral's ideas is given in Lars Rudenbeck, "Socialist-Oriented Development in Guinea-Bissau," in C. Roseberg and T. Callaghy, eds., *Socialism in Sub-Saharan Africa: A New Assessment* (Berkeley, Calif: Institute of International Studies, 1979), pp. 325ff.

17. Laurie Mylroie, *Politics and the Soviet Presence in the People's Democratic Republic of Yemen: Internal Vulnerabilities and Regional Challenges* (Santa Monica, Calif.: The RAND Corporation, December 1983), pp. 4–29; and Stephen Page, *The Soviet Union and the Yemens: Influence in Asymmetrical Relationships* (New York: Praeger, 1985).

18. Marina Ottaway, "Marxism-Leninism in Mozambique and Ethiopia," in David Albright, ed., *Communism in Africa* (Bloomington, Ind.: Indiana University Press, 1980).

19. See Lisa Anderson, "Qadhdhafi and the Kremlin," *Problems of Communism*, no. 5 (September-October 1985): pp. 29, 33ff.

20. Aldo Vacs, "Soviet Policy toward Argentina and the Southern Cone," *Annals of the American Academy of Social and Political Science*, September 1985, pp. 163–166.

21. Edward Gonzalez and David Ronfeldt, *Post-Revolutionary Cuba in a Changing World* (Santa Monica, Calif.: The RAND Corporation, December 1975), pp. 3–13.

22. See Edward Gonzalez, "Cuba, the Third World, and the Soviet Union," unpublished paper delivered at Bellagio, November 1985.

23. Edward Gonzalez, "Institutionalization, Political Elites, and Foreign Policies," in Cole Blasier and Carmelo Mesa-Lago, eds., *Cuba in the Third World* (Pittsburgh: University of Pittsburgh Press, 1979), pp. 21–22.

24. Harry Gelman, *The Soviet Far East Buildup and Soviet Risk-Taking Against China* (Santa Monica, Calif.: The RAND Corporation, August 1982), p. 92.

25. The Soviets also disapprove of Kim's desire to pass rule on to his son, a kind of "dynastic communism." See Harry Gelman and Norman D. Levin, *The Future of Soviet-North Korean Relations* (Santa Monica, Calif.: The RAND Corporation, N-3159-AF, October 1984), p. 25.

26. Brian Crozier, "The Surrogate Forces of the Soviet Union," *Conflict Studies* 92 (1978), and Melvin Croan, "A New Afrika Korps?" *Washington Quarterly* 3, no. 1 (Winter 1980).

27. Brian Crozier, "The Soviet Satellitization of Cuba," *Conflict Studies* 35 (1973).

28. Zafar Imam, "Soviet Treaties with Third World Countries," *Soviet Studies* (January 1983): p. 53.

29. For example, Egypt signed its treaty as a result of Sadat's tenuous situation in the aftermath of the June 1967 war, India just prior to war with Pakistan in 1971, Iraq prior to its nationalization of Western oil interests, and Syria during a severe internal crisis caused by Muslim fundamentalist opposition to Assad's rule. The North Yemeni treaty was apparently signed by Sanaa in hopes of attracting greater economic assistance, and contains fewer Soviet security commitments.

30. Stephen Page, "The Soviet Impact on the Arabian Peninsula," unpublished paper presented at the III World Congress for Soviet and East European Studies, November 3, 1985.

31. See Paul Henze, "Communism in Ethiopia," *Problems of Communism* (May-June 1981).

32. See the remarks quoted in F. Fukuyama, *Moscow's Post-Brezhnev Reassessment of the Third World* (Santa Monica, Calif.: The RAND Corporation, February 1986).

33. See ch. 9 in this volume.

34. This comes in a variety of forms, including outright grants and implicit trade subsidies, most notably in the case of sugar.

35. For further elaboration of this type of argument, see Elizabeth Valkenier, *The Soviet Union and the Third World: An Economic Bind* (New York: Praeger, 1983).

36. The most prominent of these was Yurii Andropov. See F. Fukuyama, *Moscow's Post-Brezhnev Reassessment of the Third World*.

37. In South Yemen, this came in spite of the fact that one fourth of the government's outlay was spent on agriculture. See Mylroie p. 33.

38. In 1957, Kwame Nkrumah of "socialist" Ghana issued a challenge to Felix Hophouet-Boigny of the Ivory Coast, suggesting that the performance of these two geographically similar countries be evaluated a decade later. Between 1960 and 1982, Ghana's per capita income fell 1.3 percent a year, while the Ivory Coast's rose 2.1 percent. See Nicholas D. Kristof, "The Third World: Back to the Farm," *New York Times*, July 28, 1985.

5. Herbert J. Ellison, "Marxism-Leninism in the Third World"

1. Joseph Stalin, *Foundations of Leninism* (New York: International Publishers, 1977), p. 20.

2. Marx had provided a dispensation for a possible Russian shortcut to communism in his preface to the Russian edition of the *Manifesto* (1882): "If a Russian revolution serves as a signal for a workers' revolution in the West, so that both complement each other, then the contemporary Russian form of land tenure may be the starting point of communist development." Lenin did not choose to use it, possibly because it suggested Russian populist notions that he rejected.

It seems unlikely that Lenin worried about the Marxist propriety of the timing of his power seizure. His prerevolutionary writing on the future revolution, including political alliances to achieve it, had left little of conventional Marxist historical stages, at least as concerned the role of the bourgeoisie. It is, however, true that he thought revolution in Europe was imminent. After surviving the civil war, the main question was whether a small minority of communists could move forward with socialism in peasant Russia. Until Stalin's concept of "socialism in one country," it still remained official doctrine that revolution in the advanced capitalist states would provide the backing for building Russian socialism.

The idea of bringing about revolution in the West by supporting the liberation movement in the colonies derives from the notion in Lenin's *Imperialism* that advanced capitalist states had postponed revolution by colonial expansion, the latter providing a needed market for their surplus production. Cutting off the colonies would hasten the capitalist collapse. In a curious way the approach leads to a further extension of the rationale for the "premature" Russian revolution, and moves even further away from the Marxian concept of the link between economic and political change. Leninist "voluntarism"—the initiation of change by political means—becomes even more pronounced.

3. V. V. Zagladin, The World Communist Movement. Quotation is from the English translation published by the Foreign Broadcast Information Service (Washington), JPRS No. UPS-84-034-L, Aug. 29, 1984, p. 202.

4. The documentation of these debates is provided in Helmut Gruber, *Soviet Russia Masters the Comintern: International Communism in the Era of Stalin's Ascendancy* (Garden City, N.Y.: Doubleday, 1974).

5. Hugh Seton-Watson, *From Lenin to Khrushchev: The History of World Communism* (New York: Praeger, 1960), pp. 129-30

6. Xenia Joukoff Eudin and Robert C. North, *Soviet Russia and the East, 1920-27* (Stanford, Calif.: Stanford University Press, 1927), p. 17.

7. Wolfgang Leonhard provides an extraordinarily interesting and useful essay on "The Political Concepts of Maoism" in his *Three Faces of Marxism: The Political Concepts of Soviet Ideology, Maoism, and Humanist Marxism* (New York: Holt, Rinehart and Winston, 1974), pp. 210-57. He dismisses the extravagant official claims for Mao's originality and independent significance within the Marxist-Leninist tradition, but emphasizes what he calls the "sinification of Marxism" in China.

8. Seton-Watson, pp. 210-27.

9. In all cases communist leaders were really fighting two battles simultaneously—against colonial authority and against noncommunist nationalists. In an important sense the latter struggle was the most vital to them. An unusually interesting account of the way this process worked in Vietnam is provided by Dennis J. Duncanson in "Vietnam: From Bolshevism to People's War," in *The Anatomy of Communist Takeovers*, ed. Thomas T. Hammond (New Haven, Conn.: Yale University Press, 1975), pp. 490-515.

10. The suspension of these offensives occurred at different dates in each country and was clearly affected by local political circumstances and needs. Certainly by the early 1950s it was clear that for the time being nothing further could be gained by a policy of political or political/military offensive against nationalist regimes, but the Vietnamese struggle, with the involvement of the French, was clearly a special case. See Duncanson.

11. Duncanson.

12. An extraordinarily interesting example of communist political action in both periods is provided by the Indonesian Communist Party (PKI) in the early postwar period and then, again, in the events leading up to the 1965 coup. See Justus M. Van Der Kroef, "The Wages of Ambiguity: The 1965 Coup in Indonesia, its Origins and Meaning," in Hammond, pp. 534-62.

13. Alvin Z. Rubinstein, *Soviet Foreign Policy since World War II: Imperial and Global* (Cambridge, Mass.: Winthrop Publishers, 1981), pp. 216-18.

14. The distinguished Egyptian journalist Mohamed Heikal has provided a remarkable portrait of President Nasser and his role in the Egyptian-Soviet relationship in his *Sphinx and Commissar: The Rise and Fall of Soviet Influence in the Middle East* (London: Collins, 1978).

15. The background of this policy in the Iraqi Ba'th party is described by Oles M. Smolansky in "The Kremlin and the Iraqi Ba'th 1968-82: An Influence Relationship," *Middle East Review* 15, no. 3-4 (Spring-Summer 1983): 63.

The stern repression of the communist parties has been a persistent problem for the Kremlin in its dealing with Moslem countries of the Middle East and Southwest Asia since the earliest days of the Comintern.

16. Congressional Research Service (CRS), *The Soviet Union in the Third World, 1980-85: An Imperial Burden or Political Asset?* (Washington, D.C.: U.S. Government Printing Office, 1985), pp. 164, 181.

17. The estimates of Soviet military personnel in Syria are between 6,000 and 7,000; those for Iraq between 1,000 and 2,200. See CRS, pp. 160, 181.

18. The recent Syrian involvement in wars with Israel in Lebanon is an impressive case in point. The heavy Syrian losses required a very large increase in arms deliveries from the USSR. Similarly, Iraq's war with Iran has increased that country's dependence on Soviet arms supplies.

19. There are, of course, recent studies that make serious and informative efforts to analyze the Soviet internal discussion of Third World policy. These include a study that is specifically focused upon the economic aspects of the subject—Elizabeth Valkenier, *The Soviet Union and the Third World: An Economic Bind* (New York: Praeger, 1983)—and Jerry Hough, *The Struggle for the Third World: Soviet Debates and American Options* (Washington, D.C.: The Brookings Institution, 1986). Much more study and serious discussion of Soviet objectives in the Third World, in all their complexity, are still needed.

20. This line of argument has, it seems to me, been rather common in journalist commentary in recent times, not in the scholarly literature dealing seriously with Soviet discussion. Both the Valkenier and the Hough studies cited in fn. 19 take note of the internal Soviet discussions of the costs of Third World economic aid, and Hough implies that they may take a more negative view of those costs than they are prepared to say publicly, especially in connection with such failed efforts as Egypt and Ghana. But Hough also notes that enterprises such as Nicaragua, Ethiopia, and Grenada bring costs that are "well within Soviet capabilities" (p. 249).

The fact is that the Soviets have, in the last two decades, moved away from economic aid and increasingly stressed military aid. See, for example, David Albright, "The Middle East and Africa in Soviet Policy," in *Soviet Foreign Policy in the 1980s*, ed. Roger Kanet (New York: Praeger, 1982) p. 304.

21. Comparative study of the historical development of the administrative structures in Soviet Central Asia with those in some of the postwar Third World communist states would be useful. The patterns of organization of the party apparatus, the mass organizations, etc., and the training of leadership cadres would doubtless show many similarities.

22. For a very interesting recent article on Nicaragua, see Jiri and Virginia Valenta, "Sandinistas in Power," *Problems of Communism* XXXIV (September-October 1985): 1–28.

23. Throughout the cited CRS study (e.g., pp. 67, 159–61) one finds mention of the importance of Soviet action in Afghanistan in creating reservations or caution about current or future collaboration. This is particularly pronounced in the Moslem countries.

24. The CRS study describes the situation in Asia as follows: "For many noncommunist Asians . . . the appeal of the Soviet Union as a development model for the 1980s had declined sharply in the preceding two decades" (p. 68).

25. The Philippines have become a major focus of Soviet East Asian diplomacy, seeking to exploit U.S.-Philippine frictions (as over U.S. bases), and stressing that the relationship is one of "neocolonialism." The wooing of the political leadership is combined with expansion of contacts through cultural and other programs.

For a more extended background on the Soviet-Philippine relationship see "Soviet Policy in Southeast Asia," in Donald S. Zagoria, ed., *Soviet Policy in East Asia* (New York: Council on Foreign Relations, 1982), pp. 87–88; 153–74.

26. The close cooperation between the Soviets, the Cubans and the East Germans in southern Africa and Ethiopia beginning in the 1970s has been a very important factor in the region. Moscow supplied arms, Cuba the military and civilian personnel (some 33,000 military and 8,000 civilian advisers by 1979), and the German Democratic Republic (GDR) specialized in security and intelligence services. See David E. Albright, "The Communist States in Southern Africa," in *International Politics in Southern Africa*, ed. Gwendolen M. Carter and Patrick O'Meara (Bloomington, Ind.: Indiana University Press, 1982), pp. 4–14; also, Melvin Croan, "A New Afrika Corps?" *Washington Quarterly* (Winter 1980): 27–28.

27. The functioning of the important International Department is thoroughly described in Robert W. Kitrinos, "International Department of the CPSU," *Problems of Communism* (September-October 1984): 47–67.

One of many examples of skillful propaganda directed at the United States and aiming to thwart American intervention in Soviet-supported Third World revolution was the recent campaign to influence opinion on El Salvador and Nicaragua. The Soviets and Cubans had clearly planned in advance a campaign aimed at discouraging aid to the Central American states in which they were supporting guerrilla forces. The plan prepared by Soviets and Cubans with Salvadoran insurgent leaders in Havana in June 1980 is particularly revealing. See Department of State and Department of Defense, "Background Paper: Central America," Washington, D. C., May 27, 1983, pp. 13 ff.

28. On the other side of the ledger, and taking the period from 1975–79 alone, one can list seven seizures of power by pro-Soviet communist parties in Asia and Africa: North Vietnam in South Vietnam and Laos (1975); Neto in Angola (1975–76); Mengistu in Ethiopia (1974); Taraki in Afghanistan (1978); South Yemen (1978); and North Vietnam in Cambodia (1979). This trend led at least one serious scholar to question whether the United States would eventually be left out of the Third World. (Donald S. Zagoria, "A New Scramble for Africa," in *The Conduct of Soviet Foreign Policy*, ed. Erik P. Hoffmann and Frederic J. Fleron, Jr. (Hawthorne, New York: OeGruyter Aldine, 1980).

29. Studies such as those of Valkenier and Hough (fn. 19 above) do much to extend understanding of the seriousness and quality of Soviet writings on Third World revolutions and opportunities for communist parties. Those who have little sense of the Soviet work on such matters would be well advised to read some of the recent literature, much of it available in English, especially to gain an insight into the intelligence and thoroughness with which Soviet specialists analyze political, social, and economic currents as well as the structure of analysis they use for measuring their opportunities and refining revolutionary strategy and tactics.

A good recent example of such work is V. F. Li et al., *Partii i revoliutsionnyi protsess v stranakh Azii i Afriki (Parties and the Revolutionary Process in Asian and African Countries)* (Moscow: Izdatel'stvo Nauka, 1984). English translation published by the Foreign Broadcast Information Service (Washington, D. C.), JPRS No. UPS-84–015-L, April 10, 1984.

6. Richard E. Ericson, "The Soviet Economic Predicament"

1. See the papers of the Joint Economic Committee (JEC), U.S. Congress, *Soviet Economy in the 1980s: Problems and Prospects* (Washington, D.C.: U.S. Government Printing Office, 1983); Richard F. Kaufman, "Causes of the Slowdown in Soviet Defense," *Soviet Economy* 1, no. 1. (1985): 9–31; and Gertrude E. Schroeder, "The Slowdown in Soviet Industry, 1976–1982," *Soviet Economy* 1, no. 1 (1985): 42–47.

2. See, for example, Marshall I. Goldman, *USSR in Crisis* (New York: W.W. Norton & Company, 1983); and M. Elizabeth Denton, "Soviet Perceptions of Economic Prospects," in JEC, pp. 30–45.

3. Discussion of these has been prominent in both the Soviet and Western press. See, for example, *New York Times*, October 14, 15, and 16, 1985, and almost any issue of *Pravda*. The texts of recent important decrees can be found in the July 26, August 4, and October 16 issues of *Pravda*.

4. See Gorbachev's speeches before Foremen and Brigade leaders, April 12, 1985; before the Central Committee of the Communist Party, June 11 and October 15, 1985; and in Tyumen and Tselinograd in early September 1985. Also see Marshall I. Goldman, "Gorbachev and Economic Reform," *Foreign Affairs* 64, no. 1 (Fall 1985): 56–73.

5. This can be seen in the claims put forth in the recent revision of the Third Program of the Communist Party of the Soviet Union, the draft of which was published in *Pravda*, October 26, 1985. The emphasis is, however, more subdued than in the original Third Program of 1961.

6. See Alec Nove, *An Economic History of the USSR* (New York: Penguin Books, 1982) for a readable survey of Soviet economic development; and JEC, U.S. Congress, *USSR: Measures of Economic Growth and Development, 1950–80* (Washington, D.C.: U.S. Government Printing Office, 1982) for a summary of recent statistics.

7. See Nove, Chs. 12 and 13.

8. There is general agreement among Western specialists that the Soviet economy was and is

in no danger of collapse. At worst it faced, and may indeed face, a prolonged period of relative economic stagnation, accompanied by growing obsolescence.

9. These arguments have been particularly prevalent in the Novosibirsk management journal *EKO*. See, for example, the Fel'tsman article in the December 1985 issue of *EKO*, and Alec Nove, "Has Soviet Growth Ceased?" paper before the Manchester Statistical Society, Manchester, England, November 15, 1983.

10. Gertrude E. Schroeder, "The Soviet Economy on a Treadmill of 'Reforms'," in JEC, U.S. Congress, *Soviet Economy in a Time of Change*, vol. 1 (Washington, D.C.: U.S. Government Printing Office, 1979), pp. 312–340, and "Soviet Economic 'Reform' Decrees: More Steps on the Treadmill," in JEC, U.S. Congress *Soviet Economy in Change* (Washington, D.C.: U.S. Government Printing Office, 1983) pp. 65–88.

11. These have been particularly associated with the Novosibirsk economists around Abel Aganbegian and the economic/management journal *EKO* published in Novosibirsk. For a clear statement see "The Novosibirsk Report," *Survey* no. 1 (Spring 1981): 88–108. Further arguments can be found in the recent articles of Zaslavskaia in *Trud*, August 28, 1984, and *Izvestiia*, June 1, 1985, and Aganbegian in *EKO* (August 1985), and *Problemy Sotsializma i Mira* (September 1985).

12. A clear discussion of these factors is contained in Herbert S. Levine, *The Causes and Implications of the Sharp Deterioration of Soviet Economic Performance* (Washington, D.C.: Wharton Econometrics, August 1983).

13. The original experiment decree appeared in *Pravda*, August 26, 1983.

14. A "conservative" reform should be understood as one that does not attempt to change the nature of the system, but merely aims at making it work better. This indeed has been the only kind of "reform" attempted in the Soviet Union. On the fate of such reforms see Schroeder, "Soviet Economy on a Treadmill" and "Slowdown in Soviet Industry."

15. An excellent brief summary of Soviet economic institutions and procedures can be found in Morris Bornstein, "The Soviet Centrally Planned Economy," in *Comparative Economic Systems*, 5th ed. (Homewood, Ill.: Richard D. Irwin, 1985), pp. 188–219. More detailed accounts are available in standard texts, e.g., Alec Nove, *The Soviet Economic System*, 2nd ed. (London: George Allen & Unwin, 1980).

16. The classic reference here is Gregory Grossman, "The 'Second Economy' of the USSR," *Problems of Communism* 26, no. 5 (September-October 1977): 25–40. Survey evidence from recent immigrants indicates that it may be quite substantial.

17. On November 12, 1985, by decree of the Supreme Soviet, five ministries related to agriculture, and SEL'KHOZTEKHNIKA, were abolished and a new State Committee for Agro-Industrial Complexes put in their place. Philip Taubman, "Soviet Overhauls Farm Bureaucracy," *New York Times*, November 23, 1985, p. 3.

18. Jerry F. Hough, *The Soviet Prefects* (Cambridge, Mass.: Harvard University Press, 1969).

19. Bornstein, p. 195.

20. There have recently been serious efforts to raise the operational significance of the five year plans by increasing their detail and making their indices binding on planners and executors. This is part of the intent of the July 1979 and succeeding decrees on "improving the economic mechanism." See Morris Bornstein, "Improving the Soviet Economic Mechanism," *Soviet Studies* 37, no. 1 (January 1985): 1–30. These efforts seem to have had little impact on the actual functioning of the economy as five years is just too long a period to be able to plan in operational detail.

21. See George Garvy, *Money, Financial Flows, and Credit in the Soviet Union* (Cambridge, Mass.: Ballinger, 1977).

22. Bornstein, "The Soviet Centrally Planned Economy," p. 201.

23. Alexander Gerschenkron, *Economic Backwardness in Historical Perspective* (Cambridge, Mass.: Harvard University Press, 1962).

24. This classification is due to Herbert Levine; Schroeder, "Slowdown in Soviet Industry," discusses the same issues from a slightly different perspective.

25. See Schroeder, "Slowdown in Soviet Industry."

26. Schroeder, "Slowdown in Soviet Industry," p. 64. The estimate of 15 to 17 percent comes from a recent Central Intelligence Agency/Defense Intelligence Agency Report to the Congress, March 19, 1986.

27. Schroeder, "Slowdown in Soviet Industry" and "Soviet Economy on a Treadmill."

28. On the latter see Bornstein, "The Soviet Centrally Planned Economy."

29. "On the Extension of the New Methods of Management and the Strengthening of Their Influence on the Acceleration of Scientific-Technological Progress."

30. For example, getting just a half hour per week additional work out of the labor force could give a 1 percent gain in output, though if that output is not truly needed it will just accumulate in inventories. See Vasilii Seliunin, "Experiment," *Novy Mir* 8 (August 1985): 173–194.

31. See, for example, Henry S. Rowen and Vladimir G. Treml, "As Oil Prices Fall, Moscow's Woes Rise," *The Wall Street Journal*, March 6, 1985.

32. A Soviet economist has noted that over one-third of the capital stock is over fifteen years old. Also, some 30 percent of newly installed equipment in the late 1970s had been in production for over ten years. See D. Palterovich in *Planovoe Khoziastvo*, September 1980, p. 105.

33. See the statement by Robert Gates before the Joint Economic Committee of the United States Congress, November 21, 1984.

7. Charles Wolf, Jr., "The Costs and Benefits of the Soviet Empire"

1. For a more extensive discussion of methodology and other matters dealt with in this chapter, see Charles Wolf, Jr., K. C. Yeh, Edmund Brunner, Jr., Aaron Gurwitz, and Marilee Lawrence, *The Costs of the Soviet Empire* (Santa Monica, Calif.: The RAND Corporation, 1983); and Charles Wolf, Jr., Keith Crane, K. C. Yeh, Susan Anderson, and Ed Brunner, *The Costs and Benefits of the Soviet Empire* (Santa Monica, Calif.: The RAND Corporation, 1986).

2. For example, see H. C. d'Encausse, *Decline of an Empire: The Soviet Socialist Republics in Revolt* (New York: Harper and Row, 1979).

3. See J. A. Hobson, *Imperialism* (New York: Golden, 1975), p. 15.

4. Compare the earlier discussion by Charles Gati in ch. 3, in which he describes Soviet dominion in Eastern Europe through the penetration of Eastern European military and security establishments (including the role of so-called "two check" employees in the East European security services), and through the appointment by Moscow of the elite *nomenklatura* in Eastern Europe. Military intervention by Soviet forces is the ultimate guarantor of control, and the threat of its use has been made credible by the incursions into Czechoslovakia, Hungary, East Berlin, Poland, and Afghanistan.

5. See Allain Besançon, unpublished paper, October 1985.

6. See Nathan Leites, *Soviet Style in War* (New York: Crane Russak, 1982), and *Soviet Style in Management* (New York: Crane Russak, 1985), as well as Leites's other writings.

7. See ch. 8.

8. For a further discussion of the role these forces play in maintaining Soviet hegemony in Eastern Europe, see Charles Gati's ch. 3 in this volume.

9. See the Appendix by Edmund Brunner, Jr., in Wolf, et al., *Costs of the Soviet Empire*, pp. 60 ff.; and Wolf et al., *Costs and Benefits of the Soviet Empire*, pp. 30–33.

10. For a strong reiteration of this Soviet position, see Henry Trofimenko, "The Third World and U.S.-Soviet Competition: A Soviet View," *Foreign Affairs* (Summer 1981).

11. See ch. 2.

12. For a more extensive treatment, see Wolf et al., *Costs of the Soviet Empire*, p. 60. See also Wolf et al., *Costs and Benefits of the Soviet Empire*.

13. Where there are joint products and joint costs, it is difficult to draw the line between the cost of the empire and the cost of maintaining the Soviet system. Hence some arbitrariness is inevitable. For example, some of the cost of Soviet covert operations and related activities abroad probably should

be viewed as concerned primarily with maintenance of the Soviet system, rather than attributed to the empire. Other categories of covert operations, such as equipping and training terrorists in Turkey to destabilize that country, should be considered costs of the empire rather than of system maintenance.

14. Costs that represent investment costs in standard national economic accounting may thus become variable costs in this context. The extra expenditure for petroleum and other lubricants and ammunition incurred in Soviet operations in Afghanistan are incremental costs in both contexts, however.

15. This component is estimated by attributing all estimated costs of Soviet intelligence (including KGB and MVD) personnel abroad and of Soviet civil and military advisers in Third World countries to cost of the empire, but none of the costs of MVD, KGB, and other backup personnel stationed within the Soviet Union. This is clearly an oversimplification because some of the personnel within the Soviet Union are engaged in activities relating to the empire's maintenance and expansion, and some Soviet agents abroad are also engaged in counterintelligence activities relating to system maintenance at home. (See Wolf et al., *Costs of the Soviet Empire*, pp. 57–66.)

16. The curves shown in Figure 1 are logarithmic regressions fitted to the mid-points of the range of cost of empire estimates for each year in the periods 1971–80 and 1981–83. The model is CSE_t # $ae^{\%t}$, where ‰ is the rate of growth (or decline) for the period, and CSE_t is empire cost in year t. I have used the same exponential growth model to fit the other curves presented here. All of the estimated growth (or decline) coefficients are significant at the 1 percent level, and the adjusted R-squares are .8 or higher.

17. For a discussion of the conversion method, see Wolf et al., *Costs and Benefits of the Soviet Empire*, pp. 9–11, and Charles Wolf, Jr., "The Costs of the Soviet Empire," *Science* (November 29, 1985): 997–1002.

18. The ruble estimates for 1980, and hence the growth rate calculations, are slightly higher than the corresponding estimates in our previous report (see Wolf et al., *Costs of the Soviet Empire*) because of upward revisions, made by ACDA since publication of our earlier study, in estimated Soviet military aid deliveries for the period 1978–80.

19. The pattern exhibited (Figures 1 and 3) by both dollar and ruble costs between 1978 and 1983 displays a pagoda-shaped curve, with bimodal peaks in 1980–81 and the 1982–83 figures declining to approximately the levels of 1978–79.

20. For the ruble GNP and military spending estimates and sources, see Joint Economic Committee (JEC), U.S. Congress, U.S. Government Printing Office, *USSR: Measures of Economic Growth and Development, 1950–80* (Washington, D.C.: 1982); and *Soviet GNP in Current Prices* (Washington, D.C.: Central Intelligence Agency, 1983). See also Wolf et al., *Costs of the Soviet Empire*, p. 26. About one-quarter of the rise in current ruble GNP is due to inflation.

21. It is important to note that, in using Soviet GNP to assess both dollar cost and ruble cost of the empire, I spoke of the ratio of these costs *to* Soviet GNP, rather than the share of the cost of empire *in* Soviet GNP. The reason for this distinction is that part of the cost of empire represents the opportunity costs of trade subsidies: namely, the implicit costs resulting from the higher prices the Soviets paid for imports from Cuba and Eastern Europe than they would have paid on world markets, or from the lower prices they charged for Soviet oil relative to the prices those exports would have commanded on world markets. These implicit subsidies represent real economic costs, but they are not included in Soviet GNP as it is usually calculated.

22. As indicated in Table 3, the 80 percent CMEA share and its division between Eastern Europe and Cuba and Vietnam is based on the total cost estimate in dollars. Ruble calculations would show a larger share for the CMEA countries because the dollar-ruble conversions raise the relative size of trade subsidies and *net* military aid, and these two components of total cost are concentrated in CMEA.

23. See Wolf et al., *Costs of the Soviet Empire*, pp. 41–42.

24. See "East European Economies: Slow Growth in the 1980s," JEC, U.S. Congress, in *Economic Performance and Policy, Selected Papers*, vol. 1 (Washington, D.C.: U.S. Government Print-

ing Office, 1985). See also Keith Crane, *The Creditworthiness of Eastern Europe in the 1980s*, RAND Corporation, January, 1985; and ch. 11 in this volume.

25. See ch. 2, this volume.

26. See above, pp. 121. See also Michael Marrese and Jan Vanous, "Soviet Trade Relations with Eastern Europe, 1970–1984," mimeographed, 1985.

27. Central Intelligence Agency, *Handbook of Economic Statistics, 1985*, p. 64.

28. See, for example, Alec Nove, "Has Soviet Growth Ceased?" paper presented before the Manchester Statistical Society, Manchester, England, November 15, 1983.

29. *Handbook of Economic Statistics*, p. 64.

30. See Abraham Becker, *Sitting on Bayonets: The Soviet Defense Burden and the Slowdown of Defense Spending*, JRS-01, The RAND/UCLA Center for the Study of Soviet International Behavior, December 1985, pp. 29–33.

31. See Wolf et al., *The Costs of the Soviet Empire*, pp. 44–46. Accepting these parameters on the premise that military procurement was only 3 or 4 percent per annum during the first part of the 1980s, a reduction of 2 or 3 percent in the ratio of CSE to GNP should have made possible increased growth of civil production of more than 1 percent in real terms per annum compared with the decade of the 1970s. Instead, the rate of growth in civil production actually decreased.

8. Bruce D. Porter and James G. Roche, "The Expanding Military Power of the Soviet Union"

1. *Statement Before the Senate Armed Services Committee on the FY 1969–73 Defense Program and the 1969 Defense Budget*, January 22, 1968, pp. 46–47.

2. V. V. Zhurkin, *SShA i mezhdunarodno-politicheskiye krizisy* (Moscow: Nauka, 1975), p. 49.

3. Richard Pipes, *Survival Is Not Enough* (New York: Simon and Schuster, 1984), p. 18.

10. Mikhail S. Bernstam, "Trends in the Soviet Population"

1. See, for example, U.S. Department of Health and Human Services, National Center for Health Statistics, *Monthly Vital Statistics Report* 34, no. 11 (February 1986): 7.

2. See, for example, *Demographic Yearbook 1980* (New York: United Nations, 1982), p. 913; *1982* (New York: United Nations, 1984), p. 459.

3. For a broader, more detailed and technical discussion of other trends and their causes and consequences, see Mikhail S. Bernstam, "The Demography of Soviet Ethnic Groups in World Perspective," *The Last Empire: Nationality and the Soviet Future*, ed. Robert Conquest (Stanford, Calif.: Hoover Institution Press, 1986); Mikhail S. Bernstam, "Competitive Human Markets, Interfamily Transfers and Below-Replacement Fertility," ed. Kingsley Davis et al., a supplement to "Below-Replacement Fertility: Causes, Consequences, Policies," *Population and Development Review* 12 (1986); Mikhail S. Bernstam, "Marxism and Birth Control in the USSR," *Novyi Zhurnal* 153, (Fall 1983): 231–61; Mikhail S. Bernstam and Peter L. Swan, "The Production of Children as Claims on the State: A Comprehensive Labor Market Approach to Illegitimacy in the United States, 1960–80," *Working Papers in Economics*, no. E-86-1 (Stanford, Calif.: Hoover Institution, 1986), pp. 9–10, 49–56.

Broader and different analyses of Soviet demographic trends can be found in Ansley J. Coale, Barbara A. Anderson, and Erna Harm, *Human Fertility in Russia Since the Nineteenth Century* (Princeton, N.J.: Princeton University Press, 1979); Murray Feshbach, "The Soviet Union: Population Trends and Dilemmas," *Population Bulletin* 37 (August 1982); Murray Feshbach, "Trends in the Soviet Muslim Population – Demographic Aspects," in Joint Economic Committee (JEC), U.S. Congress, *Soviet Economy in the 1980s: Problems and Prospects*, vol. 2 (Washington, D.C.: U.S. Government Printing Office, 1983); Roland Pressat, "Historical Perspectives on the Population of the Soviet Union," *Population and Development Review* 11, no. 2 (June 1985) 315–34; Henry P. David and Robert J. McIntyre, *Reproductive Behavior: Central and Eastern European Experience* (New York: Springer Publishing Co., 1981); Helen Desfosses, ed., *Soviet Population Policy: Conflicts and Constraints* (New York: Pergamon Press, 1981); Joseph S. Berliner, "Culture, Social Structure, and Fertility in the USSR," in *Marxism, Central Planning, and the Soviet Economy: Economic Essays in Honor of Alexander Erligh*, ed. Padma Desai (Cambridge, Mass.: The MIT Press, 1983).

4. Expectation of life at birth, or life expectancy at birth, is the average number of years remaining to be lived by the newborn person under the given year's (period's) living conditions and mortality schedule. This is the best snapshot of life conditions in the given area at the given time.

5. U.S. National Center for Health Statistics, *Vital Statistics of the United States 1980*, vol. II, *Mortality*, pt. A (Washington, D.C.: U.S. Government Printing Office, 1985), pp. 6/13–14; U.S. Bureau of the Census, *Statistical Abstract of the United States 1985* (Washington, D.C.: U.S. Government Printing Office, 1984), p. 69.

6. *Naselenie SSSR: Chislennost', Sostav i Dvizhenie Naseleniia, 1973. Statisticheskii Sbornik* (Moscow, 1975), p. 139; *Vosproizvodstvo Naseleniia SSSR* (Moscow, 1983), p. 117; and life tables in *Narodnoe Khoziaistvo SSSR v 1965 g. Statisticheskii Ezhegodnik* (Moscow, 1966), p. 45 (hereinafter *Narkhoz* 1965 or other year) and in *Vestnik Statistiki*, no. 2, 1974, pp. 94–95 (hereinafter *VS* and date).

7. See, e.g., *Vosproizvodstvo Naseleniia SSSR*, p. 273; S. V. Bakurskii, *Sotsial'no-Ekonomicheskie Problemy Demograficheskogo Razvitiia Moldavskoi SSR* (Kishinev, 1984), p. 38; I. R. Mulliadzhanov, *Demograficheskoe Razvitie Uzbekskoi SSR* (Tashkent, 1983), p. 239.

8. These are the rates that are free of the influence of the age structure changes on mortality. Thus, increases in the proportion of the elderly do not affect these rates. The same age structure (in this case, that of the USSR in 1970) is used and the area-specific age-specific death rates are applied to it, thus yielding the real trend in overall mortality values. Rates for 1958–59, 1965–66, and 1969–70 were calculated from age-specific death rates by John Dutton, Jr., "Changes in Soviet Mortality Patter, 1959–77," *Population and Development Review* 5, no. 2 (June 1979): 286. Rates for other years are published in the USSR. For 1974–75: I. Rylkova, "Prodolzhitel'nost' Zhizni Naseleniia SSSR," in *Vozobnovlenie Pokolenii Nashei Strany* (Moscow, 1978), p. 82. For 1978: *Osobennosti Demograficheskogo Razvitiia v SSSR* (Moscow, 1982), p. 94. For 1980: G. P. Kiseleva and I. N. Veselkova, "Tipy Vosproizvodstva Naseleniia v SSSR," in *Narodonaselenie SSR i Mira: Razvitie, Problemy, Issledovaniia* (Moscow, 1983), p. 77. Due to the clear misstatement of the Russian Soviet Federated Socialist Republic (RSFSR) rate for 1980, we recalculated it as a residual of the USSR's and other republics' rates, using republics' populations as weights.

9. R. H. Dinkel, "The Seeming Paradox of Increasing Mortality in a Highly Industrialized Nation: The Example of the Soviet Union," *Population Studies* 39, no. 1 (March 1985) 87–97.

10. Our estimates in Tables 3 and 4 correspond closely to the official data in A.A. Tal'chuk and G. V. Mazurenko, "Vliianie Smertnosti ot Zlokachestvennykh Novoobrazovanii na Sredniuiu Prodolzhitel'nost' Predstoiashchei Zhizni Naseleniia Belorusskoi SSR," *Zdravookhranenie Belorussii*, no. 10 (October 1985): 19. Another contributing factor of high life expectancy in Byelorussia of all European parts of the USSR is its lower level of illegitimacy (M. S. Bednyi, *Demograficheskie Faktory Zdorov'ia*, [Moscow, 1984], p. 94) and, thus, infant mortality.

11. Age-specific mortality schedules for the period 1965–1975 show steady rise. See *Narkhoz*, various years. Continuous decline of age-specific survivorship ratios in the second half of the 1970s can be observed by calculating age-specific survivorship ratios in 1974–78 relative to 1970–74. See Appendix 1 for methodology and sources of the data.

12. *Demographic Yearbook 1983* (New York: United Nations, 1985), pp. 470–90.

13. *Spravochnik Partiinogo Rabotnika* 22/1982 (Moscow, 1982), pp. 467–76.

14. G. I. Litvinova, *Pravo i Demograficheskie Protsessy* (Moscow, 1981), pp. 94–95.

15. *Narkhoz* 1975, p. 600.

16. U.S. Bureau of the Census, *Statistical Abstract of the United States 1985*, p. 76.

17. See, for example, *Vestnik Statistiki*, no. 12 (1971): 81 and no. 11 (1984): 77; M. S. Bednyi, *Demograficheskie Faktory*, pp. 154–55; V. A. Miniaev, I. V. Poliakov, *Zdravookhranenie Krupnogo Sotsialisticheskogo Goroda* (Moscow, 1979), p. 220; *Demografisheskoe i Ekonomichesko Razvitie v Regione* (Moscow, 1983), pp. 192–200; I. M. Virganskaia, "K Voprosu o Predstoiashchei Prodolzhitel'nosti Zhizni v Trudosposobnom Vozraste," *Zdravookhranenie Rossiiskoi Federatsii* (hereinafter *ZRF*), no. 7 (1984): 24–27; Murray Feshbach, "Issues in Soviet Health Problems," in JEC, U.S. Congress, *Soviet Economy in the 1980s*, 203–27.

18. See, e.g., *Vestnik Statistiki*, various years; M. S. Bednyi, *Mediko-Demogrficheskoe Izuchenie Naseleniia* (Moscow, 1979), p. 137; N. Ia. Kopyt, "Bor'ba s P'ianstvom i Alkogolizmom Vazhnyi Put' Profilaktiki Zabolevanii i Ukrepleniia Zdorov'ia," *ZRF*, no. 2 (1985): 3–4; N. Ia. Kopyt, "Mediko-Sotsial'nye Faktory Preodoleniia P'ianstva i Alkogoliza," *ZRF*, no. 12 (1985): 5; A. F. Serenko and V. K. Ovcharov, *Zabolevaemost', Smertnost' i Sredniia Prodolzhitel'nost' Zhizni Naseleniia SSSR* (Minsk, 1979), passim. These and other sources report that a significant proportion of deaths from cardiovascular diseases (over 30 percent) and of fatal accidents (over 50 percent) is alcohol-related. Other special studies show, however, that almost 90 percent of industrial injuries are caused by managerial and technological policies (e.g., V. F. Kaverin, "Nekotorye Voprosy Izucheniia Proizvodstvennogo Travmatizma na Predpriiatiiakh Derevoobrabatyvaiushchei Promyshlennosti," *ZRF*, no. 11 [1985]: 21).

The present author found no robust relationship between trends and cross sections of alcohol consumption and life expectancies. Alcohol consumption increased recently in various Western countries but life expectancy, including that at male working ages, did not decline. In the USSR, per capita alcohol consumption increased by 10.5 percent per annum in the 1950s, by 6.7 percent in the 1960s, and by 3.2 percent in the 1970s (G. G. Zaigraev, "O Nekotorykh Osobennostiakh Profilaktiki P'ianstva," *Sotsiologicheskie Issledovaniia*, no. 4 [1983]: 98). Life expectancy increased until the mid-1960s and declined since then, thus showing no meaningful relationship with trends in alcohol. There is also no significant cross-sectional relationship among republics between various measures of alcohol consumption and mortality.

One can conclude that alcoholism is a major labor problem in the USSR and Eastern Europe, but not a major mortality factor. Alcohol is a highly income-elastic product but only when opportunity costs, such as private investments, are nonexistent. This is why alcoholism is widespread in white republics of the USSR (as opposed to nonwhite republics with private agriculture and private housing), in socialist Eastern European countries, and in U.S. urban ghettos. On the rationality of behavior of alcohol addicts see George J. Stigler and Gary S. Becker, "De Gustibus Non Est Disputandum," *American Economic Review* 67, no. 2 (March 1977): 77–81. In this economic context one should not follow Eastern European literature in seeking a behavioral scapegoat for declining life expectancy so that industrial victims, not industrial policies, be blamed.

19. These recipients belong to the Soviet social security (income substitute) program. This program does not include welfare (income supplement) recipients who never had a breadwinner in the family or are otherwise destitute. See, e.g., V. A. Babkin, G. B. Smirnova, *Kommentarii k Polozheniiu o Poriadke Naznacheniia i Vyplaty Gosudarstvennykh Pensii* (Moscow, 1984), pp. 102–212; and L. Shokhina, "Razvitie Form Sotsial'nogo Obespecheniia," in *Naselenie i Sotsial'noe Obespechenie* (Moscow, 1984), pp. 15–20.

20. To be sure, in the United States the proportion of similar social security recipients is also about 5 percent, but when one excludes never-worked wives who receive benefits for their deceased husbands, the proportion drops to 3 percent of the total population (calculated from U.S. Department of Health and Human Services, Social Security Administration, *Social Security Bulletin, Annual Statistical Supplement, 1982* [Washington, D.C.: U.S. Government Printing Office, 1982], pp. 113–23). This 3 percent figure for the United States is more comparable with the Soviet 5 percent since in the Soviet Union old widows belong to the category of the old age retirees.

21. See Samuel H. Preston, "The Changing Relation Between Mortality and the Level of Economic Development," *Population Studies* 29, no. 2 (June 1975): 231–48; J. G. Williamson, "British Mortality and the Value of Life, 1781–1931," *Population Studies* 38, no. 1 (March 1984): 157–72.

22.   One can also consider U-3, that is, suburbanization. This is an important factor in the United States and other Western countries, but does not exist in the USSR.

23.   For example, *Narkhoz 1984*, pp. 32, 437. The literature calls this "the housing gap." See, e.g., Henry W. Morton, "The Soviet Quest for Better Housing—An Impossible Dream?" in JEC, U.S. Congress, *Soviet Economy in a Time of Change* vol. 1 (Washington, D.C.: U.S. Government Printing Office, 1979), pp. 790–809; and Henry W. Morton, "Who Gets What, When, and How? Housing in the Soviet Union," *Soviet Studies* 32, no. 2 (April 1980): 235–59.

24.   Thomas J. Espenshade, Leon F. Bouvier and W. Brian Arthur, "Immigration and the Stable Population Model," *Demography* 19, no. 1 (February 1982): 125–33.

25.   In 1980, U.S. marital fertility per 1,000 married females aged 15–44 was 96.4 births among whites and 94.4 births among blacks. If illegitimate children and their mothers are excluded, there were 58.0 marital births per 1,000 white women and 41.4 marital births per 1,000 black women (calculated from U.S. National Center for Health Statistics, *Vital Statistics of the United States 1980*, vol. 1, *Natality*, section I, pp. 7, 58–59, 71). For an analysis see Mikhail S. Bernstam, "Competitive Human Markets," section II.

26.   Cast and tribal systems (e.g., in India and rural Africa, respectively) produce the same effect: they provide both economic immobility and economic security on separated markets. Those individuals who choose an alternative strategy of breaking with the system and breaking into outside markets reduce fertility to low levels.

27.   See Tables 6 and 7 and, e.g., Litvinova, pp. 147–54; G. I. Litvinova and B.Ts. Urlanis, "Demograficheskaia Politika Sovetskogo Soiuza," *Sovetskoe Gosudarstvo i Pravo*, no. 3 (1982): 40–46; D. I. Ziuzin, "Prichiny Nizkoi Mobil'nosti Korennogo Naseleniia Respublik Srednei Azii," *Sotsiologicheskie Issledovaniia*, no. 1 (1983): 109–17; Ellen Jones and Fred W. Grupp, "Modernization and Ethnic Equalization in the USSR," *Soviet Studies* 36, no. 2, (April 1984): 159–84 and Nancy Lubin, *Labour and Nationality in Soviet Central Asia* (Princeton, N.J.: Princeton University Press, 1984), passim.

28.   We will not be discussing nonwhite demographic behavior outside nonwhite republics, but, predictably, about 96 percent of Central Asian and Caucasian nonwhites reside in nonwhite home areas. Judging from the 1959, 1970, and 1979 census data, their concentration in their home areas steadily increased. But this analysis does not apply to several nonwhite ethnic groups who reside in the Russian Republic and are subject to the same economic conditions as whites. These groups, such as Tatars and Bashkirs, practice virtually as low fertility as their surrounding whites. Islamic religion and other cultural variables identical with Central Asian nonwhites thus made a negligible influence on fertility relative to economic factors. For further details see Mikhail S. Bernstam, "The Demography of Soviet Ethnic Groups."

29.   This did not imply a higher share of managerial personnel in the nonwhite republics' agriculture. Looking at the distribution by occupations, one can observe that agricultural manual workers in the RSFSR in 1979 had a low ratio of educated males, 12.7 percent with secondary education, against 37.4 percent of manual workers in machine-tool and metal production. Respective ratios in the Uzbek Republic were 47.6 percent and 47.3 percent. Half of the Uzbek Republic's male *manual* workers in agriculture, as well as in procurements, utilities, supplies, trade and food industries, and 60 to 70 percent in such occupations as food production, food trade and services, shipping and storage rooms, etc., held in 1979 college degrees and high school diplomas.

30.   Ruralization took place in the United States during the Great Depression, precisely due to the same change in the relative standard of living in favor of the countryside.

31.   See, for example Ziuzin p. 110; Zh. A. Zaionchkovskaia, "Migratsiia Naseleniia SSSR za Gody Sovetskoi Vlasti," in *Na Novom Meste* (Moscow, 1984), pp. 8–9; and G. D. Moskvina, "Prizhivaemost' Naseleniia v Kazakhstane," in *Na Novom Meste*, pp. 58–63.

32.   An analysis of changes in spacial distribution and natural increase of whites from the 1970 and 1979 censuses demonstrates this. See also Ziuzin, p.115.

33.   Even in the cities, the kin network of urban and rural nonwhites engaged in the production, consumption, distribution, and sales of agricultural products makes nonwhites better off relative to

whites. Educational and promotional preferences for nonwhites work in the same direction.

34. E.g., G. I. Litvinova, pp. 151–52; Ziuzin, p. 115. If one adjusts official estimates of private plot incomes for market prices for both marketed output and household consumption, these incomes increase by a factor of 2.5. See *Sem'ia i Narodnoe Blagosostoianie v Razvitom Sotsialisticheskom Obshchestve* (ed. N. M. Rimasheuskaia and S. A. Karapetian (Moscow, 1985), pp. 84–94. With 35 percent of per capita income of nonwhite collective farmers derived from private plots, such an adjustment would raise their total per capita income by 53 percent.

35. See, e.g., Alastair McAuley, *Economic Welfare in the Soviet Union: Poverty, Living Standards, and Inequality* (Madison, Wis.: The University of Wisconsin Press, 1979), pp. 99–173.

36. M. S. Gudzenko and M. V. Shul'ga, *Podsobnoe Khoziaistvo Grazhdan* (Moscow, 1983), pp. 23–31, 113–17; A. M. Samoilovich, "Lichnoe Podsobnoe Khoziaistvo i Ego Rol' v Proizvodstve Sel'skokhoziaistvennoi Produktsii Uzbekskoi SSR," in *Regional'nye Problemy Razvitiia Lichnogo Podsobnogo Khoziaistva v SSSR* (Moscow, 1982), pp. 81–84.

37. *Narkhoz*, various years; Z. I. Kalugina, and T. P. Antonova, *Lichnoe Podsobnoe Khoziaistvo Sel'skogo Naseleniia: Problemy i Perspektivy* (Novosibirsk, 1984), p. 47; M. S. Gudzenko and M. V. Shul'ga, *Podsobnoe Khoziaistvo*, pp. 73–74; Karl-Eugen Waedekin, "The Impact of Official Policy on the Number of Livestock in the Soviet Private Farming Sector," *Radio Liberty Research Bulletin* 27, no. 24 (June 1983): 1–10; and Karl-Dugen Waedekin, "The Performance of the Private Sector of Soviet Agriculture in Recent Years," *Radio Liberty Research Bulletin* 27, no. 37 (September 1983): pp. 1–8.

38. E.g., D. I. Ziuzin, pp. 109–17; D. I. Ziuzin, "Sredniia Aziia–Vazhneishii Istochnik Trudovykh Resursov Dlia Narodnogo Khoziaistva," in *Naselenie Srednei Azii* (Moscow, 1985), pp. 90–94; V. I. Kozlov, "Dinamika Natsional'nogo Sostava Naseleniia SSSR i Problemy Demograficheskoi Politiki," *Istoriia SSSR*, no. 4 (1983): p. 27; T. M. Karakhanova and V. D. Patrushev, "Kollektivnoe Ogorodnichestvo i Sadovodsto–Rezerv Prodovol'stvennogo Obespecheniia," *Sotsiologicheskie Issledovaniia*, no. 2 (1983): pp. 82–89.

39. This regional wealth also can be treated as rent that did not dissipate over time. But higher income derived, for example, from the subterranean economy may not be conducive to higher fertility. Rising incomes over time may only increase the competition between households for children's economic mobility, thus simulating the competitive market environment of Western countries. This is probably the cause of rapid fertility decline in the southern white republics of Georgia and Armenia. Only legal private plots can generate noncompetitive child investment. In Georgia, for example, private plots were especially restricted and private livestock depleted. Private plots expansion in the Kazakh Republic and stagnation in the Azerbaidzhan Republic probably account for the fact that fertility declined more rapidly in the latter. See *Narkhoz* , various years. Also, unlike Central Asian and Kazakh Republics, higher education and other transfer programs in the Azerbaidzhan, Georgian, and Armenian Republics were not financed from federal subsidies. See, e.g., "O Gosudarstvennom Biudzhete SSSR na 1986 God," *Pravda*, November 28, 1985, p. 3.

40. Since the cost of education increases over grades and stages, the life-cycle transfer effect of public education is the same as that of social security. That is, it is another major transfer from young parents and their children to middle-aged parents and their adolescent and college-age children. Wages, bonuses, and amenities seniority is another clear transfer in the same direction.

41. To sustain zero population growth, one female child surviving by the mean age of childbearing is needed per average woman. The per woman number of female children surviving by the mean age of childbearing is called Net Reproduction Rate (NRR); the level of NRR/1.0 is called replacement. The survivorship ratio in contemporary industrial countries may vary from 0.93 in the Lithuanian SSR to 0.99 in Japan (calculated from V. Nauduizhas, "Aktual'nye Demograficheskie Problemy v Litovskoi SSR," in *Naselenie SSSR Segodnia* [Moscow, 1982], p. 58; *VS*, no. 11 (1979): 66; and *Demographic Yearbook 1981*, [New York: United Nations, 1983], p. 552; respectively). Since on the average 48.8 females are born per 100 births, the total number of children born per woman must be from $1/0.488/0.99 = 2.1$ to $1/0.488/0.93 = 2.2$ to secure population replacement in industrial countries. The average number of children born per woman in a given year is the sum of age-specific

fertility rates. This is called Total Fertility Rate (TFR). TFR is a snapshot of current fertility. It is the fertility of Ms. Japan-1986, or Ms. RSFSR-1970, or Ms. California-1958, or Ms. Uzbek SSR-1975, etc. A useful hypothetical measure of the *implied* level of natural increase in a given year can be derived from these indicators, called the Intrinsic Growth Rate (IGR). IGR = log (TFR × 0.488 × survivorship ratio) / mean age of childbearing. This is the rate of natural increase free of the influence of the age composition; this rate will prevail if both fertility and mortality rates will stabilize at the current level for over 50 years (the difference between female life expectancy and the mean age of childbearing). Thus, IGR is a prediction of the results of the continuous current demographic behavior. IGR is also useful because it can show the future population size (without migration) should the current rates continue. For example, if Soviet white fertility or any Western country's fertility will stabilize at the current West German level of TFR =1.27, in 100 years after erasing the impact of current age composition a given population will equal exp(IGR × 100) = exp{[log(1.27 × 0.488 × 0.965)/25.5] × 100} = 13.3 percent of its size at the beginning of the period. That is, there will be no Germany, no Russia, no Japan, etc. By the same measure, if Soviet nonwhite TFR will decline to 4.0 and then stabilize, this will yield an increase by a factor of 8.7, up to 500,000,000 persons. These are, of course, extreme hypothetical examples, but they demonstrate the range of the current demographic split.

42. For the latest examples see, e.g., V. I. Kozlov, "O Nekotorykh Aspektakh Demograficheskoi Teorii," in *Demograficheskaia Politika v SSSR* (Moscow, 1983), pp. 82–87; and A. B. Sinel'nidov, "Skol'ko Detei Nuzhno Imet' Chtoby naselenie Ne Stalo Umen'shat'sia?" in *Rozhdaemost': Izvestnoe i Neizvestnoe* (Moscow, 1983), pp. 50–60, 111. A long list of the earlier alarming literature is cited in Mikhail S. Bernstam, "The Demography of Soviet Ethnic Groups," footnote 2. One must underscore that awareness about depopulation and extinction prospects is much stronger in the USSR than in Western industrial countries with similar demographic trends.

43. See, for example, *VS*, no. 12 (1973): 76.

44. Ethnic age-specific fertility rates were derived from, e.g., M.K. Karakhanov, *Nekapitalis-ticheskii Put' Razvitiia i Problemy Narodonaseleniia* (Tasghkent, 1983), p. 139; *Naselenie i Trudovye Resursy Kazakhstana: Tendentsii i Prognozy* (Alma-Ata, 1979), p. 40; and R. I. Sifman, *Dinamika Rozhdaemosti v SSSR. Po Materialam Vyborochnykh Obsledovanii* (Moscow, 1974), p. 82. See also V. Belova, G. Bondarskaia, and L. Darskii, "Dinamika i Differentsiatsiia Rozhdaemosti v SSR," *VS*, no. 12 (1983): 17–18; and S. V. Bakurskii, *Sotsial'no-Ekonomicheskie Problemy*, p. 23. Births undercount was evaluated according to Ansley J. Coale et. al., *Human Fertility in Russia*, pp. 239–41.

45. On supplies and knowledge see, e.g., N. A. Shneiderman and A. A. Popov, *Mediko-Demograficheskoe Izuchenie Potrebnosti Naseleniia v Protivozachatochnykh Sredstvakh* (Moscow, 1982), p. 49; A. A. Popov, "Kontrol' Reproduktivnoi Fuinktsii Semi'i i Faktory Ego Opredeliaiushchie, *Sovetskoe Zdravookhranenie*, no. 7 (1985): 36–38; A. I. Antonov, *Sotsiologiia Rozhdaemosti* (Moscow, 1980), pp. 126–32; S. I. Golod, *Stabil'nost' Semi'i: Sotsiologicheskii i Demograficheskii Aspekty* (Leningrad, 1984), pp. 111–12. For a detailed analysis see Mikhail S. Bernstam, "The Demography of Soviet Ethnic Groups" and "Marxism and Birth Control."

46. Bassim F. Mussalam, *Sex and Society in Islam: Birth Control Before the Nineteenth Century* (New York: Cambridge University Press, 1983).

47. For a detailed econometric analysis see Mikhail S. Bernstam, "Competitive Human Markets."

48. The early control cannot be observed in the aggregate TFR data as presented in Table 10 because fertility temporarily increased among working women who practiced earlier weaning and thus reduced birth intervals. Only special tests using the Coale-Trussell techniques (especially in our modified version) can capture a significant extent of birth control among young Uzbeks, Tadzhiks, etc., already in 1966. See Mikhail S. Bernstam, "Competetive Human Markets," pp. 128–30.

49. I. Katkova and A. Mamatokhunova, "Nekotorye Aspekty Formirovaniia Sovremennykh Mnogodetnykh Semei," in *Demograficheskaia Situatsiia v SSSR* (Moscow, 1976), pp. 83–85; M. Burieva, "Formirovanie Sem'i v Sel'skoi Mestnosti Uzbekskoi SSR," in *Liudi v Gorode i na Sele* (Moscow, 1978), pp. 97–102; M. K. Karakhanov, p. 141; S. Khakimova, "Vnutrisemeinoe Regulirovanie Rozhdaemosti v Tadzhikskoi SSR," *Naselenie Srednei Azii*, pp. 36–41. Since demand for abortions

is high, but social costs for young nonwhite women are high, too, in over 50 percent of instances they resort to illegal (and expensive) abortions. See A. A. Popov, "Mediko-Demograficheskie i Sotsial;no-Gigienicheskie Prichiny i Faktory Isskusstvennogo Aborta," *ZRF*, no. 9 (1980): 28.

50. Mikhail S. Bernstam, "The Demography of Soviet Ethnic Groups."

51. U.S. Bureau of the Census, *Statistical Abstract of the United States 1985*, p. 27.

52. The U.S. ratio will, of course, decline drastically in the early twenty-first century when the baby boom generations will begin to retire.

53. V. Mozhin, "Ratsional'noe Razmeshchenie Proizvoditel'nykh Sil i Sovershenstvovanie Territorial'nykh Proportsii," *Planovoe Khoziaistvo*, no. 4 (1983): 6.

54. A. Bachurin, "Problemy Uluchsheniia Ispol'zovaniia Trudovykh Resursov," *Planovoe Khoziaistvo* no. 1 (1982): 35.

55. V. N. Ivanov, "Nekotorye Itogi Raboty ISI AN SSSR," *Sotsiologicheskie Issledovaniia*, no. 4 (1984): 6.

56. V. I. Perevedentsev, "Migratsiia Naseleniia i Razvitie Sel'skokhoziaistvennogo Proizvodstva," *Sotsiologicheskie Issledovaniia*, no. 1 (1983): 58.

57. Similar projections were made by the Foreign Demographic Analysis Division of the U.S. Bureau of the Census. Our projections differ in that they forecast a flatter trend of manpower losses: smaller decline in the second half of the 1980s and virtually no recovery in the second half of the 1990s. Compare Murray Feshbach, "Population and Labor Force," in *The Soviet Economy: Toward the Year 2000*, ed. Abram Bergson and Herbert S. Levine (London: George Allen and Unwin, 1983), pp. 94–95.

58. V. Kostakov, "Odin, kak Semero," *Sovetskaia Kul'tura*, January 4, 1986.

59. Western analysts acutely observed a weakness of the overt dissent among most nonwhite nationalities relative to the Russians and other whites. There is perhaps more to the argument that the whites will eventually revolt against transfers to the nonwhites. See Paul B. Henze, "The Spectre and Implications of Internal Nationalist Dissent: Historical and Functional Comparisons," in *Soviet Nationalities in Strategic Perspective*, ed. S. Enders Wimbush (London: Croom Helm, 1985), pp. 24–27.

Mikhail S. Bernstam, "Appendix 1"

1. The weakness of our estimates is twofold. First, the influence of economic variables may have changed in the years for which no observations were included in the OLS regression. These are the years after 1980. Second, cross-sectional values of life expectancies for all years included into derivation of the formulae were themselves derived by using the prediction estimated by Peter Mazur by regression. See D. Peter Mazur, "Using Regression Models to Estimate the Expectation of Life for the USSR," *Journal of the American Statistical Association* 67, no. 337 (March 1972): 31–35. Mazur's formula is:

$$oe_0 = 1 / \{[13.02763 + (0.32011 \, m_c - 0.20070 \, m_c \log_{10} P_{65+})^2] / 100\}$$

where oe_0 is life expectancy at birth, m_c is crude death rate per 1,000, and P_{65+} is the proportion of the population aged over 65 in percent. The standard error of this regression is 0.6 years. The m_c values we took from *Narkhoz*, various years. The age-specific data for this and consequent calculations we derived from censuses data and inter-census estimates. For 1959: *Itogi Vsesoiuznoi Perepisi Naseleniia 1959 Goda*. SSR (Moscow, 1962), pp. 50–72; 1970: *Itogi Vsesoiuznoi Perepisi Naseleniia 1970 Goda*, vol. II (Moscow, 1972), pp. 12–75; for 1975: *Narkhoz 1975*, p. 33 and *Zhenshchiny v SSSR. Statisticheskii Sbornik* (Moscow, 1975), p. 18; for 1979: Murray Feshback, "The Age Structure of Soviet Population: Preliminary Analysis of Unpublished Data," *Soviet Economy* 1, no. 2 (1985): 179–83.

2. Ansley J. Coale and Paul Demeny, *Regional Model Life Tables and Stable Populations* (New York: Academic Press, 1983).

3. In republics, population at the end of the interval was adjusted for migration. We assumed net migration to be equal to the difference between the absolute population growth within a five-year interval and natural increase within the same interval. The data was calculated from *Narkhoz* annuals.

4. We assumed the standard sex ratio at births of 105 males per 100 females. The ratio may be lower due to high Soviet rate of spontaneous abortions.

5. *Sotsial'nye Faktory i Osobennosti Migratsii Naseleniia SSSR* (Moscow, 1978), p. 128.

Mikhail S. Bernstam, "Appendix 2"

1. Another statistically highly significant variable in the equations with the inverse crude death rate as the dependent variable was the proportion of retirees. This is a trivial finding. Naturally, the aging of the population increases crude death rates. This variable was necessary as a proxy to hold the unknown age composition constant in the years for which only death rates, not life expectancies, were readily available.

2. The sign of the coefficient of this variable in column 1 of Table A2.1 is negative because the variable was regressed in the inverse form.

3. *Narkhoz 1965*, pp. 10, 615; and *1984*, pp. 9, 441.

11. Nick Eberstadt, "Health of an Empire: Poverty and Social Progress in the CMEA Bloc"

1. Morris Bornstein, "Overview: Assessing Economic Performance," in Joint Economic Committee (JEC), U.S. Congress, *East European Economies: Slow Growth in the 1980s*, vol. 1 (Washington, D.C.: U.S. Government Printing Office, 1985).

2. Charles Wolf, Jr., personal communication, April 30, 1986.

3. International Monetary Fund, *International Financial Statistics* (Washington, D.C.: International Monetary Fund, various issues); Vienna Institute for Comparative Economic Studies, *Comecon Data 1983* (Westport, Conn.: Greenwood Press, 1984); Sovet Ekonomocheskoi Vzaimopomoshchi, *Statisticheskii Ezhegodnik Stran-1985* (Moscow: Finansy i Statistika, 1985). Computations from IMF data deflate gross fixed capital formation by producer price index for industrial goods and deflate net material consumption by consumer price index.

4. Oskar Morgenstern, *On the Accuracy of Economic Observations* (Princeton, N.J.: Princeton University Press, 1963).

5. Dan Usher, "An Imputation to the Measure of Economic Growth for Changes in Life Expectancy," in *The Measurement of Economic and Social Performance*, ed. Milton Moss (New York: Columbia University Press, 1973).

6. See ch. 10.

7. Computed from United Nations, *Demographic Indicators of Countries: Estimates and Projections as Assessed in 1980* (New York: United Nations, 1982).

8. Staatlichen Zentralverwaltung fuer Statistik, *Statistiches Jahrbuch 1985* (Berlin: Staatsverlag der DDR, 1985).

9. R. H. Dinkel, "The Seeming Paradox of Increasing Mortality in a Highly Industrialized Nation: The Example of the Soviet Union," *Population Studies*, no. 1 (March 1985).

10. Shiro Horiuchi, "The Long-Term Impact of War on Mortality: Old-Age Mortality of the First World War Survivors in the Federal Republic of Germany," *Population Bulletin of the United Nations*, no. 15 (1983). Horiuchi's study touches upon the mortality patterns of Japanese men since World War II; though the postwar era has been a time of rapid health progress in Japan, and though the

Japanese teenage boys from World War II are only now entering later middle age, Horiuchi has discerned some of the same health stress patterns for them that he detailed for an earlier generation of European men.

11. P. A. Compton, "Rising Mortality in Hungary," *Population Studies* 39 (1985).

12. United Nations, *National Accounts Statistics: Main Aggregates and Detailed Tables, 1982* (New York: United Nations, 1985).

13. Charlotte Chase, "Alcohol Consumption—An Indicator of System Malfunction in Contemporary Poland," *East European Quarterly* 18 (1985).

14. United Nations, *National Accounts Statistics.*

15. Chase.

16. Compton.

17. The similarity of deterioration in the health of the Soviet and the Hungarian adult populations is all the more interesting in view of the other differences in their health strategies. Within the limited confines of the data set of Warsaw Pact countries, Hungary and the USSR represent divergent approaches to "health management": Hungary has the Pact's most developed pharmaceutical industry, and is a leading East Bloc producer of medical equipment and instrumentation, while the Soviet Union makes comparatively little use of either of these "inputs" in its national "health production function." If such differences in strategy have an impact on health progress, they are evidently overwhelmed by the factors that have made overall adult health "progress" in the two countries broadly similar.

18. See, for example, International Monetary Fund, *World Economic Outlook 1985* (Washington, D.C.: International Monetary Fund, 1985), and JEC, *East European Economies: Slow Growth in the 1980s.* Table 1 in this chapter gives some official data pertaining to this slowdown.

19. See, for example, Lawrence W. Theriot and JeNelle Matheson, "Soviet Economic Relations with Non-European CMEA: Cuba, Mongolia, and Vietnam", in JEC, U.S. Congress, *Soviet Economy in a Time of Change,* vol. 2 (Washington, D.C.: U.S. Government Printing Office, 1979).

20. United Nations, *Demographic Indicators of Countries.*

21. P. N. Mari Bhat, Samuel Preston, and Tim Dyson, *Vital Rates in India, 1961–1981* (Washington, D.C.: National Academy Press, 1984).

22. Judith Banister, "An Analysis of Recent Data on the Population of China," *Population and Development Review,* 10 no. 2 (June 1984).

23. Judith Banister, *The Population of Vietnam* (Washington, D.C.: U.S. Bureau of the Census, Series 1985).

24. Banister, *The Population of Vietnam.*

25. World Health Organization, *World Health Statistics Annual 1983* (Geneva: World Health Organization, 1983).

26. United Nations, *Demographic Indicators of Countries.*

27. United Nations, *Demographic Yearbook 1967* (New York: United Nations, 1967).

28. Lawrence W. Theriot, "Cuba Faces the Realities of the 1980s," Office of East-West Policy and Planning, April 4, 1982, Department of U.S. Commerce; quoted in *The New York Times.*

29. Kenneth Hill, "An Evaluation of Cuba's Demographic Statistics, 1930–1980," *Fertility Determinants In Cuba* ed. Paula E. Hollerbach and Sergio Diaz Briquets (Washington, D.C.: National Academy Press, 1983).

30. Christopher Davis and Murray Feshbach, *Rising Infant Mortality in the USSR in the 1970s* (Washington, D.C.: U.S. Bureau of the Census, 1980). Davis and Feshbach's adjustments attempt to bring Soviet infant mortality data into line with international infant mortality data; the Soviet criteria for "infant mortality" differ from those accepted by the United Nations agencies and most national statistical authorities.

31. See the discussions in Vladimir G. Treml and John P. Hardt, eds., *Soviet Economic Statistics* (Durham, N.C.: Duke University Press, 1972).

32. United Nations, *Levels and Trends of Mortality Since 1950* (New York: United Nations, 1982).

12. Dennis Ross, "Where Is the Soviet Union Heading?"

1. Gregory Grossman was probably the first to call attention to Soviet economic problems in "An Economy at Middle Age," *Problems of Communism* 26 (March-April 1976). For additional outlining of the Soviet problems, see Dennis Ross, "Coalition Maintenance in the USSR," *World Politics* 32, no. 2 (January 1980); and more recently, Timothy Colton, *The Dilemma of Reform* (New York: Council on Foreign Relations, 1984).

2. See Colton, p. 12.

3. Quoted in Patrick Cockburn, "Gorbachev Tightens His Grip," *Financial Times*, July 4, 1985, p. 8.

4. See "Draft Guidelines for Economic, Social Development," *Pravda*, November 9, 1985.

5. Cockburn, p. 8.

6. Alexander Yanov, *Detente After Brezhnev* (Berkeley, Calif.: Institute of International Studies, 1977), p. 26.

7. Quoted in Richard Pipes, "Can the Soviet Union Reform?" *Foreign Affairs* 63, no. 1 (1980): 54.

8. Ross.

9. Konstantin Chernenko, "The Leninist Strategy of Leadership," *Kommunist*, September 1981, p. 11.

10. See *Pravda*, June 16, 1983, p. 2.

11. Quoted in Colton, p. 37.

12. See *FBIS: USSR*, November 29, 1985, p. R-17.

13. *FBIS: USSR*, p. R-18.

14. The changes in the military are significant, particularly as senior military officers of long standing have retired. Both Marshal Yepishev and Admiral Gorshkov had held their positions since the 1950s. Gorshkov was obviously also a military leader with significant clout, having lobbied for and succeeded in turning the Soviet navy into a blue-water navy. The changes probably reflect more than just the transition to a younger military leadership; they may well reflect a decision on Gorbachev's part to put in place military leaders more compatible with his values and perhaps with his definition of Soviet needs.

15. Quoted in Cockburn, p. 8.

16. Here several experiments are likely to be extended — e.g., letting teams or brigades of agricultural workers contract out; permitting individuals on their private plots access to state materials, feed, and small machinery; making the measure of success — and the basis of bonuses — the fulfillment of contracts (not gross output); permitting managers to determine how they will reinvest the money their enterprises make, etc.

17. See Jerry Hough's discussion of the changing values and attitudes in the different generations in *Soviet Leadership in Transition* (Washington, D.C.: The Brookings Institution, 1980); also George Breslauer, *Five Images of the Soviet Future: A Critical Review and Synthesis* (Berkeley, Calif.: Institute of International Studies, 1978).

18. This is a concern emphasized by Yanov.

19. See Breslauer for an excellent analysis of future Soviet alternative patterns of internal organization.

20. For an account of this document, see Gary Lee, "Document Versus Reforms Circulating in Moscow," *Washington Post*, July 23, 1986.

21. Lee.

22. Peter Reddway has come up with this figure as a result of his current research.

23. The Soviets seek very much to get back into the Middle East peace process and seem increasingly to understand that it may not be possible without relations with Israel. To build the Israeli stake in relations and in including the Soviets in an international conference, the Soviets may well have an interest in letting Jewish emigration increase. They have been hinting as much to the Israelis and Jewish leaders like Edgar Bronfman.

24. For a discussion of these factors, see Dennis Ross, "The Soviet Union and Middle East

Diplomacy: Putting Moscow to the Test," The Washington Institute for Near East Policy, Policy Options Series, Issue ff1, November 15, 1985.

25. *Pravda*, March 12, 1985, p. 3.

26. Yanov, p. 45.

13. Henry S. Rowen and Charles Wolf, Jr., "The Future of the Soviet Empire: The Correlation of Forces and Implications for Western Policy"

1. A useful analysis, similar to ours in some respects and different in others, has been made by Harry Gelman, "Soviet Vulnerabilities and Advantages: An Attempt at a Balance Sheet," California Seminar on International Security and Foreign Policy, Discussion Paper No. 106, Santa Monica, California, August 1985.

2. Nathan Leites has pointed out that a more accurate translation is simply "relationship of forces: (*sootnoshenie sil*)." However, use of the term "correlation" is widespread, and the ideologically faithful typically treat the term as implying interdependence and causal significance.

3. See also Dennis Bark, ed., *The Red Orchestra: Instruments of Soviet Policy in Latin America and the Carribean* (Stanford, Calif.: Hoover Institution Press, October 1986).

4. "The Soviet Economy Under a New Leader," paper prepared by the Central Intelligence Agency and the Defense Intelligence Agency, for the Joint Economic Committee of the U.S. Congress, March 19, 1986.

5. See Vladimir Shlapentokh, "A Strange Gathering: The 27th Party Congress in Historical Perspective," unpublished paper, May 5, 1986.

6. See A. Shtromas, "How the End of the Soviet System May Come About," paper presented at the Second International Congress of the Professors' World Peace Academy, Geneva, Switzerland, August 1985.

7. The reported improvement might be false. Soviet statistics have always been sparse and unreliable. They are becoming increasingly sparse and there is evidence of increasing distortions in them. For example, see V. Seliunin and G. Khanin, "Dust in the Eyes," *Pravda*, December 30, 1985.

8. See Charles Wolf, Jr., K. C. Yeh, Edmund Brunner, Jr., Aaron Gurwitz, and Marilee Lawrence, *The Costs of the Soviet Empire*, (Santa Monica, Calif.: The RAND Corporation, 1983).

9. See ch. 7.

10. Even as knowledgeable an observer as Zbigniew Brzezinski repeatedly refers to the U.S. empire, although drawing a sharp contrast between it and that of the Soviet Union. See his *Game Plan: A Geo-Strategic Framework for the Conduct of the U.S.-Soviet Contest* (Boston: Little Brown, 1986).

11. See ch. 7.

12. Ronald Hingley, *The Russian Mind* (New York: Scribner, 1977).

13. John B. Dunlop, *The New Russian Nationalism* (New York: Praeger, 1985).

14. Alexandre Bennigsen and Marie Bruxop, *The Islamic Threat to the Soviet State* (London: Croom Helm, 1983).

15. A neglected question is the extent to which the Soviet Union might try to ameliorate its economic predicament by gaining control of Persian Gulf oil. Such control (leaving aside both the exact definition of "control" and the feasibility of the Soviets achieving it) would enable the Soviets to threaten the oil-importing states with vast economic disruption, greater than in the 1970s crises, and might be a source of large revenues both directly to Moscow from the Gulf and, indirectly, via the increased value of Soviet oil and gas exports. The magnitude of this threat against the Western alliances could be powerful.

16. As well as others within the Soviet system whose views are perhaps reflected in the recent reformist manifesto, whose provenance is uncertain, but which has been attributed to a group called the "Movement for Socialist Renewal." See *The Guardian* (London), July 22, 1986.

17. A recent expression of this view is by Peter Reddaway, "Waiting for Gorbachev," *The New York Review of Books*, Oct. 10, 1985.

18. Seweryn Bialer, *The Soviet Paradox* (New York: Knopf, 1986).

19. Daniel F. Kohler, *Economic Costs and Benefits of Subsidizing Western Credits to the East* (Santa Monica, Calif.: The RAND Corporation, 1985).

20. Television address by Mikhail Gorbachev, Oct. 14, 1986, as reported in *The New York Times*, Oct. 15, 1986.

21. See ch. 7.

22. For elaboration of this proposal, see Charles Wolf, Jr., and Katherine Watkins Webb, *Developing Cooperative Forces in the Third World* (Lexington, Mass.: Lexington Books, 1987).

23. Western governments have a moral obligation to spare the civilians of the area, one that has long been recognized in NATO planning. But if Warsaw Pact armed forces are attacking the West, these forces would have to be countered by NATO and widespread spillover damage to civilians would be likely. In this case, morality and self-interest—in terms of encouraging Eastern European neutrality—coincide.

24. *The Economist*, August 30, 1986.

25. For instance, the Federal Republic's exports and imports with Eastern Europe (GDR excepted) amount to around 3 percent of the total; see Central Intelligence Agency, *Handbook of Economic Statistics*, 1986. Trade with the GDR is treated as internal commerce.

26. See ch. 7.

27. The détente of the 1970s led Western banks and governments to extend large loans for reasons of overestimates of the borrowers' ability to repay, traditional European mercantilism, overarching political objectives, and a largely mistaken belief in the existence of a Soviet financial "umbrella" over the region. Because of the political motivation, Western banks had implicit—where not explicit—guarantees that their governments would protect them if the loans went sour. Currently, the total debt of all of Eastern Europe is $65–70 billion, of which $31 billion is owed by Poland. There will be little further net lending to this region that is not guaranteed by Western governments.

28. It is an open question as to whether any savings from reduced nuclear forces resulting from an agreement would be shifted to making capital equipment or to making conventional weapons. Some military leaders (including former Soviet Chief of Staff Ogarkov) have expressed an urgent need for more modern military technology—especially for conventional forces. But many in the military may agree with Gorbachev on the importance of modernizing the economy's stock of capital equipment.

29. Albert Wohlstetter and Brian Chow, "Arms Control That Could Work," *The Wall Street Journal*, July 17, 1985.

30. "Modern Audio Broadcast Facilities for the Voice of America," paper prepared by the Technical Operations Study Committee, Board on Telecommunications and Computer Applications, Committee on Engineering and Technical Systems, National Research Council, June 1986.

31. In this connection the Soviet leadership has recently announced steps to decentralize its foreign trade away from the Ministry of Foreign Trade to a large number of ministries and major enterprises. Joint ventures with Western firms are also envisioned. This attempt to promote access to Western technology and goods may not be incompatible with the Western aims advocated in the text. The importance of this goal warrants strenuous, persistent, and imaginative efforts to advance it.

Contributors

MIKHAIL S. BERNSTAM is a Senior Research Fellow at the Hoover Institution, Stanford University. His latest work is *Below-Replacement Fertility in Industrial Societies* (with Kingsley Davis and Rita Ricardo-Campbell), 1987.

VLADIMIR BUKOVSKY left the Soviet Union in 1976 after 12 years in Soviet prisons, work camps, and psychiatric "hospitals." His many writings include *To Build a Castle: My Life as a Dissenter.*

NICK EBERSTADT is Visiting Fellow at the Harvard Center for Population Studies and Visiting Scholar at the American Enterprise Institute for Public Policy Research. He is author of *Poverty in China* and *The Poverty of Communism* (forthcoming), and editor of *Fertility Decline in the Less Developed Countries.*

HERBERT J. ELLISON is Professor of Russian History and Chairman of Russian and Eastern European Studies Program at the Henry M. Jackson School of International Studies, University of Washington. He has contributed to and edited a series of books on Soviet foreign policy, which include *The Sino-Soviet Conflict: A Global Perspective* (1982), *Soviet Policy Toward Western Europe* (1983), and *Japan and the Pacific Quadrille* (1987).

RICHARD E. ERICSON is Professor of Economics at Columbia University and the W. Averell Harriman Institute for the Advanced Study of the Soviet Union. His areas of research and teaching are economic theory, economic planning and comparative systems, and the Soviet economy. He has published scholarly articles in *Econometrica*, the *Journal of Economic Theory*, and the *Journal of Comparative Economics*.

FRANCIS FUKUYAMA is a member of the political science department of the RAND Corporation. His areas of expertise include Middle Eastern and Soviet affairs, with particular emphasis on Soviet policy in the Third World. He has served as a member of the Policy Planning Council of the U.S. Department of State.

CHARLES GATI, Professor of Political Science at Union College, is also associated with the Research Institute on International Change and the Harriman Institute for Advanced Study of the Soviet Union at Columbia University. His latest book, *Hungary and the Soviet Bloc*, received the first Shulman Prize for the outstanding study on Soviet foreign policy published in 1986.

BRUCE D. PORTER is Executive Director of the Board for International Broadcasting. He previously served as a senior analyst in Soviet Affairs at the Northrop Corporation, and as a staff member of the Senate Armed Services Committee.

JAMES G. ROCHE is Vice President and Director of the Northrop Analysis Center. He was formerly a captain in the U.S. Navy, senior staff member of the Senate Armed Services Committee, and deputy director of the State Department's Policy Planning Council.

DENNIS ROSS is Special Assistant to the President, Near East and South Asian Affairs, the National Security Council. He was previously executive director of the Berkeley-Stanford Center for Soviet International Behavior.

HENRY S. ROWEN holds the Edward B. Rust Professorship of Public Policy and Management at the Graduate School of Business at Stanford, and is a Senior Fellow at the Hoover Institution. He was formerly chairman of the National Intelligence Council and president of the RAND Corporation.

CHARLES E. WATERMAN has had a long career as an official of the Central Intelligence Agency and served as deputy chairman of the National Intelligence Council. He is currently a private consultant.

CHARLES WOLF, JR. is Dean of the RAND Graduate School of Policy Studies and Director of the RAND Corporation's International Economic Policy Program.

Index